INSIGHT GUIDES

TUSCANY

D0107756

APA PUBLICATIONS L

Part of the Langenscheidt Publishing Group

✵ INSIGHT GUIDE
TUSCANY

Editor
Cathy Muscat
Cartography Editor
Zoë Goodwin
Picture Manager
Steven Lawrence
Series Editor
Rachel Fox

Distribution

UK & Ireland
GeoCenter International Ltd
Meridian House, Churchill Way West
Basingstoke, Hampshire RG21 6YR
sales@geocenter.co.uk

United States
Langenscheidt Publishers, Inc.
36–36 33rd Street 4th Floor
Long Island City, NY 11106
orders@langenscheidt.com

Australia
Universal Publishers
1 Waterloo Road
Macquarie Park, NSW 2113
sales@universalpublishers.com.au

New Zealand
Hema Maps New Zealand Ltd (HNZ)
Unit 2, 10 Cryers Road
East Tamaki, Auckland 2013
sales.hema@clear.net.nz

Worldwide
**Apa Publications GmbH & Co.
Verlag KG (Singapore branch)**
7030 Ang Mo Kio Avenue 5
08-65 Northstar @ AMK
Singapore 569880
apasin@singnet.com.sg

Printing
CTPS - China

ABOUT THIS BOOK

The first Insight Guide pioneered the use of creative full-colour photography in guidebooks in 1970. Since then, we have expanded our range to cater for our readers' need not only for reliable information about their chosen destination but also for a real understanding of that destination. Now, when the internet can supply inexhaustible (but not always reliable) facts, our books marry text and pictures to provide that much more elusive quality: knowledge. To achieve this, they rely heavily on the authority of locally based writers and photographers.

How to use this book

The book is carefully structured to convey an understanding of Tuscany:
◆ To understand the region today, you need to know something of its past. The first section covers its people, history and culture in lively essays written by specialists.
◆ The main Places section provides a full run-down of all the attractions worth seeing. The main places of interest are coordinated by number with full-colour maps. Margin notes provide background information and tips on special places and events.
◆ A special section of photographic features highlights Florentine museums and other aspects of Tuscan culture, such as Chianti and its wine.
◆ Photographs are chosen not only to illustrate the landscape and buildings but also to convey the moods of the region and the life of its people.
◆ The Travel Tips listings section provides a point of reference for information on travel, hotels, shops and festivals. Information may be located

writers who contributed to previous editions, much of whose work survives in this edition. Among the principal authors, **Lisa Gerard-Sharp**, who is knowledgeable about all things Tuscan, contributed to the original Places section and wrote sections on *Wild Tuscany, Tuscan Architecture* and the *Tuscan Spa Renaissance*. She has also kept the history chapter up to date.

Christopher Catling wrote the original history chapters, and the Renaissance art chapters were penned by **Russell Chamberlin**. Celebrated cookery writer and Italian food expert **Valentina Harris** describes the pleasures of Tuscan food and wine. **Marc Zakian**, a travel writer specialising in Italy, contributed the new essay on *Tuscany Today*. The routes on the accompanying touring map were planned and written by travel writer **Rebecca Ford**.

Other contributors to previous editions include: **Paul Duncan, Lorella Grossi, Susan Zucker, Marco de Stefani, Nicky Swallow**, and **Yvonne Newman**.

The majority of stunning pictures were taken by **Anna Mockford** and **Nick Bonetti**, regular Insight photographers. They have captured the timeless beauty of the Tuscan landscape and its historic towns.

The book was proofread by **Neil Titman** and indexed by **Helen Peters**.

CONTACTING THE EDITORS

We would appreciate it if readers would alert us to errors or outdated information by writing to:

Insight Guides, P.O. Box 7910, London SE1 1WE, England.
Fax: (44) 20 7403-0290.
insight@apaguide.co.uk

NO part of this book may be reproduced, stored in a retrieval system or transmitted in any form or means electronic, mechanical, photocopying, recording or otherwise, without prior written permission of *Apa Publications*. Brief text quotations with use of photographs are exempted for book review purposes only. Information has been obtained from sources believed to be reliable, but its accuracy and completeness, and the opinions based thereon, are not guaranteed.

www.insightguides.com

quickly by using the index printed on the back cover flap – and the flaps are designed to serve as bookmarks.

The contributors

This edition of *Insight Guide: Tuscany* was revised by **Cathy Muscat**, an Insight Guides editor specialising in Italian destinations. This new edition builds on the excellent foundations laid down by editors of previous editions, **Rosemary Bailey** and **Barbara Balletto**.

The Places chapters and Travel Tips section were updated for the latest edition by **Angela Vannucci**, and previously by **Adele Evans**, a regular contributor to Insight Guides, **Sarah Birke** and **Robert John**, former tour guide in the region.

The updaters' contributions have been blended with the expertise of

Contents

Travel Tips

THE BEST OF TUSCANY

Art, culture, food and shopping...
Here, at a glance, are our
recommendations for
your visit

CHURCHES AND MONUMENTS

- **The Leaning Tower** stands alongside the gleaming Duomo and Baptistery on Pisa's aptly named Campo dei Miracoli – Field of Miracles. *See page 155*
- **Brunelleschi's dome**. An incredible feat of engineering by father of Renaissance architecture. *See page 89*
- **Florentine churches**. San Lorenzo, San Marco, Santa Maria Novella, Santa Croce and San Miniato should all be seen. *See pages 87–96*
- **San Michele** in Lucca, a fine example of the exuberant Tuscan Romanesque style. *See page 135*
- **San Galgano**. The evocative ruins of a Gothic abbey. *See page 190*
- **Siena cathedral**. A magnificent Gothic structure of banded black and white stone. *See page 209*
- **Monte Oliveto Maggiore**. A secluded 14th-century monastery set among groves of cypress trees. *See page 217*
- **Sant'Antimo**. An abbey church built of creamy travertine and set against tree-clad hills. *See page 230*
- **Santa Maria Nuova**. The domed church just outside the Etruscan walls of Cortona is a hidden gem. *See page 255*
- **San Pellegrino in Alpe**. An ancient monastery deep in the Garfagnana mountains, with glorious views. *See page 144*

THE BEST TUSCAN HILLTOWNS

- **San Gimignano.** The medieval skyscrapers are best seen early in the morning or at dusk, when the coachloads have left. *See page 193*
- **Pienza**. The ideal Renaissance city with excellent pecorino cheese. *See page 219*
- **Monteriggioni**. The Sienese hilltown encircled by walls and 14 towers is a spectacular sight. *See page 197*
- **Cortona**. One of many Tuscan hilltowns rich in attractions out of all proportion to their tiny size. *See page 255*
- **Vinci**. The genius of Leonardo is cele-
brated in his birthplace, a tiny hilltown between Florence and Pisa. *See page 119*
- **Massa Marittima**. The ancient mining capital of the region. *See page 189*
- **Montepulciano** and **Montalcino** deserve long and leisurely exploration with frequent stops to sample their famed wines. *See pages 220 and 229*
- **Pitigliano** is situated above a dramatic cliff of soft tufa in the forgotten corner of Tuscany. *See page 242*
- **San Miniato**. An ancient town straddling three hills. *See page 119*

ABOVE The Leaning Tower of Pisa and **LEFT:** Brunelleschi's dome – two Tuscan icons.

TUSCANY FOR FAMILIES

- **Giardini di Boboli**. The gardens behind the Pitti Palace are fun for children to clamber around. There is an amphitheatre, strange statues and grottoes, and a handy café. *See page 104*
- **Trips to the Tuscan islands**. Ferries and hydrofoils sail from Porto Santo Stefano to Giglio and from Piombino to Elba. *See pages 239, 174 and 260*
- **Giardino dei Tarocchi**. A bizarre garden full of colourful fantasy figures. *See page 240*
- **Pistoia Zoo**. Compact, but one of the region's best. *See page 127*
- **Parco di Pinocchio**. At Collodi near Pisa. A hi-tech theme park it isn't, but Pinocchio's park has a certain old-fashioned charm. *See page 138*

- **Horse-riding**. Excursions on horseback are popular with families visiting Tuscany. There are over 40 equestrian centres. For recommendations *see page 283*
- **Museo dei Ragazzi**. Dressing up, model making and other fun activities for kids in the Palazzo Vecchio bring the Renaissance to life. *See page 84*
- **Ice cream**. When all else fails, an ice cream on the town square, most of which are traffic free, rarely fails to win them over.

TOP ETRUSCAN SITES

- **Volterra** has some of the best Etruscan art to be found outside Rome. *See page 185*
- **Chiusi**. Etruscan tombs are the highlight of a visit to Chiusi. *See page 226*
- **Fiesole**. An Etruscan temple and a Roman theatre a 30-minute bus ride from Florence. *See page 113*
- To see some of the most intact Etruscan ruins visit **Roselle** and **Vetulonia**, near Grosseto. *See page 235*
- **Museo Archeologico** in Florence has a fine collection of Etruscan art. *See page 93*

SEASIDE AND SPAS

- **Elba**. A beautiful island with dramatic scenery and a series of small beaches. Perfect for families. *See pages 177–183*
- **The Maremma**. One of the most unspoilt stretches of beach on the Italian coast. *See page 237*
- **Viareggio**. An appealing coastal town with plentiful fish restaurants and an atmospheric harbour. *See page 138*
- **Spas**. Tuscany's new breed of thermal spas combine sophisticated pampering with authentic water cures. *See pages 128 and 287*

FAR LEFT: on the Tuscan Riviera.
LEFT: 5th-century BC Etruscan sculpture, *L'Ombra della Sera* (Evening Shadow).

A TASTE OF TUSCANY

- **Wine-tasting**.
  Sample Vino Nobile in Montepulciano's Cantine Contucci *(see page 221)*, sip a glass of Brunello in Montalcino's Fortezza *(see page 230)* or visit the Castello di Brolio, birthplace of the modern Chianti industry *(see page 200)*.

- **Food festivals**.
  Tuscans are proud of their local produce which they celebrate with festivals *(sagre)* – white truffles, chestnuts, Valdichiana beef, wild boar and pecorino cheese all have festivals dedicated to them *(information from local tourist offices)*.

- **Cookery Courses** are big business in Tuscany. The course at Il Borghetto in the heart of Chianti is one of many to be recommended. *See page 274* Badia a Coltibuono is a "wine resort" where you can eat, sleep and learn to cook. *See page 199*

- *Cacciucco*. The famous fish stew from Livorno is best sampled in the port town and the immediate environs. *See page 107*

- **Mushrooms**.
  Around October time, mushroom-loving Tuscans head for the mountain woods to forage for *funghi*. Wild mushrooms, especially the prized *porcini* and *tartufi* (truffles), are widely available in restaurants in the autumn. *See page 69*

- **Sweet treats** include the candied fruit cake, *Panforte*, sweet almond biscuits, *Ricciarelli* and the irresistible *gelati*. *See page 102*

BEST SQUARES

- **Piazza del Campo**.
  All roads in Siena lead to the rose-pink Campo which spreads out from the Gothic town hall like a fan. *See page 207*

- **Piazza della Signoria**.
  Florence's open-air museum of statuary, where a copy of Michelangelo's *David* takes centre stage. *See page 84*

- **Piazza Grande**.
  Arezzo's main square in the old hilly part of the city, is the venue for Tuscany's biggest antiques market. *See page 245*

- **Piazza Anfiteatro**.
  Lucca's bustling square takes the shape of the Roman amphitheatre that once stood here. *See page 136*

VILLAS AND GARDENS

- **The Boboli Gardens**.
  The regal gardens of the Pitti Palace, palatial residence of the Medici and now a vast museum. *See page 104*

- **Villa Medicea Poggio a Caiano**. Thought by many to be the perfect Medici villa, with frescoed halls and beautiful gardens. *See pages 116 and 118*

- **Villa Demidoff and Parco di Pratolino**.
  The gardens here contain extraordinary Mannerist sculpture and grottoes. *See page 116*

- **Villa Medici (Fiesole)**.
  A delightful villa and garden with superb views of Florence. *See page 116*

- **Villa Medicea della Petraia**. An elegant villa decorated with wonderful frescoes. *See page 116*

- **Villa Medicea di Castello**. Beautiful Renaissance gardens. *See page 116*

- **Lucchesi villas**. The area around Lucca is rich in villas, all surrounded by beautiful parks. *See page 137*

ABOVE: Arezzo's Piazza Grande. **ABOVE LEFT:** the "rustic" raffia-wrapped Chianti flask. **LEFT:** Giambologna's *Rape of the Sabine Women* on the Piazza della Signoria, Florence. **RIGHT:** Michelangelo's *Holy Family* tondo in the Uffizi.

TUSCAN LANDSCAPES

- **The Crete Senesi**. The dramatic landscape of rounded hills, stately cypresses and isolated farms, is the Tuscany of postcards and posters. *See page 217*
- **Parco Naturale della Maremma**. Beautiful unspoilt beaches backed by steep cliffs, parasol pines and Mediterranean scrubland. *See pages 65 and 236*
- **Chianti Country**. Gentle hills cloaked in vineyards, many centred around medieval castles where winetasting is usually on offer. *See pages 63 and 202–3*

- **Parco dell' Orecchiella**. A wild mountainous area, rich in wildlife – the region's most spectacular park. *See pages 64 and 145*
- **Apuan Alps**. Behind the well groomed beaches of the Versilia is a rugged hinterland of marble quarries, mountain ridges and narrow gorges. *See pages 64 and 146*
- **The Casentino**. Ancient forests of the upper Arno valley. *See pages 63 and 249*
- **Monte Amiata** The site of an extinct volcano with a profusion of thermal springs. *See pages 228 and 242*

FESTIVALS AND EVENTS

- **Giostra del Saracino**. Jousting tournament in Arezzo. *See page 280*
- **Scoppio del Carro**. Amid colourful processions fireworks explode from a moving carriage in Florence. *See page 280*
- **Estate Fiesolana**. Music festival in Fiesole. *See page 281*
- **Effetto Venezia**. Livorno's lively 10-day festival. *See page 281*
- **Il Teatro Povero**. Drama written, acted and directed by the people of Monticchiello. *See pages 39 and 281*

- **Luminaria di San Ranieri**. Pisan festival (pictured above) when thousands of candles light up the Arno; ends with a boat race. *See pages 162 and 281*
- **Palio**. Siena's traditional horse race. *See pages 214–5*
- **Puccini Festival**. By the composer's villa on Lake Massaciuccoli. *See pages 139 and 281*
- **Carnevale**. Viareggio's carnival is one of the best in Italy. *See page 138*

RENAISSANCE ART

The Uffizi an overwhelming collection of masterpieces including Botticelli's *Birth of Venus* and *Primavera* and works by Leonardo da Vinci, Raphael, Titian and other masters of the High Renaissance. *See pages 100–3*

The Bargello A major collection of Renaissance and Mannerist sculpture in a former prison. *See pages 110–11*

The Baptistery Ghiberti's doors are so dazzling, Michelangelo called them the "Gates of Paradise". *See page 87*

Lorenzetti's frescoes in Siena's Palazzo Pubblico – an allegory of good and bad government. *See page 209*

The two Davids Michelangelo's *David* is Florence's icon, but Donatello's *David* was the first free-standing nude since antiquity. *See pages 109 and 110*

Masaccio's Florentine frescoes in the Brancacci chapel and Santa Maria Novella display all the characteristics of the Renaissance: the importance of the human form, human emotion and the use of perspective. *See pages 96 and 92*

Giotto's frescoes in Florence's Santa Croce show a departure from the flat Byzantine style. *See page 94*

Piero della Francesca's frescoes in Arezzo are marvels of pastel shades awash in cool light. *See page 246*

Orsanmichele a showcase of statuary paid for by the wealthy guilds. *See page 87*

THE TUSCAN MIRACLE

Birthplace of the Renaissance, a strong tradition of village life, a picturesque countryside: these factors and more contribute to the enigma that is Tuscany

From the top of a village tower, the Tuscan landscape lies below: the most civilised rural scene on Earth. Yet driving through southern Tuscany at night there is little sense of civilisation, still less of domesticity – even farm animals are kept indoors. In the distance, a succession of small lights trail across the black countryside: tenuous links with separate inward-looking communities. The spaces in between are remote, uncivilised. The blackness and emptiness of the countryside go back to medieval times and beyond; the "Tuscan Miracle" only illuminates the cities, leaving the gaps unfilled.

In giving birth to the Renaissance, Tuscany designed the modern world. In his painting, Giotto projected Tuscany into space. Brunelleschi crowned space with his Florentine dome, the greatest feat of Renaissance engineering. In the Carmine frescoes, Masaccio peopled space with recognisably human figures. His *Expulsion from Paradise* reveals Adam and Eve in all their naked beauty. Gone is the medieval coyness; present is the palpable suffering of a couple who have lost everything.

The Tuscan miracle, however, is not a frozen Renaissance portrait but a living procession of Tuscans at ease with their artistic setting and identity. Tuscans do have an innate aesthetic sense but the Tuscan tapestry is a rich weave that has been created by many different threads. Literary Tuscany is a strand that can be clearly traced through Boccaccio, Petrarch and Dante. Republican Tuscany is best glimpsed through its fortified town halls while humanist Tuscany is enshrined in poetry, sculpture and art, the fruits of patronage and craftsmanship. Aristocratic Tuscany still lingers in Medici palaces, villas and sculptured gardens, as well as the ancestral homes of the Rucellai, Corsini and Frescobaldi. Bourgeois Tuscany parades along Florence's Via Tornabuoni, patronises the arts and restores family farms. Peasant Tuscany traditionally takes a little of everything from the land: game, beans, chestnut flour, unsalted bread, olive oil, and, of course, the grapes needed to make Chianti and Brunello. Tuscan cuisine combines proportion and variety. Like the Tuscans themselves, it is of good peasant stock.

PRECEDING PAGES: PRECEDING PAGES: view of the Piazza del Duomo, religious heart of Florence; the skyline of San Gimignano, one of Tuscany's best-preserved medieval towns. **LEFT:** Hidden hill village in the heart of the Garfagnana.

THE MAKING OF TUSCANY

First the Etruscans and Romans left their imprint on the landscape. By the Middle Ages Tuscany had become the scene of fiercely battling city-states. Then the Medici dynasty arrived and dominated Tuscan politics for 300 years. Unification in the 19th century and the two world wars in the 20th forced a somewhat scarred Tuscany into the modern world

The story of Tuscany begins with the Etruscans, its earliest known inhabitants, whose origins are shrouded in myth and mystery. The Romantics and latter-day writers believed that the Etruscans sailed from Asia Minor. However, Dionysius, writing as the Etruscan civilisation neared its end, held that the Etruscans were natives with an indigenous culture too deeply ingrained to be oriental. Most modern scholars believe that the Etruscans migrated from Eastern Europe over the Alps and represent the flowering of the early Italic tribes. What is clear is that between the 8th and 4th centuries BC "Etruria Propria" flourished as a confederation of 12 city-states in central Italy. Northern Etruria, roughly equivalent to modern Tuscany, included Arezzo, Chiusi, Cortona, Populonia, Vetulonia and Volterra.

Etruscan seafarers and merchants first settled on the coast and began smelting iron ore from Elba and importing oriental ceramics, glass and silverware. Greek naval supremacy meant an opening to Hellenistic culture: ships sailed to Corinth with honey, gold and bronze figurines, and returned to Vetulonia and Populonia with perfume and painted wine jars. The inland cities such as Chiusi and Volterra thrived on hunting, farming and internal trade. Over the next two centuries, the Etruscans allied themselves to the developing Roman power, and by the 1st century BC all the Etruscan territory was annexed. Although Etruscan and Latin co-

existed, Etruscan culture was crushed; its role degenerated into the provision of soothsayers, musicians, dancers and fighters for Rome.

Etruscan society

The original confederation had a complex urban and social structure: each city was originally run by a king, later by local aristocrats and finally by a priestly oligarchy. The lords owned large landholdings or navies and were served by serfs and slaves. Whereas the serfs were rewarded with agricultural plots, the slaves danced and sang for their supper. With urbanisation, an independent class of artisans and merchants emerged. The granting of the same

---

LEFT: Etruscan tomb painting.
RIGHT: part of the fortification wall at Chiusi, one of Tuscany's major Etruscan sites.

Roman citizenship to the middle classes as to the aristocratic priests and magistrates was a blow to the Etruscan princely tradition.

The Etruscans were expert builders. Their cities followed the contours of the land and sited the necropolis below the city walls and the living city above. If cities of the dead predominate today, it is by accident and not by design. Public buildings, constructed of wood and clay, did not survive. From what remains of the cities, there was enough to impress Roman and Renaissance architects. Volterra's Porta all' Arco, a deep gateway inspired by Mesopotamian architecture; the huge drystone walls at Saturnia, rebuilt to defend the city against

borrowed from Greek, the language, read from left to right, is part of no known linguistic group and defies interpretation. Many claim to have found a key text equivalent to the Rosetta Stone. In Marsiliana a writing tablet was found engraved with the Greek Euboic alphabet used as a model for Etruscan.

Despite considerable progress, the unintelligibility of Etruscan is part of a glamorous myth. True, there are no external keys such as dictionaries or bilingual texts, but even by the 18th century, the sounds of most letters, names and gods had been identified and simple texts translated. Today, the core grammatical and phonetic structure is known, and, by deduction,

Roman incursions; the neat town plans of Pitigliano and Sovana – all these scattered remains are evidence of the vitality and ingenuity of Etruscan builders.

But it is the tombs that remain as a cultural testimony to the power, wealth and beliefs of their owners. Death reflected life: the poor were often buried in shallow graves or their ashes put in small urns; the rich were buried in chamber tombs and stone sarcophagi decorated with pottery.

Mystery language

The Etruscan language is as mysterious as the people's origins. Although the alphabet is

most of the 10,000 shorter texts can be read accurately. These texts are mostly funerary inscriptions and religious dedications. The one known book, a priest's manual discovered wrapped around an Egyptian mummy, has still only been partially deciphered.

Etruscan influence

The art critic John Ruskin saw an unbroken line of tradition from the tomb paintings of the Etruscans to Giotto and Fra Angelico. Certainly, the Etruscan influence on the Romans was considerable. Apart from introducing to Rome the purple toga, an abundance of gods and competent soothsayers, the Etruscans also added a set of religious, humanistic and regional values which far outlived the Roman Empire.

The Roman legacy

Rome annexed Etruria in 351 BC, and, from the 3rd until the 2nd century BC, as part of the massive road-building programme which was to transform Italy, four great Roman roads were built across the territory: the Via Aurelia, which ran up the western seaboard to Pisae and the naval base at Genua in Liguria; the Via Clodia, which stopped at Saturnia; the Via Cassia, built in 154 BC to connect Rome with Florentia; and the Via Flaminia, built in 220 BC to connect Rome to Umbria and the Adriatic.

Roman roads purposely avoided the great Etruscan cities, which slowly fell into decline, whereas the new Roman cities such as Pistoriae (Pistoia) grew in importance.

New colonies were founded at Ansedonia, Fiesole, Roselle, Populonia, Volterra, Luni and Lucca. The cultural identity of the Etruscans was gradually absorbed into that of the Romans, a process which accelerated in 91 BC when Roman citizenship was extended to the Etruscans. The Romans learned many things from the Etruscans – principally the Tuscan arch, which they developed as a key element in their extraordinary aqueducts, bridges and buildings, relegating the classical

It's hard to imagine the impact these giant engineering projects must have had on the local inhabitants, as surveyors and workmen spanned rivers with elegant stone bridges, built drains to prevent their new roads from flooding and at times even cut through the hills themselves.

Etruscan roads were all designed to connect the interior with the coast, whereas Roman roads all led to Rome, thus the axis was turned 90°, from east–west to north–south. The new

columns of Greece to a more decorative role.

The most complete remains in Tuscany are at Fiesole, Roselle and Cosa (Ansedonia); the best villas are near the coast on Elba, near Porto Santo Stefano and particularly on the Isola di Giannutri, near Grosseto. Most Tuscan cities have something to show, though sometimes a little detective work is required.

By creating the roads and major cities of Tuscany, the Romans left a permanent imprint on the landscape. A millennium later, the ruins of their great bridges, amphitheatres and city walls were the inspiration for the next great blossoming of Italian culture: Tuscany's coming of age, the Renaissance.

LEFT: the Etruscan tomb of Larthia Seianti, Chiusi, 2nd century BC.
ABOVE: the Teatro Romano in Fiesole.

Roman Tuscany

Ansedonia, the Roman Cosa, was founded as a Roman colony in 273 BC. The ancient hilltop city has been excavated, and the site contains a main street, remains of a forum, a walled acropolis and the ruined *capitolium* – a tripartite sanctuary for the triad of Jupiter, Juno and Minerva. The city's 1.5 km (1 mile) of wall is virtually intact, as are many of its 18 guard towers. The site is overgrown, and many of the ruins are covered in brambles, giving it a melancholy atmosphere.

Fiesole, which possibly dates from the 8th century BC, is an Etruscan settlement overlooking the valleys of the Arno and the Mugnone. As Faesulae, it was a Roman military colony from 80 BC and later became the capital of Roman Etruria. The Piazza Mino da Fiesole is built on the site of the Roman forum. The archaeological site, set on a hillside near the Duomo, features a remarkably well-preserved Roman theatre, still used for performances. Near by are Roman baths, and on the other side the ruins of a Roman temple, both 1st-century BC, as well as a 3rd-century BC Etruscan temple, set against the Etruscan city walls.

Detective work is necessary in Florence, the Roman Florentia; the Roman gridiron street plan is clearly visible in maps, with the Piazza della Repubblica following the outline of the old *castrum*. The perimeter of the theatre, outside the city walls to the southwest, is still described by the little streets surrounding the Piazza Santa Croce.

In Lucca, the original street plan is also still evident. Luca, as the Romans named it, began as a military colony in 178 BC and featured a 10,000-seat amphitheatre that was originally to the north of the city, outside the walls. In time, it was largely dismantled, and most of its remains are below street level. During the Middle Ages, however, houses were built using the remaining walls of the amphitheatre, thus fossilising its outline and four main entrances. Fragments of it are still visible from the surrounding lanes, incorporated in the outer walls of the houses.

Luni, called Luna by the Romans, was founded in 177 BC and was the springboard for the conquest of the Ligurian tribes. The Roman city, its forum, a number of houses and its amphitheatre have been excavated.

Another extensively excavated site is at Roselle, the Roman Rusellae. The Etruscan city was taken by Rome early in the 3rd century BC. It was originally an island, dominating the waters of the gulf. The ruins are satisfyingly complete, with a nearly intact circuit of Romano-Etruscan walls, a Roman forum, paved streets, basilicas, villas, amphitheatre and baths.

Volterra was the Etruscan city-state of Velathri. It became the important Roman municipality of Volterra in the 4th century BC. The Porta all'Arco Etrusco has a Roman arched vault on massive Etruscan bases, with three Etruscan basalt heads incorporated into the arch. The ruins of the 1st-century BC Roman theatre are outside the city walls.

Throughout the region, indeed the whole of Italy, perhaps the Romans' most significant legacy, apart from the roads, is the template they laid down for the classic town plan, with the forum – evolving into the piazza – the focal point ❑

LEFT: view from the Teatro Romano, Fiesole.

Feuds of the city-states

Between the ending of the Roman Empire in the 5th century AD and the beginning of the foreign invasions in the 16th century, the story of Italy is a catalogue of conflict between its cities, each of which was a sovereign state. Gradually, the larger absorbed the smaller. In the far south, Naples dominated the area from Rome to Sicily. In and around Rome, the popes built up a power base. In the north, Milan swallowed up all its neighbours on the Lombard plain. And in Tuscany, a three-way battle was conducted between Florence, Pisa and Siena.

In the early stages the battles between the city-states were conducted by the citizens them – dominated its neighbours. Few could control them, however, and that is why the *condottieri* system got such a bad name. The *condottieri* had a vested interest in conflict, and if there were no battles to fight then trouble was created. From being paid to fight on behalf of a city, it was a short step to blackmailing that same city into paying you not to attack them.

Some *condottieri* were bought off – Sir John Hawkwood, the infamous and piratical leader of the much-feared White Company, was given a palatial villa and a substantial estate as his reward for retiring gracefully from the fray. Hawkwood craved immortality

themselves, able-bodied men between the ages of 15 and 50 sallying forth beyond their city's walls to fight the men of the neighbouring city. When Florence crushed Arezzo in 1289 at Campaldino, the bloodshed was so great that thereafter the cities began to fight out their differences with mercenaries, the *condottieri*.

Throughout the 14th century, the *condottieri* held the balance of power. Commanding companies numbering thousands of men, they sold their services to the highest bidder. The city that could afford them – and control

ABOVE: details from Lorenzetti's *Effects of Good and Bad Government* (1338).

and wanted an equestrian statue to be erected in Florence – instead, the miserly Florentines opted for the less expensive solution of an illusionistic fresco, painted by Paolo Uccello to look like a statue, in the Cathedral in Florence.

Siena employed Guidoriccio da Fogliano as its *condottiero*, and his portrait, depicting him in ceremonial battle dress, can be seen on the walls of the Palazzo Pubblico. In the adjoining room of the palace, Lorenzetti's great fresco, *Effects of Good and Bad Government*, served as a reminder to the medieval rulers of Siena of the consequences of their decisions. Under the heading of *Bad Government*, the fresco depicts a countryside ravaged by bandits, fields left uncultivated, churches and other public buildings in ruin, and women being robbed and raped in broad daylight. By contrast, *Good Government* results in a city full of happy, well-dressed people, schoolchildren listening attentively to their lessons, and merchants prospering.

It was on these same merchants that the burden of paying the *condottieri* fell. They were caught on the horns of a dilemma, desiring domination over their trade rivals, and yet aware of the high cost of war, in terms of both taxes and economic instability. When they waged war on neighbouring cities, they often did so in the name of "Guelf" or "Ghibelline"

Outside Tuscany, many city-states fell under the dominion of a single ruler – some of them former *condottieri* who ended up rulers of the cities they once protected, founding dynasties. The Tuscan city-states and republics maintained their independence far longer, but eventually even they fell to a dynastic power, as the Medici transformed themselves from private citizens to grand dukes.

The Medici

Ruefully reflecting on the mistakes that had led him to be imprisoned and tortured before being cast from office, Niccolò Machiavelli, former Chancellor of Florence, wrote his mas-

partisanship. The Guelfs were broadly made up of the rising middle class of merchants, bankers and members of the trades guilds, who nominally supported the papacy in its long battle against the Holy Roman Emperor, and who wanted a greater role in city government. Conversely, the Ghibellines, the old feudal aristocracy, supported the emperor, because he seemed the best guarantor of their virtual autocracy. Since the emperor was often German or Spanish and an absentee ruler, paying nominal allegiance to such a distant figurehead was far preferable to the threat of the pope exercising real and temporal power closer to home.

terpiece *The Prince*, in which he admiringly recounted the ruthless methods used by the Medici to claw their way to absolute power in Tuscany, admitting that they had the gift of ruthless single-mindedness that he lacked. Even more remarkable is the way that this family threw up gifted individuals, generation after generation, and, whilst being masters of realpolitik and military strategy, also performed such an important catalytic role through their sponsorship of the arts, that Florence and Tuscany became the engine of European cultural regeneration that we know as the Renaissance.

The man who laid down the foundations for the family's meteoric rise was Giovanni de'

Medici (1360–1429), founder of the Medici bank. This was just one of 100 or so financial institutions flourishing in Florence in the 15th century, but Giovanni's master stroke was to develop a special relationship with the Church, eventually securing a monopoly over the collection of the papal revenues.

Giovanni's son, Cosimo, developed this relationship still further: one of his great coups was to attract the prestigious General Council of the Greek Orthodox and the Roman Catholic churches to Florence – the equivalent, in today's terms, of being chosen as the headquarters of the European Union, or the headquarters of a worldwide body such as the United Nations. These two great Christian churches had been at loggerheads for six centuries. Their assemblies in Florence were intended to find ways of burying their differences and creating a unified Christian church. This they failed to do, but the meetings had a lasting impact on Florence. Not only did they create a stimulating climate of theological and intellectual debate, out of which the Renaissance was to grow, but also the gorgeous dress and ceremony of the papal entourage – and the even more flamboyant and exotic manners and dress of their Greek counterparts – provided artists with a rich source of exotic subjects – the inspiration, for example, behind Benozzo Gozzoli's richly detailed fresco of the *Journey of the Magi* in the Palazzo Medici-Riccardi.

Cosimo himself eschewed such riches. He was a man who took pride in simplicity, ordering Brunelleschi, the temperamental but gifted architect of the Florence Cathedral dome, to modify his designs for the Medici palace, on the grounds that they were too ostentatious. More to his taste was the work of the architect Michelozzo, who designed the marvellously airy library in San Marco, Florence, as a repository for the Medici book collection, and as the world's first-ever public library. Such generosity was typical of Cosimo, who spent a fortune in endowing Florence with public buildings. Among his friends he counted many

of the greatest minds of the era: humanists who shared his thirst for knowledge, especially classical knowledge, for this was an era in which the lost classics of Greece and Rome – Plato, Cicero and the like – were being rediscovered and translated.

Though a devout Christian who regularly spent time in retreat in his private cell at San Marco, he believed strongly that God's grace was best leavened by a healthy dose of human intellect and reason. This made him an effective and humane ruler of the city – for that is what he was in all but name: following his father's advice to "keep always out of the public eye", Cosimo never sought public office.

Instead, he wielded immense influence behind the scenes, so that no major decision was taken in the city without his being consulted.

Lorenzo de' Medici inherited his father's love of the classical philosophers, and his gift for diplomacy. An outstanding poet in his own right, he promoted the study of Dante's works in Tuscan universities, elevating the Tuscan dialect to equal status with Latin. His greatest gift to the Italy of his day was peace. By using his diplomatic gifts to hold the great rival powers of the papacy and the Holy Roman Empire apart, Tuscany and the whole of northern Italy enjoyed a period of relative prosperity, in which merchants thrived and great

LEFT: *The Journey of the Magi,* by Benozzo Gozzoli (*c.*1460), in the Palazzo Medici-Riccardi; the central figure on horseback is a portrait of Lorenzo de' Medici. **RIGHT:** Cosimo de' Medici, Lorenzo's father, by Pontormo (*c.*1518).

fortunes were made. With the countryside no longer ravaged by war or held to ransom by lawless mercenaries, wealthy individuals began to build the villas that are still such a characteristic feature of the Tuscan countryside. Lorenzo himself led the way, retreating regularly to his rural retreats at Fiesole and Poggio a Caiano, where he enjoyed breeding racehorses and ornamental hens.

Bonfires of vanity

Prophetically, Pope Innocent VIII declared that "the peace of Italy is at an end" on learning of Lorenzo's death in 1492. From that moment on, the sounds of battle were heard again and again

were collected and smashed, or burned in what Savonarola termed "bonfires of vanity". Botticelli supported the movement, recanting of his past fondness for Neoplatonic ideas, turning from such mesmerising paintings as the *Birth of Venus* and the *Primavera* to equally complex Christian allegories, such as the mystic *Nativity*.

Michelangelo carved his *David*, the boy hero standing up to the bullying giant Goliath, as a symbol of the city's desire to rid itself of the Medici. He also helped to design and build new defences for the city, but when the combined forces of the Medici and Holy Roman Emperor held the city to siege in 1530, he took

at the gates of northern Italian cities, during a period in which the aspirations of small city-states to remain independent were dashed by powerful imperial or papal armies. Lacking the wisdom, intelligence and political acumen of earlier generations of the Medici, Lorenzo's successors were expelled from the city as Savonarola, the firebrand Dominican preacher, filled his fellow Florentines with anti-Medici zeal, shrewdly claiming that their love of pagan philosophers and fondness for the depiction of pagan gods in painting and sculpture would bring God's wrath upon the city.

Erotic art, fine clothing, secular poetry, mirrors, bronzes and sculptures of all sorts

himself off to hide – irony of ironies – in the Medici mortuary chapel, attached to San Lorenzo church. Vasari attributes his cowardice to the artistic temperament, and while he was in hiding he worked the masterly reclining figures of *Dawn*, *Evening*, *Day* and *Night*, which now adorn the tombs of two minor members of the Medici family.

Alessandro de' Medici, who led the victorious siege of the city, rubbed salt in the wounds of his fellow citizens by having himself crowned Duke of Florence, claiming absolute power for himself where his predecessors had been content with influence. When he was murdered in 1537 by his own cousin, with whom he had been having a homosexual affair, the city was relieved of one burden but faced with another – that of choosing a successor, since Alessandro had no natural heir. Various candidates were canvassed, and it was Cosimo, descended from Giovanni de' Medici via the female line, who emerged victor, partly by persuading his fellow citizens that he would appoint counsellors and consult widely before making decisions.

Once in power, Cosimo revealed his true colours, as he systematically set about destroying all opposition. Not only was he unrelenting in his pursuit of the republican leaders who had opposed his election, tracking them down in

cany into political unity and established security in the region, he also set up an effective civil service to administer the dukedom, based in the Uffizi (literally, the "Offices") in Florence, which proved effective right up to the point when Tuscany joined the United Kingdom of Italy in 1861. So effective was this civil service that Tuscany continued to be ruled effectively even when, as so often happened, Cosimo's successors proved to be corrupt, incompetent, self-indulgent or mad. Few made their mark on the city in quite the same way as the earlier generation, though Cosimo II did the world a great favour by patronising Galileo, making him court mathematician to the Medici

their exile and bringing them back to be tried and executed in Florence, he also set about conquering old enemies – Pisa, Siena, Massa Marittima, Montepulciano – with a ruthlessness and brutality that is still remembered and resented to this day. The whole story is told on the ceiling of the Palazzo Vecchio council chamber in a series of bloody frescoes painted by Vasari to honour Cosimo I in 1563–5.

To his credit, Cosimo not only forced Tus-

and providing him with a home after his trial and excommunication by the Inquisition.

The family also amassed an astonishing art collection, which Princess Anna Maria Lodovica, the last of the Medici line, bequeathed to the city of Florence at her death in 1743, along with all the Medici palaces and gardens, ensuring that many of the greatest works of the Renaissance were not sold off or dispersed, but would remain in the city that gave them birth. Today, these priceless works form the backbone of Florence's three main galleries: the Uffizi, the Pitti and the Bargello.

For more about Renaissance art and architecture see pages 43–52.

LEFT: the 15th-century Villa Medicea di Castello.
ABOVE: one of the battle scenes decorating the Hall of the Great Council in the Palazzo Vecchio by Vasari, depicting Florence's victories over Pisa and Siena.

Unification and war

Since the glories of Rome and the Renaissance, Italy has written little history. The head of Italy's Bureau of Statistics likens modern Italian history to a muddle, "a happy antheap where everyone is running about and no one is in control". The alternative is the "strong man" view of recent history, as expressed in the Florentine saying, "Whose bread and cheese I eat, to his tune I dance". But, while Rome danced to martial music, Tuscany sometimes starved or burned.

Tuscany has been buffeted rather than enriched by its recent past. Well-kept war memorials in shabby towns attest to the loss of two generations, one abroad and one at home. Look at Asciano, a village dwarfed by its Carabinieri stronghold, built by Benito Mussolini and still used to this day to maintain law and order. Visit Montisi where, for the price of a drink, locals will describe the German bombing of the village tower, a story complete with sound effects, gestures and genuine sorrow. Ask proud Florentines why the medieval houses on the south side of the Arno are lost for ever.

In 1865 Florence briefly became the capital of the newly united Italy. Although its exalted role would only last five years before Rome was then made the permanent capital, Florence underwent profound and rapid change during

THE GROWTH OF THE GRAND TOUR

Tuscany – particularly Florence – has been a magnet to foreign visitors since the 17th century, when a few adventurous eccentrics ventured forth into this strange land. By the 1700s, rich aristocrats were attracted to the region's alien psyche, perfect climate, low cost of living and undervalued works of art. Florence became an essential stop on any European tour.

But it was only in the 18th century that the middle classes joined the aristocratic dilettanti and literati on the road to Tuscany. Art was well and truly on the agenda, with foreign visitors flocking to see the Uffizi sculptures and Botticelli's *Birth of Venus*. By the 1850s, escapees

from mid-Victorian England had made Florence *"une ville anglaise"*, according to the Goncourt brothers.

At the turn of the 20th century, the Anglo-Florentine community was well established, although World War I chased many away. The Grand Tour resumed in the 1920s and 1930s, but mainly for society figures and intellectuals rather than for leisured young aristocrats. The tradition continues to this day, with sons and daughters of the Establishment coming to learn Italian and attend art courses on the Renaissance – while others come to enjoy the designer labels and the shopping rather than the artistic treasures.

this time. An ambitious plan of expansion and modernisation sadly led to the demolition of among other things the old city walls, and their replacement with a wide ring of avenues punctuated with large piazzas in keeping with the French urban taste of the times. Quarters for the middle classes and the Piazzale Michelangelo were built. Later, old areas of the centre including the Ghetto were declared to be in dangerous condition and unwholesome, and were razed; the soulless Piazza della Repubblica was created partly in their place. The square remains a bold flourish of nationhood, but when the capital was transferred to Rome, Tuscan allegiance unquestionably remained in

enough, but the end result is still only to be seen abroad or at international football matches.

Unification represented a missed chance for Italy. By failing to help shape a national identity, Tuscans also fell victim to the clearer vision of a "strong man". Even before World War I, Mussolini was making inflammatory speeches while a weak parliament practised the art of "timely resignation", a ploy used ever since to stage-manage a new coalition.

Although the pre-war Tuscan economy thrived under weak government, it was no match for growing social pressures and a deepening gulf between society and state. With few real policies, one of the last liberal

Tuscany. Unification, under the leadership of Count Camillo Benso Cavour, a French-speaking Piedmontese, was seen as a foreign threat to the de facto sovereignty of Florence and the smaller city-states. Defenders of the Risorgimento, the Movement for Italian Unification, appealed to nascent patriotism. Critics of unification cited Dante's pleas to Tuscan liberty before both sides settled down to start subverting the power of the new rulers. The welding of Tuscans into Italians started promisingly

LEFT: American Grand Tourist Allen Smith contemplating the Arno, by François-Xavier Fabre (1797).
ABOVE: Montecatini in the early 1900s.

governments blundered into World War I. Italy's unpopular late entry cost Tuscan lives and support. The pyrrhic victory was exacerbated by a power vacuum, economic problems and a revolutionary working class. Benito Mussolini, from neighbouring Emilia, wasted no opportunity in proclaiming, "Governing Italy is not only impossible, it is useless," before proceeding to govern it impossibly but fairly usefully for 20 years.

By 1922, the corporate state was literally under construction. The economic benefits lasted until 1929, but the aesthetic effects linger on in functionally "improved" cities all over Tuscany. Florence station, from which trains

Foreign Writers in Tuscany

The poet Shelley pronounced Tuscany a "paradise of exiles" tempted by art, adventure and escape from persecution. But the exiles' motives were as varied as their prose styles. Tobias Smollett (1721–71), the misanthropic Scottish writer, found nothing to admire in Tuscany. He failed to appreciate the entrepreneurial nature of the Tuscan aristocracy, finding it undignified for "a noble to sell a pound of figs or to take money for a glass of sour wine". The Romantics were more enthusiastic. Lord Byron

threw himself into Renaissance art and was "dazzled, drunk with Beauty" in Santa Croce. His friend Shelley adored Pisan landscapes and Livornese seascapes, tragically drowning near La Spezia. Tuscany soon became a pilgrimage for the later Romantic poets, such as Tennyson and Wordsworth.

Although officially a diplomat in Florence, French novelist, Stendhal, spent most of his time absorbing Renaissance frescoes and planning his novel, *Le Rouge et le Noir* (1830). As with Byron, the Santa Croce Effect sent Stendhal reeling: once outside, "I walked in constant fear of falling to the ground." This aesthetic sickness is now known as the Stendhal Syndrome.

Henry James was one of the few foreign writers able to see through Tuscany's literary and artistic veil, taking a more pragmatic approach. His *Portrait of Places* gives an opinionated but sensitive picture of the region in the 1870s.

The most romantic mid-Victorian couple was undoubtedly the poets Elizabeth Barrett Browning and Robert Browning. Robert brought his wife to Florence because of her poor health. There he cunningly used local Chianti to wean Elizabeth off her long addiction to laudanum. Their 15th-century *palazzo*, redecorated in Victorian style, is now a literary museum and writers' haunt.

The 20th century brought E.M. Forster, with his ironic analysis of the resident English community at play. Forster's *A Room with a View* is famous for its portrayal of the heroine's encounter with alien culture and passions. Virginia Woolf, along with many other writers on Tuscany, saw her own image reflected in the landscape, "infinite emptiness, loneliness, silence…", while D.H. Lawrence, living in his "grave old Tuscan villa", imagined he was communing with the original Etruscans.

World War II prevented further literary flowering, but in *War In Val d'Orcia*, Iris Origo, an Anglo-Florentine, painted a dramatic picture of the Tuscan battlefield. As a young woman Origo was part of Lawrence's artistic circle, but her understanding of the Tuscans set her apart. Soon after the war, the Welsh poet Dylan Thomas came to Tuscany for the first time and was entranced: "The pine hills are endless, the cypresses at the hilltop tell one all about the length of death, the woods are deep as love and full of goats." He apparently enjoyed a hedonistic lifestyle, vegetating in the sun and devouring strawberries and wine at only 20 lire a glass.

Tuscany still draws literary pilgrims. Frances Mayes's recent best-seller, *Under the Tuscan Sun,* has brought a fresh wave of American tourists in search of the Tuscan experience. The irony is that tourism is in danger of destroying the Tuscan idyll visitors have come in search of for centuries. ❑

LEFT: Virginia Woolf saw "loneliness".

presumably ran on time, was the first Functionalist station in Italy. At the outbreak of World War II, most Tuscans were cautiously neutral. Mussolini, despite having signed the Pact of Steel with Germany, only entered the war in 1940, after the fall of France. By 1943 the north was under German control, but the Allies were progressing northwards from Sicily. Allied bombing, German entrenchment and an emerging Tuscan Resistance transformed Tuscany into a battleground.

Anti-Fascist cells had been secretly set up by the Communists and Catholics in key towns under German and neo-Fascist control. Florence was split: while it was the intellectual centre of

winter behind the so-called "Gothic Line" in the Apennines. Apart from Florence, the partisans were very active in the Monte Amiata area, as well as in the Val d'Orcia where the writer Iris Origo, an Englishwoman married to an Italian *marchese*, sheltered many refugees and prisoners of war in her villa, La Foce.

Writing about it at the time, she grimly observed, "In the last few days I have seen Radicofani and Cortignano destroyed, the countryside and farms studded with shell holes, girls raped, and human beings and cattle killed. Otherwise the events of the last week have had little effect upon either side; it is the civilians who have suffered."

the Resistance it also harboured strong Fascist sympathisers. Even after the city was captured by the Allies, individual Fascists held out, firing from the rooftops. Surprising loyalties emerged: while the director of the British Institute was a known Fascist sympathiser, the German consul risked his life to protect Florentines who had been denounced. After the liberation he was granted the freedom of the city.

Florence was liberated in August 1943, but Mussolini and the German forces survived the

Nor were the Allies completely blameless. The modernity of Grosseto, Livorno and Pisa today owes much to Allied bombing in 1943. The British War Office reports naturally exonerated the Allies: "No damage of any significance is attributable to Allied action [in Florence]." The Allies issued their troops with booklets listing various buildings to be protected, including the tricky prospect of safeguarding the "living museum" of Florence: "The whole city of Florence must rank as a work of art of the first importance." According to one report, "The great monuments, nearly all of which lie north of the river, escaped practically undamaged because,

ABOVE: Hitler and Mussolini salute at Florence's Tomb of the Fascist Martyrs.

though the enemy held the northern bank against an advance, our troops deliberately refrained from firing upon them."

Commendable feats of Allied bravery included the penetration of enemy lines via the Vasari Corridor, a secret route used by the Medici in similar crises. Despite Allied concern and care, Florence nevertheless lost innumerable bridges, streets, libraries, churches, *palazzi*, paintings and Tuscan lives. But in contrast to the "mutilated victory" of 1919, Italy lost the war but won the peace.

Massimo Salvatore, a supporter of the partisans in Florence, saw the war as a character-building exercise: "Without it [we] would surely have sunk into a morass of low politics and intrigues." That was still to come.

"Red-belt" Tuscany

Tuscans may be conservative by nature, but they are also fiercely independent. Since World War II, they have tended to vote for right-wing governments nationally but for left-wing councils locally. Until recently, this meant Christian Democracy at national level and Communism at regional level. On the surface, this appeared a rather curious recipe for success.

Given the level of national opposition to Communists, the Communist Party evolved an aggressively pro-regionalist stance. The reward

THE FLOODING OF FLORENCE

When the Arno broke its banks in 1966, the havoc caused to the city's heritage was immediate: Santa Croce was soon under water; the Duomo lost sections of its marble façade; panels from the Baptistery doors were swept away; statues from the Arno bridges were lost; over a million antiquarian books and illuminated manuscripts were destroyed; and countless artworks were damaged. Although most works have been restored to their original state, Cimabue's *Crucifix* in Santa Croce was controversially left semi-restored. Instead of re-creating the missing sections of the work, restorers simply painted in the spaces with patches of neutral colour, intended to symbolise the city's "wound".

Since the flood, attempts have been made to ensure that the disaster will not be repeated; the river bed near the Ponte Vecchio has been deepened, and the river banks around Ponte Amerigo Vespucci have been reinforced by massive walls. Changes in the river's level are scrupulously monitored by computers and video cameras. Throughout the city, both inside and on the façades of buildings, small plaques have been mounted on the walls, showing the 1966 flood levels. This is especially striking in the area around Santa Croce, one of the lowest parts of the city. The actual water marks are still visible on some buildings which have not been repainted since the disaster.

was the "red belt" across central Italy, run by left-wing coalitions since the first regional elections in 1970. Red Tuscany formed the central strand between Emilia Romagna's model economy and rural Umbria. Despite the transformations in the "new Italy", the "red" regions survive under broad left labels as some of the most efficient of regional governments.

The Tuscan left believes in a broad but increasingly secular Church. Civic culture, regional pride and fierce individualism form the real faith. The power of the left is as much a reflection of regional hostility to Roman centralisation as an espousal of social democratic principles. Even in "red-belt" Tuscany,

ments suffered from opportunism, not lack of opportunity. *Partitocrazia* (party influence) supplanted democracy, extending from government to public corporations, infiltrating banking, the judiciary and media, and the public tacitly condoned this "old boys' network".

Corruption and terror

The early 1990s saw a series of political scandals involving bribes, and the result was the *Mani Pulite* ("Clean Hands") campaign under the fiery leadership of Antonio di Pietro, a former magistrate who became Italy's most popular public figure when he spearheaded inquiries into corrupt practices in politics, business and

the region's most popular newspaper is the right-wing but regional *La Nazione*, not the left-wing but national *La Repubblica*. How could a Roman product possibly compete with a Florentine/Sienese masterpiece?

At a national level, however, by the early 1990s, more than 50 post-war "swing-door" governments had come and gone. To many observers, the source of this crisis lay in Italy's administration and dubious morality. Senior party leaders tended to die in office, govern-

state administration. A seemingly vast network was uncovered, in which public contracts were awarded by politicians to businesses in return for bribes. Italian public life was convulsed by the scandal, dubbed *Tangentopoli* – literally, "Bribesville". Dozens of MPs and businessmen came under investigation, with some arrested and others committing suicide. The Christian Democrat Party, which had dominated Italian politics since the war, collapsed under the weight of its own corruption. Two former prime ministers – the socialist Bettino Craxi and the Christian Democrat veteran and seven times former prime minister Giulio Andreotti – were investigated.

LEFT: pictures from the Uffizi laid out for restoration after the 1966 flood.
ABOVE: Craxi and Andreotti shake hands.

Craxi slipped through the net and died in self-imposed exile in Tunisia in January 2000, with arrest warrants hanging over his head for corruption charges. Andreotti, who was instead charged with Mafia ties, was eventually let off after a mammoth trial lasting years. His acquittal was later held up on appeal by state prosecutors. The appeal judges found Andreotti to have enjoyed "friendly" and direct relations with the Mafia "up until 1980", but not later – so `Beelzebub' escaped prosecution thanks to the statute of limitations.

In the midst of the political upheaval, in May 1993 Florence suffered yet another devastating blow, when a bomb planted by the Mafia

bosses in 1998. Meanwhile, while no area of Italy appeared to have been left untouched by corruption, including Florence, in the end few, if any, *Tangentopoli* politicians served much real time in jail.

In a frank interview in July 2005, film director Bernardo Bertolucci told the *Corriere della Sera*: "Italy lost a great opportunity after *Tangentopoli*. It should have had a real examination of conscience, in order to understand how on earth it could be that there were so many corrupt figures populating our landscape, accomplices of a system which goes from small tips in return for small favours, to large *tangenti* [bribes] for big contracts. And instead we have wound up

behind the Uffizi gallery rocked the city, both physically and psychologically. Five people were killed, and priceless paintings and sculptures damaged, while a handful were destroyed. The fabric of the Uffizi's buildings was damaged, and several medieval buildings around the corner were virtually destroyed.

The Mafia's widely perceived aim was to use the attack, and others in Milan and Rome, to force the Italian state into submission, and to agree to a deal of mutual convenience with the Mob, as had been enjoyed with the Christian Democrats. The jailed Sicilian Godfather, Salvatore "Toto" Riina, was sentenced to life for the Uffizi bombing, along with other crime

with an illegal prime minister, who was elected amid conditions of almost complete control of the media." He was referring to Silvio Berlusconi, the media tycoon turned prime minister.

Silvio Berlusconi

Berlusconi, the populist, perma-tanned tycoon, was first elected premier in 1994, on an anti-corruption ticket, and has gone on to lead two further administrations. Ironically, Berlusconi's career has been dogged by charges of everything from conflict of interests to embezzlement and false accounting. His classic response is that such allegations have been politically motivated by rivals and a biased judiciary. Clowning and corruption scandals aside, Berlusconi has dominated Italian life like no other politician in recent times, as much by his over-size personality as by his vast wealth. The billionaire's business empire spans the media, entertainment, insurance, construction and sport (the tycoon owns AC Milan football club). Above all, Berlusconi's critics cite conflict of interests, including the media mogul's ownership of three private television channels, and undue influence over the public broadcasting networks.

Berlusconi's second term, from 2001-6, made him the only post-war Prime Minister to govern for a full five-year term. Despite bring-

lionaire businessman was elected on a platform of reducing public spending, lowering taxes, reforming the judiciary, and modernising the country's infrastructure. The jury is still out on the legacy of Italy's maverick leader.

Paul Ginsberg, Professor of Contemporary History at Florence University, fears Berlusconi's domination of the political scene heralds a "slow and insidious mutation" in the democratic process. But he also sees Berlusconi as a product of Italian culture, tapping into the traditions of patronage, family and clan. Such clannishness, coupled with a weak state, fosters a curious cocktail of clientelism and disaffection, at odds with the civic sense the

ing a semblance of stability, the right-wing empire-builder narrowly lost out to Romano Prodi in 2006, ceding to a fragile left-wing coalition whose eventual collapse prompted fresh elections. Disillusionment with a lack of leadership from the left led to the right regaining power in 2008, masterminded by Berlusconi's People of Freedom party. Formed by an alliance between Berlusconi's Forza Italia and the once Fascistic Alleanza Nazionale, the party won a comfortable victory. The flamboyant bil-

LEFT: aftermath of the 1993 bombing of the Uffizi.
ABOVE: Berlusconi re-elected prime minister in 2008 for the third time.

country so needs. Berlusconi's fans grudgingly feel that only a successful businessman can transform a recalcitrant country into a model business. Optimists see Berlusconi as desperately trying to get things right in his third term – and point to the leadership skills he deployed in resolving the rubbish crisis in Naples shortly after regaining office in 2008. Instead, detractors, many of them Tuscan, believe that Berlusconi entered politics to save his own skin, protect his empire and evade legal charges. Whether Berlusconi's swansong is about lining his pockets or writing his name in the history books, the great showman looks set to baffle fans and foes alike. ❏

Decisive Dates

Etruscans and Romans

800–500 BC Etruscan civilisation flourishes. Etruria Propria, a confederation of 12 states, includes Arezzo, Cortona, Chiusi, Fiesole, Populonia, Roselle, Vetulonia, Volterra.

480–290 BC Romans in power; they annex Etruria and found colonies at Ansedonia, Roselle, Volterra, Luni and Lucca.

80 BC Faesulae (now Fiesole) becomes a Roman military colony.

59 BC A colony of Roman army veterans founds Florentia (Florence) on the banks of the Arno.

AD 200–600 Region invaded by Lombards, Goths and Franks.

AD 306 Constantinople becomes capital of Roman Empire; the Byzantine period follows.

AD 476 The Fall of Rome.

Medieval Tuscany

1000–1300 German emperors conquer Italy, followed by constant warring between Guelfs (supporters of the papacy) and Ghibellines (supporters of the Holy Roman Empire).

1062 Pisan navy wins an overwhelming victory over the Saracens in a battle off Palermo.

1115 Florence is granted the status of a *comune* – an independent city governed by a council drawn from the mercantile class.

1118 The consecration of Pisa Cathedral.

1125 Florence begins its expansion with the takeover of Fiesole.

1173 Bonnano Pisano begins work on Pisa Cathedral's campanile, now known as the Leaning Tower.

1246 Work on Florence's Santa Maria Novella begins.

1250 Florence's Bargello built.

1260 Sienese defeat the Florentines in battle of Montaperti.

1289 Florence crushes Arezzo.

1294 Arnolfo di Cambio begins work on Florence's Santa Croce church.

1296 Di Cambio begins work on Florence's Duomo, which – excepting the dome – was completed in 1369.

1301–11 Giovanni Pisano sculpts the pulpit in Pisa cathedral.

1310 Siena's Palazzo Pubblico is completed.

1314 Dante Alighieri begins work on *The Divine Comedy*.

1330 Andrea Pisano is commissioned to design and cast bronze doors for Florence Baptistery.

1334 Giotto di Bondone begins work on the Florentine Campanile.

1338 Pietro Lorenzetti paints the *Good and Bad Government* fresco in Siena's Palazzo Pubblico.

*c.***1345** Florence's Ponte Vecchio is erected by Taddeo Gaddi.

1348 Black death strikes Florence, killing a third of the population.

1350 Boccaccio starts work on *The Decameron*.

1390 John Hawkwood, *condottiero*, becomes Captain General of Florence; inter-city wars fought.

The Renaissance

1406 Pisa is defeated and becomes part of the Florentine state.

1420 Papacy returns to Rome from Avignon.

1421 Florentines pay the Genoese 100,000 florins for Livorno.

1425 Masaccio paints the *Life of St Peter* frescoes in Santa Maria del Carmine.

1434–64 Cosimo de' Medici rules Florence.

1436 Brunelleschi's dome for Florence's Duomo is completed.

1452 Alberti's *Ten Books on Architecture* is published.

1469–92 Lorenzo de' Medici rules Florence.

1478 Sandro Botticelli paints *La Primavera*.

1498 "Mad monk" Savonarola is hanged for heresy in Florence's Piazza della Signoria.

1504 Michelangelo completes *David*.

1513 Niccolò Machiavelli writes *The Prince*.

1527 The sack of Rome.

1530 The Republic of Florence ends as armies of Pope Clement VII and Emperor Charles V besiege the city.

1537 Alessandro de' Medici is murdered by his cousin.

1550 Giorgio Vasari's *Lives of the Most Excellent Architects, Painters and Sculptors* first published.

1554 Florence defeats Siena and incorporates its rival into the Florentine state.

1564–1642 The Pisan Galileo Galilei discovers the principles of dynamics.

Grand Duchy Tuscany

1716 Decree issued by the Grand Duke of Tuscany defines boundaries of Chianti and establishes laws governing production and sale of wine.

1737 Gian Gastone, the last male Medici, dies.

1796 Napoleon's first Italian campaign.

1815 The Grand Duchy is absorbed into the Austrian Empire.

Wartime Tuscany

1848 The War of Independence.

1861 The proclamation of the Kingdom of Italy.

1865–71 Florence is briefly capital of Italy; the Piazza della Repubblica is built in 1865 to celebrate.

1915 Italy enters World War I on the Allies' side.

1922 Benito Mussolini comes to power.

1940 Italy forms pact with Germany and Japan, and enters World War II against Britain and France.

1943 The fall of the Fascists. Mussolini is executed at the end of the war, in 1945.

1946 Italy becomes a republic.

LEFT: Lorenzo de' Medici.
RIGHT: debris from the 1966 flood outside Santa Croce, Florence.

Modern Tuscany

1957 The Treaty of Rome; Italy is a founder member of the EEC (now the European Union).

1966 Massive flooding: the Arno overflows in Florence and many works of art are damaged.

1970 The first regional elections held.

1989 The Leaning Tower of Pisa is closed in response to its increasing tilt.

1993 A terrorist bomb in Florence kills five people and damages the Uffizi.

1994 A right-wing government ushers in the Second Republic. Silvio Berlusconi elected premier.

1996 The electorate does an about-turn and elects Romano Prodi's left-wing Ulivo Party.

1996–7 Freak fires and floods ravage much of

the region, killing at least 14 people.

2000 Top Mafia bosses Filippo Graviano and Leoluca Bagarella are imprisoned for their part in the Uffizi bombing.

2001 Silvio Berlusconi is elected prime minister. His Forza Italia party governs in coalition with the National Alliance and the Northern League.

2002 The euro replaces the lira.

2005 Pope John Paul II dies and is succeeded by Cardinal Joseph Ratzinger, elected 265th pope, who takes the name Benedict XVI.

2006 Romano Prodi leads a fragile left-wing coalition government.

2008 Berlusconi voted prime minister for the third time. ❑

TUSCANY TODAY

The challenges facing modern Tuscans are many, and include achieving a successful blend of the old and the new

Pienza is typical Tuscany. This tower-capped 15th-century village gazing imperiously over lush valleys is everything an Italophile could wish for – so much so that this town of 2,300 has 100,000 visitors a year. In the rush to enjoy rustic perfection, tourism has turned high-season Pienza into an elbow-to-elbow mêlée. And this is Tuscany's dilemma. Her beauty is in danger of becoming her beast. While Rome does government and Milan does commerce, La Toscana does cypress-lined rolling hills and the Renaissance. The region's wealth is her landscape and heritage, and the question for the 21st century is how to preserve this and at the same time find room for 10 million tourists a year.

The price of tourism

Florence's long-standing relationship with tourism is finely balanced. The city that invented the Stendhal Syndrome – the dizzying disorientation some visitors experience when they overdose on Florentine Renaissance masterpieces – is in danger of sending tourists' heads spinning from hours spent queuing to enter its famous sites.

There are also concerns that tourism could affect the city's character. Historic artisan shops are struggling with rent hikes, as landlords try to maximise profits. And landmark stops on the Grand Tour itinerary are striving to keep their dignity; Piazza Donatello's cemetery – the burial place of English poet Elizabeth Barrett

Browning – is now visited to the honking soundtrack of traffic on roads which threaten to overwhelm this once quiet oasis.

For residents and visitors alike, traffic pollution is a blot on the landscape. On hot, windless days the city is shrouded in a cloudy pall. The traffic police complain that their 600-strong force was designed to cope with Florence's 400,000 residents, not the summer population of millions. Noise and air pollution harm major buildings and modern sensibilities. In the historic centre, pollution has been reduced, but some residents complain that restrictions on traffic in the centre merely lead to the clogging of the *viali*, Florence's arteries.

LEFT: Florence draws huge crowds all year round.
RIGHT: in Tuscan villages domesticity still reigns.

A controversial new tram line currently under construction is meant to address the problems of congestion and pollution, but critics of the scheme believe it will cause irretrievable damage, particularly to the cathedral square. More environmentally friendly is the much-anticipated new bike-sharing service, modeled on the successful initiatives in Paris, Barcelona and other European cities.

Tuscany's second city, Pisa, is also grappling with the quick-fire habits of the modern tourist. With day-tripper coaches decanting passengers on a racing schedule to take in the highlights of the Campo Dei Miracoli in as short a time as possible, the rest of Pisa often

regional hub; but the town doesn't want to be Tuscany's airport lounge – Pisa needs visitors to come for more than just a photo of the tower.

In the countryside, the same problems which face Florence and Pisa are played out on a smaller scale. But for Tuscany's hill towns there is an extra resonance to the money and opportunities tourism brings.

The countryside revival

World War II shattered rural life in Tuscany – ending the feudal *mezzadria* system, with land governed by a few rich aristocrats. With the paternalistic social structure that had sustained the countryside for centuries gone, thousands of

goes unnoticed. This is not surprising. No city in the world is as closely associated with one single monument as Pisa is with her tower. Even during the 1990s, when the marble miracle was in architectural intensive care and out of bounds to visitors, most tourists still failed to notice that there was life outside the Campo.

To encourage visitors to enjoy the unhurried, bookish atmosphere of the Pisa beyond the Tower, local government has refurbished the market area around Piazza delle Vettovaglie. And the Arno river, with its boat tours and festivals, is being touted as the Pisan "left bank". The city's recent tourist trump card is the budget airlines' choice of Galileo Galilei airport as their

farmers and villagers abandoned their homes and headed for the towns and cities in search of jobs. Many left Italy never to return. Villages which had been the hub of rural life for thousands of years became ghost towns overnight.

To generate local jobs, some areas turned themselves over to industrial production. Textiles, chemicals, petroleum and fertiliser factories spread though the region. And though they provided much-needed employment for the now landless peasantry, the visual impact on the countryside was less than welcome. Today they sit uncomfortably alongside the rustic charm that characterises the region. For those who remained in their villages and farms, life was hard. Typically the older ones clung on – and with no children in the schools, or young blood to energise the economy, the countryside was drifting into a decaying slumber.

Monticchiello's response to these seismic changes was unique. Thirty-five years ago this village of 500 people in the bobbing hills of the Orcia valley decided to write and perform a play about their plight. Four decades on, the *teatro povero* is an annual event. The plays' themes have charted the fall and rise of rural Tuscan life. Early productions were pleas to the young people not to leave, and calls for the government to sustain traditional rural life. More recent dramas have dealt with the

1960s and '70s, saw the empty farmhouses as an opportunity to create a rural idyll. Not surprisingly, the peasant farmers who had abandoned their homes to posterity could not believe their luck, and news soon spread that foreigners were prepared to pay good money for crumbling piles.

The few became many, and now over 100,000 farmhouses have been brought back to life. The British presence gave birth to the nickname Chiantishire. Residents of this very English Italy (though an increasing number of Americans are buying up properties and setting up business in the area) include writers John Mortimer, Muriel Spark and Harold Pinter.

reverse phenomenon: wealthy people moving from the cities in search of an idealised Tuscan rural "lifestyle". This constant flow of newcomers into the region's peasant heartland threatens to overwhelm the character of the area. As Monticchiello's director Andrea Cresti puts it, rural Tuscany is in danger of becoming "a brand too successful for its own good".

The early days of this "brand" was pioneered by Germans and Britons who, in the

LEFT: a positive approach to Florence's pollution problem. **ABOVE:** *agriturismo* attracts families wanting a taste of the Tuscan rural lifestyle.

Tuscans protest that the Chiantishire commuters have pushed prices so high that locals can't afford to live in their native villages. Foreigners counter this by pointing out that they saved places like Sovicille near Siena, or Bugnano near Lucca from total abandonment, and that blaming *"stranieri"* is simply passport prejudice, because wealthy Florentines and Pisans are just as busy buying second homes as foreigners. Tuscan landowners themselves have benefited from the revival of the countryside. *Agriturismo* – farm stays – are increasingly popular, both as a way of making the farm pay, and as an opportunity for locals to restore or convert outhouses and barns.

Though the medieval *mezzadria* system of share-cropping was officially banned in 1978, old traditions die hard. The scale of farming in most of the region is small; apart from some large wheat and cattle farms in the Val d'Arno and Val di Chiana, much of the farming is labour-intensive, relatively unmechanised and organic. Partly through poverty and partly through tradition, Tuscany has gained itself a reputation as Europe's leading region for small-scale sustainable farming.

Tuscany's countryside traditions have deep roots. Lucca's olive trees date back to Roman times, and the region's ancient vineyards are terraced onto slopes which have been cultivated for wine for centuries. And, after decades of intensive logging which left some parts of the Casentino forest slopes bare, official protection has seen the fir, beech and maple trees recover. Even the wild wolves which were once lost to this part of the country are back.

Environmental issues

But there is still much work to be done if tourism and the environment are going to co-exist. The *legambiente* (environmental league), which monitors pollution on Italy's beaches, gives the Tuscan Riviera a mixed report: while some of the beaches are clean, others exceed pollution levels by 10 times the acceptable level.

A TUSCAN HALL OF FAME

There's a saying that Tuscany is "equally blessed by the genius of man and nature". And history has proved the proverb, with the greatest of the region's greats achieving worldwide fame. Not surprisingly, many of the province's superstars are from the world of art: Giotto, Leonardo da Vinci, Michelangelo, Donatello, Masaccio and Cellini were all born in or near Florence. And Giorgio Vasari – also a painter – is famed for his much-read *Lives of the Artists*.

Literary celebrities include the writer triumvirate Dante, Petrarch and Boccaccio (born in Paris, but raised in Florence). While in the field of music, the composer Puccini hailed from Lucca, and opera itself was born in Florence in the late 1500s. Tuscany was also home to the astronomer Galileo, father of modern mathematics, Leonardo Fibonacci, the philosopher Machiavelli, architect Brunelleschi and merchant-turned-explorer Amerigo Vespucci.

Many famous modern-day Tuscans are associated with the fashion world, such as Emilio Pucci, Guccio Gucci and Salvatore Ferragamo (a transplanted Neapolitan). While showbiz representatives include singer Andrea Bocelli, film-makers Franco Zeffirelli and the Taviani brothers, producer-cum-politician Vittorio Cecchi Gori and the Oscar-winning film-maker and comedian Roberto Benigni.

The river Arno, which flows 240 km (150 miles) through the heart of Tuscany, has suffered from decades of industrial development. A critical problem for people living near the Arno is flooding. Heavy rains bring the water up to dangerous levels, most notoriously in 1966 when it rose 6 metres (20 ft), causing death and destruction and compromising Florence's cultural heritage. After years of debate, the authorities are finally taking action by building expansion chambers to reduce the risk of future floods.

Engineers are also constructing Florence's first-ever sewage-treatment plant. Currently, waste from Florence flows directly into the Arno, in stark contravention of EU directives.

have suffered far less from the Disneyfication that has infected central Tuscany. And to the west, the Maremma is still imbued with a sense of mystery and rural isolation, its wild pine woods a reminder that Tuscany is blessed with more forest than any other region in Italy. And in these unspoilt environments lies the region's magnetic charm. True Tuscans are provincial, conservative and independent; civic culture and regional pride are their touchstones, and as a consequence the quality of life – both urban and rural – is generally good; nobody is prepared to jeopardise this by turning the region over to heavy industry. The industries Tuscans speak of with pride, such as Siena's

A treatment plant is being built at Lastra, just outside Florence, and it is hoped that a cleaned-up river will be an opportunity to revive the river banks for leisure.

Tuscany's allure

Outside the Florence–Siena axis the effects of modern tourism are far less visible. Here another Tuscany emerges; the Apuan Alps and Garfagnana region in the north with their rugged mountains, plunging valleys and marble mines,

LEFT: Tuscan-born Roberto Benigni with fellow Oscar-winning actors. **ABOVE:** alabaster craftsman in Volterra.

panforte, Carrara's marble, Volterra's alabaster and Arezzo gold, date back to medieval times.

For all its Dantesque grandiloquence and Renaissance finery, Tuscany's heart is rural. Its largest city is home to less than half a million people, and the nickname for Tuscans is *"Mangiafagioli"* (bean eaters). So it is perhaps not surprising that the province's most loved son is a child of countryside Arezzo. Italy's tragicomic clown prince – Oscar-winning film-maker and actor Roberto Benigni – speaks lovingly of his homeland as "a region of hunters and hares, of large peasant women and wild and poetic beauty". And who would argue with Tuscany's "grande Roberto"? ❏

RENAISSANCE ART

Art historians divide the Renaissance into three sub-periods: the Trecento (1300s) was the era of the workshop and fresco; the Quattrocento (1400s) welcomed a new realism featuring perspective and emotion; the Cinquecento (1500s), or High Renaissance, was a peak period followed by a sharp decline, as political and economic decay eventually took its toll

One of the great myths of history provides a kind of Hollywood scenario for the "birth of the Renaissance", linking it to the fall of Constantinople in 1453, when scholars were supposed to have escaped, clutching their precious Greek manuscripts, to Italy. There, these manuscripts became a kind of magical seed, taking root, growing and bearing fruit almost immediately as "the Renaissance".

Of course, this is nonsense; like any other human phenomenon, the Renaissance had roots deep in history. It was the political fragmentation of Italy which created the Renaissance, each little city-state contributing something unique to the whole. But the process certainly started in Florence, and the city dominated the cultural scene until the early 16th century. Again and again over the centuries, attempts have been made to analyse the causes of the Florentine flowering, with reasons ranging from the poverty of the soil to the quality of the light. But it is no more possible to "explain" this than any other mystery of the human spirit.

Defining the Renaissance

The very word "renaissance" is a Florentine invention. In his book *Lives of the Most Excellent Architects, Painters and Sculptors*, first published in 1550, Vasari, first of the art historians, remarks that the reader "will now be able

LEFT: portrait of a young man (*c.*1475), probably a member of the Medici dynasty, by Botticelli (Uffizi).
RIGHT: *The Awakening Slave* (1519–20), one of four "unfinished" *Slaves* by Michelangelo (Accademia), intended for the tomb of Pope Julius II in Rome.

to recognise more easily the progress of [art's] rebirth *(il progresso della sua rinascita)*".

But what, exactly, did Vasari mean by *rinascita*? What was being "reborn"? Vasari was referring to a rebirth of the art and architecture of classical times, that is, before Emperor Constantine transferred the seat of empire to Constantinople at the beginning of the 4th century AD, causing Byzantium to become the centre of art and culture. A distinctive architecture, based on Roman models, using bricks and featuring domes and cupolas, was developed. Byzantine artists covered the interiors with mosaics, a Roman decorative form which they developed into a sumptuous art form, the thousands of glazed-stone fragments catching the light in a way no fresco ever could. The best examples in Italy are in Ravenna, made in the 5th and 6th centuries, but the style prevailed in the 11th century in San Marco, Venice, and even in the 13th century in the magnificent Baptistery in Florence. It was the stiff formalised work of Byzantine artists that Vasari, who dismissed them as "a certain residue of Greeks", was attacking, and which was completely overthrown by the new naturalism of the Renaissance artists.

Architects drew and measured the ruins of the Roman cities, rediscovering their building techniques and their rules of proportion, the "classical orders". Vitruvius' *Ten Books on*

Architecture, the only surviving manual from classical times, was studied anew and became the basis, in the 15th century, for Alberti's treatise of the same name.

Painting, which of all the arts is preeminently *the* art of the Renaissance, owed little to antiquity, partly because no Roman examples survived to be used as models. Renaissance artists broke new ground, discovering perspective and observing the natural world which surrounded them. The 14th-century Florentine artist Cennino Cennini gave good advice to his fellow artists. "If you wish to draw mountains well, so that they appear natural," he wrote, "procure some large stones,

rocky, not polished, and draw from these." The idea of a handful of stones standing in for the Alps or the Apennines might seem ludicrous, but it was a pointer to the new road the artist was taking, the road to reality in nature.

The classical world provided the inspiration for the artist to rise above the narrow medieval world, with its emphasis on theological studies. But, once he had started, he went his own way. What was reborn was an artistic sensibility but not a re-cycled past.

The Trecento

Until the Quattrocento (15th century), the term "artist" had no particular significance, being virtually interchangeable with "artisan" or "craftsman". All were members of guilds, or *arti*: there was an *arte* for the shoemaker, no more and no less valid than the *arte* for the goldsmith, itself a sub-division of the immensely powerful Silk Guild. The guilds extended their control, as a matter of course, over the decorative as well as the useful arts. Sculptors and architects were enrolled with the masons, and painters formed a subdivision of the apothecaries, on the general principle that they had to have some acquaintance with chemistry to prepare their colours.

Far from resenting the obligation to join associations, painters and sculptors formed their own groups, or *compagnie*, created both within and across the boundaries of the larger guilds. The reasons were both social and technical. Socially, members could help each other, the group as a whole sharing both profits and losses. Technically, an increasing amount of work was done in cooperation, either on a kind of conveyor-belt system (two or three men might be engaged at successive stages in the shaping of a pillar, from rough hewing to final carving) or working side by side.

The growing popularity of the process known as *buon fresco* demanded this cooperative approach. The medium of fresco painting had been introduced about a century earlier, and time had shown that it was the most permanent of all forms of mural art, since the colouring became an intrinsic part of the plaster itself.

In addition to these large, set tasks, the workshop (or *bottega*) would produce a variety of smaller articles for sale, either on speculation or on commission, ranging from painted scabbards and armorial bearings to holy pictures and statues. There was widespread demand for religious art, which provided the bread and butter for hundreds of small *botteghe*. A peasant may have scraped together a few lire for a picture; a parish priest might have a large sum at his disposal and commission a mural or even an altarpiece, or a merchant who had made his fortune might be anxious to propitiate fate and show appropriate piety.

The potential client had little interest in the identity of the craftsmen producing his order. But, if expensive colours were used (gold, silver, or blue made from the semi-precious lapis lazuli), then the fact was clearly stated in the contract, along with the date of delivery of the finished piece. Commissioned work was almost invariably done on these written contracts which, in addition, usually specified how many figures were to appear in the finished painting, their activities and attributes. Religious paintings touched on the delicate area of religious orthodoxy, and the wise craftsman ensured that his client stated exactly what he wanted.

The identity of most of the workers in these workshops is unknown. They were conscientious and skilled, rather than brilliant, but they formed the subsoil from which the genius of the Quattrocento could flourish. The actual working pattern of the *bottega*, whereby a group of lesser men would paint the main body of a picture, leaving it to the identified master to put the finishing touches to it, would continue into the so-called High Renaissance of the Cinquecento, making it difficult and at times impossible for the most skilled art critic to say that such a painting is, beyond a doubt, the work of a particular famous artist.

Early Renaissance art

Comparing Trecento (or Gothic) paintings in any Tuscan art gallery with the work of Quattrocento (or early Renaissance) artists reveals a compelling difference: whereas Gothic paintings are iconographic, revelling in the use of celestial gold and presenting a spiritual Madonna and Child for worship and contemplation, the same subject in the hands of Renaissance painters becomes a study in living flesh, the figures of mother and child endowed with attitudes, character, emotions and psychological motivation. Scholars argue endlessly about why this great change occurred, but there is near-universal agreement on who started it: Giotto di Bondone (1267–1337), who, according to Vasari, "restored art to the better path followed in modern times".

Tradition has it that Giotto was working as a shepherd boy until Cimabue, himself a pioneer of greater naturalism in art, discovered that Giotto could draw a perfect circle freehand, and offered to train him as an artist. Pupil soon

surpassed master, and Giotto went on to create the great *St Francis* fresco cycle in the Upper Basilica in Assisi and the *Life of Christ* fresco series in the Scrovegni Chapel in Padua. In Florence his main masterpiece is in the Franciscan church of Santa Croce, where his work (and, of course, that of the *bottega* that assisted him) covers the walls of the two chapels to the right of the choir.

Despite his supposedly rural experience, even in Giotto's work nature is formalised and in the background. It is the humans who occupy the foreground, vibrantly alive.

Giotto, who died in 1337, was ahead of his time in introducing character and individuality

LEFT: detail from the *Coronation of the Virgin* (*c.*1330) altarpiece by Giotto (Santa Croce, Florence).
RIGHT: scene from the *Life of St Nicholas* (*c.*1327–30) by Lorenzetti (Uffizi).

to his art. He was not, however, entirely alone in these endeavours. Nicola (1223–84) and Giovanni (1245–1314) Pisano, the father and son team, were achieving similar advances in sculpture at the same time as Giotto was breaking new ground in art.

At the time when the Pisani were living and working in Pisa, it was the fashion for Pisan merchants to ship home Roman sarcophagi from the Holy Land or North Africa for eventual reuse as their own tombs. Scores of them still line the cloister surrounding Pisa's Campo Santo cemetery. Inspired by the realistic battle scenes carved on these antique marble tombs, the Pisani created their own versions: great

pulpits sculpted with crowded and dramatic scenes from the life of Christ, which can be seen in Pisa's Cathedral and Baptistery, and in Sant'Andrea church in Pistoia.

In architecture, the classical inspiration that helped to define the Renaissance had never disappeared to quite the same degree as it had in art. The very name Romanesque – meaning derived from or in the Roman style – indicates the essential continuity between the architecture of Rome and that of Tuscany in the 1300s. Churches were still built to the same basilican plan as those of the late Roman period, and, though the façades of many Tuscan churches look quite unclassical, they are still based on the

geometry of the Roman hemispherical arch, as distinct from the four-centred arches of Venice or the pointed arches of French Gothic. What distinguishes Tuscan Romanesque from Lombardic or Piedmontese is the exuberant use of polychrome marble to create complex geometrical patterns. Pisa was the seminal influence here – trade links with Spain and North Africa led to the adoption of arabic numerals in place of Roman, and to the fondness for surface patterning in architecture, copying Moorish tilework and textiles.

From Pisa the oriental influence spread to Lucca, Prato, Pistoia and even to Florence, where it was to pave the way for the great polychrome Campanile built by Giotto. Straddling two ages, Giotto has been claimed by rival art historians both as a Gothic artist and as the pioneer of the Renaissance. Perhaps if war and the Black Death had not ravaged Europe from the 1340s, the Renaissance might well have blossomed sooner than it did. As it was, another 60 years were to pass before the naturalism pioneered by Giotto and the Pisani was to re-emerge, this time as a mass artistic movement.

The Quattrocento

A great breakthrough took place in Florence at the beginning of the 15th century, a moment so important that it can be dated to within a few years, and a new philosophy of life flowed through the city. Until the 1470s, Florence was a kind of dynamo, providing light and energy for the entire peninsula. The city retained its dominance in art for barely a lifespan, however, because it exported so much of its native talent – which ensured the spread of Renaissance values but, with it, Florence's own relative eclipse.

The breakthrough began when the Florentine *Signoria*, or government, decided to refurbish the ceremonial centre of Florence: the group of buildings consisting of the Cathedral, the Campanile – begun by Giotto in 1334 and finished after his death but to his design in 1359 – and the octagonal Baptistery. This little black-and-white building had a special place in Florentine affections, and when, in 1401, it was decided to offer a thanksgiving for the city's escape from plague, the Baptistery was chosen to benefit. The wealthy Wool Guild announced that they would finance the design and casting of a second set of bronze doors that would be even grander than those of Pisano. The design for it was thrown open to competition.

Out of the many entrants, seven were chosen each to execute a panel on the same subject: the sacrifice of Isaac. Two of the entrants, the 21-year-old Brunelleschi, later credited as the creator of the "Renaissance style" in architecture, and the 20-year-old Lorenzo Ghiberti, produced work which caused considerable difficulty to the judges. Both the panels exist today, one preserved in the Museo dell'Opera del Duomo, the other in the Bargello museum. Comparing the two, posterity finds it impossible to say which is "better". The *Syndics*,

expected to put in a full day's work "like any journeyman".

In the later contracts, he is treated far more as a free agent, permitted to undertake other commissions. Ghiberti, too, made explicit the change by boldly including his own self-portrait among the sculptures of the door.

Learning from the ancients

Meanwhile, in Rome with his friend Donatello, Brunelleschi was discovering how the ancients had built their enormous structures. In an entirely new approach to the past, he examined originals rather than copies of copies. One of his findings – or possibly, inventions – was the

at a loss to choose, came up with a compromise, suggesting that the artists should share the work. Brunelleschi declined and took himself off to Rome, while Ghiberti began work on the doors, completing them 22 years later.

He was offered the commission to produce a second pair: these took him 27 years. During the almost half-century that he worked on the project, it is possible to see in his contracts the changing status of the artist. In the first contract he is treated essentially as an artisan,

ulivella. Intrigued and puzzled by the existence of regular-shaped holes in the huge stone blocks of the ancient buildings, he assumed that they had been made to allow the block to be gripped by some device, and designed a kind of grappling iron to fit. Whether or not the Romans had actually used such a device, it was very useful – and a demonstration of the benefits to be gained by studying the past.

Brunelleschi returned to Florence at about the time that the *Syndics* of the Wool Guild, who also had the responsibility for the Cathedral, were puzzling over the problem of completing it. Arnolfo di Cambio had begun it in 1296, and it had been completed, all except for the dome,

LEFT: *Adoration of the Magi* (1423) by Gentile da Fabriano (Uffizi). **ABOVE:** *The Battle of San Romano* (1432) by Paolo Uccello (Uffizi).

by 1369. Nobody knew how to bridge this immense gap which, for half a century, had been covered by a temporary roof.

In 1417 a special meeting was called to debate the problem and consider suggestions, and Brunelleschi put forward his solution. He was mocked for it because it dispensed with the wooden centring over which architects traditionally built their arches and vaults, supporting their weight until the keystone was in place. But, in desperation, the *Syndics* offered him the job. Brunelleschi solved the problem by building a dome that was pointed in sections, supported by ribs with the lightest possible in-filling between them. He built two

Brunelleschi introduced the columns, pediments and cornices he copied from Roman ruins into his churches, there were no surviving examples of Roman domestic architecture for the 15th-century Florentines to copy. When Rucellai, a wealthy Florentine merchant, asked Alberti to design a palace for him, Alberti took as a model the Colosseum in Rome and applied its tiers of arches to the façade of a three-storey *palazzo*. Though it was the only *palazzo* he built, and though Brunelleschi's design for the Medici Palace never got beyond the model stage, these two architects developed a new type of building, a system of proportion and an elegance of line which is still in use today.

shells, an outer skin and an inner one: one way in which the crushing weight of the dome, the problem which had prevented its construction, was considerably reduced.

The work took 16 years, and was completed on 31 August 1436. This was the first Renaissance dome in Italy, the largest unsupported dome in Europe, bigger than the Pantheon in Rome which Brunelleschi had studied, bigger even than the great dome which Michelangelo raised a century later over St Peter's in Rome.

It was Brunelleschi's successor, the scholar Alberti, who first applied the classical orders to domestic architecture and created what we now think of as the Renaissance *palazzo*. Whereas

Brunelleschi's other major breakthrough was his use of perspective. Alberti described its effect to a generation for whom it appeared almost a magical technique: "I describe a rectangle of whatever size I wish, which I imagine to be an open window through which I view whatever is to be depicted there." Donatello (1386–1466) eagerly used the technique in his bas-relief of *Salome offering John's head to Herod*. The observer is looking at a banquet where the diners are recoiling in horror from the offering. Beyond the banqueting rooms can be seen a succession of two more rooms, giving a remarkable and, for contemporaries, almost eerie sense of depth.

A new perspective

Like the difference between Giotto's mobile, dramatic figures and their static, formal predecessors, perspective gave a new vista to civilisation. Its most dramatic form was that employed by the young Masaccio. His great painting of the *Trinity*, in the church of Santa Maria Novella, is an intellectual exercise in the use of perspective that is also infused with religious awe. Beneath a *trompe l'oeil* classical arch stands the immense figure of God the Father, half supporting a cross on which there is an equally immense figure of Christ; below them are various saints and donors and a memento mori of a skeleton in a sarcophagus revealing an ancient warning: "I am what you are, and what I am, you shall be."

The huge figures stand out from the background and appear to loom over the observer. As a young man, Michelangelo used to stand before these, copying them again and again to fix the style in his mind. Eventually, therefore, some essence of this experimental period of the Renaissance found its way into the Sistine Chapel, that shrine of the High Renaissance dominated by Michelangelo's work.

The classical arch in Masaccio's painting is a pointer to a curious development which took place during the Quattrocento – the clothing of Biblical figures in a totally anachronistic way, either in classical Roman attire or in contemporary Florentine dress. The frescoes which Ghirlandaio (1449–94) painted in the Sasseti Chapel within the church of Santa Trinità supposedly concern the prophecies of Christ's birth, and the location should be Augustan Rome. But it is an Augustan Rome which bears a remarkably close resemblance to 15th-century Florence, and the people standing round waiting for the awesome news are all citizens of Florence wearing their normal clothes. Lorenzo de' Medici is there, as is his mother, his children, friends and various colleagues.

Mythological elements

Early Renaissance painters were preoccupied with technique. Their subject matter remained largely unchanged: religion was still the most

important concern. But in the second half of the Quattrocento a new, exciting and somewhat disturbing element began to appear: the mythological and the allegorical.

The supreme practitioner in this field was Sandro Botticelli, who worked with Leonardo da Vinci in Verrocchio's workshop but developed in a totally different direction. His most famous painting – certainly the most mysterious of the early Renaissance – is *La Primavera*, painted in 1478 and hung in the Uffizi.

Nine supernatural creatures are placed in an exquisite natural setting. On the left, a young man is aiming at, or pointing at, something. Next to him a group of beautiful, grave-faced

women are performing a solemn ritual dance. On the right is the only figure who seems to be aware of the observer: Botticelli's stunningly beautiful "mystery" woman with a provocative half-smile. Beside her what appears to be an act of violence adds a discordant note: a bluish figure is leaning out of the trees and clutching at a startled girl.

In the background, but dominating the whole, is the most enigmatic figure: a pale woman whose expression has been variously described as frowning, smiling, gay and melancholy; whose stance has also been described in conflicting ways, as dancing, as that of a consumptive, as pregnant and as offering a blessing. The

LEFT: *Birth of John the Baptist* by Ghirlandaio (1485).
RIGHT: *Trinity* (*c.*1425) by Masaccio, the pioneer of perspective (both in Santa Maria Novella, Florence).

figure itself has been "firmly identified" as both Venus and the Virgin Mary. What Botticelli was trying to do was to restate classical mythology in Christian terms while remaining true to the original – and true to his own quirky self. However, he was later influenced by the gloomy, savage friar Savonarola – who turned Florence into a puritan reformatory in the 1490s – and, almost overnight, ceased his joyous mythological paintings, concentrating instead on orthodox religious subjects.

The High Renaissance

Even to the untutored eye, there is a profound difference between the work produced before

for Rome with Raphael to work for Pope Julius II. Other artists followed suit: the major Florentine families – other than the Medicis – could no longer afford to make commissions, so there was no longer any kind of independent art scene.

Shortly after the sack of Rome, the Medici Pope Clement VII clamped down on his native city of Florence, ending republicanism and preparing the way for the first dukedom. Meanwhile, in the world of art, the glory was departing from Florence, as the impetus of the Renaissance shifted to Rome and Venice. From the middle of the 16th century, Florentine artists tended to be court artists, dancing

and after the 1520s in Tuscany and elsewhere, most noticeably in Florence. Partly this was the result of an immense political crisis. Italy had become a battleground invaded again and again by warring foreigners. In 1527 a savage army, composed partly of mercenaries, sacked Rome and held the pope to ransom. Italy was never to recover from that experience, which was the curtain-raiser for a period of foreign domination that would not end until the 1800s.

The peak phase of the Renaissance – in Florence, at least – was entered with the advent of Leonardo da Vinci and Michelangelo, but the decline came very soon afterwards, particularly when Michelangelo left

attendance on the Medici dukes. Among them was the artist-cum-historian Giorgio Vasari.

Until recently, Vasari's work as an artist was dismissed almost as contemptuously as his work as an art historian was received enthusiastically. However, posterity owes him a debt of thanks, both as an architect and as a painter. Not only did he build the Uffizi for Duke Cosimo I, but in his paintings in the great Salone dei Cinquecento, the parliamentary chamber of the Palazzo Vecchio, he created outstanding contemporary representations of the city and its surrounding countryside. Equally fine is his frescoed interior of Brunelleschi's dome, revealed in 1994 after a five-year restoration programme.

Leonardo

Although the glory was departing from Florence, the sunset was stupendous. It could scarcely be otherwise with two such giants as Michelangelo and da Vinci still working in the city. Leonardo, born in 1452, trained in the *bottega* of Verrocchio, thus carrying the medieval systems on into the new era. One of Vasari's anecdotes claims that Verrocchio, on seeing his young apprentice's work, laid down his brush and never painted again. Unlikely though the incident is, the anecdote shows that Leonardo was recognised as being almost a freakish genius in his own lifetime.

Leonardo left Florence for Milan at the age of 30. He came back again in 1502 when he was commissioned by the *Signoria* to create the great mural, the *Battle of Anghiari* in the Council Chamber, returned to Milan in 1506, then finally crossed the Alps and became court painter to François I of France. His contribution to the history of ideas is incalculable, but his physical contribution to Tuscan art history is relatively small. Typically, both the *Battle of Anghiari* and the *Adoration of the Kings* in the Uffizi are unfinished. And his two most famous paintings, the *Mona Lisa* (a portrait of a virtuous but otherwise undistinguished Florentine housewife) and the *Virgin of the Rocks*, are in Paris and London respectively.

Michelangelo is very different. His greatest work, the Sistine Chapel frescoes, is also outside Florence, but he did leave an enduring imprint upon his home city, in the form of the walls that gird it and the sculptures that grace it.

Michelangelo

Michelangelo was nearly a generation younger than Leonardo, born in 1475 when the Renaissance was approaching its apogee. His father was a poor but proud country gentleman who thoroughly disapproved of the idea of his son becoming an artisan or artist; in his mind there was no clear distinction. Michelangelo, too, was apt to be a little touchy on the subject. Although he served his apprenticeship in a *bottega*, he later rejected the idea that he touted for trade: "I was never a painter or a sculptor like those who set up shop for the purpose."

A Vasari anecdote describes how the young Michelangelo, then around 13 years old, made a drawing of the various tools in the workshop. His master, Ghirlandaio, was so impressed that he drew Lorenzo de' Medici's attention to the talented boy. As a result, Michelangelo entered the princely Medici household, eating at the same table and studying with the same scholars as Lorenzo's own children.

Michelangelo was just 18 when Lorenzo de' Medici died in 1492. Florence was plunged into chaos, because Lorenzo's son, Piero, was extravagant and unpopular, and the Florentines chased him out of the city. Michelangelo's ties with the Medici were no longer so advanta-

geous, and he took the road to Rome. There he undertook the work by which he is best remembered. He also worked for the next 40 years on a task he never completed: the great tomb for his patron and taskmaster, Pope Julius II. The unfinished statues for this tomb, the famous *Slaves*, are now in Florence's Accademia gallery. In them it is possible to see, five centuries later, the sculptor's technique.

As in a *bottega*, the roughing out of the figures was done by apprentices, the master giving the finishing touches. It is profoundly moving to see in some of them the shallow depressions surrounding the figure, made by the rounded head of a chisel, which seems to

---

LEFT: Botticelli's *Primavera*, 1478 (Uffizi).
RIGHT: a sketch in charcoal by Leonardo (Uffizi).

be "freeing" the figure, as though it already existed and was simply trapped in the stone.

Florence has many statues by Michelangelo; although often unfinished, they always reveal the chisel strokes of a master. They include the famous *David*, and the statues of *Dawn*, *Evening*, *Day* and *Night* in the Medici Chapel.

In the Casa Buonarroti in Via Ghibellina are displayed some of the sculptor's working drawings and a few of his earliest works. Although Michelangelo is remembered as a painter and sculptor, he was also an engineer of very considerable skill and a poet of sensitivity and insight.

on the Piazza della Signoria – a message to anyone in Florence who dared to resist the might of the Medici. But it is indicative both of Cellini and of the phase into which the art of the Renaissance was moving that his best-known work would be the elaborate golden salt cellar which he made for François I of France.

Raphael

Raphael was a gentle, handsome young man who seemed to have no enemies. He was born in Umbria in 1483 and received his basic training in the workshop of Perugino, working on frescoes in Perugia. In 1500, at the impressionable age of 17, he came to Florence, where

Cellini

Michelangelo was just 25 when Benvenuto Cellini was born in 1500. Like so many of the artists of his time, he was skilled in a number of crafts – he was, improbably enough, a gunner. He played a role in the tragic sack of Rome which, in effect, brought the Renaissance to an end. Acting as gunner in defence of the Vatican, he assured his supporters that the pope promised him absolution "for all the murders that I should commit".

In Florence, his most famous work is that beautiful but curiously heartless statue of *Perseus Slaying Medusa* commissioned by Cosimo I for the statue-filled Loggia dei Lanzi

he absorbed the works of Leonardo da Vinci and Michelangelo.

He left Florence in 1508, attracted to Rome by the fiery Pope Julius II, who was planning a series of architectural embellishments to the Vatican. There the young Raphael easily proved himself. He painted the series of rooms known as the Stanze della Segnatura and, under the Medici Pope Leo X, was placed in charge of archaeological excavations in Rome itself.

Thus, the last true artist of the Renaissance introduced into the mother city of Europe that passionate search for the past which had triggered off the Renaissance in Florence nearly two centuries earlier. ❑

Literary Classics

In a crowded field, three towering figures provide some orientation to Tuscan literature. Dante, Petrarch and Machiavelli follow each other chronologically and, because each caused, as well as recorded, great changes, it is possible to plot the course of the region's history through them.

Born in 1265, Dante was an exact contemporary of Giotto, whose work he admired. But where Giotto kept out of politics, Dante involved himself wholeheartedly and was exiled for his pains during one of Florence's upheavals. He never returned to Florence, and eventually died in Ravenna in 1321. *The Divine Comedy*, which deals with the great mysteries of religion, had a profound effect on Italian thought. It is a vivid story with a meticulous chronology, and philosophers and theologians still debate its significance.

Francesco Petrarch, though a Florentine, was born in Arezzo, where his parents had been exiled during the same feuds that caused Dante's expulsion. Petrarch was one of the first to hunt down and discover the lost classical literature without which the Renaissance could not have begun. He travelled widely, had an enormous circle of friends and kept in regular contact with them through his letters. It was as much through these letters as through any formal work that the "new learning" was disseminated. In poetry, he devised the sonnet form which took his name – Petrarchan – which was greatly to influence the poets of Elizabethan England.

Niccolò Machiavelli was born in 1469. Viewed from almost any angle, his life appears a failure. As a career diplomat, he never wielded real authority. As a republican, he was obliged to spend later years currying favour with the now openly despotic Medici. His appearance and habits were totally at variance with the personality that comes across in his political writings. There he is ice-cold, logical, in total command. In real life he was shabby, lecherous and adulterous. But he was, despite all appearances to the contrary, an idealist. *The Prince*, his notorious book on the practice of tyranny, was only one of many works, including a delightful comedy, *Mandragola*, still staged today.

Although innovations in literature were less spectacular than in art and architecture, there are a number of outstanding "firsts". Francesco Guicciardini wrote the first true *History of Italy*, and Giovanni Boccaccio (1313–75) produced Europe's first novel, *The Decameron*, a collection of tales told by 10 young aristocrats who retreat from the plague which struck Florence in 1348. Staying in a country house, they spend the time telling erotic stories and reciting poems, and

poking fun at the clergy. All the stories demonstrate Boccaccio's well-honed skills as a storyteller.

Finally, there were the truly Renaissance figures who expressed themselves in all the arts, including literature – as exemplified in Michelangelo's poetry and Cellini's swashbuckling *Autobiography*. Cellini, a brilliant sculptor and part-time soldier, was also a superb writer. He wrote a heart-stopping account of the problem of casting the exquisite *Perseus*, a bronze sculpture destined for the Loggia dei Lanzi. At a crucial moment, he ran out of metal and had to throw in the family pewter in order to complete the statue. ❑

LEFT: Raphael's *Entombment*. **RIGHT:** *Dante and the Divine Comedy*, in Florence's Duomo.

ARCHITECTURAL TREASURES

Tuscany combines rich urban heritage with a delightful rural legacy, to create a unique architectural tableau

Curiously, Tuscan architecture is characterised as much by diversity as it is by harmony: harmony in its aesthetic sweetness; diversity in its range of buildings, from Romanesque cathedrals to Renaissance palaces, town halls to tower-houses. The region is equally rich in religious and secular architecture, with the bustling urban heritage complementing the tranquil, sunny rural landscape of villas and farmhouses.

Civic architecture is particularly rich. The Tuscan town hall, with accompanying belltower, encapsulates a civic ideal. In the past, it promised a degree of democracy to the merchant guilds, the nobility and the people. The Palazzo del Comune, known by different local names, has been the seat of local government since medieval times. This imposing, fortified building dominates the square today, as surely as it has always dominated the lives of local citizens. The best-known is the fortress-like Palazzo Vecchio, Florence, its austerity belied by a palatial interior. However, even the smallest commune has a grand town hall. In the Mugello, Palazzo Vicari in Scarperia resembles Palazzo Vecchio, with its impressive 14th-century merlons and corbels. Such public *palazzi* are often studded with stemmata, stone-carved coats of arms belonging to prominent citizens or noble clans.

In numerous cities, including San Gimignano, there is also an adjoining balcony known as the *arengo*, from which politicians would harangue the crowd. Near by is usually a loggia, providing shelter from the sun or rain, as well as a meeting place, today often

used as a small market. Thus, Tuscany's grandest buildings serve much the same purpose today as they have always done.

Urbanisation

Visually, urban Tuscany is the product of medieval and Renaissance builders, even if Roman and Etruscan stones were recycled. Dismissing the Middle Ages as a period of decadence and decay does an injustice to the region's prosperity and architectural heritage. In Tuscany, the period represented a marked social rebirth, with the flowering of independent citystates in the 11th century. By 1200 most towns had become burgeoning centres with distinctive identities and a civic pride evident in the grandiose town halls and tower-houses. The medieval cathedrals and civic buildings were a testament to the citizens' refined taste, just as the ordered country estates later became a Renaissance symbol of peace and prosperity.

The medieval skyscrapers of San Gimignano signified the civilising effect of urban living, with the *signori* (feudal lords) encouraged to relinquish their castles for city life. The *borgo*, or fortified city, was also home to landowners and merchants, particularly with the rise of the *popolo grasso*, the wealthy middle class in the 14th century. The medieval city became a symbol of safety during the city-state conflicts.

retains a certain simplicity of form, contrasting the austerity of Romanesque with the traditional Tuscan love of polychrome marble patterns.

Given city rivalries, Tuscan Romanesque delights in distinctive regional variations, as in the differentiated stripes and arcading in Lucca. In San Michele, a city masterpiece, the chiselled style of the delicate colonnades emphasises the height and exuberance of the façade.

The maritime republic of Pisa was an 11th-century power, trading with northern Europe and the Muslim world. As a result, the Pisan style is a glorious hybrid: austere Norman Romanesque inspired by a Moorish Sicilian aesthetic and the Tuscan taste for marble. While the

Tuscan Romanesque

This style is less solemn, less philosophical than French, English or German Romanesque. Its hallmarks are surface decoration and space rather than sobriety and solidity, with simple bricks transformed by a marble veneer. The style, centred on Florence, favours contrasting patterns of dark and light marble as well as striking geometric designs. The form was first realised in the city baptistery, with its round-headed arches, classical proportions and a striving for weightlessness. The Florentine model

LEFT: the Palazzo Pitti, prototype of a patrician palace.
ABOVE: Pisa's glorious "Square of Miracles".

severe colonnaded galleries owe much to Norman models, Sicily inspires the seductive decorative elements such as exuberant arabesques.

Yet the colourful geometry of the multi-coloured marble is essentially Tuscan. The palette contrasts white marble from Carrara, rosy pink from Maremma and dark green from Prato. A hallmark of the style was its talent for selecting a theatrical space: in Pisa the main buildings present a unified whole, placed on the lawn like prisms on a baize cloth. The Pisan Duomo was the prototype, with its contrasting bands of colour, blind arcading, colonnaded gallery and the geometry of inlaid marble. Inspired by Pisa, the cathedrals of Siena,

Pistoia, Florence, Prato and Lucca use zebra-like stripes and an interplay of light and shade.

Medieval cityscape

Given the rich Roman heritage, Tuscans did not take to the Gothic form, with its pointed arches and sheer verticality, but preferred symmetry, balancing height with breadth. In great churches such as Santa Croce in Florence, naves and aisles are not vaulted, but use the open trusses favoured by Romanesque architecture.

However, Gothic details adorn Romanesque designs, as in the triangular pediments on the Baptistery at Pisa or the Gothic mullioned windows of Case dei Guinigi in Lucca, the final

Without question, fortifications played an important role in medieval Tuscany. Walled towns, often known as *borghi* and built on hilltops, are emblematic of the Tuscan cityscape. Anghiari, Buonconvento, Monteriggioni and Montepulciano all provide proof that preserving walls helps preserve a distinct identity. While a *castello* was either a fortified village or a castle, a *rocca* was usually a defended garrison post and a *fortezza* was a fortress of strategic importance.

The region abounds in ruined or restored examples, including castles at Poppi and Prato, and the pair of fortresses in Florence. Siena province alone boasts San Gimignano's

alongside the Romanesque round-arched arcading. Nonetheless, the Cistercian abbey of San Galgano echoes French Gothic, while the gabled Gothic church of Santa Maria della Spina in Pisa feels more French than Tuscan.

Not that Gothic gables are a guide to a medieval atmosphere. Many Tuscan towns are authentically medieval, as is the case with Cortona, Lucca, San Gimignano and Volterra. As the largest medieval city in Europe, Siena is arguably the most authentic, with strict building regulations in place since the 13th century. Certainly, its Gothic spirit is intact, from red-brick palaces to herringbone alleys, all moulded to a mystical Sienese sensibility.

Rocca and watchtowers, as well as the massive *fortezze* in Siena and Montalcino, which have both been converted into wine-tasting centres.

Tower-houses were castle-residences serving as both warehouses and fortresses, self-sufficient enclaves symbolising the wealth of the feudal nobles or prosperous merchants and their scorn for civil authority. Key features included a well for a constant water supply, an inner courtyard to provide light and ventilation, and an external staircase to the *piano nobile*, the grand residential first floor. As the great Tuscan families grew wealthy on banking and the cloth trade, their homes became more palatial and domesticated. In time, decorative details were added, notably graceful courtyards complete with sculpted wells, coats of arms, ornate arches and a loggia on the first or top floors. Despite 16th-century modifications, the Florentine Palazzo Davanzati preserves much of its medieval atmosphere. The palace is impressive, from its iron-bolted doors and formidable façade pierced by numerous small windows to an internal courtyard boasting a well with a pulley system designed to supply water to each floor. The interior presents a charming portrait of domestic life, from 15th-century frescoes and tapestries to the *cassoni*, Tuscan wedding chests, and even a privileged child's bathroom.

home and banking headquarters, a massive mansion with an arcaded inner courtyard. He also designed Palazzo Pitti (1444), the prototype of a patrician palace, boasting strict classical proportions and a rusticated façade. Yet there are lingering traces of feudal times in the Gothic windows and heavy cornices. Built for Cosimo de' Medici, Palazzo Pitti clearly symbolises the power and prestige of the owner.

However, some nobles simply modernised their feudal seats. Palazzo Spini-Ferroni, a crenellated three-tiered fortress close to the Arno, was a 13th-century watchtower before becoming a palatial home. Just around the corner looms the grandiose Palazzo Strozzi, a

Renaissance palaces

The Florentine *palazzo* was a direct descendant of the tower-house, but without an outmoded defensive function. In keeping with the new humanist spirit, architects designed gracious private palaces as proof of their revivalist skills, not simply as symbols of patrician pride. Foremost amongst the trailblazers was Michelozzi (1396–1472), who pursued the architectural principles of Alberti and Brunelleschi. Michelozzo designed the Florentine Palazzo Medici-Riccardi, the Medici

rusticated stone cube of mammoth proportions built for the greatest banking dynasty. Rustication was intended to underline the Strozzi's power. Whereas Palazzo Strozzi emphasises strength and stability, homes such as Palazzo Rucellai were more harmonious, embellished with elegant loggias, classical motifs and decorative friezes.

Florence may be the most innovative Renaissance city, but Pienza is the best-preserved. Pienza was built by Pius II as a papal city, offering both an echo of imperial patronage and a humanist memorial to his papacy. In 1462, the architect Rossellino grafted a monumental Renaissance core onto

LEFT: woodcut of Florence, *c.*1470.
ABOVE: the fortified town of Monteriggioni.

medieval grandiosity. All the elements of civic life were set on one tiny square, its geometric shape giving tension to the whole. Using a well-head as the lynchpin, the piazza embraces an episcopal palace, a dignified town hall with an open loggia, and a tower embodying Tuscan pride. In his private palace here, the pope delighted in hanging gardens, delicate loggias and rooms for every season.

Renaissance architects

As the cradle of the Renaissance, Tuscany is where the profession of architect first came into its own. Imbued with a new humanist spirit, architects of the stature of Brunelleschi, Alberti, Michelozzo, Rossellino and Sangallo made their mark on churches, palaces and villas. Florence, which saw itself as the inheritor of Roman grandeur, is the city with the greatest concentration of Renaissance monuments. Strongly influenced by Tuscan Romanesque, the buildings were models of visual restraint, dedicated to proportion, perspective and classical motifs. Brunelleschi (1377–1446), the father of Renaissance architecture, left his masterpiece on the Duomo in Florence. His dome was the fulfilment of the Renaissance ideal, a feat of Florentine engineering *(see page 48)*.

Alberti (1404–72) is considered the archetypal Renaissance man, a patrician playwright,

SACRED SITES

Religious architecture represents one of the highlights of Tuscany. Any tour would certainly include the cathedrals of Florence, Lucca, Pisa and Siena. Lesser-known gems include Barga's Romanesque Cathedral, Montepulciano's Renaissance San Biagio and the Romanesque San Miniato al Monte in the Florentine hills. In many cases, the architecture is inextricably bound up with the artistic wealth on the walls. This is true of the Gothic church of Santa Maria Novella in Florence or Arezzo's San Francesco, with its poignant fresco cycle by della Francesca. By contrast, exteriors can be austere or even unfinished, a sign that patrons squabbled or ran out of funds.

The siting is also significant, with cathedrals usually constructed on sacred spots hallowed since Roman or Etruscan times. Mendicant churches were often built outside city walls, with the surrounding square often becoming a major city market. Abbeys and monasteries, which could be as large as medieval towns, were built on virgin sites, and blended civic and Christian concerns.

Some of the most intriguing architecturally are the Romanesque abbey of Sant'Antimo, the baroque Certosa di Pisa, the Carthusian foundation of Camaldoli, the hilltop monastery of La Verna and Monte Oliveto Maggiore, a Benedictine foundation in the woods south of Siena.

humanist and philosopher, composer and lawyer, athlete and architect. He rivalled Brunelleschi in his gift for geometry and desire to revive "the immutable laws of architecture", yet also sought to respect the Tuscan taste for decoration. As an architectural historian, he revived Vitruvius' theories and put them into practice in Florence. The laws of proportion, perspective and the use of the classical orders all came into play in the Duomo and in the Florentine Palazzo Rucellai (1446). This landmark palace was inspired by the Colosseum and the buildings of classical Rome. The Roman influence is present in the porches and panelled doors as well as in the frieze, which bears the crests of the Medici and Rucellai families. The magnificent Rucellai loggia was the last to be built in 15th-century Florence, such was the profligacy it engendered. Weddings and festivities in the loggia may be no more, but the family remains ensconced in part of the palace.

Rural retreats

Tuscany's rich urban heritage risks overshadowing the delightful rural legacy of sunny villas and picturesque hilltop farmhouses. In medieval Tuscany, the traditional manor or fortified seat was bound by solid walls or battlements. This country refuge evolved into the gracious villa-residence of Renaissance times. In the 13th century, there were two forms of rural retreat, the feudal domain – the grand preserve of the landed nobility – and the *casa da signore*, the busy hub of a country estate. This was a crenellated property with a watchtower, surrounded by farm buildings and cottages, and owned by the gentry or bourgeoisie.

The villa as a country retreat was a Renaissance concept, reflecting the gracious rural lifestyle cultivated by the Tuscan nobility. The villas were generally elegant but not ostentatious, in keeping with the cultural conservatism of the Florentine nobility. However, the grandest Medici villas, such as Cafaggiolo, designed by Michelozzo, were sumptuous princely estates. Poggio a Caiano *(see Villas and Gardens, page 116)* is the model Renaissance villa, with its harmonious design and colonnaded loggia harking back to the grandeur of classical times. The rural

design reflected a desire for symmetry and a rationalisation of form and function. Embellished by porticoes, the villa was built on a square plan around an inner courtyard, with a loggia on the first floor. Set in ornamental gardens and encircled by walls, the villa enjoyed superb views, often from a hilltop.

At a time when peace reigned in the Tuscan countryside, the gardens were regarded as a bucolic retreat, an essential part of the architectural composition. The grounds consist of a *giardino segreto*, a geometrical walled garden, with formal parterres and topiary, kitchen and herb gardens, lined by stately avenues of cypresses or lemon trees. The design, enlivened

by water gardens, was set in the 16th century, when the Mannerist style acquired colonnades and statuary, grottoes and follies.

By the 17th century, the crisp geometry of the gardens was matched by formal terraces, virtuoso waterworks and sculptures of sea monsters cavorting with mythological figures. In their ease and openness, the gardens were in harmony with the house and with the patrician owner. As the Renaissance architect Alberti declared, "Only the house of a tyrant can look like a fortress: an ideal home should be open to the world outside, beautifully adorned, delicate and finely proportioned rather than proud and stately". ❑

LEFT: Arezzo's stately main square.
RIGHT: Villa Medici, a rural retreat built by Michelozzo.

WILD TUSCANY

Nature-lovers sated by the art treasures of the region will find plenty of wild refuges in which to rest or roam

Classic Tuscany is a civilised scene of silvery olive groves, vine-cloaked hills, sunflowers shimmering in the heat and dark silhouettes of cypresses, arranged in double file along timeless avenues. The Welsh poet Dylan Thomas, who was no stranger to life on the wild side, praised the Florentine countryside – "The pine hills are endless, the cypresses at the hilltop tell one all about the length of death, the woods are deep as love and full of goats" – a seductive rural image that has lured so many visitors to find their version of earthly paradise.

Given the civilisation of the landscape, "wild Tuscany" might seem a misnomer. Yet, beyond the classic chessboard of vineyards, a rugged wilderness awaits. Tuscany is Italy's most thickly wooded region. Mountains soar, and in the northwest there are woods as thick as rainforests, while on the west coast the Maremma marshlands remain the emptiest and ecologically purest stretch of Italian coastline. The south, meanwhile, has the primeval emptiness of the Sienese moonscape.

The animals are indeed in flight given Italian hunters' fondness for the chase. The power of the hunting lobby has severely depleted their numbers, with the exception of wild boar. Outside designated reserves, bird-watchers and animal-lovers fare less well than botanists and nature-lovers. Hawks and golden eagles still enjoy the majesty of the mountains, but life is no pastoral idyll for deer, ravaged by hunting. But, against the odds, Apennine wolves have

made a comeback in mountainous regions, encouraged by the profusion of their favourite dish, shaggy mouflons (mountain sheep).

Rural pursuits

Away from the cultural crowds, nature-lovers and adrenalin junkies can indulge in trekking and skiing, horse riding and mountain biking, climbing and caving, gliding and paragliding, sailing and surfing. Riding is very popular in Tuscany, with more riding stables and well-trodden mule tracks than anywhere else in Italy. It is also a rambler's paradise. Better mapped than most Italian regions, the variety of trails from relaxed to rigorous is vast. Serious hikers

LEFT: Evening primrose in the Apuan Alps.
RIGHT: negotiating a suspension bridge near Pistoia.

can follow the long-distance trails run by the Italian Alpine Club (CAI). Garfagnana Trekking and Apuane Trekking are key paths in the Apuan Alps, while the Grande Escursione Appenninica (GEA) is a 25-day trek to Emilia and Umbria along the ridges of the Apennines.

The Apuan Alps, Lunigiana and Garfagnana

This mountain chain, with its awe-inspiring landscape, runs parallel with the coastline and the Apennine ridge. Behind the well-groomed beaches of Versilia, on the western side of the chain, lurks a rugged hinterland of marble quarries and mountain ridges, narrow gorges

Lunigiana, the mountainous area north of Carrara, is wedged between Emilia and Liguria. The region is criss-crossed by streams, with canoeing carried out in the clear waters of the river Magra. From Aulla, a convenient base, there are organised tours of glacial moraines, karst gorges, caves and botanical gardens.

Garfagnana lies on the borders of Emilia Romagna and northern Tuscany, between the Apuan Alps and the Apennines. Parco dell' Orecchiella is the region's most spectacular park. While closely resembling the Apuan Alps, it is higher and wilder, with a mixture of woodland and pasture, picturesque clearings and mountain streams.

and thermal springs. This desolate landscape was devastated by floods in 1996, but has recovered. Lago di Vaglia, in the heart of the mountains, is a reservoir containing a drowned medieval village that can be seen periodically. The underground landscape is equally inspiring, with caves often as deep as mountains are high, and notoriously long and labyrinthine. In Fornovolasco, east of Forte dei Marmi, the Grotta del Vento represents the region's most fascinating caverns, riddled with steep gorges and secret passages, slowly revealing stalagmites and stalactites, fossils and alabaster formations, crystal pools and echoing chambers.

The Apennines

While the Apuan Alps are more varied, the Apennines have not been ravaged by quarrying. They include the range on the Emilian border, the loftiest in the northern Apennines, as well as those in the Casentino and Mugello. Centred on the resort of Abetone, the rugged northern range is ideal hiking country.

Abetone, commanding the mountain pass separating Tuscany and Emilia, is the most important winter-sports resort in central Italy. Fortunately, the mountain air also makes Abetone invigorating in the most stifling Tuscan summer, when the cable car takes walkers up to the leafy heights. Despite the ravages of hunting, the forest is home to roe deer, mouflons and marmots, with golden eagles swooping over the crags. One of the most rewarding stretches of the rugged long-distance path (GEA) lies between Abetone and Cisa. Yet Abetone is also suitable for less energetic walkers, who can stroll along well-marked paths in the woods.

The Casentino, north of Arezzo, forms a series of razor-like crests and deep woods which straddle Emilia and northeast Tuscany. Centred on Bibbiena in the Upper Arno, these ancient forests are the region's finest. While the Emilian side is characterised by steep bluffs and stratified outcrops, the Tuscan side is softer, with picturesque waterfalls and streams. Hikers and pony-trekkers can follow the long-distance trail (GEA), but should bear in mind that the rescue services are often required in these treacherous forests. Fallow deer and mouflon were introduced in 1870 for hunting purposes, and again in the 1960s after local depredations. Today, sightings of the shaggy sheep, badger or porcupine are more frequent than glimpses of the eagle owl, deer, weasel, wildcat or wolf.

The Mugello, the hilly region north of Florence, resembles a landscape painted by Giotto, whose homeland this was. The Mugello can be explored on horseback, by following the old bridle paths between Bologna and Florence. The valleys along the Sieve, the main tributary of the Arno, are dotted with villages, olive groves and vineyards. The transition from valley to mountains means that olive groves give way to chestnut and oak forests before culminating in beech woods and waterfalls. Upper Mugello is a harsh, wild landscape of mountain peaks and passes, with ridges and ravines carved by rivers over the years.

Classic Chianti

While the Florentine Chianti is devoted to wine, the Sienese side is wilder, with vineyards gradually giving way to slopes covered in holm oaks, chestnuts and juniper. A 15-km (9-mile) hilly hike from Greve in Chianti to Panzano covers the Via Chiantigiana and its offshoots, passing farms, cypresses and chestnut groves.

In subtle Siena province, much is classic Tuscany, with olive groves, gently rolling hills

and dark cypresses standing sentinel. However, stretching from Siena to Montepulciano is a singular moonscape known as Le Crete Senesi, the strange hillocks marking the Sienese badlands. Barren or virtually treeless, this is beguiling territory nonetheless, with solitary farmhouses marooned on the crests of hills. This seemingly empty terrain is home to foxes, badgers and wild boar. Monte Amiata, the site of an extinct volcano further south, presents the province's wilder face, with a profusion of thermal springs bubbling amidst the beech and chestnut groves. With its mossy banks and majestic grandeur, the mountainous setting is suitable for hiking, horse riding and skiing.

Marshy Maremma

Maremma, the southern coastal strip, is a composite of natural Tuscany. The Parco Naturale della Maremma, with its soft whale-backed hills parallel to the coast, is dotted with Spanish watchtowers, parasol pines and coastal dunes. Waymarked paths connect the shoreline and steep cliffs. On La Spergolaia ranch near by, the legendary *butteri*, the last of the Maremman cowboys, break in sturdy wild horses. The Maremma sustains around 600 beasts, a mixture of semi-wild ponies and white long-horned cattle. The park can be explored on horseback, on foot or by bus from Alberese *(see page 237)*. ❑

LEFT: The Garfagnana.
RIGHT: Le Crete Senesi, after the harvest.

Nature Parks

Parco Nazionale Appennino Tosco-Emiliano
The Apennine ridges that form the border between northern Tuscany and Emilia Romagna are rich in contrasting landscapes, from moorlands and lakes to craggy summits and waterfalls. Golden eagles, wolves, mouflons and roe deer roam, and rare botanic species transform whole areas into wild botanical gardens. *The visitor centre is in Reggio Emilia (Piazza 1 Maggio 3, Cervarezza Terme di Busana; tel: 0522-890111, freephone 800-945007). www.appenninopark.it*

Parco Nazionale delle Foreste Casentinesi, Monte Falterona, Campigna
This protected area lies along the Apennine ridge forming the border between eastern Tuscany and Emilia Romagna. Its beech and chestnut woods are among the largest and best-preserved in Italy. They are home to a rich variety of flora and fauna, such as deer, wolves and golden eagles. Also of interest are the secluded monasteries of Camáldoli and La Verna. There are eight waymarked nature trails – "Sentieri Natura" – within the park. A small and practical guide (on sale in the visitor centres) highlights the region's wildlife and points of interest.

The park headquarters is in Pratovecchio (Via G. Brocchi 7, tel: 0575-50301, www.parco forestecasentinesi.it). There are information offices at Camáldoli (tel: 0575-556130) and Campigna (tel: 0543-980231). Outside the park, the Arezzo tourist office (by the train station; tel: 0575-377678) also has information on the park. www.parks.it

Parco Alpi Apuane
The park extends for over 20,000 hectares between the coastal plain and the rivers Magra, Aulella and Serchio. The Apuan Alps differ from the Apennines, with deep valleys, steep slopes and mountains of glistening white marble. Forests of chestnut and beech give cover to some 300 species of birds and a rich diversity of wild flowers. Shy marmots can often be spotted on the higher slopes. It is an ideal environment for trekking, walking, mountain climbing, cycling and horse riding.
The park headquarters is at Seravezza, (Via Corrado del Greco 11; tel: 0584-75821). Visitor centres are at Castelnuovo di Garfagna (Piazza Erbe 1; tel: 0583-644242) and Forno (loc. Filanda; tel: 0585-315300). Park guides are available for hikes and visits to caves. www.parcapuane.it

Parco Naturale dell'Orecchiella
The mountains of the Orecchiella park in the Garfagnana region are higher than the neighbouring Apuan Alps, but the landscape is tamer, though no less beautiful for that, and criss-crossed by a network of hiking trails. The area is centred on the high broad plain of Pania di Corfino, overlooked by a dramatic limestone peak that dominates the Serchio valley. There is a wide variety of rare flora, and the wildlife includes deer, wild boar, mouflons, badgers, otters, weasels and wolves. The monastery of San Pellegrino offers fabulous views and houses a folk museum. San Romano in Garfagnana is a good base for exploring.
The visitor centre is near Corfino (tel: 0583-619002). For walks, contact the Club Alpino Italiano – www.cai.it

Parco Regionale di Migliarino, San Rossore, Massaciuccoli

This regional park covers the coastal hinterland behind the beach resorts and campsites between Viareggio and Livorno, and includes the forest of San Rossore and Lake Massaciuccoli. Huge holm oaks, maritime pines and common oaks grow right up to the beach and are home to wild boar, fallow deer and countless species of native and migratory birds. While the Macchia Lucchese, Lago di Massaciuccoli and Tenuta Borbone are freely accessible, entrance to other areas is restricted. The archaeological area of San Rossore, where a fleet of Roman ships was unearthed, can be visited by appointment.

There is a visitor centre at Coltano (Villa Medicea, Via Palazzi 21; tel/fax: 050-989051), and the Tenuta San Rossore organises walking and cycling tours (tel/fax: 050-530101). Boat tours of Lake Massaciuccoli depart from Torre del Lago. www.parcosanrossore.it

Parco Regionale della Maremma

This beautiful, unspoilt nature park covering over 100 sq. km (40 sq. miles), stretches along the Tyrrhenian coast from Principina a Mare to Talamone. It is centred on the Monti dell'Uccellina (Mountains of the Little Bird), which rise from the sea. The rugged landscape is a mixture of marshland, mountains and virgin coast backed by umbrella pines, interspersed with rocky outcrops and coves. There are no human settlements, and just one access road links Alberese (the main point of entry) to Marina Alberese, a beautiful seaside stretch. A variety of migratory birds stop here en route to Africa. The dense vegetation provides the perfect habitat for wild boar, symbol of the Maremma, while herds of Maremma cattle and horses of the *butteri* (local cowherds), roam on its plains. Waymarked paths connect the shoreline and steep cliffs.

The main entrance and visitor centre are at Alberese (Via Bersagliere 7, tel: 0564-

407111, www.parco-maremma.it), but Talamone also has an access point.

Parco Nazionale Arcipelago Toscano

This protected area is Europe's largest marine park. It covers the seven islands of the Tuscan Archipelago: Elba, Capraia, Gorgona, Pianosa, Montecristo, Giglio and Giannutri *(see page 182)*. The coastline and seabed vary enormously from island to island, hence the variety of flora and fauna. Seabirds such as shearwaters and black-headed gulls proliferate. More rare is Audouin's gull, an endemic species. These waters, which are popular among

divers, are home to a great many species of fish, including swordfish and tuna. Dolphins, sperm whales and even the rare monk seal may also be sighted by the lucky or the very patient.

The main office of the marine park is on Elba (Via Guerrazzi 1, Portoferraio; tel: 0565-919411; fax: 0565-919428). www.isoleditoscana.it, www.islepark.it

Useful References

www.parks.it (official website of the Italian Federation of Parks and Nature Reserves) www.wwf.it/oasi (World Wildlife Fund reserves in Italy) ❑

LEFT: horses can be hired in many locations.
RIGHT: poppies brighten the fields in spring.

A TASTE OF TUSCANY

Purity and simplicity: Tuscan cooking makes full use of bountiful local products to create dishes that are as much a joy to prepare as they are to taste

Tuscany has everything to offer the visitor in terms of food. There is a rich selection of fruit and vegetables from the prolific countryside, and a fantastic bounty from the sea – everything from red mullet to mussels, tender beef and pork, excellent oil with which to cook and dress it and superb wines with which to wash it down. To finish off, there are hearty cheeses and divine cakes and desserts.

What is immediately striking about Tuscan food is that, no matter what you are eating or where you are eating it, it is always very rustic, very simple, designed to nourish the soul and the spirit as much as the body. Tuscan cooking is never elaborate or excessive; there are no fussy decorations, complicated reductions of sauces or subtly blended flavours. But there is a basic, honest simplicity about the dishes which has made them popular for centuries the world over.

Tuscany produces its own inimitable versions of Italian staples: pasta dishes with gamey sauces of hare, wild boar, even porcupine; polenta with fresh *funghi*; rabbit or roast baby goat. But along with a particular attitude to food, Tuscany also has many dishes and delicacies unique to the region, most available the year round, others – such as chestnuts, truffles and wild mushrooms – more seasonal.

Hunting is a popular local sport, resulting in plentiful offerings of *cinghiale* (wild boar), which comes in many guises. Despite conservationists' pleas, numerous small birds, from sparrows to quail, are still considered fair game.

Hearty stews and barbecues

Legumes are used widely throughout Italy, but are a particular mainstay in Tuscany, where *cannellini*, or white kidney beans, are favoured. Tuscans, in fact, are known as *Toscani Mangiafagioli* – bean eaters, because the pulse is used so much in local specialities, adding a smooth texture as only well-cooked beans can. Thick soups and hearty bean stews are served in terracotta pots often enhanced by a trickle of olive oil which is added at the table.

Tuscan cooks favour methods that can be carried out on a large scale and preferably out of doors – a grill over an open wood fire is something you will come across behind chic

LEFT: ingredients for a perfect holiday.
RIGHT: preparing *bistecca alla Fiorentina*.

Florentine restaurants or in the garden of rural *trattorie*. Fresh herbs like sage, rosemary and basil are used, as they grow, in abundance.

The most important Tuscan meat dish is the excellent *bistecca alla Fiorentina*, a vast, tender, juicy and succulent beef steak – preferably from cattle raised in Val di Chiana. It is brushed with a drop of the purest virgin olive oil and grilled over a scented wood fire of oak or olive branches, then seasoned with salt and pepper before serving. In good Florentine and Tuscan restaurants in general, you will be able to see the meat raw before you order.

Another famous Tuscan meat dish is *arista alla Fiorentina*, consisting of a pork loin highly

seasoned with chopped rosemary and ground pepper. The origin of this dish goes back to the 15th century. At the Ecumenical Council of 1430 in Florence, the Greek bishops were served this dish at a banquet and pronounced it "*aristos*", which in Greek means very good. The name stuck, and it has become a feature of Tuscan cuisine ever since. It is a particularly useful dish because it keeps very well for several days and is even better cold than hot.

Soups are made of the ubiquitous beans, and include *acquacotta*, a vegetable soup with an egg added before serving, and *pappa al pomodoro*, a thick soup of bread and tomatoes. Also well known in this category is the Florentine speciality *ribollita*, meaning "boiled again": a second boiling of the soup increases the density and improves the flavour.

Although beef- rather than bean-based, a special stew is *peposo*, a fiery blend of meat and vegetables from Impruneta, a town near Florence that is famous for its terracotta.

The coastal province of Livorno produces the delicious *cacciucco*, an immense seafood-and-fish soup claimed to be the original bouillabaisse. The story goes that the soup originated in the port after a tremendous storm that left a widowed fisherman's wife desperately trying to feed her many children. The children were sent begging for something to eat. As the fishermen had nothing else to give, the children came home with handfuls of mussels, a few shrimps, half a fish and some fish heads. The clever mother put them all in a pot, added herbs and tomatoes from her garden and created the glorious *cacciucco*. While *zuppa di pesce* can be eaten all over Italy, *cacciucco* can be eaten only in Livorno and surrounding areas. It is ladled over a thick slice of toasted bread flavoured with garlic.

Cheese

The cheeses available in Tuscany are plentiful and varied. There is a delightful overspill of cheeses from neighbouring Emilia Romagna, including, of course, the King of Cheeses, *parmigiano reggiano*. It is used extensively to complement Tuscany's marvellous pasta dishes and soups. Other cheeses made locally include *marzolino*, a ewe's-milk cheese made in March, when milk is most plentiful in the Chianti valley; *mucchino*, cow's-milk cheese made in and around Lucca by the same procedure as pecorino; *brancolino* from the town of Brancoli; the delectable *formaggette di Zeri*, made with half ewe's and half cow's milk in Massa Carrara; and all the local rustic *cacciotte* and ricotta made with cow's, goat's and ewe's milk.

Chestnuts, mushrooms and truffles

Chestnuts are a staple of the region, particularly in mountain areas, where they are made into flour, pancakes, soups and sweet cakes like *castagnaccio*, flavoured with rosemary and pine nuts. The season peaks around mid-October, when chestnut – and steam-train – lovers can travel on a restored 1920s steam

is awaited impatiently, as the spoils are highly prized both for their pungent flavour and the handsome price they will fetch in the market.

There are many different varieties of wild mushrooms growing in abundance amongst the trees in the Tuscan hills – although the type of mushroom found will depend very much upon the type of tree it is growing next to or under – but the most sought after is the perfect *porcine (boletus edulis)*, which grows to enormous size and thickness.

If you want to try your hand at picking them yourself, make sure you go with someone who knows what they are doing, as many types are poisonous. If you don't want to take the risk,

train from Florence's Santa Maria Novella station to Marradi's *Sagra delle Castagne*, or chestnut festival, to partake in the celebrations.

In the autumn, when the rains fall, the hills become a target for family outings. Long lines of cars park along the side of the mountain roads – particularly in the Maremma, Garfagnana and Mugello areas, where little groups of people don stout shoes and arm themselves with baskets and hooked knives, searching for the delectable harvest of *funghi*. The wild-mushroom season

LEFT: picking olives, as pictured by a 15th-century artist. **ABOVE:** *The Fruit Vendor*, a 16th-century still-life by Vincenzo Campi, shows the region's harvest.

just purchase some from a roadside market during the August–October season.

Fresh wild mushrooms can be prepared in a number of ways, but perhaps the best is to grill the large *porcini* in the Tuscan way, like a steak: rub each with a slice of lemon, stick them with slivers of garlic and sprigs of thyme – or, even simpler, just brush them with olive oil and salt. Dried *porcini* are even tastier, as the dehydration concentrates the flavour. When regenerated by soaking in lukewarm water, they are ideal for use in risottos or pasta sauces.

If there is one food item that causes more excitement in Italians than wild mushrooms, it is the *tartufo*, or truffle – particularly the white truffle, which begins to form in early summer and matures by the end of September, with a season lasting until the middle of January. Truffles are "underground fungi", developing close to the roots of oaks, poplars, hazelnut trees and certain pines. But the exact location of a "truffle trove" is a well-guarded secret, with truffle hunters regarding their talented dogs, who unearth the strong-smelling delicacy, as highly important members of their families.

Truffles are sold by the gram and handled as carefully as if they were gold nuggets – and expect to pay as if they *were* gold, for these are precious commodities. Although it is nearly impossible to describe the taste, true Italian food connoisseurs will tell you that there is nothing on earth like a plate of plain, buttered tagliatelle with a sprinkling of parmesan and liberal shavings of white truffle on top.

While the most highly prized (and strongest-smelling) white truffles are to be found in the Piedmont region, Tuscany also has its share, mainly centred around the town of San Miniato, which produces 25 percent of Italy's crop and hosts a truffle festival in November.

Other truffle-related activities and fairs held in the San Miniato area at this time include the *Sagra del Tartufo Bianco* at Corazzano and, at Balconivisi, *Il Palio del Papero* (a parade culminating in a goose race).

EATING ITALIAN-STYLE

Italians love their food, and Tuscans are no exception. But there are "rules" to be followed if you want to "eat as the Italians do". Cappuccino in the afternoon? You'll be branded a tourist. Salad *before* the main course? Never.

Usually, breakfast consists of just an espresso or cappuccino, drunk on the hoof in a local bar if not at home, perhaps with a *panino* (filled bread roll) if you are really hungry. Dinner, too, is generally a fairly minor event, with perhaps a light soup or *frittata*, sometimes eaten as late as 10 or 11pm. Lunch, however, is a different story. This is a truly gastronomic event, to be shared and savoured with friends and family at leisure – which is why for sev-eral hours in the middle of the day you'll find churches locked, museums shut, shops closed and streets empty. All attention is on the table.

Traditionally, a full-blown, no-holds-barred Italian meal will begin with an antipasto – a bit of salami or some roasted peppers, for example. Then follows the first course, *il primo*, usually a pasta, risotto or soup. *Il secondo* is next, consisting of meat or fish accompanied by vegetables. Salad is always served after this, effectively cleansing the palate in preparation for *i formaggi* (cheese) and *i dolci* (dessert), the last often being fruit-based. Top it off with an espresso. *Buon appetito!*

Sweetmeats

Siena is famous for the Palio, for its Gothic beauty, and for its incredibly wide selection of sweetmeats. *Cavallucci* are delicious little hard biscuits which are usually served at the end of a meal and dipped into glasses of Vin Santo.

Panforte, an Italian Christmas speciality, is unmistakable in its brightly coloured octagonal cardboard box. It is a rich, sweet cake of candied fruit, nuts, spices, honey and sugar, sandwiched between sheets of rice paper.

Ricciarelli are delightful, diamond-shaped almond cakes, also saved for the Christmas celebrations, along with the delicious, rich, golden rice cake called *torta di riso*. The local

receive a blessing from the saint. Prato has *biscottini di Prato* made from almonds, eggs, flour and sugar, delicious dipped into the local Vin Santo. In Livorno they make gorgeous, light, golden buns called *bolli*. A speciality of Lucca is a ring-shaped plain cake known as *buccellato*, and an unusual sweet tart of spinach and chard with pine nuts. Finally, in Florence, around carnival time you find *schiacciata alla Fiorentina*, a simple, light sponge cake.

No visit to Florence would be complete without a taste of its ice cream. You can see why Florentines claim to have invented *gelato*, for the city is awash with a rainbow of flavours. Always look for the sign *Produzione*

pasticcerie are filled with these and many other delectable varieties. In other areas of the region, different specialities appear. At Castelnuovo della Garfagnana they make a wonderfully simple cake of chestnuts called *torta garfagnina*; on the borders with Emilia Romagna they bake a delicious apple cake, the *torta di mele*.

Pistoia produces the pretty *corona di San Bartolomeo* for the feast of St Bartholomew on 24 August, when mothers lead their children to church wearing this cake "necklace" to

Propria (home-made). But taking pride of place amongst Tuscany's sweet specialities is the *zuccotto*, a sponge cake mould with a filling of almonds, hazelnuts, chocolate and cream. Once eaten, it is never forgotten. Literally translated as "small pumpkin", *zuccotto*, being a dome-shaped Florentine speciality, is thought by some to refer affectionately to the Duomo – or is perhaps a slightly irreverent allusion to the clergy. In the Tuscan dialect, a cardinal's skullcap is also called a *zuccotto*.

Tuscany is truly a food-lover's paradise. But remember, this is not the region to seek out complicated or intricate dishes. The food of Tuscany is a pure and simple art.   ❑

LEFT: *bruschetta*, the ubiquitous appetiser; fresh *funghi*. **ABOVE:** making a meal of your ice cream – one of the great pleasures of a Tuscan holiday.

PLACES

A detailed guide to the region, with the
principal sites clearly cross-referenced by
number to the maps

Stretching from Carrara marble quarries, to the Maremma wilderness; from Livorno's rugged coastline to the mountainous Casentino, through the wooded slopes of Monte Amiata, the Sienese craters, the Chianti hills and Mugello valley – Tuscany's evocative landscapes are a powerful mixture of the wild and the tamed. For many travellers, Tuscany is the true Italy – that is the Italy they know from romantic novels, glossy brochures and the Merchant-Ivory film adaptations of E.M. Forster novels – a land of swaying cypress trees, olive groves and vineyards, scattered with medieval castles and Medici villas. Tuscans themselves are more pragmatic about the rural idyll so beloved of foreign visitors. They have a deep relationship with the land, but recognise the tough realities of rural life. They are also innately sociable and will always prefer living in large villages or small towns to an isolated farmhouse, however idyllic.

The appeal of Tuscan towns is that they appear to go against the current of modern homogeneity and internationalism and remain much as they were a few hundred years ago. Florence, the city that gave birth to the Renaissance, retains a huge number of the art works that were created there. Gazing at its skyline from the Piazzale Michelangelo it is evident how little the cityscape has changed since its artistic heyday. Variety is also the secret of Tuscany's townscapes: from medieval hill-top towns to Etruscan villages; from *fin de siècle* spa towns to sophisticated mountain resorts; from the splendour of a Renaissance cathedral to a stark Romanesque church.

But for all its artistic and architectural riches, most visitors to Tuscany would agree that as much, if not more pleasure can be derived from a simple lunch on the shady terrace of a rustic trattoria and a bit of banter with its owner, as a meeting with Michelangelo's *David* and Botticelli's *Venus*. As Forster observed: "The traveller who has gone to Italy to study the tactile values of Giotto, or the corruption of the papacy, may return remembering nothing but the blue sky and the men and women who live under it." And there's nothing wrong with that.   ❑

PRECEDING PAGES: a lone farmhouse and cypress trees – a classic Tuscan scene; Porto Santo Stefano, on the Argentario peninsula. **LEFT:** a cypress copse in Le Crete.

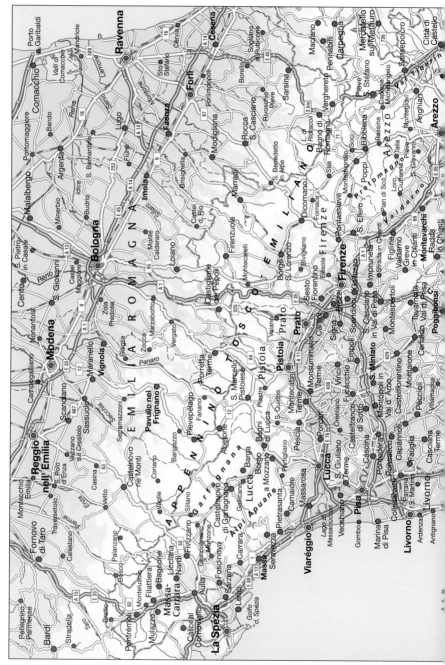

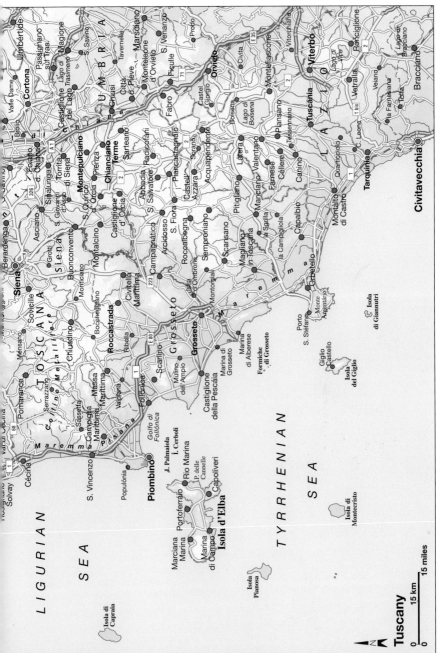

Tuscany

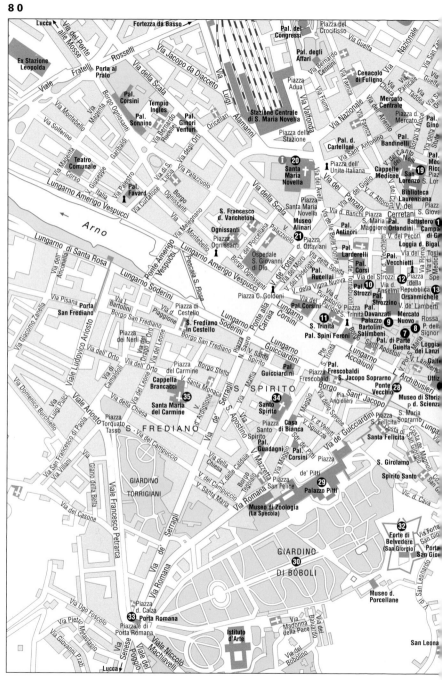

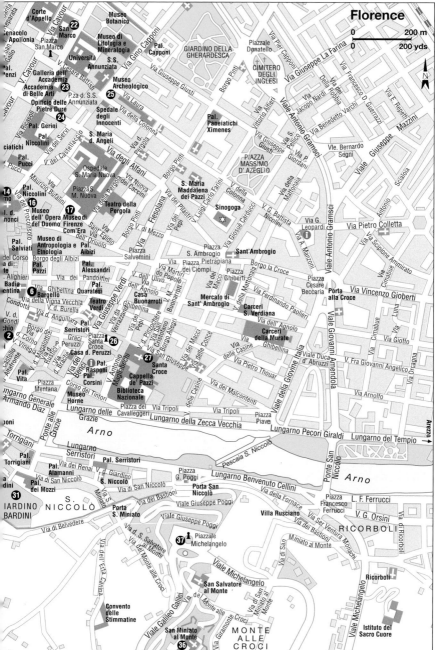

Florence

THE CITY OF FLORENCE

The throbbing heart of Tuscany and the cradle of the
Renaissance, Florence is a truly outstanding city – in a
country full to bursting with spectacular sights

Viewed from the surrounding hills, Florence seems to be floating in a bowl which, at dusk, is tinged violet. The honey-coloured walls and myriad, rose-coloured roofs of the city combine to make a unity which is dominated by a single, vast building, the Cathedral, or Duomo. It is by far the biggest building for miles around, with its roof and dome in the same subtle colour-range as the surrounding smaller buildings, above which it seems to float like a great liner among tugs. There are few towers or spires. Giotto's multi-coloured Campanile next to the Duomo, plain in outline but intricate in detail, and the thrusting tower of the Palazzo Vecchio, elegant and sombre, soar above a generally low profile. The overall impression is not that of a city, composed of tens of thousands of units, but of one single, vast building, a majestic palace.

Close contact with the city can be at first disconcerting, even disappointing and claustrophobic. The streets are narrow, hemmed in by towering, plain buildings. There is no delicate filigree, as in Venice, or cheerful baroque, as in Rome, to tempt the eye. Some of the buildings resemble 19th-century warehouses – grim structures that were erected at a time of social unrest, their pri-

mary function being as fortresses. In any case, Florentine taste runs to the understated and the restrained.

However, gradually, the visitor comes to terms with a city which, though sharing basic characteristics with the larger family of Italian cities, is a unique mixture. The no-traffic laws in the historic centre – while often abused – have, for the most part, given Florence back to pedestrians. The streets are again part of the city's fabric, simultaneously discharging the role of stage-

Map on pages 80–1

LEFT: the rooftops of Florence seen from Brunelleschi's dome.
BELOW: San Miniato by moonlight.

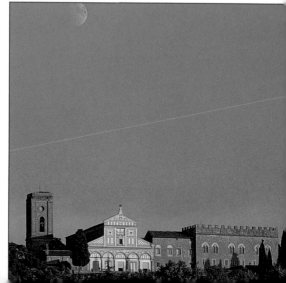

TIP

Florence is one of many Italian cities to implement a new bike-sharing scheme to help cut down on pollution and traffic. Set to start in spring of 2009, the service will include over 750 high-tech bicycles linked to hubs around the city. After registering online or at designated offices and obtaining a rental pass, you can pick up a bicycle at one hub and drop it off at another. The first half hour is free. More information is available from Tourist Information points throughout the city.

BELOW: crowds outside the Uffizi.

set and communication link. It's a liberating atmosphere: you are free to wander, stop, and wander again, absorbing all the city has to offer.

For the visitor to attempt a comprehensive survey of Florence on a single visit will simply invite fatigue, then boredom. The monuments and localities which figure in the following bird's-eye view are chosen on a necessarily arbitrary basis. Some, of course, select themselves; others have been included because they can stand as an example for their class as a whole, or illustrate some particular point of the Florentine story.

The city has been grouped into four sections, starting with the area around the Palazzo Vecchio, followed by the area around the Duomo and then by three important religious foundations (which, though physically scattered around the city, have been grouped together in this chapter). The final section is the river Arno and beyond. Nearly all the places are within easy walking distance of one another – despite Florence's size, its historic centre is reasonably compact.

The civic heart

Of all the great Italian city squares, Florence's is the most perversely irregular. There is nothing in the **Piazza della Signoria ❶** to compete with the harmony that makes Venice's San Marco a vast, unroofed hall. There is nothing here of the grace of Siena's curved Campo, or the simple majesty of Rome's Capitol. Instead, the buildings follow each other around the perimeter of the piazza in no particular order. Tucked on one side is the **Palazzo Vecchio ❷** (open Fri–Wed 9am–7pm, Thur until 2pm; entrance fee; tel: 055-276 8224), the seat of government for the past six centuries. Next to it stands the elegant **Loggia dei Lanzi ❸**, crammed with statues. The huge fountain in the centre is the subject of amiable mockery by the residents of Florence themselves, and no two buildings in the piazza seem to have the same façade.

With a despot's love of order, Cosimo I tried to impose an artificial unity on the square, but his schemes came to nothing, leaving the piazza as a perfect illustration of Florentine "unity in diversity".

Battle for the Uffizi

Plans to add a radical new loggia to the Uffizi were recently sent back to the drawing-board by the Minister for Culture. The design by Arata Isozaki, the architect behind cutting-edge buildings in Barcelona, Turin and California, is part of an ambitious project to expand the exhibition space and double visitor numbers. The 'New Uffizi' is due for completion in 2013, but the mooted extension is highly controversial. Traditionalists who see the city solely as 'the cradle of the Renaissance' are pitted against the progressives who say that the city has to embrace change if it is ever to escape its stifling 16th-century strait-jacket. Who will win the battle remains to be seen.

Despite the absence of an overall plan and the individuality of the buildings, the piazza as a whole does come together. It has changed little over the centuries, as is evident in the contemporary painting (in the Museo di Firenze Com'Era) of the execution of Savonarola, the anti-Medici Dominican preacher, which took place on the piazza in 1498 *(see pages 92–3)*.

The **Marzocco**, the lion symbol of the city which prisoners were forced to kiss, can be found here, as well as a copy of Michelangelo's immense statue of *David* (the original is in the Accademia, *see page 109*), commissioned in 1501 to mark an important change in the constitution.

Nearby is a statue of the first Medici duke, Cosimo I. The Loggia dei Lanzi (named after the *landsknechts* or mercenaries employed by Cosimo) has an impressive statue of a triumphant Perseus holding the severed head of Medusa *(see page 52)*, which Cosimo commissioned from Cellini. Most stunning among the other statues in the loggia is Giambologna's *Rape of the Sabine Women* on the opposite side.

The interior of the Palazzo Vecchio itself, begun in 1299 and finished in 1314, belies its grim exterior. The courtyard, with its copy of an enchanting fountain by Verrochio, is a delight. The portentous **Salone dei Cinquecento** was built for the Republican Council of 500 introduced by Savonarola in 1496. It was transformed into a throne room for Cosimo I by Vasari, who produced vast, rather tasteless but historically fascinating frescoes lauding the exploits of the Medici. Finally it served as the first parliament of a united Italy when Florence briefly became the Italian capital in 1865.

Although the Palazzo still functions as Florence's town hall – you might even catch the incongruous sight of a wedding party, as it is very much a working building – most of the historic rooms, including the Medici suite and the grim little cell where Savonarola was held before his execution in the piazza below, are usually open to the public.

The **Museo dei Ragazzi**, on the ground floor, organises special palace visits for children with actors who bring its history to life.

The Uffizi

Adjoining the piazza are the immense galleries of the **Uffizi ❹** *(see pages 100–103)*. Originally built to house the city's administration offices *(uffici)*, the building now contains the world's greatest collection of Renaissance art, with paintings by Giotto, Botticelli, Michelangelo, Leonardo, Raphael, Titian and Caravaggio among other great masters.

Just behind the Uffizi is the **Museo di Storia della Scienza ❺** (open winter: Mon, Wed–Sat 9.30am–5pm, Tues until 1pm; summer: Mon, Wed–Fri 9.30am–5pm, Tues and Sat until 1pm; entrance fee; www.imms.fi.it), which is undergoing renovations and will be partially closed until late 2009.

Map on pages 80–1

The intricately decorated ceiling in Palazzo Vecchio's Sala d'Udienza.

BELOW: A copy of Michelangelo's *David* outside the Palazzo Vecchio.

Milan may be the fashion capital, but Florence has its fair share of home-grown designers of international repute. Nearly all have their outlets at the southern end of Via de' Tornabuoni, including the shoemaker, Ferragamo.

BELOW: arcades on the Piazza della Repubblica.

This museum, housed in the 14th-century Palazzo Castellani, makes a refreshing change after an over-indulgence in the arts. The collection of scientific instruments shows that Renaissance Florence was pre-eminent in Europe as a centre of scientific research as well as of painting and sculpture. Amid the museum's prized collection of Galileo's instruments, the mathematician's middle finger of his right hand is displayed like the relic of a Christian saint.

The Bargello

Chronologically, the Palazzo Vecchio is the second city hall of Florence. Its predecessor, the **Bargello** ❻ *(see pages 110–11)*, was built 50 years earlier in 1250 as the seat of the chief magistrate, the *Podestà*. The Bargello was, in effect, the police headquarters, and its courtyard was often the scene of public executions. The building is now a wonderful museum specialising in sculptures with a rich collection of works by artists such as Michelangelo, Cellini, Donatello and many others – and is not nearly as bewildering as the Uffizi.

Four centuries of history

Just west of the Piazza della Signoria is a loosely associated group of three buildings which takes you across some four centuries of Florentine history, from the embattled Middle Ages to the era of ducal control. The **Palazzo di Parte Guelfa** ❼ (just off Via delle Terme) was the headquarters of the all-powerful Guelf Party which, after the defeat and expulsion of the Ghibellines, completely ruled the city. The Palazzo was built in the 13th century, but was enlarged by Brunelleschi in the 15th century and given its external staircase by Vasari in the 16th. It now houses a library.

Nearby, is the lively **Mercato Nuovo** ❽ – also known as the "Straw Market". "Nuovo" is only relative, for the elegant covered market was built in around 1550. It is still a popular shopping place, full of high quality leather goods and tourist "tat". Here is the **Porcellino**, the amiable bronze boar whose snout is polished to gleaming gold by the rubbing of visitors, who touch it as a means of ensuring a return to the city on the Arno.

Also referred to as the Museo dell'Antica Casa Fiorentina, the **Palazzo Davanzati** ❾ (only partially open owing to restoration; daily 8.15am–1.50pm; closed 1st, 3rd and 5th Mon, 2nd and 4th Sun of the month; entrance free during restoration) is the earliest example of a patrician home, and gives a fascinating insight into life in medieval Florence. Built about 1330, its painted walls and ceilings are excellent examples of Trecento work serving to soften and brighten domestic architecture, turning a fortress into a home.

From Palazzo Davanzati, Via de' Sassetti leads into Piazza Strozzi. Here stands the grandiose **Palazzo Strozzi** ❿, (open daily during exhibitions) testament to the overweening pride of the powerful merchant and banker, Filippo Strozzi. Construction of the building began in 1489; it was

still not complete 47 years later, in 1536, when Strozzi died leaving his heirs bankrupt. The Palazzo Strozzi is now a major cultural destination, hosting high-profile international art exhibits. Beneath its delightful court-yard **La Strozzina**, is an exciting new space which stages challenging contemporary art exhibitions, often showcasing emerging artists.

Worth a visit while you're in the vicinity is the Romanesque church of **Santa Trinita ⓫** (open Mon–Sat 8am–noon, 4–6pm, Sun 4–6pm), which features a fresco cycle of the life of St Francis painted in 1483 by Domenico Ghirlandaio.

East of Palazzo Strozzi, **Piazza della Repubblica ⓬** was laid out over the medieval market quarter and Ghetto, which were demolished in the 19th century. The plan to develop central Florence was con-ceived between 1865 and 1871, when the city was briefly the capital of Italy. The ancient and "squalid" buildings were to be swept away and replaced by broad avenues, symbolic of the new age of the United King-dom of Italy. Thankfully the scheme was abandoned. The square, with its swish cafés, department stores and billboards, remains a modern intru-sion into the heart of the city.

The religious centre

The main artery of the city, the street which links the two great monuments of the Palazzo Vecchio and the Duomo, is still known as the Street of the Hosiers – Via dei Calzaiuoli – after the stocking-knitters who plied their trade here. It still specialises in footwear. The guilds were concen-trated in this area. The guild church of **Orsanmichele ⓭** (open Tues–Fri 10am–5pm) was built on the site of the 9th-century San Michele ad Hor-tum. Its exterior is, in effect, an open-air sculpture gallery, with various statues displayed in individual niches set into the wall of the building.

Holding up to 20,000 people, the enormous size of the **Duomo ⓮** (open daily, Sun pm only) is empha-sised by the smallness of the square in which it is placed, and the narrow-ness of the streets which enter it. At no point can one take in the whole.

The Baptistery

Despite the Duomo's dominating presence, the little **Battistero ⓯** (open Mon–Sat noon–7pm, 1st Sat of each month 8.30am–2pm, Sun 8.30am–2pm; entrance fee) in front of it easily holds its own. The oldest building in the city, it was built on, or reconstructed from, a 7th-century building sometime between 1060 and 1120 and served as the cathedral of Florence until 1228, when it was rel-egated to the role of baptistery. Dante was among the eminent Florentines baptised there, and the wealthy Wool Guild *(Calimala)* lavished vast sums on its interior. In particular, they com-missioned the superb Venetian mosaics decorating the cupola.

The *Calimala* then turned its atten-tion to the three great doors, first commissioning Andrea Pisano to

TIP

In peak season, to avoid queuing for hours for the Uffizi, Bargello or Accademia, you can book your ticket and a time slot for entry either online, through your hotel or by phoning the museum directly (tel: 055-294883). For up-to-date information on all the state museums in Florence, visit www.polomuseale. firenze.it. A ticket booth on the Via dei Calzaiuoli side of Orsanmichele also sells tickets to these museums.

BELOW: the cupola mosaics of the Baptistery.

The south doors of the Baptistery were the work of Andrea Pisano (c.1270–1348) – goldsmith, sculptor and architect rolled into one.

BELOW: Moses receiving the Commandments, as depicted on the Baptistery's east doors by Ghiberti.

create bronze doors for the south entrance, then initiating a competition for the other doors, which was won by Lorenzo Ghiberti. There is no mistaking the second pair (the east doors, facing the Duomo) – which took Ghiberti 27 years to create, and which Michelangelo described as the "Gates of Paradise" – for there is always a little knot of people standing staring at them. But the present panels are copies. The original panels are in the **Museo dell'Opera del Duomo** ⓰ on the east side of the Piazza del Duomo (open Mon–Sat 9am–7.30pm, Sun 9am–1.40pm; entrance fee), while the competiton panels are in the Bargello.

The two doors are divided into 10 panels, each representing a scene from the Old Testament. Round the panels are heads of the Sibyls and the Prophets. To get an idea of the incredible detail, and the precision to which Ghiberti worked, look for his self-portrait. It is halfway down on the right-hand side of the left-hand door and, though only a few inches high, is a perfect portrait – a little, balding man peering knowingly out.

It took the Florentines over 400 years to decide just what kind of façade they wanted for the west front of the Duomo – the side immediately facing the Baptistery. Again and again both artists and the city fathers came up with some scheme which satisfied nobody (when the first Medici pope, Leo X, visited his native city in 1515, they even erected a cardboard front for it). The present front was designed in 1887 and has inevitably come in for criticism.

Inside the Duomo

After the multicoloured splendour of the freshly restored exterior, the interior of **Santa Maria del Fiore** (the Duomo's official name) comes at first as a disappointment. Many of the treasures have been removed and are now in the Museo dell'Opera del Duomo. The overall colour scheme of the interior is muted, coming to life only at the time of religious festivals, when immense crimson banners are hung on the walls and pillars.

But the relative lack of architectural detail allows the eye to pick out the remaining treasures which highlight the city's history. High on the wall immediately to the left of the entrance are two large murals of soldiers. The right-hand one is of an Englishman, John Hawkwood, a mercenary soldier or *condottiero* who first attacked Florence for his paymasters and then became the city's Captain-General in 1375. The original intention was to erect a monument to him, but thriftily the *Signoria* settled for this clever chiaroscuro imitation, painted by Uccello in 1436, which gives the impression of a three-dimensional monument.

Further along the aisle is the painting *Dante Declaiming the Divine Comedy* by Michelino. On Dante's right in the painting are Hell and Purgatory, while on his left is a contemporary view of the city's major monuments. For years, readings from

the *Comedy* used to be given in the Duomo during Lent, a fact which would doubtless have given Dante wry amusement, and in 1465 this painting was commissioned to mark the second centenary of his birth.

The Duomo's greatest treasure is Michelangelo's *Pietà*, which is now in the museum. He sculpted it for his own tomb in 1550, though it was never finished. It is entirely different from his earlier, more famous *Pietà* in St Peter's in Rome; where that is all calm, resigned acceptance, this is simply the utter defeat of death.

Lorenzo the Magnificent took refuge in the nearby **New Sacristy** on Easter Sunday morning in 1478 when the Pazzi Conspirators wounded him and murdered his brother Giuliano during High Mass. Although you can't actually walk in the New Sacristy, you can observe the artwork (including a Lucca della Robbia terracotta relief) through glass doors.

The dome and bell tower

If you have a head for heights, ascend to the gallery of the **dome** (open Mon–Fri 8.30am–7pm, Sat 8.30am–5.40pm; entrance fee). It is not for vertigo sufferers: the gallery is narrow and the balustrade low, but only here can Brunelleschi's stupendous achievement be fully appreciated. The original intention was to cover the interior of the dome with mosaic, which would have emphasised its soaring majesty; instead Vasari was commissioned to cover it with bold allegories.

Scarcely less tall, at 85 metres (278 ft), is the **Campanile** (open daily 8.30am–7.30pm in summer, June–Oct Fri–Sat until 11pm; daily until 4.30pm in winter; entrance fee) alongside, begun by Giotto shortly after he was appointed chief architect in 1331 and finished off after his death in 1337 by Andrea Pisano and then Talenti. Work was eventually completed in 1359. The climb to the top is worth the effort for intimate views of the Cathedral's upper levels and the panoramic city views.

East of the Duomo, on Via dell' Oriuolo, is the **Museo di Firenze Com'Era** ⓱ (open Mon–Wed 9am–2pm, Sat until 7pm; entrance fee). The historical-topographical

If you're thinking of climbing up to the dome, it is probably best to do it early in the day, when you still have some stamina: there are 464 spiralling stairs to negotiate before reaching the top. But once there, the view of the city is fabulous.

BELOW: the magnificent outline of Giotto's Campanile and Brunelleschi's dome.

BELOW: San Lorenzo's unfinished façade.

museum of "Florence as it was" is best seen once you have familiarised yourself with the city, so you can recognise the buildings depicted in the collection. One of the most fascinating exhibits here is a 19th-century copy of the huge and famous woodcut *Pianta della Catena* made around 1470, which shows an early view of the city *(see page 56)*.

Memories of the Medici

A few streets to the northwest of the Duomo is the heartland of Medicean Florence: the **Medici Palace** and the church of **San Lorenzo**.

The palace – now known as the **Palazzo Medici-Riccardi ⓲** (open Thur–Tues 9am–7pm; entrance fee) – is dignified but not ostentatious. It still has the look of a fortress about it, particularly in the façade of the ground floor, with its massive blocks of "rustic" masonry. Today it is the Prefecture of Florence, but the **Cappella dei Magi** and the Medici Museum are open to the public.

The museum contains various mementoes of the family, including the poignant death-mask of Lorenzo,

but it is the chapel which contains one of the brightest jewels in the Medici crown, *The Journey of the Magi* by Benozzo Gozzoli (*c.*1460; *see page 22*). This painting has been reproduced again and again, for it breathes the spirit of the Florentine Renaissance in its mixture of real figures of identifiable people, historical re-creation and delight in colour. The immense procession, winding its way through a delightfully improbable landscape, is led by a handsome, richly dressed youth on horseback – the young Lorenzo. Behind him comes his grandfather, Cosimo, soberly dressed, attended by a black servant. Other members of the family are in the group – which includes the painter himself, with his name inscribed on his hat. In the distance is the Medici country Villa Cafaggiolo – and a couple of camels to remind the observer that the picture is set in the Middle East!

San Lorenzo

The church of **San Lorenzo ⓳** (open Mon–Sat 10am–5.30pm, in summer also Sun 1.30–5.30pm;

entrance fee) is one of the earliest and most harmonious of all Renaissance churches, representing a break with French Gothic and a return to an older, classical style. The church's façade is rough and unfinished, but the interior is outstanding, a gracious composition of the grey stone *pietra serena* and white walls. Giovanni, father of Cosimo de' Medici, commissioned Brunelleschi to design San Lorenzo in 1419, but progress was halting and neither lived to see it complete. Thereafter, successive members of the Medici family continued to embellish it, commissioning the greatest artists of their age to add frescoes, paintings and – ultimately – their mausoleum.

Of particular note in the basilica are Donatello's pulpits with bronze reliefs of the Passion, and the Old Sacristy adorned with sculptures by Donatello.

The quiet cloister to the north of the church, with its box-lined lawns and pomegranate bushes, leads to the **Biblioteca Laurenziana** (open for exhibitions only, hours variable; tel: 055-211590). Designed by Michelangelo between 1524 and 1534, the library houses more than 10,000 manuscripts (including the famous 5th-century Virgil codex) from the Medici collection.

The Medici chapels

The entrance to the **Cappelle Medicee** (open daily 8.15am–5.50pm; closed alternate Sun and Mon; entrance fee) is outside the church, in the Piazza della Madonna degli Aldobrandini. You go in via the crypt, where a floor slab commemorates Anna Maria Ludovica (died 1743), the last in the Medici line. Stairs lead to the opulent **Cappella dei Principi** (the mausoleum of the Medici grand dukes) and the **New Sacristy** (the Medici tombs), the latter Michelangelo's first architectural commission. The two New Sacristy tombs of Giuliano (son of Lorenzo the Magnificent) and Lorenzo (his grandson) are graced with the reclining figures of *Dawn*, *Evening*, *Day* and *Night*, conveying to the observer an unforgettable feeling of uneasiness, of sadness, of loss.

The Mercato Centrale, Florence's main food market, open Mon–Sat 7am–2pm.

BELOW: a Florentine news-stand.

St Thomas Aquinas, depicted on one of the stained-glass windows of Santa Maria Novella.

BELOW: Giotto's *Crucifix* in Santa Maria Novella.

Santa Maria Novella

The three great buildings of Santa Maria Novella, San Marco and Santa Croce are widely separated in the city – the first near the Stazione Centrale, the second on the far eastern side of the city, and the last in the north. They are grouped together here because they illustrate a truth about Florence, in the absence of which even the most splendid buildings lose something of their significance. The truth is that religion was a driving force – probably even stronger than commerce or the desire for self-aggrandisement – a force that nearly drove the city to destruction.

The church of **Santa Maria Novella** ⑳ (open Mon–Thur, Sat 9am–5pm, Fri, Sun 1–5pm; at time of press the façade was being restored as part of the ongoing refurbishment of the Piazza Santa Maria Novella, so expect to find the square torn up), begun in 1246, was designed by Dominican monks. Though dignified and indeed majestic, it reflects their gloomy preoccupations: striped like a tiger, the family chapels are sombre and overwhelming, their murals little more than illustrations of sermons. The **Spanish Chapel** carries this to extremes, with its murals dedicated to the 13th-century theologian, Thomas Aquinas, who was, of course, a Dominican. The chapel now lies within the **Cloister Museum** (open Mon–Thur, Sat 9am–5pm; entrance fee) adjoining the church, as do Uccello's frescoes. In the church itself is Masaccio's *Trinity (see page 49),* and the chapel is frescoed by Fra Filippino Lippi and Ghirlandaio.

Decorations in the church were carried out well into the Renaissance, with work by Brunelleschi, among others, so there is a lightening of the spirit. But the overall impression is a somewhat gloomy one, with a rather threatening air. It was in Santa Maria, incidentally, that Boccaccio's seven young maidens met in the spring of 1348, where they were joined by three young men and launched the comedy of *The Decameron.*

At the southern end of Piazza Santa Maria Novella, the **Museo Nazionale Alinari Fotografia** ㉑ (open Sun–Tues, Thur–Fri 9.30am–7.30pm, Sat until 11.30pm; www.alinarifondazione.it; entrance fee) has one of the best photographic collections in Europe. Founded in 1852, the Alinari brothers' photographic studio supplied 19th-century Grand Tourists with prints, postcards and art books. The museum features special exhibits and an archive of 900,000 vintage prints.

San Marco

Ironically, the convent of **San Marco** ㉒ was almost entirely rebuilt with money provided by Cosimo de' Medici; the irony lies in the fact that San Marco became the headquarters of the friar Girolamo Savonarola, who was the greatest and most determined enemy of Cosimo's grandson, Lorenzo. Cosimo engaged his own favourite architect, Michelozzo, who

had designed the Palazzo Medici, to build San Marco, and spent more than 50,000 florins on it, as well as presenting it with a magnificent library.

Savonarola was Prior of San Marco from 1491 until his execution in 1498. During those years he totally dominated Florence, nearly succeeded in overthrowing the Medici and even presented a challenge to the papacy. The vivid portrait of him by Fra Bartolomeo, which can be seen in San Marco, shows a man with a forceful but ugly face, a great beaked nose and burning eyes.

The convent of San Marco is now a **museum** (open Mon–Thur 8.15am–1.50pm, Fri until 6pm, Sat and Sun until 7pm; closed alternate Sun and Mon; entrance fee). The prize exhibits are the murals of Fra Angelico, himself a Dominican, but one who brought a delicacy to his work quite at variance with the austere tenets of that order. Each of the friars' cells is graced by one of his murals, and at the head of the stairs is the most famous of them all, the *Annunciation*. Savonarola's cell is laid out as he knew it, complete with desk and elegant but rather uncomfortable-looking chair.

In the immediate vicinity of San Marco are several sites of note, the first and foremost being the **Galleria dell'Accademia** ㉓ (see pages 108–9), often identified by the enormous lines outside (at times even longer than those at the Uffizi). Its star attraction – and the focal point of the entire museum – is the colossal statue of *David*, which was carved between 1501 and 1504 from a single piece of marble, and established Michelangelo as the foremost sculptor of his time before the age of 30. The statue now standing in front of the Palazzo Vecchio is an equally impressive copy.

Near to the Accademia, with its entrance on the Via Alfani, is the **Opificio delle Pietre Dure** ㉔ (open Mon–Wed, Fri–Sat 8.15am–

2pm, Thur until 7pm; entrance fee), where restoration of artistic treasures takes place. Exhibits include inlaid semi-precious stones used in *pietra dura*, as well as workbenches and instruments once used by the craftsmen.

The **Museo Archeologico** ㉕ (open Mon 2pm–7pm, Wed, Fri–Sun 8.30am–2pm, Tues and Thur 8.30am–7pm; entrance fee) in Piazza S.S. Annunziata features an important collection of Greek, Egyptian, Etruscan and Roman art.

Santa Croce

The great **Piazza Santa Croce** ㉖ was a favoured place for such large-scale activities as horse races and tournaments. *Calcio Storico*, a historic football match, continues to be played here. Featuring many souvenir and leather shops, the square is now dominated by a statue of Dante.

Although the façade of **Santa Croce** ㉗ (open Mon–Sat 9.30am–5.30pm, Sun opens at 1pm; entrance fee) dates from the mid-19th century, Arnolfo di Cambio began work on the church in 1294. With the light-

Map on pages 80–1

TIP

One little-known sight worth discovering is the Cenacolo di Sant' Apollonia (Via XXVII Aprile; open daily 8.30am–1.50pm; closed 1st, 3rd and 5th Sun, 2nd and 4th Mon of the month), a Renaissance refectory *(cenacolo)* set in a Benedictine convent now occupied by the University of Florence. On the main wall is Andrea del Castagno's dramatic version of *The Last Supper*.

BELOW: Fra Angelico's *Last Judgement* in San Marco.

TIP

From 6.30–9pm most bars in Florence offer a set price for drinks and free access to a buffet. The buffet laid on in some bars is substantial enough to provide a cheap substitute for supper, for those with smaller appetites or following a big lunch.

BELOW: Ponte Vecchio.

ness and elegance associated with Franciscan churches, it is the Pantheon of Florence – and, indeed, of Italy, since this is where so many of the country's illustrious dead were laid to rest. The tomb of Michelangelo, designed by Vasari, is here and invariably has a little bunch of flowers laid upon it. Here also are the graves of Ghiberti and Galileo; and of Machiavelli, who died in 1527. Crowning all are the frescoes painted by Giotto and his school.

This area, which is the lowest in the city, recorded water levels in the piazza itself as high as 6.2 metres (20 feet) in the 1966 flood. The watermarks are still visible today on some buildings. The cloisters, designed by Brunelleschi, lead to the highly original **Pazzi Chapel**, which contains 12 terracotta roundels of the Apostles by Luca della Robbia.

The **Museo dell'Opera di Santa Croce** (open Mon–Sat 9.30am–5.30pm, Sun opens at 1pm; entrance fee) houses the beguiling *Tree of the Cross* by Taddeo Gaddi and Cimabue's world-famous 13th-century *Crucif*ix, which was badly damaged in the flood. It has only been partially restored, but this was intentional, so that the work remains a poignant reminder of the city in peril.

Across the river

The Florentines look upon their river with decidedly mixed feelings. It has brought wealth but it has also brought danger, for it is entirely unpredictable. In summer it can shrink to nothing more than a trickle along a dried-up bed. In winter, however, the Arno becomes a raging brown torrent.

The **Ponte Vecchio** ❷⓿ was erected by Taddeo Gaddi sometime after 1345 and has become virtually a symbol of Florence itself. Fortunately, the Germans spared it when they blew up every other Florentine bridge during World War II. It bears the same appearance that it has borne for six centuries. Even the goldsmiths and jewellers who throng it today were established there in the mid-16th century. Before the goldsmiths, the shops on the bridge were occupied by butchers and tanners, who used the river as a dumping ground until they were evicted in 1593.

It was for Ferdinando's father, Cosimo I, that Vasari built the extraordinary **Vasari Corridor** *(see page 100)* in 1565. Running from the Uffizi to the Pitti across the Ponte Vecchio, the private walkway made a physical as well as symbolic link between the two centres of Medicean power. In his film *Paisà*, Roberto Rossellini shot an unforgettable sequence of the fighting that took place along this gallery during the German retreat, which caused damage so severe that the gallery has been closed until recent years.

The Pitti Palace

The part of Florence south of the river, the **Oltrarno**, has a character all of its own. In the 15th century, this area was the centre of opposition to the Medici, spearheaded by the Pitti family. It was they who built the **Palazzo Pitti** ㉙ *(see pages 104–7),* the most grandiloquent of all Florentine buildings, which, by the irony of history, eventually became the seat of government for the Medici dukes themselves. Today it is home to museums and art galleries, the foremost of which is the **Galleria Palatina**. Here, in an opulent setting, are hung some masterpieces of the Medici collection by artists such as Raphael, Rubens, Van Dyck and Titian.

Adjoining the gallery are the **Appartamenti Monumentali** or **Reali** (State Apartments), lavishly decorated with impressive works of art. The palace also contains the **Galleria d'Arte Moderna**, the **Galleria del Costume** and the **Museo degli Argenti**.

An excellent antidote to the overwhelming splendours of the Pitti are the enchanting Boboli Gardens or **Giardino di Boboli** ㉚ *(see page 103),* attached to them.

Also included in the Boboli ticket is the **Giardino Bardini** ㉛, accessible from Via dei Bardi 1r or Costa San Giorgio 2 (open 8.15am–sunset, closed 1st and last Mon of month). The park offers stunning vistas and quiet spots for meditation among the beautiful floral displays.

Continue up Costa San Giorgio to the **Forte di Belvedere** ㉜ (open Tues–Sun 3–7pm), a 16th-century fortification designed by Buontalenti for the Grand Duke Ferdinando I de' Medici. The fort, which commands one of the most breathtaking views over Florence, hosts modern art and photography exhibits.

The Porta Romana

The **Via Romana**, which begins just past the Palazzo Pitti in Piazza San Felice, goes to the **Porta Romana** ㉝, providing an artery from the city centre, via the Ponte Vecchio, to the outside world. The gates of Florence were more than a means of entry and exit. The larger ones, like the Porta Romana, built in 1328, were both a garrison and a customs post, collecting dues on all the goods that came into the city. You can now walk a section of the ramparts near Porta Romana.

Map on pages 80–1

Resting outside the Palazzo Pitti – much time and energy are needed to do this vast repository of art and the adjacent Boboli gardens justice.

BELOW: fountain on Piazza Santa Trinità.

Map on pages 80–1

The Expulsion from Paradise *by Masaccio (c.1427) in the Brancacci Chapel. They are among the most powerfully emotive figures ever painted in Western art.*

BELOW: café on Piazzale Michelangelo.

Oltrarno churches

Three churches of note are also situated on this south side of the city, each remarkable in its own way. The first, not far from the Ponte di Santa Trinità, is **Santo Spirito** ㉞ its modest 18th-century façade masking the beautiful and harmonious interior designed by Filippo Brunelleschi in the 15th century. The numerous paintings inside provide an insight into the work of some of the lesser-known masters of the Renaissance period. Unfortunately Santo Spirito has been a victim of theft and vandalism, forcing staff to open the church only a few hours a day.

To the west of Santo Spirito is the church of **Santa Maria del Carmine** ㉟, which contains one of the greatest treasures of Italian painting – the **Brancacci Chapel** frescoes (open Mon and Wed–Sat 10am–5pm, Sun 1–5pm; reservation required; tel: 055-276 8224; entrance fee). Considered by many to rival even Michelangelo's Sistine Chapel in Rome, the work of Masolino (including *The Temptation of Adam and Eve*), Masaccio (including *The Expulsion from Paradise* and

The Tribute Money) and Filippino Lippi is truly magnificent. Unfortunately, due to the popularity of the frescoes, visitors are only allowed 15 minutes to see them.

Further east, dominating a hilltop (and battling a subsidence crisis), is **San Miniato al Monte** ㊱ (daily, summer 8am–7pm, winter 8am–noon, 3–6pm, Sun pm only). A building stood on this site as early as the 4th century; the present structure was started in 1018 and is a fine example of Florentine Romanesque architecture. Of particular interest inside are the **Cappella del Crocifisso**, a tiny vaulted temple, and the 11th-century crypt, which houses the relics of St Minias. You can hear the monks chanting each afternoon at 4.30pm.

San Miniato towers above the **Piazzale Michelangelo** ㊲, which is most easily reached from the Porta Romana along the enchanting Viale dei Colli, or else by climbing up from the river, past the Porta San Niccolò, taking the winding paths through the gardens to the piazzale.

Adorned with bronze copies of Michelangelo's statues, the piazzale is one place that no visitor should miss. From it the entire city is visible.

On the edge of the city

This southern section of Florence outside the remainder of the city wall is a reminder, though a rapidly fading one, that Florence is a country town: a brisk walk along Via di San Leonardo will take you from the very heart of the city out into vineyards, olive groves and maize fields.

The area north of Florence is also succumbing to urban sprawl. Fiesole (*see page 113*) is a prime example. In its heyday it was one of the chief towns of Etruria Propria and could claim to be the mother of Florence itself; now it is little more than a refined suburb of the spreading city it overlooks from its steep hilltop vantage point. ❑

RESTAURANTS, BARS AND CAFÉS

Restaurants

VERY EXPENSIVE (€€€€)

Alle Murate
Via del Proconsolo 16r
Tel: 055-240618
www.allemurate.it
Dine beneath the beautifully restored frescoes of this elegant restaurant set in the old Palace of Judges and Notaries. An audio guide at the end of your meal will lead you down into the basement where a Roman laundry house has been discovered. Closed Mon.

Enoteca Pinchiorri
Via Ghibellina 87
Tel: 055-242777
www.enotecapinchiorri.com
Elegant dress and a jacket are required at "Italy's finest restaurant" (three Michelin stars). It occupies a 15th-century palace with a fine courtyard for alfresco meals. Expect excellent nouvelle cuisine, rare wines... and a hefty bill. Reservation essential. Closed Sun and Mon, and lunchtime on Tues and Wed.

Il Cibrèo
Via Andrea del Verrocchio 8/r
Tel: 055-234 1100
www.cibreo.com
Justly famed, elegant but relaxed restaurant, one of the most popular in the city. Pure Tuscan cuisine, with a creative twist. No pasta, but a selection of superb soups and other *primi* (first courses). Closed Sun and Mon.

Relais Le Jardin, Hotel Regency
Piazza Massimo d'Azeglio 3
Tel: 055-245247
www.regency-hotel.com
Top-notch food in exclusive hotel restaurant, overlooking a garden. Elegant dress and reservation required.

Targa Bistrot
Lungarno Cristoforo Colombo 7
Tel: 055-677377
www.targabistrot.net
Very pleasantly set restaurant on the north bank of the Arno, some way from the centre, with a wood-panelled interior. Imaginative food. Closed Sun and 3 weeks in Aug.

Taverna del Bronzino
Via delle Ruote 25/27r
Tel: 055-495220
Classically comfortable restaurant in a quiet side street, some way from the centre. Elegantly served traditional food. Try the black *tortellini*, flavoured with truffle. Closed Sun and Aug.

EXPENSIVE (€€€)

Beccofino
Piazza degli Scarlatti 1r
Lungarno Guicciardini
Tel: 055-290076
www.beccofino.com
Fashionable restaurant with great wine list and original dishes. Tasty desserts. Closed Mon.

Cantinetta Antinori
Piazza Antinori 3
Tel: 055-292234
www.antinori.it

Restaurant in a 15th-century *palazzo*, serving typical Tuscan snacks and meals with wines from the well-known Antinori estates. A good place for a light lunch at the bar or a fuller meal in the elegant dining room. Closed weekends and Aug.

Godò
Piazza Edison 3–4r
Tel: 055-583881
A little out of town, but on the bus route to Fiesole, Godò lays on a wonderful breakfast, lunch and dinner. The *gnocchi al pomodoro* are sumptuous and the salads generous.

Golden View Open Bar
Via dei Bardi 58r
Tel: 055-214502
www.goldenviewopenbar.com
Touristy by day, fashionable jazz bar by night. Great view of Ponte Vecchio with live jazz almost every night and good food, although not cheap.

Osteria Caffè Italiano
Via Isole delle Stinche 11/13r
Tel: 055-289368
www.caffeitaliano.it
Under the same management as Alle Murate (*above*). Short menu but high standards. Open 10am "till late". Closed Mon.

Osteria dei Centopoveri
Via Palazzuolo 31r
Tel: 055-218846
Don't be put off by the number of tourists in this cosy osteria: the food, a mixture of Tuscan and Pugliese, is excellent.

Ristorante Nove
Piazza Degli Scarlatti 1r
Tel: 055-230 2756
Newly opened restaurant with pleasant atmosphere. Dishes are simple but feature ingredients of superb quality.

Terrazzo Rossini
Via Solferino 2
Tel: 055-284273
The restaurant on Hotel Kraft's terrace offers traditional Italian cuisine with a modern twist. The fish tasting menu is excellent.

MODERATE (€€)

All'Antico Ristoro di Cambi
Via S. Onofrio 1r
Tel: 055-217134
www.anticoristorodicambi.it
Busy, rustic trattoria serving genuine Florentine food, popular with local academics. Terrace in summer. Closed Sun, and a week in mid-Aug.

Alla Vecchia Bettola
Viale Ludovico Ariosto 32–34r
Tel: 055-224158
South of the river, away from the centre: the marble-topped tables, wooden benches and convivial atmosphere

PRICE CATEGORIES

Average cost of a three-course meal per person with a half-bottle of wine:
€ = under €30
€€ = €30–45
€€€ = €45–65
€€€€ = more than €65

make this a popular place with Florentines filling up on good, rustic food. Closed Sun and Mon.

Acqua al Due
Via della Vigna Vecchia 40r
Tel: 055-284170
www.acquaal2.it
A real dining experience which requires booking ahead due to its popularity. Try the *assaggio di primi* (five pasta dishes as chosen by the chef) followed by the *assaggio di dolci* (a selection of the desserts of the day).

Coco Lezzone
Via del Parioncino 26
Tel: 055-287178
Traditional food of the highest quality. Ingredients are always very fresh, and the menu changes with the seasons. Closed Sun and Tues at lunch.

Coquinarius
Via delle Oche 15r
Tel: 055-230 2153
www.coquinarius.it
A stone's throw from the Duomo. Very friendly staff. Great for lunchtime salads and delicious desserts. Always crowded, so reservation recommended.

Da Ruggero
Via Senese 89
Tel: 055-220542
Excellent restaurant just outside the Porta Romana. Popular with the locals, so best to reserve. Great *ribollita* and other Tuscan fare.

Da Zà Zà
Piazza del Mercato Centrale 26r
Tel: 055-215411
www.trattoriazaza.it

Good, earthy food and delicious home-made puddings. The riotous atmosphere is enjoyed by both locals and tourists.

Gustavino
Via della Condotta 37r
Tel: 055-212421
www.gustavino.it
Classy restaurant with an open kitchen so you can watch the chefs in action. The food is creative without being too fancy and is beautifully presented. Look out for the speciality food-and-wine evenings, which can be booked via the website. Closed Mon.

La Pentola dell'Oro
Via di Mezzo 24–26r
Tel: 055-241808
www.lapentoladelloro.it
As well as being unique, this is one of the friendliest restaurants in the city. Chef Giuseppe Alessi is more than willing to explain the dishes; the recipes – published in the restaurant's book – are inspired by medieval and Renaissance cookery. Closed Sun.

Napoleone
Piazza del Carmine 24
Tel: 055-281015
www.trattorianapoleone.it
This new trattoria in the trendy Oltrarno neighbourhood features simple Tuscan fare with Mediterranean influences. Same owners as the popular Zà Zà. Open for dinner.

Omero
Via Pian dei Giullari 11r
Tel: 055-220053
www.ristoranteomero.it
Located in the hills just outside the city centre, this restaurant

specialises in Florentine cuisine. Great view and good wine selection. Closed Tues.

Osteria dei Baroncelli
Via Chiasso dei Baroncelli 1
Tel: 055-288219
Tucked away down an alley off Piazza della Signoria, this restaurant offers professional service and good food. Try the *crespelle* and the *bistecca alla fiorentina*. Best to come at dinner, as large tourist groups tend to stop here for lunch.

Pane e Vino
Via di Cestello 3r
Tel: 055-247 6956
www.ristorantepaneevino.it
Pleasant, informal restaurant with an interesting menu (including a daily "Menu Degustazione" with six courses) and excellent wines. Closed Sun.

Perseus
Viale Don Minzoni
Tel: 055-588226
Popular restaurant among Florentines, near Piazza Libertà. Famous for their *bistecca alla fiorentina*. Reasonable prices.

Vico del Carmine
Via Pisana 40r
Tel: 055-233 6862
Friendly Neapolitan pizzeria, serving up thick crusted pizza, and Neapolitan desserts and wines. Closed Mon.

INEXPENSIVE (€)

Borgo Antico
Piazza Santa Spirito 6r
Tel: 055-210437
A cosy restaurant where a standard menu is supplemented by an extensive

range of daily specials. Try the ravioli for a rich filling pasta dish, or one of the *secondi* from the specials menu. Lovely terrace for summer dining.

Cantinetta da Verrazzano
Via de' Tavolini 18–20
Tel: 055-268590
Pleasant, wood-panelled coffee house and wine bar in the centre of town. Delicious sandwiches and snacks; wines from the Verrazzano estate. Closed Sun.

Da Nerbone
Mercato di San Lorenzo
Tel: 055-219949
Authentic, very good market eatery as old as the market itself. Dishes like tripe and *lampredotto*, as well as the usual trattoria fare. There are few tables. Closed evenings and Sun.

Da Sergio
Piazza San Lorenzo 8r
Tel: 055-281941
Big, airy trattoria, hidden behind a row of stalls. A haunt of market workers and discerning tourists. Short, simple, seasonal menu; fish is featured Tues–Thur. No desserts served. Open for lunch only; closed Sun.

Il Pizzaiuolo
Via dei Macci 113r
Tel: 055-241171
The pizzas are wonderful, but there's plenty more besides. Try the *antipasto della casa*. Popular. Closed Sun and Aug.

Il Vegetariano
Via delle Ruote 30r
Tel: 055-218624

The imaginative use of fresh vegetables in its dishes makes Il Vegetariano the city's best vegetarian eatery. The laid back, informal atmosphere is halfway between diner and cafeteria. Closed Mon, weekends at lunch.

La Casalinga
Via del Michelozzo 9r
Tel: 055-218624
One of the best-value eateries in town. Plentiful helpings of home cooking attract locals as well as visitors. Family run. Closed Sun.

Le Mossacce
Via del Proconsolo 55r
Tel: 055-294361
Trattoria between the Cathedral and the Bargello, serving pasta dishes and basic Tuscan fare. Popular with office workers at lunchtimes. Closed Sat and Sun.

Mario
Via delle Rosine 2r
Tel: 055-218550
www.trattoriamario.com
Intimate and down to earth, this is a great place to experience fast food, Tuscan-style. A good selection of meals. Open for lunch Mon–Sat.

Ristorante Al Tranvai
Piazza T. Tasso 14r
Tel: 055-225197
www.altranvai.it
This neighborhood locale offers communal seating and daily specials in a very lively atmosphere. They also offer options for gluten-free diets.

Ruth's
Via Carlo Farini 2a
Tel: 055-248 0888

Pleasant and airy restaurant serving kosher Middle Eastern food. Closed Fri pm.

Santa Lucia
Via Ponte alla Mosse 102r
Tel: 055-353255
Authentically Neapolitan, no-frills trattoria, serving the best pizzas in town. Good seafood, too. Booking essential.

Trattoria Cibrèo
Via dei Macci 122r
Tel: 055-234 1100
www.cibreo.com
Annexe of Il Cibrèo (see above), but with meals at half the price. Few frills, but the food is basically the same as in the main restaurant. No bookings. Closed Sun and Mon.

Bars, Cafés and Ice-Cream Parlours

A frothy cappuccino and a buttery brioche at **Robiglio** (five branches including Via dei Servi and Via dei Tosinghi) is a must in Florence. A hot chocolate or *aperitivo* at **Rivoire** (Piazza della Signoria) is also worth experiencing just once. People-watch at **Paszkowski**, **Gilli** or the **Giubbe Rosse** (Piazza della Repubblica), or for a view of the rooftops and Brunelleschi's dome, go to the bar at the top of **La Rinascente** department store. **Caffè Italiano** (Via della Condotta), just behind Piazza della Signoria, is a cosy place to indulge in a slice of cake or a cocktail. Satisfy your sweet

tooth at **GROM** (Via delle Oche), whose *gelati* change according to seasonal ingredients. Head for **Chiaroscuro** (Corso) for a buffet lunch, evening *aperitivo* and coffee from all over the world. Further along is **I Visacci** (Borgo degli Albizi), a cheerful place in which to relax and drink a *prosecco*. On your way to Piazza della Signoria, join the crowd at **I Fratellini** (Via dei Cimatori) for a glass of wine and little *panino* right in the street. North of Santa Croce, **Caffè San Ambrogio** (Piazza San Ambrogio) is suitable at any time of day and has outside seating in the square. **The Jazz Club** (Via Nuova de'Cascini, off Borgo Pinti) is an underground cavern with live music. Near Piazza Santa Croce,

Finesterrae (Via dei Pepi) is a Moroccan restaurant and bar with a sultry atmosphere. **Gelateria dei Neri** (Via dei Neri) makes creamy ice cream and *granite* to beat the summer heat. In the other direction, towards the Arno, **Moyo** is a chic bar and restaurant. The elegant and pricey bars lining the river are where Florentines go to be seen. On the south bank, drink wine at **Caffè Pitti** (Piazza Pitti) or have a cocktail at **Il Rifrullo** (Via San Niccolò).

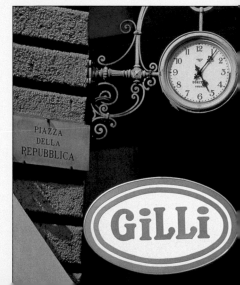

GLI UFFIZI

The greatest collection of Renaissance art to be found anywhere in the world

Tuscany's foremost gallery (open Tues–Sun 8.15am–6.50pm; July–Sept Tues, Wed until 10pm; entrance fee) is housed in a U-shaped building whose former use as administrative buildings gave it its name "The Offices". It now holds the highest concentration of Renaissance art in the world, including famous works by Botticelli, Leonardo, Michelangelo and Raphael. The majority of the collection originates from the Medici family, dating from the latter half of the 16th century, when Francesco de' Medici decided to convert the second floor into a museum. The gallery was left to the city at the end of the dynasty line. It also contains the **Gabinetto Disegni e Stampe degli Uffizi** (Collection of Prints and Drawings; entrance included), the **Contini Bonacossi Collection** (by appointment only; tel: 055-294883; entrance fee) and the **Corridoio Vasariano** (Vasari Corridor; by appointment only; tel: 055-265 4321 for information), an overhead passageway connecting the Uffizi to the Palazzo Pitti via the Ponte Vecchio. There are three different entrances into the museum for groups, individuals and individuals with tickets. The chaotic lines outside make it worthwhile buying tickets with a scheduled entry time in advance (055-294883 or www.florenceart.it).

The main collection is on the second floor, with some important rooms (and temporary exhibitions during construction) on the first floor. The paintings are arranged chronologically by schools – moving from the predominantly Italian collection to works by German, Flemish and Dutch masters.

ABOVE: The Botticelli Rooms (10–14) are the most popular exhibit in the Uffizi, containing the world's best collection of work by the artist. Here are the famous mythological paintings which fused ideas of the spiritual and the secular: the *Birth of Venus*, painted around 1485, and *La Primavera*, painted some five years earlier. The meaning of the latter remains a subject of fervent discussion, while Venus has overtones of the Virgin Mary.

ABOVE: Room 15 exhibits Leonardo da Vinci's early works – including the *Annunciation* (1475) and the unfinished *Adoration of the Magi* (1982) – and also paintings by Perugino and Signorelli.

THE EASTERN CORRIDOR

The two corridors from which the 45 rooms lead off are filled with sculptures, while the strip connecting the sides allows magnificent views down the river and towards the Ponte Vecchio. Rooms 2–4 are dedicated to works from Siena and Florence during the Duecento and Trecento (13th and 14th centuries), exhibiting the decorative and iconographic pre-Renaissance style. Notable works are the interpretations of the Madonna by Giotto and Duccio, as well as that of Cimabue, Giotto's master.

Room 7 is dedicated to the early Renaissance and its founders and leading figures, who include Masaccio and Uccello and, later, Fra Angelico. The Filippo Lippi Room (8) holds the Franciscan monk's lovely *Madonna with Angels*, as well as a number of other celebrated works, and is worth visiting for Piero della Francesca's portraits of the Duke and Duchess of Urbino I *(pictured above)*. Room 9 holds works by the Pollaiuolo brothers, whose paintings show no distinctive style but are nonetheless decorative.

After a room of sculpture, the Tribuna (Room 18) is an octagonal room lit from above, with a mother-of-pearl-encrusted ceiling, designed by Buontalenti. This room's structure and decor was designed to allude to the four elements and used to exhibit the objects most highly prized by the Medici. It holds a collection of portraits and sculpture, as well as Rosso Fiorentino's super-famous *Putto che Suona*, or *Angel Musician (pictured opposite)*. The circular route around the room unfortunately renders it somewhat difficult to appreciate the art from a good distance or to linger in front of the portraits.

BELOW: Rooms 5–6 form the International Gothic Rooms, whose paintings exhibit a more conservative and less lavish approach, in keeping with the medieval mindset. Lorenzo Monaco's *Crowning of Mary* provides a good example of this by one of the main practitioners of the era.

ABOVE: The High Renaissance continues in Room 19, which exhibits Perugino and Signorelli's work. These Umbrian artists worked during the 15th and 16th centuries, and the latter's tondo (circular painting) *Holy Family* is reputed to have inspired Michelangelo's version. Room 20 is a break from Italian art, with work by Dürer (including his *Madonna and the Pear* pictured here) and Cranach. The last few rooms on the eastern corridor hold works from the 15th and 16th centuries: the Venetian school in Room 21, followed by Holbein and other Flemish and German realists (22) and more Italian work by Mantegna and Correggio in Room 23. Room 24 contains a collection of miniatures.

THE WESTERN CORRIDOR

The western corridor starts with the Michelangelo Room and his vivid *Holy Family* tondo *(below)*. This prelude to Mannerism was produced for the wedding of Angelo Doni to Maddalena Strozzi, and the depth of the figures betrays Michelangelo's penchant for sculpture. Early works by Raphael – such as the glowing *Madonna of the Goldfinch* – and Andrea del Sarto's *Madonna of the Harpies* can be seen in the next room. Room 27 is the last room to focus on Tuscan art before moving on to other regions of Italy.

LEFT: Room 28 displays work by Titian, including the erotic *Venus of Urbino (left)*. Rooms 29–30 focus on Emilia Romagnan art and the Mannerists Dosso Dossi and Parmigianino. Veronese's *Annunciation* is in Room 31, while Tintoretto's sensual *Leda and the Swan* hangs in Room 32. A number of rooms are now dedicated to minor works of the Cinquecento (16th century) before the Flemish art of Rubens and Van Dyck in Room 41 (currently closed for restoration). The Sala della Niobe has reopened and holds sculpture, while Room 44 has works by Rembrandt.

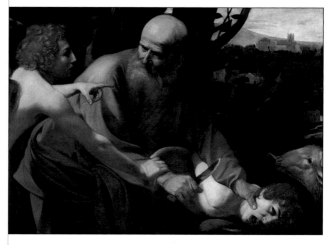

On the first floor are five rooms of paintings, as well as the Verone sull'Arno – the bottom of the U-shaped corridor which looks over the Arno and the Piazza degli Uffizi the other side.

The Sala del Caravaggio holds three paintings by the troubled artist whose style is characterised by his realism and use of light *(see his* Sacrificing of Isaac, *right)*. His method inspired the works by other artists contained in the same room and the next three: the Sala di Bartolomeo Manfredi, the Sala di Gherardo delle Notti and the Sala dei Caravaggeschi.

The last room adjacent to the Verone is the Sala di Guido Reni, where three paintings by the classicist artist of the first half of the 17th century are displayed.

Gabinetto and Contini Bonacossi Collection

The Gabinetto, recently situated on the first floor, holds a number of important and precious drawings – including works by Renaissance masters (such as Fra Bartolommeo's *Portrait of a Young Woman, right*), some of which are only viewable for academic study purposes. The Contini Bonacossi Collection (temporarily closed) was recently installed in the Uffizi (moved from its previous home in Palazzo Pitti) and contains paintings, furniture, majolica and coats of arms.

Galleria degli Uffizi

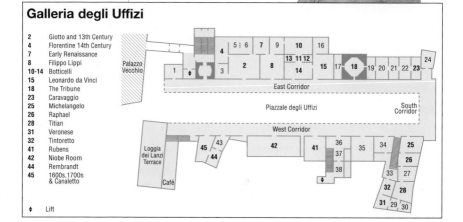

PALAZZO PITTI AND GIARDINO DI BOBOLI

The gigantic Palazzo Pitti and the Boboli Gardens were once the royal residence

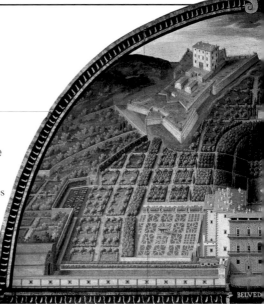

The Pitti houses seven museums, and provides access to the splendid gardens that became a model for Italian landscaping. The imposing Renaissance palace is built of large, rough-hewn stones; set in its own piazza, it dominates the area to the south of the Ponte Vecchio. The gardens, which lead up to Forte Belvedere, escape being overshadowed thanks to the hill, which allows them to rise, to give glorious views over the city to the north and countryside to the south.

A visit to one or two museums combined with the gardens will take up at least half a day, and a three-day ticket offers value for money. Tickets are purchased in the right wing of the palace, and entrance to all the museums is from the internal courtyard. The **Appartamenti Reali**, **Galleria Palatina** and the **Galleria d'Arte Moderna** (Royal Apartments/Palatine Gallery/Gallery of Modern Art) combine luxurious rooms with spectacular works of art. A ticket to the **Giardino di Boboli** (Boboli Gardens) includes admission to the **Museo degli Argenti**, the **Museo delle Porcellane**, the **Galleria del Costume** and the **Giardino Bardini** (Silver Museum/Porcelain Museum/Costume Gallery/Bardini Gardens). These smaller museums are worthwhile for a second visit or if you have a specific interest.

The **Museo delle Carrozze** (Carriage Museum) can be visited by appointment only (tel: 055-294883).

ABOVE: At the end of the Medici reign in 1737, the *palazzo* became the home of the Lorraines, and its elongated cubic form was further extended by the wings which curve round to frame the paved square at its front. Work on the outside was paralleled by alteration to the interior decor, which exhibits the ostentatious tastes of the period of the Lorraines and the Savoys, the next to take up occupancy within its walls. The history of the *palazzo* includes brief tenure by the Bourbons and the Emperor Napoleon before the last ruling monarch, Vittorio Emmanuele III, transferred the house to the public.

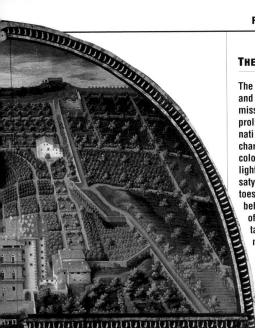

THE GARDENS

The gardens (open daily 8.50am–sunset; closed 1st and last Mon of the month; entrance fee) were commissioned by Cosimo I and created by a range of prolific figures of the day, from Vasari and Ammannati to Buontalenti. One of the most compelling characteristics of Boboli is the shadowy dark-green colour of the cypress and box which serve to highlight the numerous statues of amorous nymphs, satyrs and statuesque deities, as well as the grottoes and fountains. The steps lead up to the terrace behind the palace and in front of Susini's fountain of 1641. The amphitheatre surrounding the fountain occupies the site of a quarry used to obtain much of the stone for the palace, and contains an Egyptian obelisk. A series of terraces leads up the hill to the Neptune Fountain, round to the Rococo Kaffeehaus and up to the statue of *Abundance*. At the summit lies the Giardino del Cavaliere, or Knight's Garden. This delightful garden – with its low hedges, rose bushes and little cherub fountain – gives open views of San Miniato to the left and the village of Arcetri to the right, rising above a valley dotted with villas and olive groves. This is where the Museo delle Porcellane is located.

The cypress-statue-lined avenue known as il Viottolone *(see left)* leads to the Vasca dell'Isola (Island Pool) with its Oceanus Fountain (by Giambologna), murky green water, ducks, fish, strange mythical creatures and circular hedge. The route from here to the exit leads past the Grotta di Buontalenti, named after the sculptor who created this cavern in 1583–8. Copies of Michelangelo's *The Slaves* (the originals are on display in the Accademia; *see page 109*) are set in the four corners. Finally, on the right as one exits and nestling below the wall of the corridor, is the naked, pot-bellied Pietro Barbino, Cosimo I's court dwarf, seated on a turtle *(see opposite)*.

ABOVE: The Palazzo Pitti was commissioned in the 15th Century by Luca Pitti, and was designed by Brunelleschi, although he never lived to see the final results. The Medici family took over ownership in 1549, when Eleonora di Toledo, wife of Cosimo I, purchased the *palazzo* when the Pitti family ran into financial strife. She transferred her family from the Palazzo Vecchio to this more tranquil location, though still close to the political heart of the city. This link was strengthened by the Vasari Corridor, which directly connects the residence with Piazza della Signoria by way of the Uffizi and the Palazzo Vecchio. Under the Medici family, work on the *palazzo* continued, substantially increasing its size and grandeur. Ammannati was given architectural control, and he constructed the inner courtyard and redesigned the outer façade, which was later further extended.

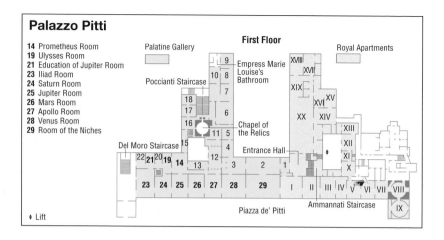

Palazzo Pitti

First Floor

14 Prometheus Room	Palatine Gallery
19 Ulysses Room	
21 Education of Jupiter Room	Empress Marie Louise's Bathroom
23 Iliad Room	
24 Saturn Room	Pocciantii Staircase
25 Jupiter Room	
26 Mars Room	
27 Apollo Room	Chapel of the Relics
28 Venus Room	Del Moro Staircase
29 Room of the Niches	Entrance Hall

Royal Apartments

Piazza de' Pitti

Ammannati Staircase

✦ Lift

The **Galleria Palatina** on the first floor (open Tues–Sun 8.15am–6.50pm; closed Jan; entrance fee) houses an extraordinary range of paintings collected by the Medici family. In the west wing of the building are the rooms comprising the **Royal Apartments** (same times as the gallery). They are garish and ostentatious, decked out in heavy carpets, wallpapers, fabrics and furnishings, and overstuffed with treasures. Several of the rooms are named after the colour in which they are themed, and contain paintings and portraits fitting with the mood, followed by the Queen's Apartments, the King's Apartments and a ceremonial room, all filled with exquisite furniture.

ALLEGORICAL FRESCOES

The most important rooms, named after the planets, are frescoed by Pietro da Cortona to allegorise the stages of Prince Ferdinando's education: Sala di Saturno, Sala di Giove, Sala di Marte (during restoration paintings have been moved to the Sala delle Nicchie) and Sala di Venere. These contain works such as Rubens's *The Consequences of War* (Sala di Marte), Raphael's *Portrait of a Lady* (*see left*: Sala di Giove). Other important paintings, such as Raphael's *The Pregnant Lady* (Sala dell'Iliade), Lippi's tondo of *The Madonna and Child* (*see above*: Sala di Prometeo) and *Sleeping Cupid* by Caravaggio (Sala dell'Educazione di Giove) are found in smaller rooms.

SILVER AND PORCELAIN

On the ground floor, the Museo degli Argenti is in the left-hand corner of the courtyard, whilst the Museo delle Porcellane is situated in the Boboli Gardens (both open daily 8.15am–sunset; closed 1st and last Mon of the month). The former contains much more than silver, ranging from antique vases much loved by Lorenzo the Magnificent to baubles encrusted with semi-precious stones and jewellery. The frescoed rooms alone make a visit worthwhile – in particular the Sala di San Giovanni which formed part of the summer apartments. The frescoes by the artist after whom the room is named depict the reign of Lorenzo de' Medici, portrayed as a great patron of the arts. The latter museum displays pottery as well as objets d'art.

The **Galleria d'Arte Moderna** contains mainly Italian works from the neoclassical and Romantic movements, dating from the 18th century to the period after World War I (including this fine portrait of *The Artist's Daughter-in-Law* by Giovanni Fattori). The most notable feature of the second-floor collection is its holding of paintings by the Macchiaioli, late 19th-century Italian Impressionists. Also situated on the second floor is the **Galleria del Costume** (both open daily 8.15am–1.50pm; closed 1st, 3rd and 5th Mon, 2nd and 4th Sun of the month; entrance fee), whose 6,000-piece holding of clothing, theatrical costumes and accessories is supplemented by frequent special exhibitions.

ABOVE AND RIGHT: One of the finest rooms is the Sala di Apollo, in which hang important works by Andrea del Sarto (including his *Lamentation of Christ*, 1522–3, *above*). The Sala di Venere includes works by another master of the High Renaissance, Titian (notably his *The Interrupted Concert*, *c.*1510, *right*).

THE ACCADEMIA

Originally the world's first school of art, the gallery is now home to Michelangelo's most famous work, *David*

Michelangelo's *David* is the main attraction of the Galleria dell'Accademia (open Tues–Sun 8.15am–6.50pm; entrance at No. 60; entrance fee includes entry to the Museo degli Strumenti Musicali), but the rest of the art is equally worthy of attention.

The museum was originally part of the world's first art school, the Accademia delle Belle Arti, an institution established by Cosimo I de' Medici and of which Michelangelo was a founding academician. The current gallery was consolidated in the late 18th century by Grand Duke Pietro Leopoldo next to the art school housed in the same row of buildings.

The collection contains sculpture and early Renaissance religious art, and has recently been expanded to incorporate a display of musical instruments. On entry, the Sala del Colosso contains the plaster cast of Giambologna's *Rape of the Sabines* (on display in the Loggia dei Lanzi – *see pages 84, 111*) and a collection of colourful religious art from the late 15th and early 16th centuries.

While the exit to the right of the entrance leads to the Museo degli Strumenti Musicali, the Accademia continues through the door to the left. The view of Michelangelo's *David* from the end of the corridor-shaped Galleria dei Prigionieri is stunning, the domed Tribuna di Michelangelo at its far extent framing the huge statue.

ABOVE: Among the most notable pieces is Fillipino Lippi's striking *Deposition from the Cross*, which was finished by Perugino on the former's death. Other highlights are *Christ as a Man of Sorrows* – a poignant fresco by Andrea del Sarto – and Fra Bartolomeo's *Prophets*.

Off to the left of the Tribuna di Michelangelo are three small rooms – the Sala del Duecento e del Trecento, the Sala dei Giotteschi and the Sala degli Orcagna. These all hold early Florentine works, including works by Taddi and Daddi. The *Tree of Life* by Buonaguida is one of the best-known and most impressive works in the small collection. Stairs lead to the first floor and four further rooms. The first two contain attractive work from the late 14th century. The following room is dedicated to Florentine painter Lorenzo Monaco, whose work shows the bridge between Gothic and Renaissance art – the key to understanding the Florentine style.

LEFT: The approach to the Tribuna is lined with four unfinished sculptures by Michelangelo. Known as *The Prisoners* or *The Slaves*, the pieces were intended for the tomb of Pope Julius II, but became the property of the Medici family instead.

DAVID

Standing at over 4 metres (13 ft), Michelangelo's *David* is one of the most iconic works in Western art. It was sculpted between 1501 and 1504 as a symbolic commemoration of the start of republican Florence, through its depiction of the young boy who slew Goliath. Originally placed in front of the Palazzo Vecchio (a copy stands in the former position), the statue was moved to the Accademia in 1873 for reasons of preservation. The marble from which *David* was carved was famously rejected as faulty by other artists, but the then 29-year-old Michelangelo sought to embrace its faults and patches of discoloration. *David* is celebrated for being of perfect proportions – hailed as a testament to Michelangelo's eye for detail. The artist's attention to minutiae is evident in the muscle contour of the legs and the veins in the arms, which can be appreciated from every angle thanks to the way in which the statue is displayed.

But this timeless icon of masculine virility is under threat and may yet be on the move again. After the discovery of cracks in the 500-year marble, the statue has been declared at risk of toppling over. The cracks in the statue's ankles are believed to have developed after David spent over a century leaning forward dangerously from his proud perch on Piazza della Signoria. The weight of the marble, bearing down on David's left ankle, is also partly to blame, as are the vibrations from the traffic and road works outside the gallery. Fortunately, the experts have declared that Florence's most famous statue is not in danger of imminent collapse, but as a precaution, there is talk of transferring the symbolic statue to a purpose-built site on the outskirts of the city.

ABOVE: Botticelli's delightful *Madonna and Child* is in the Sale del Quattrocento Fiorentino, as is Paolo Uccello's masterpiece *Scenes of a Hermit Life*.

THE BARGELLO

The Bargello holds Florence's most important collection of sculpture from the Medici and private collections

The *palazzo* was transformed into a museum in 1865, its previous uses as the seat of the city's chief magistrate and later as a prison reflected in features of the building such as the decor, and in the street names of the surrounding area. Entry into the rooms of the museum (open daily 8.15am–6.50pm, ticket office closes at 5.30pm; closed 2nd and 4th Mon, 1st, 3rd and 5th Sun of the month; entrance fee) takes the visitor through the medieval courtyard, adorned with emblems of the city wards, magistrates and governors. *Oceanus* by Giambologna is one of the sculptures housed under the vaulted cloisters, which lead off to the right of the staircase into the Sala del Cinquecento. The entrance to this room – which contains a range of Renaissance statues, busts and bas-reliefs in marble and bronze – is flanked by two lions. Of particular note are a number of works by Cellini, a Florentine bronze sculptor of lesser fame, while 16th-century contemporaries such as Ammannati and others complete the collection in this room. An external staircase leads to the second floor and a number of bronze sculptures of birds on display in the loggia, originally made by Giambologna for the Medici Villa di Castello.

ABOVE AND BELOW: The Bargello museum (above in an 18th-century painting by Giuseppe Zocchi) is situated in an impressive Gothic *palazzo* constructed in the mid 13th-century on Via del Proconsolo, the heart of the ancient city.

ABOVE: Donatello's recently restored *David* (from 1430–40) is on display in the Donatello Gallery – a small bronze most renowned for being the first nude since antiquity. It differs dramatically from Michelangelo's masterpiece not just in size and material, but also in its coyness and melancholy, which some view as more faithful to David's youth.

ABOVE RIGHT: Four of Michelangelo's early sculptures are on display in the Sala del Cinquecento: *Bacchus Drunk*, the Pitti Tondo – a depiction of the Madonna and Child shown here – *Apollo-David* and *Brutus*.

ABOVE: In the Donatello Room are the bronze panels submitted by Ghiberti and Brunelleschi *(above)* for the Baptistery doors.

THE DONATELLO AND BRONZE GALLERIES

The Salone del Consiglio Generale is often nicknamed the Donatello Gallery. Apart from *David*, other works by Donatello in the room worth paying attention to are *Saint George*, which was designed for the Orsanmichele church, and *Cupid*. The walls* of the room figure several glazed terracotta works by Luca della Robbia, while the first floor chapel (the Cappella Maddalena) features attractive frescoes depicting hell: look out for the figure on the right dressed in maroon thought to be a depiction of Dante. Also on the first floor is a corridor displaying an eclectic group of 5th- to 17th-century objets d'art, including ivories and Islamic treasures.

Upstairs (currently open afternoons only), the Verrocchio Room displays Tuscan sculpture from the late 15th century, including portrait busts of notable Florentines and an interpretation of *David* by the artist who lends his name to the room, Andrea del Verrocchio. The adjoining rooms are filled with work by members of the della Robbia family – predominantly Andrea and Giovanni – dominated by the often overbearing large reliefs coloured in yellow, green and blue.

The last major room in the museum is the Bronze Gallery. This has one of the most rewarding displays in the Bargello. The sculptures generally depict mythological tales or Greek history, in the form of both models and more functional articles such as candelabra. The model for Giambologna's *Rape of the Sabines* (on display in the Loggia dei Lanzi) stands out, as do two other of his statues: *Kneeling Nymph* and *Hercules and Antaeus*.

Completing the second floor is a collection of medals.

RIGHT: Giambologna's bronze of Mercury is in the Sala del Cinquecento.

AROUND FLORENCE

The region surrounding Florence was the most advanced in Europe throughout the Middle Ages and the Renaissance, resulting in an important agricultural, historical and artistic heritage for its people

The province of Florence is full of towns and villages perched on steep, cypress-covered hills. Below them, straggling down to the bottom of the valleys, are the vineyards that have been producing some of the most famous wines in Italy since the Renaissance – red Chianti and Carmignano and white Malvasia and Trebbiano. Just north of the city lies the Mugello, the fertile Apennine region that forms the border between Tuscany and Emilia Romagna. The best view of the mountains is a seat in the Roman theatre of Fiesole, a delightful hill town 8 km (5 miles) northeast of Florence.

Hilltop retreat

Fiesole ❶ was first settled by Etruscans probably in the 8th century BC. The Romans who followed named the place Faesulum – praising it for its freshwater springs and its ideal location for controlling the entire valley. Despite this, the town was repeatedly attacked by the Goths and the Byzantines, and in 1125 it was destroyed by Florentine troops – only the Cathedral and the bishop's palace were saved. During the 15th century Fiesole became a city suburb where wealthy Florentines built their villas. Today, a villa on the slopes of Fiesole's verdant hill is one of the most sought-after addresses.

The main route from the centre of Florence is the Via San Domenico (the No. 7 bus goes from Piazza Stazione or Piazza San Marco, but beware pickpockets who target tourists on this route), which climbs up to Fiesole's centre. The views on the way up reveal a landscape of extraordinary beauty, dotted with Renaissance villas perched on the slope of the hill.

Everything you will want to see in Fiesole lies a short distance from the Piazza Mino da Fiesole, the main

Map on page 114

LEFT: olive trees and views over Florence.
BELOW: attractive villas cling to the hillsides above the city.

The Teatro Romano, with its numbered seats, could originally accommodate an audience of up to 2,000 people. It is in a remarkable state of repair, and is still used for dances and shows during the summer festival season.

square. A lane leads north to the **Teatro Romano**, where you can buy tickets for Fiesole's **Zona Archeologica** (open Thur–Mon 10am–5pm in winter, daily until 7pm in summer), entered from the ticket office and comprising the city's 1st-century BC Roman theatre, public baths of the same era, and an Etruscan temple, built in the 4th century BC and dedicated to Minerva, goddess of wisdom and healing. Also within the complex, the **Museo Archeologico**, built in the style of a Roman temple, is packed with finds from excavations in Fiesole. Included in the ticket is entry to the **Museo Bandini**, behind the cathedral on Via Duprè – a small art gallery with a fairly wide and representative selection of paintings from the early and middle Renaissance.

On the square, the huge **Cattedrale di San Romolo** (open daily) is almost completely unadorned except for four frescoes, which include a serene portrait of *St Sebastian* by Perugino (early 16th century). The Cathedral's jewel is the marble funerary monument to Bishop Leonardo Salutati, by Mino da Fiesole (1429–84), with a realistic portrait bust of the smiling bishop.

From the southwest corner of the square, Via Vecchia Fiesolana leads to the **Villa Medici** ➋ *(see page 116)*. Take any of the downhill paths from here to reach the hamlet of **San Domenico** ➌, about a 15-minute walk. The church of San Domenico (1406) contains a restored *Madonna with Angels and Saints* (1430), an early work of Fra Angelico who began his monastic life here before transferring to San Marco.

Opposite the church, the Via della Badia dei Roccettini descends to the **Badia Fiesolana** (open Mon–Fri 9am–6pm, winter until 5pm, Sat 9am–noon, Sun 10.30am–12.30pm), once a monastery and now home to the European University. The un-

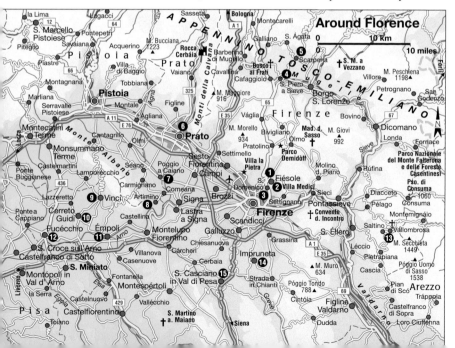

finished brick-and-stone façade of the huge church (dull inside, so don't worry if it is closed) incorporates the lovely green-and-white Romanesque façade of an earlier and smaller church. The No. 7 bus can be caught in San Domenico for the return journey to Florence.

The Mugello valley

Just a few kilometres north of Florence, the Apennine foothills and Sieve river basin form the Mugello region (www.mugellotoscana.it). Like Chianti, only less well trodden, it is characterised by gentle hills and fertile valleys, olive groves, vineyards, oak and chestnut woods. The landscape is at its most picturesque in the western Sieve valley.

The Mugello has great associations with the Medici, who originated from here and lavished a lot of attention on the region. In 1451 Cosimo il Vecchio had Michelozzo alter the old fortress of Cafaggiolo just west of **San Piero a Sieve** ❹ to create a country retreat, where Lorenzo il Magnifico spent part of his childhood, and writers and artists were lavishly entertained.

The palace was modified by the Borghese family, who acquired it in the 19th century. The recently restored **Villa Cafaggiolo** (open to the public: Sat and Sun 10am–12.30pm and 2.30–6.30pm; from mid-Apr to mid-Oct also open Wed and Fri 2.30–6.30pm; at other times by appointment; tel: 055-847 9293; www.castellodicafaggiolo.it) is now privately owned and used for weddings, events and a cooking school.

A little further south, **Castello del Trebbio** (guided visits every morning Mon–Fri by appointment only; tel: 055-845 6230), received similar treatment at the hands of Michelozzo, and, more than any other 15th-century Tuscan villa, retains the feudal atmosphere of a Medici villa.

Overlooking San Piero a Sieve, high on a thickly wooded outcrop, is the **San Martino** fortress built in 1569 by Lanci and Buontalenti to enable Cosimo I to defend the Florentine state. This massive pentagonal castle is currently being restored, though you can walk along its walls.

Just north of San Piero a Sieve is the town of **Scarperia** ❺. Its spot-

Map on page 114

Badia Fiesolana, former monastery and now home to the European University. From the terrace in front of the church there are views down the Mugnone river valley back to Florence.

BELOW: Villa Medici.

Villas and Gardens

The idea of a country retreat, so popular in Tuscany today, originated with the Romans. The villas were either working farms, which supplied the townhouses with produce, or were planned purely for pleasure. They would be visited for a day's outing and many did not even have bedrooms. In the 15th century the idea of the country villa was revived by the Medici family, who commissioned magnificent residences and elaborate gardens, modelled on classical ideas. In 1452 Leon Battista Alberti laid down the essential ingredients for a truly well-appointed country retreat: it had to be on a slope, full of light and air, with rooms grouped round an inner hall. The villas and gardens described here are all easily accessible from Florence.

The **Villa Medici** (Via Vecchina Fiesolana; gardens open for visits by appointment only Sat–Sun 9am–1pm; e-mail: com.toscana@airc.it) at Fiesole, which has been described as "the first true Renaissance villa", was designed by Michelozzo for Cosimo il Vecchio between 1458 and 1461. It commands a superb view of Florence.

On the outskirts of Florence, the 15th-century **Villa la Pietra** (guided tours of the villa

Fri pm, tours of the garden Tues am; advance booking necessary; tel: 055-500 7210; e-mail: villa.lapietra@nyu.edu; www.nyu.edu/global/lapietra) belonged to Sir Harold Acton, doyen of expatriate writers in Florence, who bequeathed it to New York University. The villa contains a fine collection of Renaissance art.

Another American-owned villa in the Florentine hills is the historic **Villa i Tatti** (closed for refurbishment; normally by appointment tel: 055-603251; www.itatti.it), by the pretty village of Settignano. Formerly the home of art collector Bernard Berenson (1865–1959), who landscaped the gardens and restored the villa to house a collection of Renaissance paintings, it is now the Harvard University Center for Renaissance Studies.

Nearby, the **Villa Gamberaia** (gardens open daily 9am–7pm; villa by appointment only; tel: 055-697205; www.villagamberaia.com) is another fine Renaissance villa which survives with most of its original garden intact.

The **Villa Medicea Poggio a Caiano** *(see page 118)* is often dubbed the perfect villa. The façade was modelled on a Greek temple by Sangallo to satisfy the tastes of Lorenzo the Magnificent. In the 19th century the gardens were converted according to the fashionable English style, with romantic temples, fountains, an aviary and a mock Gothic ruin.

Set on a steeply sloping hill, the **Villa Medicea della Petraia** (loc. Castello; open daily 8.15–sunset; villa by guided tour only, every 45 mins from 8.30am; closed 2nd and 3rd Mon of the month; entrance fee) was designed by Buontalenti for Ferdinando de' Medici as an elegant villa suitable for sumptuous entertaining. The interior is marred by the pretentious taste of the house of Savoy, but the Italianate gardens are a delight.

Only the gardens of the **Villa Medicea di Castello** (open daily 8.15am–sunset; closed 2nd and 3rd Mon of the month; entrance fee) can be viewed. Grottoes and statuary abound.

Another villa with attractive surroundings is the **Villa Demidoff and Parco di Pratolino** (open Apr–Sept Thur–Sun, Mar and Oct Sun, 10am–sunset; entrance fee), whose Mannerist gardens were restructured in the English romantic style. ❑

LEFT: cypress avenue leading to Villa la Pietra.

less monuments are rarely visited, yet there is much to see. **Palazzo de Vicari** in the main street is one of the finest examples of 13th-century civil architecture in Tuscany, similar in style to Florence's Palazzo Vecchio. The outer façade, decorated with the coats of arms of local notables, carved in stone or worked in della Robbia terracotta, faces the **Oratorio della Madonna della Piazza** in the small square, which has a *Madonna and Child* by Taddeo Gaddi. At the bottom of the main street, near the entrance to the town, is the **Oratorio della Madonna dei Terremoti**, dedicated to Our Lady of Earthquakes, which contains another fresco of the *Madonna and Child*, said to be by Filippo Lippi.

Scarperia is famous as a centre of knife-making. In local workshops traditional methods are still used to fashion knives by hand. There is even a museum dedicated to the craft, the **Museo dei Ferri Taglienti** (Museum of Cutting Tools) in the Palazzo dei Vicari (open mid-June–mid-Sept Sat–Sun 10am–1pm, 3.30–7.30pm, Wed–Fri 3.30–7.30pm, mid-Sept–mid-June Sat–Sun 10am–1pm, 3–6.30pm; entrance fee), and in September the town hosts an international knife exhibition.

Scarperia is also known for the racetrack on its outskirts. The scenic "Mugello" circuit is used as a Ferrari F1 test centre and hosts the Italian motorbike grand prix in June.

A turning on the left of the southern approach to Scarperia wends its way through dense woodlands to the remote **Bosco ai Frati** convent (open daily; ring the bell and one of the monks will usually be happy to let you in; tel: 055-848111). This Franciscan retreat retains the peace and solitude of the Franciscan ideal that places like Assisi lack; no touring hordes, no postcard-sellers, only the peace and quiet offered by a church and its convent in a clearing in the woods. The monastic buildings were restructured by Michelozzo around 1440 for Cosimo il Vecchio. They house a little-known, large wooden *Crucifix*, attributed to Donatello, one of the greatest masters of the Italian Renaissance.

Prato

Prato ❻, to the northwest of Florence, is the third-largest city in Tuscany, and long-time rival of Florence. It is renowned for its textile manufacturing industries, with numerous factory outlets selling fine fabrics, cashmere and designer clothes. Although the trade has made contemporary Prato a rich city, it was already an important centre for textiles in the 12th century and its magnificent monuments are evidence of its former wealth. Amid the industrial estates lies a compact *centro storico*, contained within medieval walls.

The city possesses an extraordinary relic: in the delightful green and white **Duomo** (open Apr–Oct Mon–Sat 7.30am–7pm, Sun 7.30am–noon, 1–7pm, Nov–Mar Mon–Sat 7am–7pm, Sun 7am–noon, 1–8pm) is

Map on page 114

While painting the fresco cycles in Prato's Cathedral, Fra Filippo Lippi famously seduced a nun, Lucrezia Buti, who was modelling for his Madonna. The nun and friar ran away together and had a son, Filippino Lippi, who became an important fresco painter in his own right. It is said that the face and figure of Salome dancing at Herod's feast in the John the Baptist cycle are those of Lucrezia.

BELOW: a Henry Moore sculpture in Prato's Piazza San Marco.

The Pulpit of the Holy Girdle on Prato's Duomo.

what is believed to be the girdle of the Virgin Mary. The legends surrounding this relic have been celebrated by Agnolo Gaddi, whose frescoes cover the walls of the Chapel of the Holy Girdle. Above the high altar are fresco cycles of *The Life of St Stephen* and *The Martyrdom of St John the Baptist* by Filippo Lippi. Outside the Duomo is the Pulpit of the Holy Girdle, decorated with dancing cherubs by Donatello, where on Christmas Day and several other holy days in the year the girdle is displayed. The **Museo dell' Opera del Duomo** (Wed–Mon 9.30am–12.30pm, 3–6.30pm, Sun am only; entrance fee) in the cloister contains paintings, sculptures and reliefs by Donatello, Fra Lippi and others.

Other notable monuments in Prato's small historic centre include the church of **Santa Maria delle Carcere** (open daily 7am–noon, 4–7pm), built by Giuliano Sangallo in typical no-frills Brunelleschian style. In front of the church is the **Castello dell' Imperatore** (open Wed–Mon, Apr–Oct 9am–1pm, 4–7pm, Nov–Mar 9am–1pm; entrance fee), built by Frederick II Hohenstaufen in the first half of the 13th century, and unique in Tuscany, taking as its model the Norman castles of Puglia. A walk along its ramparts offers a good view of Prato.

In Via Rinaldesca is the 14th-century frescoed **Palazzo Datini** (open Mon–Sat 9am–12.30pm; entrance fee), former home of Francesco Datini (1330–1410), better-known as the Merchant of Prato, the title and subject of Iris Origo's historical biography. Datini, a successful wool merchant, died one of the richest men in Europe, leaving his money to city charities, and is commemorated in statues around the town.

Further north in the Piazza Comune is the **Palazzo Pretorio**, once Prato's seat of government, now housing the Museo Civico (temporarily closed for restoration – its main works have been transferred to the Museo di Pittura Murale in Piazza San Domenico).

For a break from Renaissance art, the **Centro per l'Arte Contemporanea Luigi Pecci** (10am–7pm, summer closed on Tues, autumn and winter closed on Mon; entrance fee; www.centropecci.it) lies on the edge of town. It exhibits a modest collection of contemporary works by internationally renowned artists.

Outside the historic centre is the excellent **Museo del Tessuto** (Via Santa Chiara 24; open Mon–Fri 10am–6pm, Sat 10am–2pm, Sun 4–7pm; entrance fee), dedicated to the fine textiles that made Prato's fortune. Gorgeous masterpieces of antique cloth are on display, and the skills that led to their production are not lost, as the section on contemporary textiles clearly demonstrates.

Leonardo country

A gentle meander into the countryside due west of Florence takes in some lovely views, a few small towns and Leonardo's birthplace at Vinci.

Head west out of Florence on the SP66 (in the direction of Pistoia), and turn south at **Poggio a Caiano** ❼, site of Lorenzo the Magnificent's favourite retreat, built by Sangallo (1480–85). It is one of the most magnificent and best-preserved of Florentine rural retreats (open daily 8.15am–sunset; villa by guided tour only, hourly from 8.30am; closed 2nd and 3rd Mon of the month).

The walled village of **Artimino** ❽, about 11 km (7 miles) from Poggio a Caiano, is the setting for another huge Medicean villa (open by appointment only; tel: 055-875 1427), this one built by Bernardo Buontalenti as a hunting lodge for Ferdinando I in 1594 and curious for the number of tall chimneys stuck on the roof. It has been beautifully restored, and converted into a distinguished hotel and conference centre, complete with a restaurant specialising in dishes with Medici origins. Part of the villa is open to visitors, including a small Etruscan museum.

A tortuous road leads through olive groves and vines from Artimino to **Vinci** ❾, alleged birthplace of Leonardo. Here, the 13th-century castle in the centre of town houses the **Museo Leonardiano** (open daily 9.30am–7pm in summer, 9.30am–6pm in winter; entrance fee), which has a vast selection of mechanical models built to the exact measurements of Leonardo's drawings. In **Anchiano**, near his rustic birthplace, another museum features more prosaic mementoes of his life.

Five km (3 miles) southwest of Vinci is the hill town of **Cerreto Guidi** ❿. Once owned by the Guidi counts, it now produces a good Chianti Putto wine and boasts yet another Medici villa, the austere **Villa di Cerreto Guidi** (open daily 8.15am–7pm; closed 2nd and 3rd Mon of the month; entrance fee), built in 1564 for Cosimo I as a hunting lodge. It contains some fine portraits of the Medici family. Isabella, daughter of Cosimo I, is said to have been murdered here by her husband for her infidelities.

West of Florence

To the west of Florence, the first major stop along the *superstrada* is **Empoli** ⓫, a prosperous, modern

San Miniato is famous for the highly prized white truffle *(tuber magnatum pico)*. The Association of Trufflers of the San Miniato Hills issues a map showing where to find the aromatic plant, which is dug out of the ground with a type of pole called a *vangheggia*. Truffling season runs from mid-September to Christmas. On weekends in November a huge market and exhibition display the best of the season.

BELOW LEFT: San Miniato.

San Miniato

The ancient town of San Miniato, whose origins go back to Etruscan and Roman times, is set on the top of three hills and gazes out upon magnificent views. The nature and history of the town have always been closely linked to its geographical position, equidistant from the important cities that played a decisive historical role: Pisa, Florence, Lucca, Pistoia, Siena and Volterra. High on the hillside are the two towers of the **Rocca** (open Apr–Sept daily 10am–7pm, Oct–Mar 10am–5pm), which was rebuilt in the 12th century by Frederick II. The oldest tower of the fortress, the Torre di Matilde, was converted into a bell-tower when the **Duomo** (open daily 8am–6pm, until 4.30pm in winter) was added, with its Romanesque brick façade and later restructuring. The **Museo Diocesano d'Arte Sacra** (open Apr–Sept Tues–Sun 10am–7pm, Oct–Mar Tues–Sun 10am–5pm; entrance fee), in the old sacristy of the Duomo, exhibits art and sculpture, including works by Lippi, Verrocchio and Tiepolo. Built by the Lombards in the 8th century, the magnificent church of **San Francesco** (open daily 8am–12.30pm, 3–7pm) is the oldest building in San Miniato.

Map on page 114

The Padule di Fucecchio is the largest inland marsh in Italy and the habitat for a variety of rare birds and wetland flora.

BELOW: Impruneta, just south of Florence, is an important centre of terracotta production.

market town with a small *centro storico* and a superb Romanesque church, the **Collegiata Sant'Andrea**. The green-and-white-striped façade is reminiscent of Florence's San Miniato, and the small **museum** (open Tues–Sun 9am–noon 4–7pm; entrance fee) contains a surprising amount of precious Florentine art.

A few kilometres west of Empoli is **Fucecchio** ⑫, the ancient core of which is surrounded by more modern outskirts.

The **Padule di Fucecchio**, to the north of the town, is Italy's biggest inland marsh, covering 1,460 hectares (3,600 acres). The area was a Medicean fishing ground in the 16th century, and Cosimo I had a bridge and weirs built to facilitate the sport. It is now home to rare birds and a variety of flora. The land is privately owned, but the wetland centre in **Castelmartini di Larciano** (tel: 0573-84540) organises guided tours.

Valdarno

East of Florence, off the SS70, a narrow pass climbs up the western slope of the Pratomagno hills to the monastery of **Vallombrosa** ⑬, founded in the 11th century, but remodelled over the centuries. The reward for making the journey is not so much the monastery itself as the splendid beech wood that surrounds it. Romanesque churches worth visiting in the vicinity include **San Pietro** in **Cascia** and **Sant'Agata** in **Arfoli**. Near by, the tiny village of **Saltino** is handy in the winter for the ski runs of **Monte Secchieta**.

Towards Chianti

Not far south of Florence, towards Chianti, is the town of **Impruneta** ⑭, an important sanctuary in the early medieval period when a shrine was erected here to house an image of the Virgin Mary, thought to have been the work of St Luke and believed to be capable of performing miracles. This shrine, the **Basilica di Santa Maria**, with its terracotta tabernacle by Luca della Robbia in Michelozzo's Chapel of the Cross, underwent numerous alterations over the centuries, and was bomb-damaged in World War II. Subsequent restoration and repair to this and other pre-17th century buildings has meant that Impruneta has retained a great deal of its early character, though without the patina of age. Brunelleschi insisted that the tiles for the roof of the Duomo in Florence be supplied by Impruneta, which is still important as a centre for terracotta production.

West of Impruneta, **San Casciano in Val di Pesa** ⑮ is a quiet old Chianti town, enlivened every February by a carnival. The town's reputation today rests solely on the great quantity of art held by the Collegiata church, the convent, the church of St Francis and the church of the Misericordia – paintings by Simone Martini, Ugolino di Neri, Taddeo Gaddi and Fra Bartolomeo.

We are now in the Chianti region covered on pages 197–200. ❑

RESTAURANTS

Artimino

Biagio Pignatta
Paggeria Medicea,
Viale Papa Giovanni XXIII
Tel: 055-875 1406
www.artimino.it
This restaurant is part of a four-star hotel, Paggeria Medicea, which occupies the former stables of a Medici villa. Dishes with historical origins a speciality. Closed Wed evening and Thur lunch. €€–€€€

Da Delfina
Via della Chiesa 1
Tel: 055-871 8074
www.dadelfina.it
Seasonal ingredients of high quality are served in this elegant setting, overlooking the Medici villa. Tuscan food, often with a twist. Closed Mon, Tues lunch, and Oct–May Sun evening. €€–€€€

Barberino di Mugello

Cosimo de' Medici
Via del Lago 19
Tel: 055-842 0370
A well-respected restaurant, serving Tuscan and international food of a consistently high standard. Closed Sun evening and Mon. €€

Borgo San Lorenzo

Ristorante degli Artisti
Piazza Romagnoli 1
Tel: 055-845 7707
www.ristorantedegliartisti.it
Not far from Scarperia, this restaurant in the hills features delicious Tuscan fare. Traditional dishes

include wild hare, wild boar, served with fresh, seasonal vegetables. Closed Wed, most of Jan, 3rd week in Aug. €€€

Cerbaia, Val di Pesa

La Tenda Rossa
Piazza del Monumento 9/14
Tel: 055-826132
www.latendarossa.it
One of the best restaurants in the Florence area, serving elegant and creative food in modern, refined surroundings. Excellent wine list. Worth the trek for a special treat. Closed Mon lunch, Sun and Aug. €€€€

Fiesole

La Reggia degli Etruschi
Via San Francesco 18
Tel: 055-59385
www.lareggia.org
The patio of this restaurant has a wonderful view over Florence. The food, if not quite as breathtaking as the view, is nonetheless good, solid Italian fare. Oct–May closed Tues. €€

Pizzeria San Domenico
Piazza San Domenico 11
Tel: 055-59182
This is a simple restaurant with a huge selection of pizzas and pastas and friendly service. If you don't fancy a carbohydrate blow-out, try the big salads followed by a coppa della casa (the house sweet) for dessert. Closed Mon outside summer months. €–€€

Vinandro
Piazza Mino 33
Tel: 055-59121
Tiny rustic wine bar that offers simply prepared meals and good wine. Reservations recommended. Open air seating. Closed Mon. €

Galluzzo

Bibe
Via delle Bagnese 1r
Tel: 055-204 9085
Above-average rustic trattoria in this unremarkable Florentine suburb, with a delightful garden for alfresco meals. Closed Mon–Fri lunch and all day Wed. €€

Prato

Il Baghino
Via dell'Accademia 9
Tel: 0574-27920
This traditional establishment in the historic heart of Prato serves local specialities to a faithful clientele. Closed Aug, Sun, and Mon lunchtime. €–€€

Osvaldo Baroncelli
Via Fra Bartolomeo 13
Tel: 0574-23810
Acclaimed restaurant which mixes traditional and innovative choices. Good wine list. Booking advised. Closed Sun. €€€

San Casciano in Val di Pesa

Trattoria Mamma Rosa
Loc. Calzaiolo
Tel: 055-824 9454
Off the beaten track, this unpretentious but

elegant trattoria serves some of the best Tuscan food in the region, using locally sourced and seasonal ingredients. Excellent wines. The proprietor-chef also runs a cooking school in the nearby Il Borghetto hotel. Closed Wed. €–€€

San Miniato

Il Convio – San Maiano
Via San Maiano 2
Tel: 0571-408114
A pleasant, rustic restaurant with views over the hills and service in summer. Traditional meaty Tuscan fare. Closed Wed. €€

Settignano

La Capponcina di Settignano
Via San Romano 17r
Tel: 055-697037
www.capponcina.com
In the hills just outside Florence, this restaurant has great, reasonably priced food. The terrace offers an outstanding view of Florence. Try the risotto with zucchini flowers and buffalo mozzarella. Closed Mon in autumn/winter. €–€€

PRICE CATEGORIES

Average cost of a three-course meal per person with a half-bottle of wine:
€ = under €25
€€ = €25–40
€€€ = €40–60
€€€€ = more than €60

PISTOIA PROVINCE

The smallest Tuscan province, Pistoia is sandwiched between Lucca and Florence and was fought over for centuries by both. Today it enjoys a more peaceful existence

Pistoia province is part fertile plain and part mountains, bordered in the north by the Apennines where Abetone, a popular ski resort, is little more than an hour's drive from the city of Pistoia. The other major town in the province is Pescia, cradled in the plain of the Valdinievole and famous for its flower production. The province is also important for railway construction, embroidery, furniture-making and shoe manufacture. Here, too, is Montecatini Terme, an elegant international spa town.

Pistoia ➊ is only 37 km (22 miles) from Florence and rather unfairly neglected as a result. Its historic heart is a delight, and it has enough good hotels tucked away in the medieval streets, as well as excellent restaurants and elegant shops, to make it an attractive alternative base.

The citizens of Pistoia take great pride in their many historic monuments and churches. There are shops as glamorous as in Florence or Lucca, and when dusk falls, the lamp-lit shadowy streets of Pistoia still have an authentic medieval atmosphere. Church bells peal, Franciscan monks stride along in their unmistakable brown habits and rope belts, and the stone slabs outside the shops are laid out with goods for sale just as they were in the Middle Ages.

A rich history

Pistoia was originally a Roman town, founded as a staging post on the Via Cassia, but it was razed to the ground in AD 400 by the invading Lombards. It flourished as a banking centre during the Middle Ages when most of its important buildings were constructed, but it suffered during the wars between Florence and Lucca, eventually falling under the dominion of Florence.

The impressive trapeze-shaped walls with bastions and four gates

Maps
City: 124
Area: 126

LEFT: Pistoia's 12th-century Cathedral of San Zeno and campanile. **BELOW:** detail of the Duomo's façade.

that still encompass the centre of the city were built by the Medici during the 15th century. A number of streets around the central **Piazza del Duomo** have been pedestrianised, and when not full of bustling market stalls (Sat and Wed), the piazza is a good quiet place to take stock of Pistoia's riches.

The **Cattedrale di San Zeno** Ⓑ (open Mon–Sat 8am–12.30pm, 3.30–7pm, Sun 8am–1pm, 3.30–7pm) originated in the 5th century, but was rebuilt in the Romanesque style in the 12th century with a splendid façade of green-and-white marble stripes. A marble porch was added later and decorated with an exquisite blue-and-white Andrea della Robbia bas-relief.

Inside are many medieval frescoes, an impressive *Crucifix* (1274), Renaissance paintings and – most glorious of all – the massive, ornate silver altar in the **Chapel of Saint James** (Dossale di San Jacopo; open Mon–Sat 10am–12.30pm, 3.30–

Majolica plaque on the Ospedale del Ceppo, which was named after the offertory boxes in which alms for the poor were collected.

5.30pm, Sun 8–9.30am, 11–11.30am, 4–5.30pm; entrance fee), decorated with bas-reliefs and statues over a period of two centuries by many different artists, including Brunelleschi. Next door in the Palazzo dei Vescovi (Bishops' Palace) and above the helpful tourist office (tel: 0573-21622) is the **Museo della Cattedrale** Ⓒ (open Tues, Thur and Fri; guided tours only 10am–1pm, 3–5pm; entrance fee).

Beside the Duomo is the soaring **Campanile**, originally a watchtower, to which have been added three tiers of green-and-white Pisan arches, reflecting the Duomo façade. You can climb the bell-tower for magnificent views over the town (open Sat–Sun by reservation at the tourist office). Opposite is the 14th-century octagonal **Baptistery** of San Giovanni in Corte, designed by Andrea Pisano (open daily 10am–6pm).

The piazza is lined with a number of fine Renaissance palaces, includ-

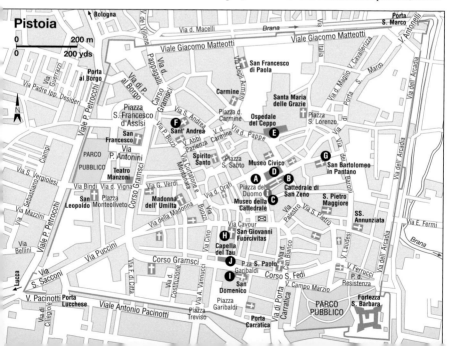

Maps
City: 124
Area: 126

ing the **Palazzo del Podestà**, still the city's law court, with a finely decorated inner courtyard. Opposite is the **Palazzo del Comune** (Town Hall), with a harmonious façade of arches and delicately pointed windows, decorated with the ubiquitous Medici crest and a grim black marble head. Inside is a courtyard and sweeping stairway, and sculptures by local artist Marino Marini, many of them based on his favourite theme of riders and horses. Upstairs in the first- and second-floor rooms is the impressive art collection of the **Museo Civico** ❶ (open Tues, Thur–Sat 10am–6pm, Wed 4–7pm, Sun 11am–6pm, winter Tues, Thur–Sat 10am–5pm, Wed 3–6pm, Sun 11am–5pm; entrance fee), which includes a rare 13th-century painting of St Francis and many delightful polychrome wooden sculptures.

To the north of the Piazza del Duomo in Piazza Giovanni XII is the **Ospedale del Ceppo** ❸. It was founded in 1287 and still functions as a hospital. Above the external loggia, added in 1514, is a brilliantly coloured majolica frieze by Giovanni della Robbia. In rich colours it depicts the *Seven Works of Mercy (Sette Opere di Misericordia)*: worthy citizens handing out food to the poor, comforting prisoners and the sick and washing the feet of dusty travellers. The figures are realistic, and sometimes even humorous, despite the gravity of their occupations.

A congregation of churches

Pistoia has a large quantity of churches, many of great architectural interest, some with notable artworks – in particular the Pisano pulpits, which are the great pride of the town.

Sant'Andrea ❹ (open 7.30am–6pm), in the Via Sant'Andrea, has an arcaded façade and reliefs above the central door. Inside is a richly painted wooden ceiling and narrow nave, well lit from the upper clerestory. Here is one of the famous pulpits by Giovanni Pisano, created between 1298 and 1301, modelled on the Nicola Pisano pulpit in the Pisa Duomo. The sharply carved marble reliefs border on the melodramatic in their depiction of *The Life of Jesus* and *The Last Judgement*.

TIP

On one corner of the Piazza del Duomo is the Café Guardingo. Set in an old building with a beautiful vaulted ceiling, this is good place for an *aperitivo* and to nibble on the tasty savouries provided.

BELOW: Della Robbia's majolica frieze above the Ospedale del Ceppo loggia.

A single ticket is available which covers all Pistoia's museums; it costs €6.50 and is valid for three days.

San Bartolomeo in Pantano  (St Bartholomew in the Swamp; open 8am–7pm), in the Piazza San Bartolomeo, is one of Pistoia's oldest churches, built in the 12th century with a five-bay façade and rich in marble carvings and reliefs. Inside there is a pulpit by Guido da Como (1250) with marble reliefs showing *Christ's Nativity*, the whole construction resting on the backs of men and lions carved out of marble.

In the pedestrianised Via Cavour is the 12th-century church of **San Giovanni Fuorcivitas** (open 7.30am–noon, 5–6.30pm), thus named because it was built outside the city walls. It has an elaborate green-and-white-striped marble façade and walls in the Pisan style. The fine works of art inside include the pulpit created in 1270 by Fra Guglielmo da Pisa, a pupil of Nicola Pisano, a water stoup by Giovanni Pisano and a touchingly beautiful white-glazed terracotta of *The Visitation,* by Luca della Robbia.

The church and monastery of **San Domenico** (the permanent exhibition is open Mon–Sat 8–11.50am, 4.30–6pm, Sun 8am–12.30pm, 4.30–7pm; for guided tours tel: 0573-32046), in Piazza Garibaldi, is a good illustration of what not to do to a church (due to rebuilding after damage in World War II). Its original windows have been filled in and new ones inserted, but there are a number of colourful original frescoes and works claimed to be by Rossellino and Bernini.

Opposite San Domenico is **Cappella del Tau** (open Mon–Sat 8.15am–1.30pm). This former chapel is now an artistic monument, with darkly dramatic Gothic frescoes on its walls and vaulted ceilings, including a fine fresco of *The Fall*. The Palazzo del Tau is now home to the **Museo Marino Marini** (open Mon–Sat 10am–5pm; entrance fee), named after Pistoia's most famous 20th-century son. Marino Marini

BELOW: Pistoia's market is set up on the pretty Piazza della Sala.

(1901–80) left an important bequest to the city of his sculptures, etchings, prints and drawings based on the recurring themes of horses and riders. He later diversified into a series of portraits of famous people including Stravinsky, Marc Chagall, Thomas Mann and Henry Miller, which are also on view here. In the courtyard next door is the museum's lovely café.

Other churches worth including in a visit to Pistoia are the **Basilica della Madonna dell'Umiltà**, with its dome by Vasari, **San Francesco**, with a wooden ceiling reminiscent of early Florentine churches, **San Paolo**, on via Silvano Fedi and with a large impressive façade, and the baroque Jesuit church of **Spirito Santa**, whose altar was designed by Bernini.

Pistoia is famous for its tradition of embroidery, fine examples of which can be seen in the **Museo del Ricamo**, set in the Palazzo Rospigliosi (via Ripa del Sale 3; open Tues–Sat and 2nd Sun of the month 10am–1pm, 3–6pm; entrance fee).

The main shopping streets, with high-quality clothes, shoes, leather and jewellery stores, are the Via Cavour, Via Cino, Via Ateo Vannucci and Via Orafi. At what was the centre of the Lombard town is the Piazza della Sala, a very attractive square. The town fruit-and-vegetable market is here, set out around an old well. At night the piazza is home to a number of lively bars.

About 5 km (3 miles) outside the town, in Via Pieve a Celle, is **Pistoia Zoo** (open Mon–Sat 9am–6pm, Sun until 7pm; entrance fee; www.zoodi pistoia.it), set in a large pine forest.

The spa towns

West of Pistoia, and most easily accessible via the A11 autostrada, are the spa towns, the grandest of which is **Montecatini Terme ❷**, famed throughout Europe for its elegance and luxury. It was rebuilt by Grand Duke Leopold of Tuscany in the 18th century and has since become a company town, with whole avenues of huge spa buildings dispensing waters to drink and treatments ranging from baths and inhalation to the famous mudbaths. You can stroll through the magnifi-

Maps
City: 124
Area: 126

Decorative stained glass at the Terme Tettuccio, one of nine spa establishments in Montecatini.

BELOW: the funicular to Montecatini Alta.

The Spa Renaissance

Taking the waters' has become fashionable once more. Water cures, popular since Etruscan and Roman times, have always been part of local culture. In the first century AD, Emperor Augustus' physician issued a prescription to the poet Horace to visit the Tuscan spas, which is one of the first medical prescriptions on record. The Romans saw spas as both curative and civilising, distinguishing their citizens from the Barbarians, who didn't know how to combine warm water with warm company and well-being. Thermal spas were also recreational in the days of the Tuscan Grand-Dukes, when resorts such as Bagni di Pisa welcomed the crowned heads of Europe to wallow in the waters, gamble in the casino and dance in the ballrooms. But somewhere along the line, the spas languished, lost their sparkle, and became the province of technicians performing obscure `liver-boosting water cures' in echoing marble halls.

The scary-white-coats brigade have been banished from the best Tuscan spas, or at least given a charm makeover rather than full colonic irrigation. The grand dames, such as **Montecatini Terme**, have survived, and retain an Art Nouveau elegance more in keeping with the monumental spas of Mitteleuropa. Smaller, old school spas, such as **Bagni di Filippo**, float along on faded charm and a Fellini-esque blend of a surreal setting, cheerful improvisation and larger-than-life characters.

But the new breed of thermal spas marks a return to Roman roots: these are both pampering and restorative spas which bathe body, mind and spirit. While not throwing the baby out with the bathwater, spas such as **Grotta Giusti**, in Monsummano Terme, manage to combine gracious 19th-century living with superb massage, thermal pools, sprawling grounds, and steamy grottoes dubbed 'the eighth wonder of the world' by the operatic Giuseppe Verdi. Health-seekers don bizarre boiler-suits to follow the Dante-esque route into 'Inferno', where grottoes named Purgatory, Paradise and Hell induce a surreal detox. After sweating in Hell, there's floating under the thermal jets in the giant pool, Ayurvedic massage or sneaky golf sessions.

Set at the foot of low-slung mountains, **Bagni di Pisa** is a delightful retreat with a view of the Leaning Tower. This romantic 18th-century resort is charmingly nostalgic, with vaulted bedrooms, a winter garden, frescoed halls, and a folly Byron was fond of. But the rooftop thermal pool and pampering treatments suit spa babes rather than Byronic adventurers. The hammam is a steamy, couples-only cavern and stone-clad pool with a 38-degree temperature conducive to chilling out, detoxing and lowering the blood pressure.

Fonteverde, floating on a sea of hills in Val d'Orcia, is a terraced spa resort clustered around a late Renaissance villa. The stylishly simple estate is dotted with thermal pools but, as a destination spa, it also delivers Oriental massage, Watsu, skin consultation, dietary advice, yoga, spiritual healing - all presented clearly, without pushiness or psycho-babble. Behind the spa philosophy is a belief in the curative powers of thermal waters, a bespoke approach to well-being, and a determination to deliver what you need. It may be a simple massage, a float in the spa but, in such a setting, even a 'simple' massage dissolves disharmony.

For a full list of spas offering health and beauty treatments, see page 287. ❑

LEFT: working up a sweat in the caves of Grotta Giusti.

cent parks, or sip the waters in marble pavilions – or, of course, you could commit yourself to a complete cure *(see page 128)*.

Montecatini Alto is the original medieval fortified town above the thermal springs, and can be reached by funicular railway or by road. Although full of wealthy tourists in high season, it is still a charming and restful place to visit, with a shady walk of chestnut trees around the lower terrace of the village and panoramic views over the plain of the Valdinievole.

The main square, **Piazza Giuseppe Giusti**, has large open cafés. Little remains of the original fortress, although its walls and towers are being restored. The adjacent church of St Peter has Romanesque origins, but has been hideously restored with its columns and exquisitely carved capitals barely visible.

Monsummano Terme ❸ is the birthplace of the poet Giuseppe Giusti (1809–50) and the site of a particularly extraordinary spa, Grotta Giusti Spa Resort *(see left and page 287)*, where you can bathe in thermal

pools or sweat it out in a bizarre steamy grotto, both experiences best savoured on an overnight stay.

Driving north of Montecatini along the N633, you arrive at **Marliana ❹** via a stunning mountain road. Marliana has the remains of a castle, and a campanile from which there are magnificent views.

A little further on, **Vellano** is well worth exploring. Still a working village, little changed since medieval times, it's a handy place for lunch, as it has a number of good family restaurants overlooking the valley slopes and olive terraces.

Floral town

Pescia ❺ has the largest flower market outside Holland. The market itself can be visited, but you have to get there early because it is all over by 8am. Pescia is a prosperous town, surrounded by nurseries, greenhouses and olive groves.

Elegant villas sheltered by cypresses are visible in the hills beyond Pescia, many of which can now be visited or rented. The town itself, most of which is 13th-century in ori-

Maps
City: 124
Area: 126

In the spring, the peach blossoms of Pescia are outstanding; every September in even-numbered years, Pescia hosts the colourful Biennale del Fiore – Festival of Flowers.

BELOW: cheeky decorative tiles at Tettuccio Terme Montecatini.

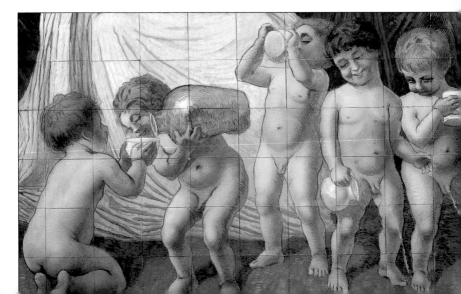

gin, is divided by the river Pescia, and at its centre is the Piazza Mazzini, dominated at one end by the Oratory of the Madonna di Pie di Piazza, which dates from the 17th century. It has a finely carved wooden ceiling, embellished with gold leaf, by Giovanni Zeti, and there is a delightful little painting beneath the altar illustrating 17th-century Pescia.

At the opposite end of the piazza is the Palazzo Comunale, with its fortified tower, still used as the town hall. On the other side of the river the 17th-century baroque Cathedral retains its 14th-century bell-tower.

Pescia's most prized works of art are the earliest known paintings of St Francis in the church of San Francesco (Via Battisti). In the church of Sant' Antonio are frescoes by Bicci di Lorenzo. In the hills above Pescia is the Convento di Colleviti, a peaceful Renaissance monastery, accessible by footpath from Pescia.

Contrasting villages

Just south of Pescia are two villages worth visiting, though they are in dramatically different states of repair. **Uzzano** ❻ is a pretty hill village with winding streets, but it is not in good shape, and many of the houses are in danger of collapse. However, it has an interesting gateway and a curious church right at the crest of the hill which has a rose window and an elaborate Pisan doorway.

Buggiano ❼, by contrast, has been carefully restored. If you head towards the church and campanile you will find a very fine *palazzo*, where a proud caretaker will appear and show you round for a small consideration. The building has massive oak beams and lovingly preserved frescoes on the walls, and houses a store of documents from the town which date back to 1377.

Mountain pursuits

The drive up into the mountains to the north of Pistoia is stunningly beautiful, especially in autumn, when the colours of the trees rival those of New England. But winter-sports enthusiasts will prefer it with a good covering of crisp snow.

The grand Palazzo Pretorio in Cutigliano.

BELOW: Ski runs from Monte Gomito, Abetone.

The main town here is **San Marcello Pistoiese** ❽. It is traditionally known for the *Mongolfiera*, or hot-air balloon, which is launched every year on 8 September to mark the end of the summer. Near to San Marcello, at Mammiano, is a spectacular foot suspension bridge, 220 metres (720 ft) long, connecting the village with the road across the river Lima.

Cutigliano ❾, further down the valley, is a typical mountain village, surrounded by fir trees, with limited skiing on 13 km (8 miles) of pistes and nine ski lifts (the more dedicated skier will probably prefer Abetone). Cutigliano has a surprisingly grand 14th-century Palazzo Pretorio, with numerous shields emblazoned on the façade, includ-ing a Medici coat of arms. Opposite is a quiet loggia, with arcading and stone seats.

Abetone ❿, about 90 minutes' drive from Pistoia, is 1,400 metres (4,660 ft) above sea level and is the most popular ski resort in the Apennines. It offers a wide range of pistes served by 25 ski lifts, has three ski schools and a wide variety of accommodation. In the absence of good snow, the recently installed artificial snow machines can cover 40 km (25 miles) of slopes. In the summer this is a good centre for climbing and walking expeditions in the surrounding pine and chestnut woods. *Rifugi*, or mountain shelters, are dotted around the area, supplying basic shelter and sometimes restaurants as well. ❑

Maps
City: 124
Area: 126

TIP

Abetone is well supplied with mountain restaurants, which command wonderful views of the dramatic landscape and supply hearty food and restorative drinks. A local speciality is *Grappa di mirtilli*, a strong spirit made from mountain bilberries.

RESTAURANTS

Abetone
Da Pierone
Via Brennero 556
Tel: 0573-60068
Rustic restaurant. Good cooking based on traditional mountain fare. Closed Mon, 15–30 June, 20 Oct–early Nov. €€

Montecatini Terme
Enoteca Da Giovanni
Via Garibaldi 25
Tel: 0572-73080
The wine list is extensive, but the food is the main attraction. Excellent meat and fish. The annexe, known as the Cucina da Giovanni, serves more traditional Tuscan fare and is cheaper. Closed Mon and last 2 weeks in Feb and Aug.
€€€–€€€€

Pescia
Cecco
Via Forti 96
Tel: 0572-477955
www.ristorantececco.com
Mushrooms, asparagus and truffles feature highly here, and the fish is also good in this historic and welcoming trattoria. Closed Mon in winter. €€

Monte a Pescia
Località Monte a Pescia
Tel: 0572-490000
This trattoria specialises in meats grilled over an open fire. Lovely terrace overlooking olive trees and hills. Closed Wed. €€

Pistoia
Al Posto Giusto
Via Mammianese 399
Tel: 0572-69247
Outside Pistoia, this non-touristy restaurant offers excellent food at a moderate price. The drive out takes you along winding country roads. Very friendly owners. Closed Wed. €

La Limonaia
Via di Gello 9a
Tel: 0573-400453
Appealing, rustic trattoria a little way from the centre of town. Unusual herbs and flavourings pep up the Tuscan food. Closed Mon and Tues. €

Lo Storno
Via del Lastrone 8
Tel: 0573-26193
A tiny eatery, with a few tables on the street, just off Piazza della Sala. Local Pistoian dishes are the speciality here. Closed Sun. €

Osteria Boccon di Vino
Corso Gramsci 83
A central, pleasant restaurant serving simple but tasty food. Closed Mon. €

Ristorante San Jacopo
Via Crispi 15
Tel: 0573-27786
www.ristorantesanjacopo.it
One of the best restaurants in Pistoia, set in the *centro storico*. It serves dishes from Pistoia and elsewhere in Tuscany, with particularly good seafood and juicy *bistecca alla fiorentina*. Closed Mon. €€

Trattoria dell' Abbondanza
Via dell'Abbondanza 10–14
Tel: 0573-368037
Traditional restaurant with recipes from the surrounding region such as *farinato* (a hearty Tuscan soup). Closed Wed and Thur lunch. €€

● ● ● ● ● ● ● ● ● ● ● ●
Average cost of a 3-course dinner and half-bottle of wine:
€€€€ = over €60, €€€ = €40–60, €€ = €25–40,
€ = under €25.

LUCCA AND THE VERSILIA

Take some mountains and spas, add a few grand
villas and beaches, blend in an underrated city
full of character, and you begin to paint a picture
of Lucca province

Often bypassed by those intent on visiting Pisa, nearby Lucca is one of the least appreciated Italian cities. Its pinky-gold buildings, tree-topped walls, enchanting churches, and its renowned olive oil and wine production, are all good reasons to spend time here. To the west of the walled city is the Tuscan Riviera, known as the Versilia, a broad strip of land between the sea and the Apennines which contains a rich playground of villas and hotels. To the north is the steeply mountainous Garfagnana region *(covered in the next chapter)*. In 1996, the province was hit hard by floods and subsequent landslides. Although many areas were affected to some extent, worst hit were the small villages high up in the hills, where people lost homes, businesses, even families. Scars are still clearly visible around the province today.

The provincial capital

Lucca ❶ sits on a marshy plain between the Apennines and Monte Pisano, which has been inhabited since ancient times. Little remains of the Etruscan city of Luk, but evidence of the thriving Roman colony of Luca is seen in the grid layout of streets and more obviously in the elliptical Piazza Anfiteatro, around which houses were subsequently

built. Under the Lombards, Luca became a ducal residence and the capital of Tuscia. In the 11th century it became the commune of Lucca and spent the next 400 years defending itself against an ever more belligerent Florence. Even though the Florentines won the title of capital of the region, Lucca never ceded its political and economic autonomy. It remained an independent republic, apart from a brief period of Pisan rule, until the Napoleonic invasion of 1796.

Maps
City: 134
Area: 144

LEFT: smart bathing huts at Forte dei Marmi.
BELOW: Piazza Anfiteatro, Lucca.

The Palio di San Paolino – a medieval celebration of Lucca's patron saint, with costume parades, flag-throwing and crossbow-shooting competitions.

This graceful and prosperous provincial capital, 77 km (47 miles) west of Florence on the A11, is a city of many seductive charms, not least the walls encircling the city. They were built after 1500 to keep Lucca's enemies at bay. In 1817, the massive ramparts were planted with a double row of plane trees, which now shade the broad avenue running along the top of the walls, used by Lucca's citizens as a playground, a jogging and cycle track and a promenade.

The Cathedral square

A path from the walls takes you to the front of the **Duomo di San Martino** Ⓐ (open Mon–Fri 9.30am–6pm, Sat until 6.45pm, Sun until 4.45pm, closes 1 hr earlier in winter; free). The Cathedral's striking façade is decorated with a sculpture of St Martin dividing his cloak (the original sculpture is now just inside the church), and with the inlaid marble designs that typify the Tuscan

Romanesque style: hunting scenes figure large, with dogs, boars, and huntsmen on horseback. Flanking the central portal are scenes of the Labours of the Months and the Miracles of St Martin.

Inside is the domed *tempietto* that contains a larger-than-life *Crucifixion* in carved and painted wood. Known as the *Volto Santo* (Holy Face), the Romanesque carving was once believed to be a true and accurate portrait of Christ, carved by Nicodemus, who witnessed the Crucifixion (in fact, the highly stylised figure is probably a 13th-century copy of an 11th-century copy of an 8th-century original). Each year, on 13 September, this greatly revered relic is paraded through the streets at dusk. Off the south aisle is the **Sacristy** (open Mon–Fri 9.30am–5.45pm, Sat until 6.45pm, closes 1 hr earlier in winter, Sun open between services; entrance fee). This contains another celebrated image: the tomb of Ilaria

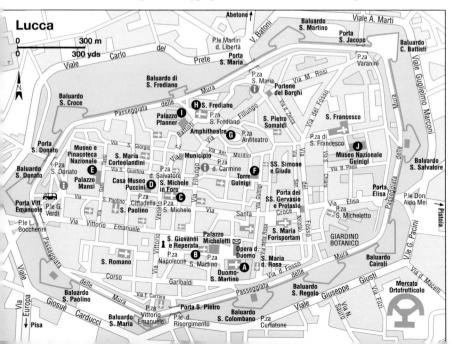

del Carretto, who died in 1405, a masterpiece of realistic carving by Jacopo della Quercia. Ilaria was the wife of the then ruler of Lucca, Paolo Guinigi; she died two years after their marriage, at the age of 24, following the birth of their second child. It's a tender portrayal, and the little dog at her feet is a touching symbol of fidelity.

Across the Cathedral square is the church of **Santi Giovanni e Reperata ❸** (open mid-Mar–2 Nov daily 10am–6pm, 3 Nov–mid-Mar Sat–Sun only 10am–5pm; entrance fee). The now-redundant church has been comprehensively excavated, and beneath the modern floor there is a wealth of Roman and medieval structures. The earliest is a 1st-century BC mosaic floor, part of a house that was superseded by a 2nd-century Roman bathhouse, which itself gave way to a 5th-century baptistery, later joined by a series of churches, culminating in the present 12th-century building.

Via del Duomo leads west of the Cathedral to Piazza del Giglio, home to the city's theatre and opera house. Adjoining the square is the far larger Piazza Napoleone, where you'll find a choice of outdoor restaurants, shaded by tall plane trees.

Pisan Romanesque to Puccini

Heading north out of the square takes you to Piazza San Michele, ringed by Renaissance arcades. At the centre of the square, the church of **San Michele in Foro ❻** (open daily 7.40am–noon, 3–6pm; free) built on the site of the old Roman forum, has one of the most spectacular Pisan Romanesque façades in Italy. The four storeys of arcades are decorated with delicate motifs and allegories; hunting scenes carved in green and white marble, with animals both exotic (bears, dragons and elephants) and domestic (a rabbit, a duck and a crow eating grapes). The

church is topped by a huge gilded statue of Archangel Michael slaying the dragon, flanked by two angels.

Turning your back on the façade, take Via di Poggio, which leads past the **Casa Museo Puccini ❹** (closed for restoration until further notice; normal opening hours June–Sept daily 10am–6pm, mid-Mar–May, Oct–Dec Tues–Sun 10am–1pm, 3–6pm; entrance fee), the birthplace of Lucca's celebrated composer, Giacomo Puccini (1858–1924).

Decorative art

Heading west, feel your way through Lucca's maze of medieval alleys to Palazzo Mansi, in Via Galli Tassi, which houses the **Museo e Pinacoteca Nazionale ❺** (open Tues–Sat 8.30am–7pm, Sun 8.30am–1pm; entrance fee). Deities and allegorical figures romp across the ceilings of the splendidly furnished 17th-century home of Cardinal Spada (1659–1724). Upstairs, at the end of a sequence of rooms decorated around the theme of the Four Elements is a sumptuous bedchamber dedicated to Fire. This fire is not

Maps
City: 134
Area: 144

Lucca is full of lanes too narrow for cars, so people get about by bicycle. This, combined with Lucca's reputation for culture and intellectual pursuits, has earned the city the nickname of "Cambridge in Tuscany".

BELOW: Pisan Romanesque façade of San Michele, Lucca.

TIP

The Bar San Michele on Piazza San Michele is a great place to stop for a drink and admire San Michele in Foro, Lucca's chief attraction. Alternatively, head for Via Fillungo, Lucca's main shopping street and evening strolling ground, for an ice cream or traditional pastry at the *belle époque* Antico Caffè di Simo (no. 58, closed Mon in winter). Try the local speciality, *buccelato* – a sweet bread with raisins and aniseed – either with a coffee or sweet Vin Santo wine.

BELOW: bird's eye view of Lucca and the Apuan Alps beyond.

a destructive one, but the flame that burns when Eros strikes with his arrow. The room features a gorgeous double bed, its lovely hangings decorated with birds and flowers.

Wealth and splendour

The wealth of Lucca, like that of Florence, was based on banking and its silk industry. As early as the 12th century, bankers were plying the waters of the Mediterranean or travelling north to Bruges, Antwerp and London, buying and selling silk and woollen cloth. Successful bankers, like the Guinigi family, built substantial city homes. To demonstrate their prosperity some of them erected towers, although only one of these, the 14th-century **Torre Guinigi ⓕ** (open daily Mar–Sept 9am–8pm, Oct 10am–6pm, Nov–Feb 9am–5.30pm; entrance fee), remains. This is a rare example of the kind of defensive tower that was once commonplace in medieval Tuscany, built as a status symbol and place of retreat in times of trouble. If you climb the tower you will see, as well as views of the nearby countryside, the outline of

Lucca's Roman Amphitheatre (Anfiteatro), perfectly preserved in the buildings that were constructed against it in the Middle Ages.

For a closer look at what is now a remarkable egg-shaped **piazza**, turn right out of the tower, and first right in Via delle Chiavi d'Oro. Passing the Art Deco baths (now a cultural centre), keep going until you reach the curving wall of the **Amphitheatre ⓖ**. Ringed by pavement cafés, restaurants and souvenir shops, the Amphitheatre is an atmospheric place to put your feet up and enjoy an ice cream or linger on for dinner.

Exit through the opposite archway, and follow the curve of the Amphitheatre to Via Fillungo, Lucca's main shopping street *(see left)* and the church of **San Frediano ⓗ** (open Mon–Sat 8.30am–noon, 3–5pm, Sun 10.30am–5pm), with its huge gold-and-blue façade mosaic of Christ in Majesty. The treasure of this church is its Romanesque font carved with scenes showing Moses and his entourage of camels, leading his people (dressed in medieval armour) through the divided Red Sea.

To the rear and left of the church is the **Palazzo Pfanner ❶** (open daily Mar–Oct 10am–6pm; entrance fee), a delightful 17th-century residence. Without paying, you can get a sneak view of the wonderful garden and exterior staircase at the rear of the palace by climbing onto the city walls at the rear of San Frediano church and walking left for a short distance. Highlights inside include examples of exquisite 17th-century Lucchese silk in the bedrooms and beer-making equipment in the cellar – the palace was used as a brewery until 1929.

The Guinigi were not the only ones to display their wealth by creating towers. A picture hanging in the **Museo Nazionale Guinigi ❶** (open Tues–Sat 8.30am–7.30pm, Sun and holidays 8.30am–1.30pm; entrance fee) shows that the city was once, like San Gimignano, a forest of towers, and illustrates just how wealthy medieval Lucca was. Among the artistic treasures here is a *Madonna and Child* in bas-relief by Matteo Civitalli, a contemporary of Donatello and Lucca's most renowned sculptor.

Lucchesi villas

The area surrounding Lucca is rich in villas: the patrician Villa Torrigiani, the baroque Villa Mansi and the Villa Reale at Marlia are all surrounded by beautiful parks. Most of these villas are still in appreciative private hands, and often the gardens can be visited even if the house is not open to the public. Wandering through fragrant shrubbery and cool grottoes, past whimsical statuary and fountains, is a delightful diversion on a hot summer's afternoon.

Leave Lucca on the SS12 in the direction of the Garfagnana, and after passing through Marlia, turn off at **Villa Reale ❷** (gardens open to the public with guided tours every hour on the hour Tues–Sun Mar–Nov 10am–noon, 3–6pm, Dec–Feb by appointment only; entrance fee). It

was built in the 17th century by the noble Orsetti family, and substantially remodelled by Elisa Bacciocchi, Napoleon's sister. There is a lush park with a lake, which surrounds the formal Italian gardens. Most wonderful of its many fine features is the *teatro verde*, an outdoor theatre surrounded by clipped yew hedges, the setting for concerts during Lucca's summer festival.

Continue on through a fairly built-up area to Segromigno in Monte and the charming **Villa Mansi ❸** (open Mar–Sept Tues–Sun 10am–1pm, 3–6pm, best to call first, tel: 0583-920234; entrance fee), with beautifully landscaped gardens. Just 2 km away in Camigliano, **Villa Torrigiani** (open Mar–2nd Sun in Nov daily 10am–1pm, 3pm–1 hr before dusk; entrance fee) is a fine example of baroque architecture.

Equally splendid is the **Villa Garzoni** (villa closed for renovations; gardens open: Mar–2 Nov daily 8.30am–sunset, rest of year Sat–Sun 9am–sunset, 20 Dec–11 Jan open daily; entrance fee) in the village of **Collodi ❹**, with a glorious

Maps
City: 134
Area: 144

Christin Majesty mosaic on the façade of San Frediano. Every year on 27 April, a flower market is held outside the church to honour St Zita, patron saint of maidens, whose mumifed body lies within.

BELOW: ornamental gardens of the Villa Reale.

TIP

In Viareggio, a recently opened carnival museum, the Museo della Cittadella (Via Santa Maria Gorretti 16; Mon, Wed, Fri 10am–noon; tel: 0584-51176), on the site where the floats are made, tells the story of the origins and characters of the famous *carnevale*.

BELOW: Villa Garzoni gardens at Collodi.

baroque garden full of mythical monsters modelled in terracotta, fountains and topiaried animals. The steep terraces of the 17th-century garden lead to some memorable viewing points.

If you were entranced as a child by the adventures of a wooden puppet with a remarkable nose, you may recognise the name of this town as being that of the author of *The Adventures of Pinocchio* (1881). Carlo Lorenzini adopted Collodi as his penname because he had fond memories of staying here as a child. The town now has a **Children's Park** (same hours as Villa Garzoni gardens) devoted to Pinocchio, consisting of mosaics, mazes and statues based on scenes from the story. Contemporary children, accustomed to virtual reality and snazzy theme parks, may find it rather tame, but there are plans to enhance the attractions at the nearby Villa Garzoni.

The Versilia

This coastal region of Italy has always attracted the attention of scholars, poets, writers and artists. It is the area west of Lucca, squeezed between the Apuan Alps in the east, the sea and the mouth of the Cinquale river in the north, and Lake Massaciuccoli in the south. The flat, pine-covered landscape has lost a lot of its earlier rustic and remote appeal now that it has been developed and built on so heavily. The sea can be reached only if you pay an entrance fee and want to lie on a sunbed among rows of others, on sand carefully raked and flattened for your added comfort.

Viareggio ❺ is the oldest of the coastal towns in the Versilia. Its origins are Roman, and in the Middle Ages it was an important sea landing. In the 19th century it was reputed to build some of the best boats ever launched on the Tyrrhenian Sea, and the boatyards are still very much active. Today, Viareggio is more famous for its February Carnival. Floats are built to a specified theme and are usually spiced up with political satire and irony. The whole town joins in the football matches, masked balls and fireworks.

Viareggio reached its heyday at the beginning of the 20th century; there are a number of buildings of this period remaining in the town, such as the **Bagni Margherita** on the seashore, as well as a great many Art Nouveau hotels on the seafront boulevard, the **Passeggiata Margherita**. Look out for the Liberty-style Gran Caffè Margherita (Viale Margherita 30) – Puccini's favourite. During the summer months there is a very lively atmosphere here; the town attracts foreigners and Italians alike, and the stretch of coastline going towards Forte dei Marmi is well known as a playground for the Milanese.

Lakeside retreats

Just south of Viareggio, along the Viale dei Tigli, is **Torre del Lago Puccini ❻**. The approach to this lakeside resort passes through one of Viareggio's two pine forests, of which the **Macchia Lucchese** is the more

beautiful. On **Lake Massaciuccoli** ❼ at Torre del Lago Puccini is Giacomo Puccini's villa, in which were written all his operas except *Turandot*. The area has been rather over-popularised, but when Puccini first came here it was a peaceful backwater where he was able to indulge not only in composing but in his other favourite pastime, which was shooting birds and animals.

Puccini's **villa** (Tues–Sun, June–Oct 10am–12.30pm, 3–6.30pm, until 5.30pm in winter, until 6pm in spring; guided tours every 30 minutes; entrance fee) displays his musical instruments as well as his guns. Puccini is buried in the nearby chapel. Each August, Torre del Lago holds a festival of his operas here in a very atmospheric setting – a stage is built by the lake near his house.

The lake and some of the neighbouring wetlands form a nature reserve and haven for birdlife – the **Parco Regionale di Migliarino-San Rossore** (tel: 050-525500; e-mail: info@sanrossore.toscana.it). You can take a pleasant boat trip around the lagoon.

Seaside resorts

Continuing north from Viareggio, the resorts fall into line in quick succession. **Lido di Camaiore** ❽ is slightly more downmarket than the other places further north, but then access to the beach is easier – being virtually free of pay-as-you-enter stretches of sand. From this part of the shore it is easy to reach **Camaiore** ❾ (to the Romans, *Campus Maior*), which is about 7 km (4 miles) to the east. The town has an interesting range of architecture, of which the 8th-century **Badia dei Santi Benedetti**, with a monumental 14th-century portal, and the Romanesque church of **Santa Maria Assunta** are the most important.

From Lido di Camaiore the subsequent pockets of watering holes are collectively known as Marina di Pietrasanta. **Pietrasanta** ❿ itself is about 8 km (5 miles) inland from the sea; its name, "Holy Stone", refers to the town's chief product, marble. Not much happens in Pietrasanta today except for the celebration of the town's main product. It is the Tuscan centre for stone sculptors, who come

Maps
City: 134
Area: 144

Giacomo Puccini, composer of La Bohème, Tosca *and* Madame Butterfly, *lived and died at Torre del Lago, where his villa is now a museum dedicated to his life and work.*

BELOW: Lake Massaciuccoli at Torre del Lago.

Fresco by the 20th-century Colombian artist, Botero, in Pietrasanta's church of Sant'Antonio.

BELOW: luxury villa at Forte Dei Marmi.

here in droves to work the marble in the privacy of rented studios. It has long been a magnet for famous sculptors and painters, including Henry Moore and Joan Miró. A fine white dust covers everything in Pietrasanta, even the wineglasses in the bars of the Piazza Carducci.

While this town has some of the loveliest monuments in the Versilia, including the 13th-century marble **Duomo** and the church of **San Biagio and Sant'Antonio**, the **marina** down on the shore is unexceptional. The two are joined by a tree-lined avenue which reaches the marina at Fiumetto. The marina is really a series of former villages – **Fiumetto**, **Tonfano**, **Montrone** and **le Fucette**. Each offers something different. Fiumetto has a pretty park.

Luxurious villas

The gem of the Versilia is **Forte dei Marmi ⓫**, still further to the north. Here the rich old villas of the late 19th century are still occupied as private residences, some Art Nouveau, some ornate and ugly, all forming a suitable backdrop to lives of the utmost luxury. The Agnellis, owners of Fiat, have houses here. So do holidaying industrialists from Turin and fashion magnates from Milan, and the number of expensive sports cars seen cruising the streets in the early evening is directly proportional to the number of bulletproof vests required by the drivers and their bodyguards.

Forte dei Marmi grew up around a fort built in 1788 by Leopold I of Tuscany, the remains of which survive in the main square of the town. The shops and cafés around the square somehow still manage to retain something of a small-town atmosphere, even if they do sell some of the most expensive items money can buy.

There are no high-rise buildings, unlike Lido di Camaiore. The highest things are the pine trees in the gardens of the villas, and in the backstreets there is still the quiet that artists and writers found here in the late 19th century. Patches of beach are freely accessible, while the remainder is made up of smart bathing huts and tropical-style bars, perched on the fine pale-grey sand. The gently sloping shore means bathing is safe. ❑

RESTAURANTS

Bagni di Lucca

Corona
Via Serraglia 78
Tel: 0583-805151
www.coronaregina.it
Overlooking the Lima river, this charming restaurant specialises in local cuisine and seafood dishes. Pleasant terrace for alfresco dining. Closed Wed and mid-Jan–mid-Feb. €€–€€€

Forte dei Marmi

Lorenzo
Via Carducci 61
Tel: 0584-89671
Expensive, chic Michelin-starred restaurant where the speciality is fish. Popular with well-heeled Milanese. Must book. Closed Mon and lunchtime July–Aug. €€€€

Lucca

Buca di Sant'Antonio
Via della Cervia 1/3
Tel: 0583-55881
www.bucadisantantonio.it
Renowned restaurant serving Lucchese and Garfagnana classic dishes (try the fettuccine with pigeon sauce), alongside dishes with a more modern slant. Closed Sun evening, Mon and periods in Jan and July. €€€

Gli Orti di Via Elisa
Via Elisa 17
Tel: 0583-491241
www.ristoranteliorti.it
Good choice for a quick lunch: a busy trattoria with a wide choice of pasta and pizzas, plus a self-service salad bar. Closed Wed dinner and Sun. €

La Mora
Via Ludovica 1748
Località Sesto di Moriano
Tel: 0583-406402
www.ristorantelamora.it
The 15-minute drive north of Lucca (on the Barga road) is worth the effort for the superb food. Seasonal local ingredients are inventively prepared and beautifully presented. Closed Wed. €€€

Ristorante Giglio
Piazza del Giglio 2
Tel: 0583-494058
www.ristorantegiglio.com
Charming restaurant specialising in fish and Tuscan meat dishes, Tables spill out onto the piazza. One of Lucca's best restaurants, and very popular with locals. Closed Wed lunch, Tues and 2nd half of Nov. €€

San Colombano Ristorante/Caffeteria
Baluardo San Colombano 10
Tel: 0583-464641
www.caffetteriasancolombano.it
Excellent restaurant on the city walls with superb views over the city. Typical Lucchese dishes change with the season. The café serves good snacks throughout the day and is a lovely spot for an *aperitivo*. Closed Mon. Reservations recommended. €€€

Pietrasanta

Enoteca Marcucci
Via Garibaldi 40
Tel: 0584-791962
This fashionable wine bar has a vast choice of wines. The food is simple but good and freshly prepared. Must book. Closed Mon and lunchtime (except July–Aug) and Nov. €€–€€€

Torre del Lago

Butterfly
Belvedere Puccini 24/26
Tel: 0584-341024
A restaurant with rooms overlooking the lake. Sardinian dishes feature alongside Tuscan and fish specialities. Good value. Closed Fri. €€

Viareggio

Barcobestia
Via Coppino 201
Tel: 0584-384416
Affordable seafood restaurant. Delicious raw or fried fish appetisers, and tagliolini with anchovies and artichokes as a first course. Closed Mon. €€

Cabreo
Via Firenze 14
Tel: 0584-54643
Pleasant family-run restaurant specialising in traditional cuisine with the emphasis on the "catch of the day". Closed Mon and Nov. €€

Il Puntodivino
Via Mazzini 229
Tel: 0584-31046
Young and buzzing atmosphere; serves full meals as well as snacks and wine tastings in the *enoteca* (wine bar). Closed Mon. €€–€€€

L'Oca Bianca
Via Coppino 409
Tel: 0584-388477
www.oca-bianca.it
Possibly Viareggio's finest restaurant, with a creative and original seafood menu. Exquisite service; exceptional wine list. Near the port. Closed Tues (except July–Aug) and lunch Fri–Sun. €€€–€€€€

Osteria Giordano Bruno
Viale Europa 7
Tel: 0584-392201
Enoteca with good wine selection, and modern cuisine with Italian, French and Japanese influences. Great desserts. Open daily for dinner, Oct–May also for lunch. €€€

Ristorante al Porto
Via Coppino 118
Tel: 0584-383878
www.alporto.it
Good quality fish restaurant, famous for its visually spectacular steamed crustaceans. Closed Sun evening and Mon. €€€

PRICE CATEGORIES

Average cost of a three-course meal per person with a half-bottle of wine:
€ = under €25
€€ = €25–40
€€€ = €40–60
€€€€ = more than €60

THE GARFAGNANA AND LUNIGIANA

The northern corner of Tuscany is one of its wildest, most beautiful, yet least explored areas – a dramatic landscape of pine-covered mountains, craggy ravines, remote castellated villages and marble peaks. This is excellent walking country

The coastal lowlands of the Versilia give way to a dramatic hinterland of snowcapped mountains, terraced hillsides, deep gorges and mountain streams, populated by deer, wild boar, mouflons, badgers, stone martens and wolves, not to mention the flocks of walkers, rock climbers, cavers and canoeists. Tuscany's northernmost tip is an untamed rocky region known as the Lunigiana, bordered by the Apuan Alps in the south and sharing frontiers with Liguria in the west and Emilia to the east. Bordering it to the south is the Garfagnana, cut through by the Serchio river that flows between the Apuan Alps and the Apennines. Together they make up one of the wildest, most beautiful, yet least explored parts of Tuscany.

An ideal base for exploring the Garfagnana is the lively town of **Castelnuovo di Garfagnana ⑫**, about 64 km (40 miles) north of Lucca. This fortress town once controlled the route from Genoa to Lucca and Pisa, and was ruled by the Este dukes of Ferrara until Italian unification. The town was also of strategic importance during World War II, when a great deal of its town centre was destroyed. However, the Duomo survived, and so did the town walls surrounding the church of San Michele, which contains a 14th-century *Madonna* by Giuliano di Simone da Lucca. The **Rocca**, or governor's palace, which dates from the 12th century, is now the town hall. In the 16th century, it was the home of Ludovico Ariosto, the quintessential Renaissance man who combined his talents as a poet with the functions of soldier and statesman. The 14th-century Monte Alfonso fortress at the top of the hill offers magnificent views. The tourist office provides maps and information on local excursions.

Map on page 144

LEFT: the Devil's Bridge spanning the river Serchio.
BELOW: Montefegatesi.

Scenic routes

Northwest of Castelnuovo di Garfagnana, a scenic road runs from Poggio to Vaglia alongside the river Edron and **Lago di Vagli** ⓭. It leads first to **Vagli di Sotto** and then on to **Vagli di Sopra**. The old stone houses and parish church in Vagli di Sotto are worth seeing, but the main attraction is the artificial lake. In the 1940s the river Edron was dammed up, submerging the medieval village of Fabbrica di Careggine, parts of which can be seen peeking through the surface, depending on the water level. Every 10 years the village is entirely exposed when the lake is drained to service the dam. The next emptying is scheduled for 2014.

Just north of Castelnuovo, at the foot of the pass which leads up through the rugged heart of the Garfagnana, are the thermal springs of **Pieve Fosciana** ⓮. Among the treasures displayed in Fosciana's church is a terracotta *Annunciation* by Luca della Robbia.

From here the road winds its tortuous way through mountain scenery for about 18 km (11 miles) to **San Pellegrino in Alpe** ⓯, an ancient monastery housing the

Museo Etnografico Provinciale (open Tues–Sun, Apr–May 10am–1pm, 2–4.30pm, June–Sept 10am–1pm, 2–6.30pm, also Mon in July–Aug, Oct–Mar Tues–Sat 9.30am–1pm, Sun 10am–1pm, 2–4.30pm; entrance fee), an interesting museum documenting peasant life in the Garfagnana. Views from its mountainside perch are magnificent.

San Romano in Garfagnana is an interesting town with a large medieval castle and stunning views across the Alta Garfagnana, whose barren beauty is best appreciated with a visit to the **Parco Naturale dell' Orecchiella** *(see page 64)*, now part of the newly created Parco Nazionale Tosco Emiliano (www.appennino park.it). This nature park, laced with waymarked trails and cycling paths, is the preserve of rare flowers, wild boar and deer, in the embrace of the grandiose peaks of the Apennines.

Other places worth keeping an eye out for in the vicinity include **Sassorosso** (an atmospheric red-stone village), **Castiglione di Garfagnana** (an impressive medieval fortress), **Villa Collemandina** (a Romanesque

church) and **Corfino** (a small resort at the foot of Pania di Corfino with fabulous views from the Apuan to the Apennine Alps).

A scenic route to the coast from Castelnuovo di Garfagnana goes along the spectacular **Túrrite Secca** through the Parco Naturale delle Alpi Apuane, via the **Marmitte dei Giganti** ("Giants' Cooking Pots"): – 23 huge hollows (20 metres/65 ft in diameter) made by Ice Age glaciers – and through the Galleria del Cipollaio, a long tunnel carved out of the marble. From here the road winds down to Seravezza and Forte dei Marmi on the Versilia coast *(see page 140)*.

Barga

Pretty, fashionable **Barga** to the south is by far the most interesting town in the district. Leave your car outside the old city walls and head through the gate to explore the old town, with its narrow, winding streets lined with Florentine-style *palazzi* overlooked by the Romanesque **Duomo**, which commands fine views of the Garfagnana from

Map on page 144

TIP

Barga's best bar is the historic Caffè Capretz (Piazza Salvo Salvi), a favourite meeting place for poets and politicians at the end of the 19th century. It has a terrace with a view at the back and tables laid out under the loggia at the front.

BELOW: colourful façades of Barga's backstreets.

Ruins of an aqueduct near Barga.

BELOW: Eremo di Calomini in the Apuan Alps.

its hilltop position. Inside is an extraordinary marble pulpit, carved in the 13th century by Guido Bigarelli, a highly original sculptor from Como, and a Lombardic polychrome figure of St Christopher. The annual opera festival brings the old town to life in July and August.

The Apuan Alps

From Barga, cross the Serchio valley to Gallicano. Just after the village, look out for signs to the 13th-century **Eremo di Calomini**, a gleaming white hermitage clinging to a rocky slope between the trees. Another 9 km (5½ miles) of steep and winding road brings you to the village of Fornovalasco and the **Grotta del Vento** ⓲ (Cave of the Wind; open daily; guided tours only, departing on the hour; entrance fee), in the Apuan Alps, a labyrinthine system of tunnels, caves and secret passages full of dramatic stalactites and stalagmites, underground lakes and echoing chambers. There are guided tours of one, two and three hours. The three-hour itinerary (departing at 10am and 2pm) is the most dramatic

(and strenuous). The caves are consistently chilly, even in summer, so be sure to take some warm clothing.

There are more than 1,300 caves in the Apuan Alps, most of which lie within the boundaries of the **Parco Apuane**, a regional park founded in 1985. The largest and most important cave system in Italy is here: the **Antro del Corchia** (open daily, July–Aug 10am–5pm, guided tours on the hour, including night tours in Aug; reduced opening hours in spring and autumn; tel: 0584-778405; www.antrocorchia.it) at Levigliana di Stazzema, just west of the Grotta del Vento, only recently opened to the public, is over 1,200 metres (3,900 ft) deep and extends over 50 km (31 miles).

The Serchio valley

Nestled in a valley at the confluence of the Lima and Serchio rivers is **Bagni di Lucca** ⓳, a fashionable spa town in the 19th century. Shelley, Byron and the Brownings all bathed in its warm, sulphurous waters. There are 19 springs in the town, as well as two steam-vapour grottoes which easily sustain temperatures of up to 47°C (118°F). The open season for the springs lasts from May to September, and they are said to be particularly good for anyone suffering from arthritis and rheumatism. The tourist office is full of useful information on the local thermal baths and all the treks, trails and natural highlights of the surrounding area.

An upward detour from Bagni di Lucca takes you to the picturesque, high-lying village of **Montefegatesi**. From here a roughish road leads to the white-water gorge of **Orrido di Botri**, an authentic wilderness with a rich variety of flora and fauna. The canyon can be explored on a gentle two-hour trek or more arduous four-hour trek.

The road continues to **Coréglia Antelminelli**, a small town surrounded by chestnut woods with a small crafts museum and a couple of Romanesque churches.

From Bagni di Lucca the road continues along the banks of the river Serchio to **Borgo a Mozzano** ⑳ and the 14th-century Ponte della Maddalena, also known as the Ponte del Diavolo – Devil's Bridge *(see page 142)*. The splendid five-arched bridge was built by Countess Matilda of Tuscany (1046–1115), who also financed the building of the Romanesque churches of Diecimo and San Giorgio di Brancoli.

Massa Carrara

Bordering on Liguria, the province of Massa Carrara has been part of Tuscany only since the middle of the 19th century, and is very different from the archetypal image of the Tuscan landscape. Inland, Lunigiana is a little-known region of pine-covered mountains, craggy ravines and remote castellated villages. The coast is a predictable, overdeveloped continuation of the Versilian Riviera, but overshadowed by the marble industry. The beaches are dominated

by the majestic marble peaks of the Apuan Alps glittering deceptively like snow in bright sunshine.

The towns of Massa and Carrara have both prospered as a result of the still thriving marble trade, although the resulting industrial development has blighted great swathes of the surrounding area. **Marina di Massa** ㉑ is a popular resort, with fine wide sandy beaches interspersed with groves of pine trees and a promenade of pretty pastel-shaded holiday villas. The ribbon of development extends up to and beyond **Marina di Carrara**, where the beach is divided by the sight and sound of the mighty port out of which ships carry marble all over the world.

Massa ㉒ is a busy modern town but has a well-preserved medieval centre, built by the dukes of Malaspina who ruled Massa for three centuries, holding sway over the entire region. The core is the Piazza degli Aranci, edged with orange trees and presided over by the elegant 17th-century Palazzo Cybo Malaspina, with airy courtyard loggias where cultural events are staged in summer. Beyond

Map on page 144

The impressive Ponte della Maddalena that spans the Serchio just south of Bagni di Lucca is also known as the Ponte del Diavolo, or Devil's Bridge. Legend has it that the bridge-builder appealed to the devil for assistance. The devil agreed, but in return demanded the soul of the first to cross the bridge. The shrewd builder kept his promise by sending a dog across.

BELOW: the Serchio river at Bagni di Lucca.

TIP

Between Carrara and
Marina di Carrara is a
marble museum, the
Museo Civico di Marmo
(open Oct–Apr Mon–
Sat 9am–5pm, May,
June and Sept Mon–
Sat 10am–6pm, July
and Aug 10am–8pm;
closed Sun; entrance
fee). Displays include
many varieties of
marble and granite,
geographical and
historical exhibits as
well as some modern
sculptures.

BELOW RIGHT: cutting
giant blocks of marble.

a cluster of narrow winding streets
stands the Duomo. It was begun in the
13th century, but now has a baroque
interior and a modern marble façade.
The crypt, where the Malaspinas
were entombed, is a museum.

Massa is dominated by the magnificent Renaissance **Castello
Malaspina** (open mid-June–Sept
Tues–Sun 9.30am–12.30pm, 5.30–
8pm, Oct–May Sat 9.30am–
12.30pm, Sun 3–6.30pm; entrance
fee). Beyond the narrow old streets
of the town, walk on up through leafy
lanes past decaying villas dotted over
the mountainside. The walls of the
old fortress provide marvellous
views, and welded onto it is a graceful Renaissance palace, its delicate
marble pillars and frescoes providing
a powerful contrast to the grim towers of the original castle.

The main evidence of the famous
marble quarries in **Carrara** ㉓ is the
river of white mud that flows through
the town, which has a dusty, dis-
affected air about it. It is a working
town, not a monument to marble;
there are few fine marble statues to be
seen. Even the **Duomo** – with dis-

tinctive features like its 14th-century
rose window, Pisan-style façade and,
inside, the 14th-century statue of the
Annunciation – is in need of cleaning.

The interesting sights are within
a few streets of one another. Worth
visiting is the **Accademia delle
Belle Arti** (open Tues–Sat 9.30am–
12.30pm; free), a 16th-century Malaspina residence built around an older
medieval castle. To view the galleries
you need permission from the director, but a brief reconnaissance will
reveal splendid marble bas-reliefs on
the walls and sculptures from the Roman site of Luni, as well as a Roman
altar found in the marble quarries.

In nearby Piazza Alberica are two
imposing 17th-century *palazzi,* and
here every July there is a massive
symposium of work in marble. Carrara also holds a biennial sculpture
exhibition and an annual International Marble and Machinery Fair.

Finally, in a scruffy area off the
Via Aurelia north of Carrara, there
is **Luni,** the original Roman settlement from which marble was
shipped**.** There is an amphitheatre
and museum, and excavations have

Marble Mountains

The fine-grained pure white marble for which Carrara is
renowned has been quarried here since Roman times. Italian
medieval churches are decorated with marble from Carrara, and
it has supplied artists from Michelangelo to Henry Moore with raw
material. Formed from limestone, hardened by great pressure and
heat, Carrara marble is still the world's single largest and most
important source of the stone. About 200 quarries are still func-
tioning, while over a thousand have been worked out or abandoned. They are scattered across three steep valleys: the
Colonnata, Fantiscritti and Ravaccione. Here the villages cling to
the mountainside that has been sliced away like chunks of
cheese.There are extraordinary views down into the quarries,
where precarious-looking staircases are strung across the sides,
and massive trucks trundle across the marble surface far below.
Since the Parco Apuane has been given national park status, opposition by environmentalists to the speed of extraction has height-
ened. However, the quarry owners continue to fight back in
protection of their tough and fearless employees.

revealed columns, capitals, mosaic floors and tomb fragments.

Just on the border of Tuscany before heading inland is **Sarzana** ㉔, a bustling market town which has been colonised by artists and is being carefully restored. There is a large market in the Piazza Matteotti, which is surrounded by arcades of Romanesque arches sheltering smart little cafés.

Lunigiana

Luni gave its name to **Lunigiana**, "the land of the moon", an almost undiscovered part of Tuscany which sees few tourists and makes little provision for them. It has always been a main trading route, however, and its many castles were built to extract tolls from pilgrims and merchants by the powerful Malaspina family who controlled the region.

Lunigiana was in the front line of fighting at the end of World War II, and this has left its mark. Since then there has been inevitable rural depopulation, with many people emigrating to the United States. Now, an enlightened attitude to

tourism promises new hope for the area, villages and castles are being restored and the roads are in good repair. There are enough hotels, pensions and local restaurants to make a visit comfortable, but the area's attractions are unlikely ever to generate mass tourism; this will probably help preserve its charm.

It is a mountainous region of steep winding roads, deep wooded valleys and unpolluted, rushing streams. On the lower slopes of the hills vines and olives grow. Narrow valleys are dotted with tiny villages; higher up are forests of oak and the chestnut trees which have provided a staple of the local diet for centuries, and there are deer and wild boar *(cinghiale)* in abundance. The terrain ranges from the busy, productive flat valley of the river Magra to the profound silence of deep river gorges.

The region is famous for its Romanesque churches and intact medieval villages, as well as its castles, many of which are in the process of being restored through government grants. A number have been taken over by artists and sculptors,

Map on page 144

TIP

In August, one of the most important Italian antique markets, *"La soffitta nelle strade"* (the open-air attic), is held in Sarzana, and in August the Cittadella hosts the National Antique Exhibition.

BELOW: a Carrara marble quarry in the Garfagnana.

The fortress at Fosdinovo is one of the region's best-preserved castles.

and are used both as private homes and cultural centres.

The inhabitants of Lunigiana are proud and insular, in rural areas still growing most of their own food, wine and olives, and regarding all other produce with some suspicion. They will buy in grapes from Chianti, making the wine themselves rather than buy an unknown finished product from foreigners.

Fortified villages

Fosdinovo ㉕ is the first fortified village you arrive at as you drive towards Aulla on the winding road from Sarzana. Its little piazzas are shaded by huge chestnut trees, and the steep twisting streets are dominated by the magnificent castle. It is one of the best-preserved castles in the region, despite the fact that it was damaged by Allied fire during World War II. The Germans had a command post there, exploiting its superb strategic position with views from all sides. It was constructed by the Malaspina family between the 13th and 14th centuries with a complicated network of corridors and

loggias. Beautiful frescoed walls and ceilings and furniture have been restored; it is sometimes used for cultural events and is one of the few castles with an interior open to the public on a regular basis (open for guided tours Wed–Mon: summer 11am, noon, 3.30pm, 4.30pm, 5.30pm, 6.30pm, winter 10am– noon, 4–6pm; entrance fee).

Aulla ㉖ itself is the gateway to the Lunigiana region, where the rivers Magra and Taverone meet, but much of it is war-damaged. Of the 10th-century abbey of San Caprasio only the original apse survives. **Brunella**, the *fortezza* of Aulla, broods over the town. It was originally built in the late 15th century as a defensive rather than a residential castle, with walls 3 metres (10 ft) thick, narrow windows and vaulted ceilings. It was restored earlier last century by Montagu Brown, the British consul in Genoa, and now houses a small **Natural History Museum** (open Tues–Sun 9am– noon, 4–7pm summer, 9am–noon, 3–6pm winter; entrance fee). It is accessible up a steep driveway off

Map on page 144

the main Via Nazionale from Aulla, and surrounded by a large park of holm oaks and heather.

Fivizzano ㉗, a few kilometres east of Aulla along the 63 road, is an attractive market town full of elegant Renaissance palaces. The young people of Fivizzano are prominent in the movement to revive folk traditions, and they participate in colourful flag-waving performances, dancing and mock duels, and travel all over Tuscany giving demonstrations.

Near by is the enchanting castle of **Verrucola**, a completely fortified settlement on the banks of the river which has been superbly restored. Little red-roofed houses and narrow medieval streets cluster around the fortified square keep, with geraniums spilling from window boxes and gardens full of zucchini, beans and tomatoes crammed right down to the river's edge.

The castle is thought to date back as far as the 11th century and is distinguished by its two separate fortified towers, erected when the town was divided between two rulers. The 15th-century church, with its peaceful arched loggia, is open to the public on Friday afternoons, but the privately owned castle can only be visited by appointment (tel: 0585-992466).

To the northwest of Fivizzano is **Licciana Nardi** ㉘, an 11th-century fortified town. Much of the town wall is still visible, with narrow passageways running through immensely thick walls into the village. In the Piazza del Municipio, the imposing 16th-century castle dominates the square, and is joined to the graceful baroque church by a small bridge spanning the narrow street. There is a small market held Sunday mornings in the leafy main square.

Above the nearby Taverone river are the hill villages of **Bastia** and **Cisigliana**, good bases for walking, with high meadows and wonderful views out to sea, perfect for picnics and mushrooming. Bastia has a 15th-century fortress built by the Malaspinas, now privately owned.

Along the valley from Licciana is **Crespiano**, with a Romanesque church, Santa Maria Assunta di Crespiano, so old that it was restored in 1079.

Comano ㉙ is an important base for walking and riding, and near by is the Castello of Comano, a ruined, malevolent-looking tower surrounded by a tiny farming community, with ducks and chickens wandering the streets, and steep steps up to the tower.

Remote villages

At the end of the valley is **Camporaghena** ㉚, the last outpost before the Apennines, where there is a sad war memorial in the church. When German soldiers came hunting escaped prisoners of war and partisans, the priest rang the church bell as a warning and was summarily shot for his brave deed.

Monti is a tiny village with a particularly charming domesticated

Lunigiana is a popular area for property hunters, although the locals still find it hard to understand the appeal of a ruined farmhouse. One English purchaser, deciding that the farmer's cowshed spoilt his view, offered to buy it along with the farm. But the farmer wanted more money for the shed than for the farm; the house was his grandparents', falling down and no use to him, but the cowshed was his livelihood!

BELOW: cooling off in the river near Pontrémoli.

The church of Pieve di Sorano, near Filattiera.

BELOW: Bagnone.

castle, complete with geraniums, lace curtains and even a street number on the door. It is well restored, with its original gateway, keep and towers, and is apparently still used as a summer residence by a surviving member of the Malaspina family. The church of Santa Maria Assunta di Venelia has an apse in *pietra serena* (the local grey "sacred stone") dating from the 12th century.

Pallerone is famous for its crib, which can be seen in the church on request. It is an extraordinary clockwork nativity scene which changes from night to day and has a huge cast of busy clockwork characters, the Holy Family, angels, millers, blacksmiths and fishermen.

A 16-km (10-mile) drive south of Fivizzano brings you to **Equi Terme**, a popular spa resort smelling strongly of sulphur, with restorative waters that are claimed to have radioactive properties. If you follow the path through the old village tucked into the mountain gorge, you reach a bridge and a waterfall and the high-roofed caves called **Buca del Cane** (guided tours daily June–Sept, Sun only Oct–May or by appointment; tel: 0585-948269), where the remains of palaeolithic men, dogs and even lions and leopards were found.

Close to Aulla is another fine castle, **Podenzana** (private; closed to the public), a well-proportioned, triangular white building, massively restored in the 18th century after an explosion in the powder room. The castle is at the top of a steep hill, and near by is an excellent local restaurant which specialises in the regional dish of *panigacci*, chestnut-flour pancakes cooked over an open wood fire and served with creamy cheese and home-cured meats. Every year, from 5–15 August, the Sagra del Panigaccio (Festival of the Panigaccio) is celebrated in Podenzana.

The Magra valley

Along the main road (SS62) up the Magra valley between Aulla and Pontrémoli are many fascinating villages and castles, all within just a few kilometres. The small villages tend not to have facilities such as shops, restaurants or even bars, so if in need of refreshment try Villafranca or Bagnone.

Villafranca in Lunigiana ㉛ lies in a strategic position near a ford over the River Magra and has some remaining medieval streets. But its 12th-century castle is in ruins, destroyed during World War II, and only parts of the keep and outer walls remain. The church of San Francesco has a terracotta of the school of della Robbia, and there is an interesting **Ethnographic Museum** (open Tues–Sat 9am–12.30pm, 3–6pm; entrance fee) in an old watermill near the river, which specialises in exhibits of typical local rural activities such as weaving, crafts and woodwork.

Bagnone ㉜ is a large, attractive town of Renaissance palaces, wide streets and cool shady arcades with a number of little bars and cafés. A

honeycomb of houses, arches and passageways leads down to the river bank and tiny gardens. The 15th-century village of Bagnone is clustered on the hillside above, surrounding the cylindrical tower of the Castello and a fine 15th-century campanile. There is an exquisitely carved wooden pulpit in the church of San Nicolò a Bagnone.

Nearby **Filetto** is a delightful, totally symmetrical, square-walled village with a tower at each corner. Almost every street is linked by covered overhead passages or bridges. Originally a defensive structure, it is now quite cosy, with cats snoozing in corners and village women passing the time of day.

Malgrate and **Filattiera** ㉝ are also worth a detour, and near by, next to the main highway, is a magnificent Romanesque church, **Pieve di Sorano.** The nave is ruinous and has been turned into a cemetery, but in the main apse is a very simple and beautiful little chapel.

Mulazzo ㉞ was the headquarters of a branch of the Malaspina family which had territories to the west of the river Magra; their arms are emblazoned over a fine arched doorway which guards the steep steps up to the town. Fragments of the original walls are left, and in the upper part of the town the narrow streets widen into charming little squares which are overlooked by elegant loggias and their inhabitants.

The town of **Pontrémoli** ㉟ was once divided in two to separate the warring factions of the Guelfs and Ghibellines, and the Castruccio fortress, built in 1332, similarly divides the town. There are rich medieval townhouses, and the church of the Annunziata has a 16th-century octagonal marble temple by Sansovino.

The **Castello del Piagnaro** houses the fascinating **Museo delle Statue-Stele** (open Tues–Sun 9am–12.30pm, 3–6pm in summer, 9am–12.30pm, 2.30–5.30pm in winter; entrance fee). Some 20 pre-historic statues or menhirs found in the area are on display, the oldest of which date from 3000 BC. Pontrémoli is also famous for its travelling booksellers, and awards the Bancarella literary prize each July. ❑

TIP

At almost every turn there are more medieval villages, more castles, more breathtaking views. One of the best ways to see this rich and varied region is to take the little train between Aulla and Lucca on its slow journey through the mountains.

Map on page 144

RESTAURANTS

Carrara

Il Trillo
Via Bergiola Vecchia 30
Località Castegnetola
Tel: 0585-46755
www.iltrillo.net
A restaurant in the hills above industrial Massa, 7 km (4 miles) south of Carrara, Il Trillo is set in a lemon grove with sea views. The food is traditional and plentiful. Closed Sun and Mon lunch in summer, Mon in winter. €€

Ninan
Via Lorenzo Bartolini 3
Tel: 0585-74741
Sophisticated gourmet dining, where the young chef, Marco Garfagnini, has won a Michelin star for his excellent Tuscan cuisine. Must book. Closed Mon. €€€€

Bagni di Lucca

Corona
Frazione Ponte a Serraglio
Tel: 0583-805151
Overlooking the Lima river, this charming restaurant specialises in local cuisine and seafood dishes. In warm weather there is a pleasant terrace for alfresco dining. Closed Wed in winter, mid-Jan–mid Feb. Must book. €€–€€€

Marina di Massa

Blue Inn
Via Fortino di San Francesco 9, Località Partaccia (4 km from Massa)
Tel: 0585-240060
Modern creative cuisine from a young chef whose speciality is fish. The extensive wine list includes regional offerings, as well as the great Tuscan reds. Closed Sun, Mon in summer, 2–15 Jan and 1–15 Nov. €€€

Pontrémoli

Cà del Moro
Via Casa Corvi 9
Tel: 0187-830588
Charming restaurant serving regional Tuscan specialities. Popular with golfers. Also has rooms. Closed Sun evening and Mon, two weeks Jan and Nov. €€–€€€

● ● ● ● ● ● ● ● ● ● ● ●
Average cost of a 3-course =
dinner and half-bottle of wine.
€€€€ = over €60, **€€€** =
€40–60, **€€** = €25–40,
€ under €25

PISA AND ENVIRONS

Beyond the iconic Leaning Tower and "Field of Miracles", this ancient city and its province have much to offer

Firenze
Pisa

Threw the Leaning Tower draws tourists to Pisa like a magnet, many of them pausing to appreciate the religious architecture, others to enjoy the glorious art and history of this Tuscan city. Once a thriving Roman port, Pisa's harbour had silted up in the 15th century, and it now stands on the Arno river, 10 km (6 miles) from the coast. Great sea battles were fought during the Middle Ages, with the city-state of Pisa becoming first an ally then a rival of a number of other states, including Genoa, Lucca, Venice and Florence. At its height, Pisa's power extended to Sardinia, Corsica and the Balearic Islands. Trade with Muslim Spain, North Africa and the Lebanon proved a rich source of money and ideas. Arabic numerals were introduced to Europe through Pisa, and the city's major architectural monuments – the Leaning Tower, the Duomo and Baptistery – show the clear influence of Islamic architecture.

Pisa ❶ is split in two by the gently curving river Arno, its steep stone banks coloured by floating green algae. Elegant 16th-century *palazzi* along the banks hide the less imposing buildings and general decay in the narrow streets and alleys behind. Crossing the original city bridge, Ponte della Citadella, the Via Nicola Pisano leads to the **Campo**

dei Miracoli (Field of Miracles), a green swathe of manicured grass in the northwestern corner of the city walls with probably the most perfect assemblage of religious buildings anywhere. The Campo dei Miracoli ticket office (open daily 9.30am–30 min before last Leaning Tower climb) to the north side of the Leaning Tower sells tickets to all the sites.

The Leaning Tower

Visitors flock from all over the world to marvel at the phenomenon of the

Maps
City: 156
Area: 160

LEFT: Italy's icon.
BELOW: Pisa's eventful Regatta di San Ranieri, held in June.

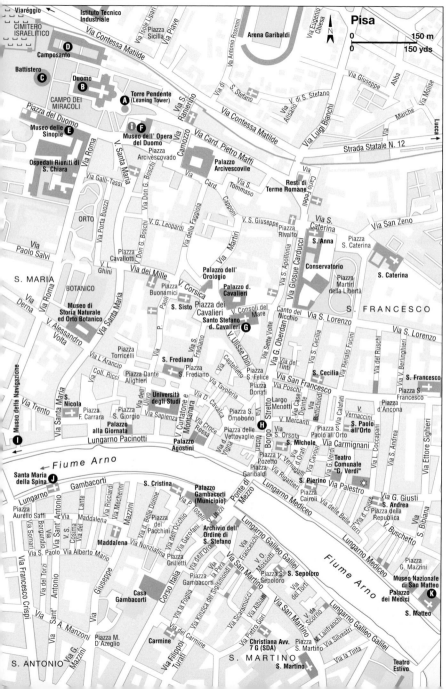

Pisa

Torre Pendente (open daily Apr–Sept 8am–8pm, Mar, Oct 9am–6pm, Nov–Feb 10am–5pm; advance bookings www.opapisa.it/boxoffice; it may be possible to buy tickets on the day from the Campo dei Miracoli ticket office on the north side of the Tower, open daily 9.30am–6.30pm; no entry to children under eight, and children between eight and twelve must be held by the hand; *see right*). The best place to catch your first sight of the 12th-century Campanile is through the archway of the Porta Santa Maria, otherwise known as the Porta Nuova. When the sun is shining, the whiteness dazzles; when raining, it glistens.

The Cathedral

The **Duomo** ⓑ (open Nov–Feb Mon–Sat 10am–1pm, 2–5pm, Sun and hols 3–5pm; Mar Mon–Sat 10am–6pm, until 8pm from 21 Mar, Sun and hols from 1pm; Apr–Sept Mon–Sat 10am–8pm, Sun and hols from 1pm; Oct Mon–Sat 10am–7pm, Sun and hols from 1pm; entrance fee – free on Sun and hols), built between 1068 and 1118, is one

of the major monuments in Italy. The beautiful white-marble façade, the model for the Pisan Romanesque style, is set with mosaics, inlaid marble and glass stones.

The tomb of Buscheto, the architect of the building, is set above eye level on the left of the façade, designed by Rainaldo and built in the early 12th century. The 16th-century bronze doors are surrounded by frames enlivened by animals. The main entrance to the Duomo was intended to be through the bronze transept doors of the Porta di San Ranieri, near the Tower. The work of Bonanno Pisano, dating from 1180, they are decorated with 24 New Testament vignettes, including such delightful scenes as shepherds in their conical caps playing their pipes to soothe the newborn child, and the figures of the Apostles under swaying palm trees.

The rich complexity of the Cathedral interior is created by the forest of pillars rising to arches of banded white-and-grey stone, and the colourful mix of altar paintings and Cimabue's apsidal mosaic, from

Maps
City: 156
Area: 160

TIP

The number of visitors to the Leaning Tower is strictly controlled, and each tour is restricted to 30 minutes. There are 181 steps to the first observation gallery, 36 steps to the second, 35 very narrow steps to the third, and the final flight of 37 steps is up a very narrow spiral staircase to the top balcony. No bags or containers are allowed while climbing the tower.

BELOW LEFT: climb to the top of the Tower for fabulous views.

Halting the Tilt

Pisa's landmark building, the Torre Pendente, really does lean to a frightening degree. Detractors have often accused Pisa of deliberately building the tower on a slant to attract attention. In reality, the unstable subsoil that underlies the Piazza dei Miracoli has caused all the buildings to tilt and subside to dizzying effect. Just to the right of the entrance to the Tower is a date stone inscribed ANDMI MCLXXIII (standing for Anno Domini 1173), the year in which building work started on the Campanile. But work stopped at the third stage because the building was already collapsing. A century later, three more stages were added, deliberately constructed to tilt in the opposite direction, so the Tower has a decided kink as well as a tilt.

By 1989 the Tower was leaning to such a perilous degree that it was in danger of collapse. It was promptly closed to the public, and an international team of engineers spent the next decade in a battle to save it. In 2001, work to stabilise the Leaning Tower was pronounced a success, and, after more than a decade under wraps, the Tower reopened to the public.

TIP

Pisa's annual Anima
Mundi festival is a
celebration of sacred
music, with concerts
by world-class musi-
cians staged in the
Duomo. This acclaimed
event runs from mid-
Sept to the mid-Oct.
For information and
bookings tel: 050-387
2229/2210, or visit
www.opapisa.it.

BELOW: the pink glow
of sunset on the
Campo dei Miracoli.

1302. The beautiful **marble pulpit**
by Giovanni Pisano (1301–11) is a
masterpiece. Supported by figures
representing prophets, Sibyls and
allegorical figures, its crowded and
dramatic marble panels depict
scenes from the *Life of Christ*.

Hanging from the westernmost
arch of the great dome is Galileo's
Lamp, so called because its pendu-
lum movement is said to have
inspired Galileo to discover the rota-
tion of the earth (in reality, the lamp
wasn't here in Galileo's time).

The Baptistery

Across from the Rainaldo façade is
the third building of the Duomo
complex: the **Battistero** ⓒ (open
daily, Apr–Sept 8am–8pm, Oct
9am–7pm, Nov–Feb 10am–5pm,
Mar variable hours; entrance fee),
the largest baptistery in Italy, with
richly decorated exterior niches and
statues of saints. The interior is far
plainer, but it has one great treasure:
Nicola Pisano's **pulpit** of 1260,
carved with scenes from the *Life of
Christ*, clearly influenced by ancient
Roman art (the source for which we

shall see next, in the Camposanto).
Mary, for example, has the long
neck, veil and ringlets typical of
middle-aged matrons in Roman portraiture. You may be lucky enough
during your visit to hear one of the
attendants demonstrate the Baptistery's remarkable acoustics – they
tend to do it when groups of visitors
are present. As four or more individual notes are sung, the long echo
allows them to build up to a complete chord that rings eerily round
the dome.

Camposanto

The fourth element of the Duomo
group is the **Camposanto** ⓓ (opening hours same as the Baptistery;
entrance fee), one of the world's
most beautiful cemeteries. The
graceful white-marble cloister is
paved with the grave slabs of
medieval Pisans, carved with coats
of arms or tools of their trade.
Roman sarcophagi, imported from
the Holy Land and reused as coffins
for wealthy Pisans, line the walls,
carved with the mythological scenes
that inspired the pulpits of Nicola

and Giovanni Pisano. Frescoes damaged by incendiary bombs during World War II have been restored to their original positions. They include a grim series of images (1360–80) inspired by the Black Death, on the themes of the *Last Judgement* and the *Triumph of Death*.

On the opposite side of the Piazza dei Miracoli is the **Museo delle Sinopie** **E** (open daily Nov–Feb 9am–4.30pm, Mar, Oct 9am–5.30pm, Apr–Sept 8am–7.30pm; entrance fee), where you can learn more about the Camposanto frescoes and how they were created by laying down a sketch on the plaster undercoat using red paint (called *sinopia* because the pigment came from Sinope on the Black Sea). When the final thin layer of white plaster was applied, the *sinopia* sketch showed through and guided the artists as they completed the fresco in full colour.

The fire which followed the bombing of the Camposanto destroyed some of the frescoes and left the others in so precarious a condition that it was necessary to remove them – but that was how the immense *sinopie* lying beneath the frescoes came to light and were salvaged, and now carefully restored.

The Cathedral Works Museum

Last on the itinerary of the piazza is the **Museo dell'Opera del Duomo** **F** (same hours as Baptistery; entrance fee) – the Cathedral Works Museum. Room 1 contains casts of the foundation stones of each of the buildings and a chronology, which begins in 1064 with the start of work on the Cathedral, followed by the Baptistery in 1154, the Campanile in 1173, and the Camposanto a century later, in 1277. This short burst of fireworks was followed by swift decline as the city's harbour silted up. (Recent excavations have revealed Roman and medieval boats, complete with cargoes, preserved in the waterlogged silt, now exhibited in the maritime museum; *see page 161*). By 1406, the city had been conquered by Florence and was about to be eclipsed culturally by that city's determination to build

Maps
City: 156
Area: 160

TIP

A couple of minutes' walk from the Campo dei Miracoli is the Orto Botanico di Pisa (Botanical Gardens; Via L. Ghini 5; tel: 221 1316; open Mon–Fri 8am–1pm, 2–5.30pm, Sat 8am–1pm; entrance fee). Founded in the 1540s, these are the oldest botanical gardens in Europe. Now part of Pisa University, they offer a tranquil place to relax, right in the heart of Pisa.

BELOW: souvenir-hunting nuns.

Around Pisa, Livorno and the Maremma Pisana

even bigger and bolder monuments.

The museum is packed with 12th–15th-century sculptures and paintings: Giovanni Pisano's ivory *Virgin and Child* (1299) is one of the highlights, using the natural shape of the ivory tusk to give the Virgin her naturalistic stance. There are models to show the construction techniques used to build the domed Baptistery, and to explain the marble-inlay technique used to give all the buildings their intricate exterior decoration. Best of all, the rooms of the museum open out onto a quiet shady cloister, with a spectacular view of the Leaning Tower and the Cathedral.

Piazza dei Cavalieri

Students often congregate on the **Piazza dei Cavalieri**, one of the most attractive squares in the city. This was the centre of activity of the Pisan Republic. It was in one of the towers of the Palazzo dell'Orologio (the building with the clock to the north of the square) – so we learn from Dante's *Inferno* – that Count Ugolino, wrongly convicted of treason in 1284, was left to starve to death with his sons. The square is named after the order of knights *(cavalieri)* founded by Cosimo I (1561), to fight the Turks in the Mediterranean. The duke gave its members the **Palazzo della Carovana**, the former council chambers of the Pisan Commune. The magnificent sgraffito decoration (floral patterns, coats of arms, symbols) and the next-door church of **Santo Stefano dei Cavalieri** Ⓖ (open summer daily 10am–7pm, winter Mon–Sat 11am–4.30pm, Sun 11.30am–5.30pm, the church often closes unannounced during these times; entrance fee) were based on plans by Vasari (1511–74). In 1606 Giovanni de' Medici added the marble façade and placed the knights' emblem above the great doorway. Displayed inside are trophies and spoils of war from Pisan naval victories against the Ottomans.

To the Arno

The lively area of alleyways and shopping streets between the square and the Arno is known as the **Borgo Stretto quarter** . The arcaded Borgo Stretto opens out at Piazza Garibaldi and the Ponte di Mezzo.

To the west, some distance along the river, the **Museo delle Navi Romane** ❶ (Lungarno Simonelli; closed for restoration at time of publication; entrance fee) in the Medici Arsenale, the old Medici shipyards, houses the finds from the ongoing excavation of Pisa's ancient port, buried by silt in the 15th century. In 1998, workers expanding the railway station stumbled on the site where the remains of 10 ancient Roman ships and their contents (including the skeleton of a sailor) have been unearthed. These docklands where the sea met the Arno were probably composed of marshy flatlands and lagoon, very similar to Venice. Proclaimed a "marine Pompeii", excavations and restorations continue so this remarkable archaeological site is called an "exhibition in progress".

On the opposite bank of the Arno, across the Ponte Solferino, stands the church of **Santa Maria della - Spina** ❿ (open Mar–Oct Tues–Sun 10am–1.30pm, 2.30–6pm, Sat and Sun until 7pm, Nov–Feb Tues–Sun 10am–2pm). Don't worry if it is closed when you visit: it is the vivacious exterior that is the most important feature, a tour de force of Gothic pinnacles and niches, crowded with statues of saints carved by members of the Pisano family from 1230. Back in the days when Pisa was a port, before its harbour silted up, seafarers came to pray before setting sail.

The chapel once guarded what was believed to be a thorn *(spina)* from the crown of Jesus, but that relic, plus the original statues, are now housed in the **Museo Nazionale di San Matteo** ⓚ (Lungarno Mediceo; open daily Tues–Sat 9am–7pm, Sun 9am–12.30pm; entrance fee), downriver. Set in rooms around the cloister of a medieval church, the museum contains such treasures as Masaccio's *St Paul* (1426), a contemplative man with a high brow, hooked nose

Maps
City: 156
Area: 160

TIP

Borgo Stretto is an elegant street in the old town, lined with shops and cafés. Off its southern end, the arcaded Piazza delle Vettovaglie, is the site of a daily produce market. In the evening the reasonably priced bars and cafés are the haunt of students from Pisa University.

BELOW: Piazza dei Cavalieri.

TIP

In mid-June Pisa holds its Regatta di San Ranieri, where boat races (with competitors in medieval costume) and processions of brilliantly decorated boats are held on the river Arno. The evening before the regatta is the Luminaria di San Ranieri, at which tens of thousands of candles and torches are placed on the buildings along the river – a stunning sight.

BELOW: the Arno cuts Pisa in two.

and patriarchal beard; Donatello's bust reliquary for San Rossore; and a whole room of glowing Renaissance paintings by such artists as Gozzoli and Ghirlandaio. There is a collection of antique armour used in the *Gioco del Ponte* (a medieval tug-of-war held annually on the last Sunday in June), which comprises breastplates, helmets and other pieces dating from the 15th and 16th centuries.

The Pisan coast

The pretty road from Pisa to the coast pauses here and there at railway crossings as it follows the Arno to the sea. About 6 km (4 miles) southwest of Pisa, it passes **San Piero a Grado**, a magnificent basilica which would once have overlooked the sea. Legend has it that this is the spot where St Peter first set foot on Italian soil. The fresco cycle in the nave shows scenes from the Apostle's life.

The road reaches the sea at **Bocca d'Arno ❷**, where hanging trawl nets and the rods of silent fishermen evoke the atmosphere captured by artists like Nino Costa and Gabriele

d'Annunzio. To the south, the pleasant old-fashioned bathing resort of **Marina di Pisa** is a fascinatingly run-down place. There's not much beach left, and swimming isn't recommended these days because of pollution from the Arno estuary. But a stroll along the beach promenade or a cappuccino in one of the many cafés can be quite enjoyable. On a clear day the two offshore islands of Gorgona and Capraia can be made out in the distance.

Five kilometres south down the coast at **Tirrenia ❸** is a stretch of Mediterranean pine forest – the one place where building has been prohibited. The trees act as a natural barrier against the *libeccio*, a strong southwesterly wind, reducing it to a light, scented breeze of pine and juniper which cools the air on hot summer days. As a much larger resort than Marina di Pisa, Tirrenia offers luxury hotels, boarding houses and campsites. Nightclubs, restaurants and sporting facilities for golf, tennis, horse riding, fishing, windsurfing, sailing and rowing are enjoyed by Tuscans, but few for-

eigners take holidays along this coast. Each year colourful regattas and boat races are held, and the training centre for the Italian National Olympics is based in Tirrenia.

Inland retreats

Midway between Pisa and Lucca, at the foot of the Pisan mountains, is the spa town of **San Giuliano Terme ④**. Olives, chestnuts and pines grow in the surrounding fertile countryside, wild horses roam the hills and a number of ruins are dotted among the valleys. San Giuliano is renowned for the curative powers of its thermal springs and mud. A good place to try out a thermal spa treatment, or simply indulge in some pampering, is the atmospheric Bagni di Pisa spa resort *(see page 287)*.

Set in lush green countryside, near Calci 10 km (6 miles) east of Pisa, is **Certosa di Pisa ⑤** (open Tues–Sat 9am–6.30pm, Sun 9am–noon; entrance fee), the Charterhouse of Pisa, founded in 1366. From the end of that century modifications and additions were continually made to the Carthusian monastery,

until the final touches were finished in the early 18th century.

The Carthusians were one of the new strict orders who believed the increasing prosperity of the Cluniac orders was accompanied by a decline in religious observance. Their architecture reflected this; the monks lived in separate cells within a main enclosure. The centre of monastic life was the Great Cloister, of which the Certosa di Pisa has a particularly fine example. Work on the frescoes of the church walls began in 1701 and in 1718 workmen from Carrara carved the marble and renovated the church façade. In 1981 a part of the Charterhouse was allotted to the University of Pisa to house the **Museum of Natural and Regional History** (open mid-July–mid-Sept Tues–Fri 10am–7pm, Sat and Sun until 8pm, Aug Tues–Thur 4–8pm, Fri 4pm–midnight, Sat–Sun 10am–midnight; mid-Sept–mid-July Mon–Sat 9am–6pm, Sun 10am–7pm; entrance fee).

Entering **Cascina ⑥** past fields of sunflowers, grapevines and maize, the roads are lined with plane trees. Cascina is proud of its solid stone

Maps
City: 156
Area: 160

The spa waters of San Giuliano Terme have been famous since Roman times, and are supposed to be especially good for the treatment of rheumatism and arthritis. Montaigne, Byron and Shelley were among famous visitors of the past.

BELOW: trawl nets at sunset.

Maps
City: 156
Area: 160

The original spa building at Casciana Terme was designed in 1870 by Poggi, but a direct hit from a bomb in World War II left only the façade and the hall intact. In 1968 the spa (pictured below) was completely rebuilt around the remains of the original structure.

BELOW: Casciana Terme's modern spa.

walls, dating from 1142, which are depicted in Vasari's energetic painting of the *Battle of Cascina*, now hanging in the Palazzo Vecchio in Florence. The town is centred round the production of wooden furniture. At the end of the arcaded main street, Corso Matteotti, there is a large factory with *MOSTRA DEI MOBILI* displayed in huge letters and containing a permanent furniture exhibition. Yet most of the workshops are tucked away in the pretty side streets. To find out more about the town's tradition of wood craftsmanship, visit the **Museo dei Mestieri e Arti del Legno** (Via Tosco Romagnolo, 238; tel: 050-701530; open Mon 9.30am–12.30pm, Tues–Sun 9.30am–12.30pm, 3–8pm; free).

Leaving the Mostra and walking up Corso Matteotti, the tiny chapel of **Suore di Carmelitane di Santa Teresa** on the left has beautifully detailed frescoes. The nearby church of the Saints Casciano and Giovanni, *c.*970, is a graceful building with a simple interior.

Casciana Terme ⓐ, less than 40 km (25 miles) from Pisa, is surrounded by flourishing vineyards, olive groves and peach orchards. The beautiful hillsides and the mild climate provide a relaxing atmosphere. The town exists solely for the **spa** (www.termedicasciana.it; tel: 0587-64461), and the pace of life is leisurely. The thermal waters attract people seeking a break, as well as those "taking the cure".

The country around Casciana Terme is good for walking, especially in the nearby pine woods of Pineta della Farnia. The village of **Colle Montanino di Ceppato**, which has a 1,000-year-old tower, and **Pariascia,** which has a fortress, are both within easy reach, and a visit to the **Sanctuary of the Madonnina Dei Monti** might serve to restore the spirit.

At **Crespina ❽** and **Fauglia ❾** are several magnificent 19th-century villas, as well as the church of **Chianni** and the nearby **Lari Castle** (opening times vary; tel: 0587-684085; e-mail: info@castellodilari .it; www.castellodilari.it), which is heavily adorned with medieval coats of arms and family crests. ❑

RESTAURANTS

Marina di Pisa

Da Gino
Via delle Curzolari 2
Tel: 050-35408
Excellent fish restaurant near the sea; dishes simply prepared and delicious. Popular with both locals and tourists. Closed Mon and Tues and Sept. €€–€€€

Foresta
Via Litoreana 2
Tel: 050-311116
www.ristoranteforesta.it
Overlooking the sea, this little family-run restaurant serves gourmet cuisine. The specialities are fish and seafood. Must book as covers are limited. Closed Sun evening and Thur. €€€

Pisa

A Casa Mia
Via Provinciale Vicarese 10
Ghezzano (just outside Pisa)
Tel: 050-879265
Very pleasant, family-run restaurant set in a little villa. Freshest ingredients form the basis of the traditional Tuscan cuisine, but with creative flourishes. Closed Sat lunch and Sun, 1–7 Jan and Aug. €€

Al Ristoro dei Vecchi Macelli
Via Volturno 49
Tel: 050-20424
Famous restaurant with a cosy ambience. Try the *Menu di Primi*, which involves a succession of

pasta dishes. Must book. Closed Sun lunch and Wed. €€€

Da Bruno
Via Bianchi 12
Tel: 050-560818
www.anticatrattoriadabruno.it
Tuscan and Pisan flavours are the hallmarks of the cuisine in this atmospheric and popular restaurant. Closed Mon evening and Tues. €€–€€€

Il Campano
Via Cavalca 19
Tel: 050-580585
Set in a quiet spot by the marketplace, this restaurant dating back to medieval times specialises in fish, seafood and pasta. In summer its terrace is a pleasant setting for dining alfresco. Good wine list. Closed Wed and Thur lunch. €€

La Clessidra
Via Santa Cecilia 34
Tel: 050-540160
Typical Tuscan flavours feature at this pleasing and popular restaurant in an elegant part of town. Booking advised. Closed Sat lunch, Sun, Christmas–early Jan and Aug. €€

Osteria dei Cavalieri
Via San Frediano 16
Tel: 050-580858
www.osteriacavalieri.pisa.it
Modern restaurant near Piazza dei Cavalieri where fish is the speciality. A simpler menu is offered at lunchtimes.

Excellent value. Booking essential. Closed Sat lunch, Sun and Aug. €€

Osteria del Porton Rosso
Via Porton Rosso 11
Tel: 050-580566
A brother-and-sister team create excellent fish dishes in the centre of Pisa. Booking recommended for this rustic and gastronomic find. Closed Sun. €€

Sergio
Via Aurelia, Località Madonna dell' Acqua (4 km/2 miles out of town on the SS1)
Tel: 050-894068
One of the old glories of Italian restaurants and one of the best in Tuscany. Impeccable service is matched by excellent dining with specialities from both land and sea. Reservation advised.

Closed Sun, Mon lunchtime and 22 Dec–mid-Jan. €€€–€€€€

Tirrenia

Dante e Ivana
Via del Tirreno 207c
Tel/fax: 050-32549
www.danteeivana.com
Pleasant fish restaurant with an open kitchen and a tank from which to choose the ingredients of your meal. Closed Sun and Mon, 20 Dec–end Jan. €€€

RIGHT: fresh pasta, fresh pesto – the simpler the better.

LIVORNO AND THE MAREMMA PISANA

There's more to the unsung province of Livorno than the grimy ports that mar its reputation. Scratch beneath the surface and you'll find Etruscan ruins, scenic coastal stretches, forgotten hill towns and great fish restaurants. Even the industrial landscapes have their own fascination

The central coastal area of Tuscany is dominated by the busy comings and goings at the port of Livorno, just south of Pisa. This is the Tuscan gateway to the sea and a city crossed by canals. South of here is the area known as the Maremma Pisana – once a mosquito-infested swampland but now transformed – and the Etruscan coast, the "Costa degli Etruschi". Over 60 miles of coastline, Etruscan sites, medieval villages, hills, valleys and wild woods make this lesser-known part of Tuscany unique.

With barely enough Renaissance art to enliven an overcast beach holiday, Livorno should be on the defensive. In fact, the province is as varied as its famed fish soup, *cacciucco*. The fishy ingredients, a little of everything in the right proportions, apply to Livorno's seascapes. Captured in moody canvases by the Tuscan Impressionists, the rocky northern coast is as dramatic as the southern coast is soothing. The mainland stretches from wild, marshy Maremma to the rugged, hilly interior, or the Elban mountains. It was from Livorno that Shelley set sail on his fatal journey of 8 July 1822.

Livorno province is no architectural desert: a coastline of Pisan watchtowers and Medicean fortresses hides the occasional Roman villa or Etruscan necropolis. Inland, the neglected hilltop villages inspired equally romantic verse from Carducci, Livorno's greatest poet. Livorno is rich in Romanesque and baroque architecture, but the lone sanctuary or homely red-painted farmhouse are truer to the province's individuality.

Livorno city

Livorno , now Italy's second-largest port after Genoa, owes its existence to the silting up of Pisa in the

Map on page 160

LEFT: the old port of Livorno. **BELOW:** a Livornese fisherman inspecting his nets.

15th century; the Livornese joke that, unlike their rivals, the Pisans, they will never be so careless as to let the sea slip away from them. The rivalry between Pisans and Livornese is legendary and very much alive today. There is a saying in Livorno: *"Meglio un morto in casa che un Pisano all'uscio"* – "It is better to have a dead body in your house than a Pisan on the doorstep."

In 1421 the Florentines paid the Genoese 100,000 florins for Livorno, a vast sum for such a malaria-infested and mosquito-ridden village. It was the enlightened Cosimo I who, in 1575, transformed Livorno into the greatest Medicean port. Cosimo was aided by Buontalenti, whose plan for the "ideal city" envisaged the present star-shaped port with its five bastions. Grand Duke Ferdinando employed Robert Dudley, the great naval engineer, to build the harbour walls and administer the port. Dudley benefited from Livorno's status as an "open city", with free trade, tax exemption and shelter from persecution. As late as the 19th century it was an enterpris-

ing yet patrician city. Cosmopolitan salons, elegant avenues, Renaissance and baroque villas made it a fashionable port of call for the Grand Tourists. But after 80 bombing raids in World War II, Livorno resembles a modern necropolis.

The port

Visitors soon realise that the city lives on commerce, not tourism. A baffling one-way street system and gruff hotel and restaurant service do not encourage you to linger, and most tourists who choose to spend the night here are en route to the islands, the hills or to Florence. Livorno is often described as a *città particolare*, an unusual city, and it is hard to visualise it as a medieval town or an attractive seaside resort.

Except for the oyster beds laid down by Cosimo, the Medicean port is unchanged. The crumbling redbrick **Fortezza Vecchia** is a patchwork of Livornese history: Antonio da Sangallo and Buontalenti's masterpiece has Roman remains in its vast Medicean dungeons; 14th-century Pisan walls enclose a small

BELOW: ship-painting, Livorno.

Medicean house and are topped by a Romanesque tower. The **Fortezza Nuova** (open daily 8am–8pm, winter until 5pm; free), built in 1590, completed the Medicis' ambitious fortifications. The murky canals encircling it once led to Pisa. Now restored, the New Fortress hosts conferences, festivals and children's romps through the gardens.

"New Venice"

Between the fortresses is the **Quartiere di Venezia Nuova**, an ill-lit, seedy area not unlike working-class Venice. The canals are lined with 17th-century *palazzi*, crumbling warehouses, fish stands and workshops. The area is not without its charm, however: the Effetto Venezia festival is held here in late July/August with performances, concerts and films. Restaurants serve *cacciucco* all day and are open until late. The area also comes alive in July with the Carnevale Marinaro, more of a water pageant than a race. Escorted by swimmers in carnival masks, bedecked boats follow the maze of canals between the two fortresses and sail under the main square, Piazza Repubblica.

Livorno's museums

South of the centre (1 km / ⅔ mile), the Villa Mimbelli houses the **Museo Civico Giovanni Fattori** (Via San Jacopo in Acquaviva 65; open Tues–Sun 10am–1pm, 4–7pm; entrance fee), near the naval college, a gallery dedicated to the "Macchiaioli Movement", Italy's Impressionist counterpart, led by the artist Giovanni Fattori. While Florence's Pitti Palace has a fuller collection Signorini, Lega and Fattori are well represented here.

The **Centro di Documentazione di Cultura Ebraica** (Via Micali 21; open Sept–June 1st Sun of the month 3–5pm, other days on request, closed Sat; entrance fee) also deserves a mention. The museum dedicated to Tuscany's most important Jewish community has a varied collection of sacred objects, furniture, books, and documents and fragments of the synagogue, destroyed in World War II.

The rocky west coast

Most of the city's artistic and literary pretensions lie in **Ardenza** ⓫ and **Antignano** ⓬. These elegant coastal resorts are part of the Etruscan coast south of Livorno, and merge into their bigger, uglier sister. Most of the beaches are private and fee-paying, and are extremely popular during the summer months. This area was home to much of what the Livornese called "Leghorn's British Factory". The sea views and the dramatic summer storms revived Shelley enough to enable him to work on his blank-verse drama, *The Cenci,* and write his famous "Ode to a Skylark". Byron, living in Ardenza, was a frequent visitor. Ardenza is now a fashionable coastal resort flanked by palms, box hedges and Liberty villas.

From prosperous Antignano, once a mere creek at the foot of the Montenero hills, a road or solar-

Map on page 160

TIP

Trips to the sleepy volcanic island of Capraia are worth looking into if you want to discover somewhere new. It's 64 km (40 miles) off the coast of Livorno – a 2½-hour boat-ride from the port. Ferry services are run by Toremar (www.toremar.it). For more information on the seven islands of the Tuscan Archipelago, *see box on page 182.*

BELOW: the rocky coast south of Livorno.

For a fabulous fish lunch with a sea view, this truck stop on the coast road a few kilometres north of Quercianella is worth knowing about (see page 175).

BELOW: Castiglioncello beach.

powered funicular railway climbs to the **Sanctuary of Madonna di Montenero** (open daily; closed 12.30–2.30pm; free), the patron saint of Tuscany. For those who dare to look, there are spectacular views of Livorno, Elba and even Corsica. Between 1345 and 1774 the original shrine was transformed into a church, which is always full of votive offerings from relics to crutches and gold hearts to hand-written promises. Beside the sanctuary is a deep series of watery grottoes. Outside, elixirs are on sale to gullible visitors who hail from beyond the Madonna's parish.

The high coastal road from Ardenza to Castiglioncello offers some delightful scenic stretches as it hugs the cliffs' edge and dips in and out of tunnels. The coast becomes progressively more rugged, and the road winds past Medici castles, watchtowers and follies. **Castello del Boccale**, encircled by gulls and rocky paths to the shore, is a Medicean fort converted into a private villa. At **Calafuria ⑬**, an isolated Medicean tower and distorted rock formations pro-

vided the Macchiaioli painters with a dramatic setting. But their favourite spot was **Romito**, a grand ducal castle later occupied by the French in 1799. It looks like a whimsical folly, a miniature bandstand perched over the sea, but is not open to visitors.

After exposed Romito, the coastline becomes wild and wooded. As the small bathing resort of **Quercianella ⑭** comes into view, pine woods run down to the water's edge; small coves, shingle beaches and a narrow harbour struggle for space.

Flat sands

Quercianella is followed by the popular rocky resort of **Castiglioncello ⑮**, which the Livornese seem to favour above the long but monotonous stretches of sand below **Cecina**. The Livornese also know that there are sandy bays tucked into the rocks. Cosimo's fort, built on the pine-clad promontory, was designed to keep the pirates at bay, but since the 19th century has drawn to it all the great Italian Impressionists. In the 1930s, Castiglioncello was very popular with film stars. It may not

Map on page 160

have the same cachet today, but it's nice enough for a dip and a cheap lunch at one of the dockside bars.

Rural Maremma

Ignoring Cecina and the vast **California** beach, take the inland road to see the real Maremma. Quiet lanes trace through marshy countryside dotted with red farmhouses and occasional herds of placid white Maremman cattle, and spiral up into the hills. The sun-baked hill town of **Casale Marittimo** ⓰ offers views back across the Livorno coast and out to Elba. **Bibbona** ⓱ is a higgledy-piggledy medieval village traditionally linked to Volterra *(see page 185)*. One of its simple churches, Santa Maria della Pietà, has the odd inscription, *Terribilis Est Locus Iste* (Terrible Is This Place) – either written after a touch of Livornese fever or because the church is built on a precarious slope.

From Bibbona it is a short drive to medieval **Bolgheri** ⓲, the land beloved by Giusè Carducci, one of Italy's finest poets. So potent is his work that Tuscans still tend to see the intensely green valley through Carducci's brooding eyes. The landscape is a shrine to a poet loved as much for his revolutionary fervour and commitment to national unity as for his melancholic verse.

The gateway to the village is the ancient door to the Gherardesca castle. The poet's home was in the village, as was the home of his first love, Maria Banchini. A square called Piazza Bionda Maria recalls his poem, "If Only I'd Married You, Blonde Maria", a lament which sounds marginally more poetic in Italian. Lines of Carducci's verse in Bolgheri are as common as Dante inscriptions are in Florence. Busts of Carducci are available, sold alongside bottles of Sassicaia, one of Italy's most costly wines, which comes from the Marchesi Incisi estate.

Bolgheri and **San Guido**, at the crossroads with the Via Aurelia, are linked by a magnificent avenue of cypresses, almost 5 km (3 miles) long, planted in 1801 by Camillo della Gherardesca. In Carducci's celebrated poem the tall trees are *quasi in corsa giganti giovinetti*, "galloping young giants" or ranks of upstanding Tuscan soldiers waiting in double file for inspection. The flatness beyond the trees is broken by low farmhouses, olive trees and the village vineyards. San Guido lies on the Strada del Vino, a wine trail linking the vineyards of the Etruscan coast *(see tip on page 173)*.

Nearby is the **Oasi di Bolgheri** (open mid-Oct–mid-Apr; tours Fri and Sat 9am, 11am and 2pm, Apr–May additional tour at 4pm; by appointment only), a nature reserve and bird colony. It is a place apart, neither sea nor land. The "Oasis", part of the San Guido estate, is home to moorhens, wild ducks, herons, egrets and migratory birds.

Castagneto Carducci ⓳ was once a Gherardesca stronghold and a scene of more childhood misery for

The church of Santa Maria della Pietà in the pretty inland village of Bibbona.

BELOW: open country in the Maremma.

October in Sassetta is a month of celebrations. A costumed Palio is held on the first Sunday of the month. The second sees a giant polenta cooked in the main square. The third Sunday is the sagra del tordo, a celebration of the thrush – this is a place where hunting is both a religious cult and a hobby, carried out in all seasons, legally or otherwise. A torchlit procession is followed by a banquet of roast thrush served with chestnut-flavoured polenta.

BELOW: good wines are on offer at the Enoteca Savio, a cosy wine bar in Bibbona.

the young Carducci, but is an attractive hilltop village in its own right. Superficially, little has changed since the Gherardesca lords drained the land, planted the vines and encircled the castle with high stone walls. From its rocky balcony, the town surveys pine forests, plains, golden beaches and two castles. On summer evenings the town is popular with *bourgeois* families tempted by the views – and the aromas of sizzling sausages, roast pigeon and hare. Olive oil from this town is among Italy's best.

Mountain villages

Sassetta ⓴, a bird's nest of a village, was once accessible only to local warriors who thrived on feuds and a diet of game. The area was damned in Dante's *Inferno* as "an impenetrable thicket without paths, leafy patches or apple trees". Since then, Sassetta has sat on its mass of red marble and waited for visitors to penetrate the deep chestnut woods.

Despite the serenity, few have visited its medieval Castello, parish church and alleyways. The locals are no longer ferocious except towards

their traditional enemy, Monteverdi Marittima, with whom they share a patron saint, Sant'Andrea, but nothing else. It is a hardy, self-sufficient community, with a tradition of weaving, embroidery and pipe-making.

From Sassetta a winding road through olives, oleanders and woodland leads to **Suvereto ⓴**, another well-preserved village which advertises itself under the banner: *La Mattina al Mare, il Pomeriggio ai Monti* ("Mornings at the Sea, Afternoons in the Mountains"). Suvereto was the first "free commune" in Maremma, and is proud of its fine 13th-century Palazzo Comunale, with its intact loggia and crenellated tower. The early Romanesque church of San Giusto combines decorated Byzantine portals with a Pisan façade. Many churches and houses are vividly decorated with the local red, brown or grey variegated marble, which has been quarried since medieval times.

Suvereto's urban design, based on rising concentric circles, is simple but effective: each level corresponds to a street, from San Giusto

to the towering Rocca above. The steep ascent winds through a rabbit warren of covered passageways. The sedate village pours onto the streets for the evening *passeggiata* and, in season, for the *sagra del cinghiale*, a wild-boar feast combining food, folklore and spectacle.

This area is **Val di Cornia**, an enchanted region of gently wooded hills, hot springs, lush valleys and old quarries. Orchids and anemones grow on the rocky outcrops, while a mix of myrtle, broom and yellow saxifrage covers the slopes. Up towards **Monte Calvi**, the "Macchiaioli" artists liked to paint the cork trees: the contrast of the fragile leaves and gnarled branches occupied them for days. Wildlife often trotted into the picture, particularly white Maremman oxen and sad-eyed Chianina cows.

At **Montioni** ㉒, a village and spa southeast of Suvereto, Elisa Bacciocchi, Napoleon's sister, used to bathe nude in the hot springs. Pauline, his favourite sister, similarly scandalised the Elban natives *(see page 179)*. The ancient baths at **Terme di Caldana** are even more impressive than those at Montioni. Both the lake and pool contain ferrous sulphates and natural radioactivity which is apparently "guaranteed to restore youthful vigour in one session".

Mining town

In spite of its name, **Campiglia Marittima** ㉓ is a small market and mining town set in the hills. As a "free commune" it was fought over by the Florentines, Pisans and Sienese, all of whom have left heraldic traces on the town walls, four gateways and imposing Rocca. Coats of arms surmount the Gothic arches of Palazzo Pretorio. The Romanesque church of San Giovanni has an equally turbulent past. When San Fiorenzo's relics were found near by, Piombino and Campiglia disputed ownership. A test

was devised to establish the saint's posthumous sense of home: the relics were put on a cart and the oxen, left to decide where to go, trudged uphill to the saint's present resting place. Naturally the oxen were Campigliese.

Campiglia's mineral past is never far from the surface. In the quarry area of **Madonna di Fucinaia** and **Rocco San Silvestro** an archaeological mining museum park has been built (open 10am–sunset, June and Sept Tues–Sun, July–Aug daily, Oct–May Sat–Sun only; entrance fee). Recent excavations have revealed traces of copper, lead, silver and tin, proving that this site has been quarried since Etruscan times. The Campigliese boast that their marble contributed to Florence's Duomo is to be taken lightly: claiming ownership of national monuments is a regional habit.

Although mining is an important cultural tradition, food plays a bigger role in the local economy. The simple peasant dishes reflect Campiglia's traditional poverty and dignity. Many dishes – probably the most famous being the *zuppa Lombarda*, a soup of

Map on page 160

TIP

Sassicaia, Ornellaia, Grattamacco and Le Macchiole are among the best of the Costa degli Etruschi's DOC wines. Many estates in the area welcome visitors for wine-tasting and vineyard tours (except during the grape harvest). For more information, visit the Strada del Vino office in San Guido or go to www. lastradadelvino.com.

BELOW: Suvereto.

Map on page 160

Most of the contents of the Etruscan tombs in Populonia are now kept in Florentine Museums, but a tiny Etruscan Museum (erratic opening hours; entrance fee) in Populonia contains some of the sacred objects found here.

BELOW: windswept Baratti Bay.

bread and beans – were imported by the so-called Lombardi, seasonal workers from the Emilian or Pistoian hills. These shepherds and woodcutters lived in tenements near the swamps, but came inland in the evenings to mix with the locals. In exchange for kindness and dinner, the Lombardi introduced those in the Val di Cornia to their regional favourites, such as chestnut polenta, rice soups and *raviolini*. Local game, sausages and *funghi porcini* were easily incorporated, and Campigliese cuisine has never looked back. The dynamic Suvereto and Campigliese tourist offices will suggest restaurants and *agriturismo* farm stays where these delights can be sampled.

The Etruscan coast

For sightings of flamingos sheltering under umbrella pines, the **Rimigliano Nature Reserve** , hugging the coast between San Vincenzo and Populonia, is where to head. If the coast beckons, San Vicenzo's metallic sands and monotonous strip of bungalows can be sacrificed to Populonia's Etruscan city. The Etruscans very considerably had themselves buried by a pine-fringed beach, reason enough to visit the only Etruscan city built on the coast.

Behind the sweep of **Baratti Bay** lie the substantial remains of **Populonia** ㉕, the last of the 12 Etruscan cities to be founded. The ancient city was divided into two parts: the "acropolis" – the religious centre clustered high around the village – and the maritime and industrial centre around the bay. The necropolises cover the slopes between the two centres.

Thanks to its proximity to Elba and to the metal-bearing Campigliese hills, Populonia became a rich industrial city. While Elban iron ore was smelted and then traded within the Etruscan League, minerals from Campiglia were shipped to Corsica, Sardinia and France. In the ancient "industrial zone", excavations have uncovered a blast furnace and sophisticated metalworking equipment dating back to the 6th century BC. Foreign slave labour was used to dig water channels, operate the furnace and mint coins. In the 6th century BC Populonia was the first Etruscan city to mint gold, silver and bronze coins. Sadly, many tombs lie buried or collapsed under the weight of ancient slag heaps. Others have been looted.

From Populonia there are smoky views of **Piombino** ㉖, which has been ruled by the Pisans, the noble Appiani family, the ignoble Cesare Borgia and, most effectively, by Elisa Bacciocchi, Princess of Piombino and Lucca and Napoleon's sister. Today, it's a grimy, relentlessly urban city, and the only reason most visitors come here is to catch a ferry to Elba, but it's not to be dismissed entirely. Vestiges of grand old Piombino remain in Piazza Verdi's town walls and in the heavily restored Palazzo Comunale and fortress. Best seen on foot, the city's genteel, dilapidated charm lingers on in quiet squares and Art Deco bars. ❑

RESTAURANTS

Antignano

Il Romito
Via del Littorale 274
3 km from Antignano
Tel: 0586-580520
Roadside restaurant suspended above the sea, with fabulous views from its spacious semicircular terrace. Service is brisk, but the dishes, predominantly fish-based, are presented with pride. Closed Wed in summer. €€

Trattoria In Caciaia
Via dei Bagni 38
Tel: 0586-580403
Set on a quiet piazza, this pleasing trattoria offers a great selection of typical Livornese fish dishes. Closed Mon and Tues, weekday lunchtimes and 1 week in Sept. €–€€

Ardenza

Ciglieri
Via Ravizza 43
Tel: 0586-508194
www.ristoranteciglieri.it
The warm, inviting decor is matched with excellent cuisine using only seasonal specialities. Must book. Closed Wed. €€€€

Oscar
Via Oreste Franchini 78
Tel: 0586-501258
Historic restaurant with modern designer ambience and a pleasant garden for alfresco dining. Fish predominates, with cacciucco a speciality

(must be ordered in advance). Extensive wine list. Closed Mon and 20 days from 27 Dec. €€€

Castagneto Carducci

Da Ugo
Via Pari 3/A
Tel: 0565-763746
Family-run restaurant that lives up to its well-earned reputation. Robust dishes feature wild boar, wood pigeon, rabbit and porcini, and there's an excellent choice of local wines from their well-stocked cellar. Closed Mon. €€

Livorno

Da Galileo
Via della Campana 20
Tel: 0586-889009
Trattoria specialising in fish and authentic Livornese cuisine at very reasonable prices. Book ahead. Closed Sun evening and Wed and last two weeks in July. €€

Osteria del Mare
Borgo dei Cappuccini 5
Tel: 0586-881027
Characterful tavern in the port area. Two small but welcoming dining rooms offer a good selection of seafood at prices that won't melt the plastic. Closed Thur and 25 Aug–10 Sept. €€–€€€

Ristorante Albergo Bar Montallegro
Piazza Montenero 3
Tel: 0586-579030
Set in a panoramic spot

near the Sanctuary of Madonna di Montenero. Cacciucco features every day of the year, with other traditional specialities. There is a very pleasant frescoed dining room and a terrace for warmer weather. Closed Tues in winter. Reservation recommended. €€–€€€

Trattoria Antica Venezia
Piazza dei Domenicani 15
Tel: 0586-887353
Typical Tuscan trattoria in the heart of Livorno's Venezia neighborhood. Offers traditional livornesi recipes including possibly the best cacciucco in town. €

Trattoria Cantina Senese
Borgo dei Cappuccini 95
Tel: 0586-890239
A characteristic trattoria near the port, with reasonably priced livornesi dishes. The locals order the house speciality: carbonara di mare. €€

San Vincenzo

Gambero Rosso
Piazza della Vittoria
Tel: 0565-701021
Elegant restaurant overlooking the sea; one of Tuscany's best. Fish features prominently. The wine list is around 100 pages long. Closed Mon–Tues. €€€€

RIGHT: cacciucco – Livornese fish soup.

ISOLA D'ELBA

Every August the beaches of "Tuscany's island" are invaded by sun-worshipping Italians. For the rest of the year, its rocky roads, wooded slopes and sandy bays belong to intrepid tourists who make the short sea crossing in search of unspoilt nature, crystal waters, Napoleonic landmarks and good food and wine

Firenze

Known to the Etruscans as *Ilva* ("Iron") and to the Greeks as *Aethalia* ("Soot Island"), Elba has exploited its mineral wealth for more than 3,000 years. As the European powers occasionally took an interest in the island's attractive strategic position, waves of Romans, Pisans and Genoese were followed by Spanish, Turkish and French invasions. In 1548, the powerful and vainglorious Medici duke, Cosimo I, fortified the capital and named it Cosmopolis, after himself. His great military architect, Giovanni Camerini, designed the star-shaped defensive system and the two Medicean forts, Forte della Stella and Forte Falcone, to keep the Saracens at bay. Today, Portoferraio's horseshoe harbour, backed by a cluster of sun-baked pastel houses, is more welcoming than forbidding, as ferries, fishing boats, yachts and pleasure cruisers glide in and out of its embrace.

Napoleon's Elba

Portoferraio ❶ is inextricably linked to that other great imperialist, Napoleon Bonaparte. He made his official home in two converted windmills above the charming Forte della Stella. Under the terms of the Congress of Vienna in 1814, Elba became a principality of the fallen sovereign. Napoleon's great empire

shrank to his faithful "old guard", pragmatic mother and libertine sister Pauline. Most Elbans were proud to have him improve the administration, build new roads, develop the mines and expand the island's fleet. The foreign commissioners, however, rightly feared that the "Eagle" might spread its wings: after nine months Napoleon flew, with the connivance of the Elbans. He escaped with no less than 1,000 troops, the Elbans' affection, his sister's diamond necklace and his mother's

Map on page 178

LEFT: Portoferraio.
BELOW: an Elban fishing boat.

MAREA LIVORNO

The emblem of Elba's most famous resident seen at San Martino villa, Napoleon's country residence during his 10-month exile on the island. A requiem Mass is said for him here on 5 May each year, and an empty black coffin is carried in a solemn procession down to the waterfront.

curt blessing, "Go and fulfil your destiny." His **Palazzina dei Mulini** (open Mon, Wed–Sat 9am–7pm, Sun 9am–1pm; entrance fee) was lined with silver and books from Fontainebleau and furniture from his sister Elisa's house in Piombino. Most of its charm lies in the period furnishings and Italianate gardens.

The 17th-century **Misericordia** church on the Via Napoleone, a broad stairway near by, displays one of Napoleon's bronze death-masks.

A few kilometres inland from Portoferraio is the emperor's country residence, **San Martino** (open Tues–Sat 9am–7pm, Sun 9am–1pm; entrance fee), purchased with one of Pauline's handy diamond necklaces. The villa's classical façade was installed in 1851 by the Russian emigré Prince Demidoff. But after the grand cypress-lined avenue and grandiose façade, the house itself seems a spartan affair, and is quickly visited. In one room, Napoleon's Nile

campaigns of 1798–9 are recalled in the Egyptian-style frescoes, painted in 1814. In another, his tiny bed is a reminder of just how short he was. Information on the emperor's life and times is thin on the ground here (though souvenir stands are not), but the fine garden, shaded by evergreen oaks and terraced vineyards, is pleasant to stroll through.

Portoferraio to Marciana

The scenic drive westward from Portoferraio to Marciana Marina passes a number of popular beaches. Le Ghiaie, the nearest beach to the town, is noted for its multicoloured pebbles, but it's worth going the extra distance to **Capo d'Enfola ❷**. The road to the cape ends at Porto di Sansone, a tiny isthmus flanked by two small pebble beaches and a couple of restaurants. Formerly restricted for military use, the cape itself remains closed to traffic, but is popular among walkers. **Viticcio** is

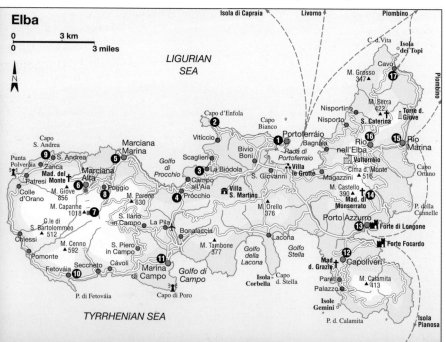

Map on page 178

another pretty cove, but sand-seekers head for **La Biodola** ❸, considered the chic-est beach on Elba, dominated by expensive resort complexes filled with rich bronzed Florentines in Valentino swimwear. At La Biodola and **Procchio** ❹, a more egalitarian paradise, the rocky ocean bottom means clear, sediment-free water.

Between Procchio and Marciana Marina is "La Paolina", an islet named after Napoleon's sister, whose passion for nude sunbathing would scandalise the natives.

Marciana Marina ❺ has evolved smoothly from fishing village to elegant resort, set amidst magnolias, palms and oleanders at the end of a long valley. The thin, pastel-coloured houses in the old quarter are reminiscent of those on the Ligurian coast. On 12 August the port explodes in a firework display to honour Santa Chiara, the patron saint.

Marciana Alta ❻, perched above, is the island's best-preserved medieval town. Chestnut woods frame the red-tiled rooftops, narrow alleys and the crumbling Pisan fortress. The local "Antiquarium" displays Etruscan sacred objects, as well as Roman oil lamps and ivory statues found in shipwrecks.

Twin peaks

From the foot of Marciana, a cable car, the Cabinovia del Monte Capanne (mid-Apr–mid-Oct 10am–12.15pm, 2.30–6pm, June–Aug until 6.30pm) lurches over crags and chasms up to the summit of **Monte Capanne** ❼. On a clear day (when the peak is free from the clouds that frequently shroud it), the views from up here are all-encompassing. Even in high summer, this wooded mountain area is wonderfully quiet and breezy. Depending on the season, patches of orchids, snapdragons and helianthemums are as common as the cedars and chestnuts. Even the coastal vegetation is more exotic than in the east: eucalyptus and magnolia rather than vines or rough maquis.

The high road from Marciana to the south side of the island winds past the quiet, neglected village of **Poggio** ❽ to **Monte Perone** nature

Heading up to the heights of Monte Capanne in the cable car.

BELOW: a cloud-covered Poggio.

reserve (for a scenic walk on the mountain, stop off at Poggio and follow the waymarked trail), vineyards and the plains behind Marina di Campo, the only part of the island flat enough for an airport.

The "Other Elba"

The northwestern corner of Elba is a protected area of wild, natural beauty. Granite cliffs, thick holm oak and chestnut woods, and dense *maquis* make it a property developer's nightmare and a nature-lover's dream. Tagged by the tourist board as the "Other Elba", this craggy corner attracts the active and eco-conscious. The sea here is ideal for snorkelling, diving and kayaking, while the surrounding mountains are exploited by mountain bikers, birdwatchers, trekkers and climbers. A long, winding road leads down past houses and hotels to **Capo Sant'Andrea ❾**, a tight bay with a small port protected from westerly winds by the surrounding cliffs. This is an ideal base for exploring the area, starting with the walk from Capo Sant'Andrea to the next bay at Cotoncello.

The coast road from Sant'Andrea to Marina di Campo clings to the edge of the island, an exhilarating and occasionally heart-stopping drive. Wherever you see a cluster of parked cars, chances are there's a rocky cove below, where those in the know gather to swim and sunbathe. This section of the coast is good for diving and snorkelling; most of the diving schools can be found in and around **Pomonte**.

As you round the southwestern corner, the first visible stretch of sand at **Fetovaia ❿** comes into view – a pretty, child-friendly sweep of beach, edged by trees, that gets very crowded in summer. Between Fetovaia and **Cavoli**, another small, pleasant enough resort, the low rocks make perfect sunbathing platforms.

The south

With its expanse of golden sand, **Marina di Campo ⓫**, in the south, is the largest resort on the island, full of bars and buzzing with nightlife. Often overlooked are two dusty medieval villages nestling in the hills behind. Fortified by the Pisans in the

12th century, **San Piero in Campo** and **San Ilario** conceal Romanesque churches and hermitages.

Capoliveri ⓬ is a traditional inland village, with a Roman and medieval past as dramatic as its location high on the southern promontory. Carved into the iron mountain of **Monte Calamita**, Capoliveri is also an old mining village. The black, iron-bearing lodestone still plays havoc with the compasses of passing ships, but is ideal for the production of sweet red Aleatico, said to be the favourite wine of Napoleon Bonaparte. Often independent, Capoliveri was the only village to reject Napoleon in 1814. The story is that only the intercession of a local beauty saved the village. It soon became part of Napoleon's hunting estate, and to this day is noted for its dishes of woodcock, pheasant and hare.

The hills are covered with heath, fern and juniper; the scent of thyme and rosemary are never far away. Roads from the hills to the sea often turn into cart tracks but are worth pursuing unless specifically marked *strada privata*; this is often the only

access to the loveliest beaches, as most of this southeastern headland is privately owned. **Innamorata** is a sandy inlet linked to the romance between a nymph and a fisherman. Believing her lover drowned in a shipwreck, the nymph drowned herself; he survived and asked the gods to turn him into a seagull so he could seek her out.

The east

Capoliveri also surveys fashionable **Porto Azzurro** ⓭, the main town on the east coast of Elba and once part of the Spanish protectorate. The vast Forte Longone, constructed in 1603 as a Spanish naval base, is now a top-security prison. Visitors can purchase crafts from the prison shop, the scene of a mass breakout in 1987. Forte Focardo, its sister fortress across the bay, has uninviting ramparts running down a sheer cliff. By day, Porto Azzurro has a rather uninspiring seafront. In the evening, however, it is a favoured place for a leisurely promenade (the famous *passeggiata*), designer shopping and people-watching. It is also a top place for

Elban wine is known for its distinct flavour, due to the mineral-rich and fertile soil. The dry whites, Chianti-like reds and Aleatico and Ansonica dessert wines are all excellent accompaniments to traditional Elban dishes.

BELOW: the pretty resort of Marciana Marina *(see page 179).*

Map on page 178

The island of Elba was long known as a mineralogical paradise. Semi-precious stones such as green quartz, black onyx and pink or pale-green beryl, can all be found here. The proper mineral name for most gem tourmalines, in fact, is "Elbaite".

sampling some of the local seafood specialities, such as a *cacciucco* (soup) of octopus, scorpion fish, dog-fish and prawns; *riso nero* or "black rice" (risotto made with the dark ink of cuttlefish or squid), perhaps followed by *schiaccia briaca* ("drunken cake"), made with hazelnuts and Aleatico wine. After enough Elban wine, one's impressions of Porto Azzurro are of harbour lights, cheerful bustle and gently bobbing boats.

Behind Porto Azzurro is the most mystical spot on the island, the remote sanctuary of **Madonna di Monserrato ⓐ** (open daily mid-July–mid-Sept, closed noon–3pm). It was built in the Toledan style by a Spanish governor, Ponce de León, in 1606. A steep, rocky track leads high up the mountain to the tiny red-domed church precariously balanced among the crags. Despite mountain goats cavorting on impossible ledges, the place has great solemnity and few visitors, and is the most important shrine on Elba. The Spanish façade and bell-tower find echoes in the Black Madonna inside, which is a copy of an early

Spanish painting. Every September, an Elban pilgrimage celebrates the *Festa della Madonna* with a walk past ravines and isolated grottoes to the church.

Elba's iron heart

To the east of Portoferraio is Elba's iron heart. The island's mineral wealth has been exploited since Etruscan times; the swords of Roman legionaries were famously made of Elban iron. But the last mine was closed in 1984, and the island's economic mainstays are now tourism, agriculture and fishing.

The workaday town of **Rio Marina ⓑ** was once the centre of the mining activity. Surrounded by hills rich in ferrous oxide, the whole port has a pinkish hue, including the 16th-century tower of San Rocco overlooking the harbour. More than 700 mineral exhibits are on display in the **Museo Mineralogico** (open Apr–June, Sept–Oct daily 9.30am–12.30pm, 3.30–6.30pm, July–Aug 9.30am–12.30pm, 4.30–7.30pm; in winter by request; tel: 0565-962168; entrance fee).

Inland, **Rio nell'Elba ⓒ** is a strange, rather wild village perched on a couple of ledges among desolate mountain slopes and scattered remains of mines. A few kilometres west, on the road to Portoferraio, a steep road leads uphill to **Volterraio** and the ruins of an 11th-century Pisan fortress, perched on a rock.

From Rio nell'Elba to the small beach resort of **Cavo ⓓ** in the northeast, the picturesque road cuts through woods and moorland. Paths trail through gorse, heather and the wild flowers of the maquis. Like the northwestern corner of the island, Elba's northeastern tip has unspoilt stretches of natural beauty, and is less crowded in summer than most of the island. Just north of Cavo, the remains of a Roman villa can be seen at **Capo Castello**. ❑

The Tuscan Archipelago

Elba is the largest island in a chain of seven islands between the Ligurian and Tyrrhenian seas, all protected as part of the Arcipelago Toscano national marine park. On a clear day, Pianosa, Gorgona, Montecristo and Capraia are visible from the island's highest reaches. Pianosa, just 14 km (9 miles) from Elba, was a maximum-security prison until 1997. It is now a marine nature reserve. Montecristo, 34 km (21 miles) away, is also a nature reserve, uninhabited but for its four guardians. So as not to disturb the fragile environments, the number of visitors is restricted. Gorgona, the smallest and northernmost island in the archipelago, is still a prison. Capraia is a miniature Elba without its history or architecture. It is a two-hour ferry ride from Livorno *(see page 167)*.

Giglio, the second-largest island in the archipelago after Elba, and its sister Giannutri, are the southernmost islands in the chain. Giglio is popular with weekending Romans and daytrippers. Both can be reached from Porto Santo Stefano *(see page 239)*. For further information, visit www.arcipelago.turismo.toscana.it.

RESTAURANTS

Capo d'Enfola

Da Giacomino
Loc. Viticcio
Tel/fax: 0565-915381
www.ristorantedagiacomino.it
A small, family-run trattoria, a short drive from the island capital. Sunsets from the terrace across the bay are memorable. Pizzas served in the evening. Closed Tues lunch, Oct–Easter. €–€€

Ristorante Emanuel
Porto di Sansone,
Tel: 0565-939003
The road to Capo d'Enfola promontary ends at a pebble beach with a couple of restaurants. Emanuel is a good option for a snack lunch, and one of few places to offer a vegetarian menu. Closed Wed Sept–Oct and Nov–Easter. €–€€

Marciana Marina

Affrichella
Piazza Santa Chiara
Tel: 0565-996844
Intimate restaurant, tucked down a backstreet away from the seafront bustle, offering an inventive fish-based menu. €€–€€€

Borgo al Cotone
Via del Cotone 23
Tel: 0565-904390
Romantic harbourside restaurant where fish and seafood come grilled and gratinated, or in more adventurous concoctions such as lasagne with chickpeas and clams. Closed Oct–early Mar. €€–€€€

Ristorante Capo Nord
Loc. La Fenicia
Tel: 0565-996983
The island's top restaurant, where you will be fed exquisite Tuscan food by impeccably dressed and deferential waiters. Dress up and book. Ask for table 5 or 6. Closed Mon in autumn and Nov–Easter. €€€–€€€€

Marina di Campo

La Lucciola
Viale degli Eroi
Tel: 0565-976395
www.lalucciola.it
Brush the sand off your feet and step onto the wooden-decked terrace of this relaxed beach bar/restaurant, where you can enjoy a drink, a big summer salad or go for the full works including the catch of the day. Closed Tues and mid-Apr–Oct. Reservation recommended. €€€

Poggio/Marciana Alta

Publius
Piazza XX Settembre
Tel: 0565-99208
Nestled on the mountainside, Publius has a well-established reputation on the island, and offers fine views from the terrace. Elban wines and fish and game dishes. Closed Mon. €€–€€€

Porto Azzurro

I Quattro Gatti
Piazza del Mercato 4
Tel: 0565-95240
A cosy and convivial restaurant decorated with copper pots, beaded lamps, old wirelesses and other knick-knacks. The menu is equally eclectic with offerings like herrings with apple, carpaccio of cod and fish ravioli. In a resort town full of bright and brash restaurants, this is a real find. Closed Mon in low season. €€–€€€

Portoferraio

Da Lido
Salita Falcone 2
Tel: 0565-914650
Set back from the port area, this consistently good and constantly bustling trattoria is one of Portoferraio's best. Closed Sun in low season, mid-Dec–mid-Feb. €€

Osteria Libertaria
Calata Matteotti 12
Tel: 0565-914978
Traditional hostelry overlooking the marina. Grab one of the two outdoor bench tables and watch the boating bustle over a pasta or fish dish. Open daily Apr–Nov. Best to book. €–€€

PRICE CATEGORIES

Average cost of a three-course meal per person with a half-bottle of wine:
€ = under €25
€€ = €25–40
€€€ = €40–60
€€€€ = more than €60

RIGHT: the traditional Osteria Libertaria overlooks Portoferraio's marina.

VOLTERRA AND THE COLLINE METALLIFERE

Perched on a windy plateau overlooking the Sienese hills, Volterra has some of the best Etruscan art outside Rome. The terrain south of Volterra goes from the dry and desolate crags of Le Balze to the dense, eerie forests of the "Metal-Bearing Mountains"

One of the most important towns in Tuscany is **Volterra ❶**, which has a richly layered history with abundant evidence of its 3,000 years of civilisation. It commands a beautiful, windswept and majestic position on a steep ridge 545 metres (1,780 ft) above sea level between the valleys of the Era and Cecina rivers. Walking round the ancient defensive walls is an excellent way to view the town, the Roman remains and the wide sweep of countryside below.

Volterra was the Etruscan city-state of Velathri, one of the confederation of 12 city-states which made up Etruria. It became an important Roman municipality (Volterrae) when Rome annexed Etruria in 351 BC. It followed the new faith of Christianity, and at the fall of the Roman Empire in AD 476 it was already the centre of a vast diocese.

The modern city of Volterra sits within the walls of a much larger Etruscan predecessor. Wherever archaeologists dig in the city, they turn up new treasures. Sometimes they do not even need to dig, since parts of the city, built on soft tufa and undermined by subterranean springs, have been slipping slowly down the hillside for centuries, revealing the remains of an extensive necropolis.

Exploring Volterra

The **Porta all'Arco** (the Arch Gate) is the best-preserved Etruscan gateway in Italy, dating from the 4th century BC (though partly rebuilt by the Romans in the 1st century BC), with sides of huge rectangular stone blocks and three mysterious carved basalt heads above the gateway, thought to represent Etruscan gods.

From the arch, a pretty road winds its way uphill to the **Piazza dei Priori**. Evidence of the Middle Ages is demonstrated not only in Volterra's

Map on page 186

LEFT: Volterra sits majestically on a steep ridge. **BELOW:** the Palazzo dei Priori.

BELOW:
a 13th-century lion
stands guard outside
the Palazzo dei Priori.

urban structure but also in its buildings, the most important of which
are clustered around the main
square. It is dominated by the tall
Palazzo dei Priori (1208) the oldest
town hall in Tuscany, and said to be
the model for Florence's Palazzo
Vecchio. Across the square is the
13th-century **Palazzo Pretorio**, with
its crenellated Torre del Porcellino
(Tower of the Little Pig), so named
due to the decorative relief of a boar.

To the south of the square, Via
Turrazza leads to the 12th-century
Duomo (Piazza San Giovanni; open
daily 7am–12.30pm, 2–6pm in winter, 7am–7pm in summer; free),
which houses works of art from the
Middle Ages to the Renaissance. The
sculpture of the *Deposition* is an
extremely rare and unusual Romanesque woodcarving, simple in execution but full of dramatic pathos.

The bishop's palace next door
houses the **Museo d'Arte Sacra** (Via

Roma; open daily 9am–1pm, 3–6pm,
Nov–mid-Mar 9am–1pm; entrance
fee), a collection of gold reliquaries,
church bells, illuminated manuscripts
and some 13th-century sculptures of
the Sienese school. The octagonal
Baptistery opposite has an elegant
marble doorway with a fine baptismal font sculpted by Sansovino.

Heading back towards the square,
Via Roma leads into Via Buonparenti and the Pisan-style **Casa Torre
Buonparenti**, a pair of so-called
house-towers (13th-century).

At the top of Via Buonparenti, the
Pinacoteca e Museo Civico in the
Palazzo Minucci-Solaini (open daily
9am–7pm, until 1.30pm in winter;
entrance fee) houses valuable paintings of the Sienese and Florentine
schools, including an *Annunciation*
by Signorelli and *Christ in Glory* by
Ghirlandaio. The most famous painting in the collection is the *Deposition
from the Cross* by Rosso Fiorentino

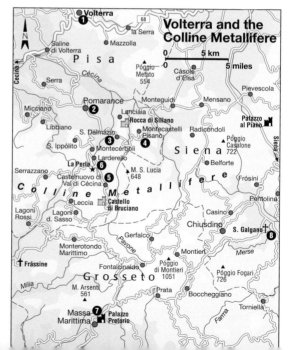

(1495–1540), considered by many to be his greatest masterpiece.

The **Palazzo Incontri-Viti** on Via dei Sarti (open Apr–Oct 10am–1pm, 2.30–6pm, winter by appointment only; tel: 0588-84047; entrance fee) is another impressive building whose façade is attributed to Ammannati, who worked on the Palazzo Pitti in Florence. This and other Renaissance buildings, such as the Palazzo Minucci-Solaini, blend gracefully with the medieval Volterran houses.

The Etruscan museum and Roman theatre

The best of the city's ancient treasures are displayed in the **Museo Etrusco Guarnacci** (Via Don Minzoni; open daily 9am–7pm, until 1.30pm Nov–mid-Mar; entrance fee). This is packed with ancient Etruscan funerary urns. The *Married Couple* urn is a masterpiece of realistic portraiture, and even more stunning is the bronze statuette known as *L'Ombra della Sera* (Evening Shadow), resembling a Giacometti sculpture but cast in the 5th century BC. The mysterious elongated figure does indeed resemble the shadow of a human being thrown by the low beams of the setting sun.

Volterra is dominated at its highest point by the **Fortezza Medicea**, a magnificent example of Renaissance military architecture – today it serves as a prison. Near by, on the site of the former Etruscan acropolis, the **Parco Archeologico** (open daily 10.30am–5.30pm in summer, weekends only 10am–4pm in winter; entrance fee) is an ideal spot for a picnic.

On the north side of town, just below the city walls, is the excavated **Roman Theatre** (open daily 10.30am–5.30pm in summer, weekends only 10am–4pm in winter), the impressive remains of a complex built during the reign of Augustus, behind which lie the ruins of a 3rd-century Roman bathhouse.

Le Balze

The countryside around Volterra is one of gentle, undulating hills, interrupted in the west by the wild and awe-inspiring spectacle of abrupt crevasses known as **Le Balze** (the Crags). Over the centuries, these deep gullies, created by the continual erosion of layers of sand and clay, have swallowed up churches and settlements along with Etruscan and early Christian remains. Today an 11th-century abbey, the Badia, sits on a precipice, awaiting its inevitable fate. For the perfect view of this dramatic landscape, exit through the western San Francesco Gate, passing the Borgo San Giusto and its remains until you reach the Le Balze campsite (a 20-minute walk).

Metal mountains

The wide vistas of the dry, desolate terrain just south of Volterra seem a world away from the cosy green hills of Chianti. At Saline di Volterra, an industrial suburb that has developed around its railway terminus and salt mine, the SS439 leads south to Massa Marittima and the coast, cutting

Map on page 186

TIP

Walk along the remains of Volterra's Etruscan walls at the northwestern edge of town, for lovely views at sunset.

BELOW: Larderello, at the centre of geothermic activity.

TIP

There are some excellent walks in the Forestali Berignone-Tatti, near Pomarance, especially in the autumn, when the leaves of the sweet chestnut turn golden-yellow and the forest becomes carpeted with bright pink cyclamen. Bicycle tours and horse-riding excursions can be booked through Pomarance's tourist office (in the car park on the SS439).

BELOW:
Massa Marittima.

through the Colline Metallifere, or Metal-Bearing Mountains. Beyond the Upper Cecina valley the landscape transforms into one of dense forests of chestnut, beech and oak, punctuated at intervals by fumaroles, cooling towers and gleaming silver pipelines, making for a strange and distinctly un-Tuscan picture.

The first noteworthy town on this surreal route is **Pomarance ②**, which retains vestiges of its prosperous medieval past, including two 14th-century town gates. La Piazza della Pretura is dominated by the church of San Giovanni, with a Romanesque façade, and a short walk away the Via Roncalli is lined with *palazzi*, one of which houses the **Bicocchi Museum** (open Thur and Sun 3.30–6.30pm in summer, rest of year by appointment only; entrance fee), a well preserved early 19th-century home, whose lavish decorations evoke the lifestyle of the rich, upper-class families whose fortunes were mostly made exploiting the region's mineral wealth. Pomarance makes a good base for exploring the local countryside.

A little further along the road is the small settlement of **San Dalmazio ③**. From here, a short but steep walk (2 km/1¼ miles) takes you to the impressive ruins of the 11th-century castle **Rocca Sillana**, a viewpoint offering commanding views over the surrounding provinces.

Across the valley, the medieval hamlet of **Montecastelli Pisano ④** is dominated by the Torre dei Pannocchieschi. Like the Rocca Sillana, this settlement was the object of many an inter-city-state battle, the Florentines finally winning out in the 16th century. Follow the signs to Castelnuovo Val di Cecina and the "Buca delle Fate", a small but well-preserved 6th-century BC Etruscan tomb, just outside the village.

The road south from Montecastelli Pisano offers the best views of the medieval village of **Castelnuovo Val di Cecina ⑤**, which is built on the side of a steep ridge and surrounded by woodland. A short walk east of the village leads through chestnut woods and down to the river Pavone, where you can swim in the rock pools, overlooked by two medieval bridges.

Geothermic activity

At the heart of this vast geothermic area, the industrial village of **Larderello ⑥** has been valued for its healing spring waters for centuries. It was named after the French industrialist François de Larderel, who set up a factory here to produce boric acid. The village was built to house the factory workers. There is a public pool fed by the thermal waters, and the **Geothermal Museum** (open mid-Mar–mid-Sept Mon–Fri 9am–noon, 1.30–5.30pm, Sat–Sun 10am–noon, 1.30–6.30pm, mid-Sept–mid-Mar Mon–Fri 8am–noon, 1.30–4.30pm, Sun 9am–noon, 1.30–5.30pm; free) dedicated to the history of the community and its important resource. There's an impressive view of the power plant from the SS439 as it

Map on page 186

crosses the hill towards Castelnuovo Val di Cecina.

Heading south along a back road from Larderello, two small villages worth a look are **Leccia** and **Sasso Pisano**, linked by a narrow, winding road that cuts through a landscape of steaming fumaroles. Just outside the hamlet of Leccia are the ancient baths of Bagnone, a vast Etruscan-Roman bathing complex from the 3rd century BC. The medieval village of Sasso Pisano is built on a rocky outcrop above the Cornia river. This strangely appealing place is often shrouded in clouds of steam from the surrounding fumaroles and the air is heavy with the smell of sulphur. The road through the village leads back to the SS439.

As the main road continues to wind south towards Massa Marittima it passes through steep wooded hillsides and up to the summits of the Colline Metallifere. It is an area of outstanding natural beauty, with dense forest and large open views across to Maremma and the Gulf of Follonica; on a clear day, the islands of Elba and Corsica are visible.

Massa Marittima

Massa Marittima ❼ is about 24 km (15 miles) inland, despite its maritime name. It is one of the most astounding Tuscan cities, perched on top of a high hill on the edge of the Colline Metallifere. It was the most important town in the Maremma until the 17th century, when the land silted up.

Massa Marittima was built around the 10th century, after the decline of ancient Populonia *(see page 174)*, which was too exposed to coastal malaria and plundering by pirates. It was known for its copper and silver mines even in Etruscan times, and the rich variety of metals available was a major factor in its economic development. The affluence of medieval Massa Marittima, and pride in its republican status (in 1225 the city overthrew its feudal lord, declaring itself a free commune), are reflected in the concentration of public buildings around the Duomo.

In the main square – the spectacular **Piazza Garibaldi**, one of the finest squares in Tuscany – are Palazzo Vescovile (seat of the bishop), Palazzo del Podestà (seat of

The mountains south of Volterra are rich in metal ores, and for centuries provided Tuscany with the precious commodities of silver, copper, lead and zinc. However, by the end of the 19th century mining and related industries had fallen into decline, and now these hills are a remote and lonely region. The ruins of mines and factories engulfed in thick forest littered with heaps of coloured metals present a surreal picture.

BELOW: a classic Tuscan snapshot.

TIP

A memorable experience – and a lot easier to see than Siena's *Palio* – is the traditional Balestro del Girifalco, every last Sunday in May and every second Sunday in August. The three *terzieri* of Massa (old city, new city and the outer Borgo) hold a shooting contest using mechanical falcons with ancient crossbows.

BELOW RIGHT: the Gothic ruins of San Galgano.

the governor, now an archaeological museum), Palazzo del Comune (town hall), Zecca Cittadina (the mint), Fonte Pubblica (public fountain) and Palazzo dell' Abbondanza (the public granary). The **Duomo** is an example of Pisan Romanesque architecture, with marvellous reliefs of the *Madonna delle Grazie*, ascribed to Duccio di Buoninsegna (1316) and the *Arca di San Cerbone* (St Cerbone's Ark), a masterpiece of the Sienese school of sculpture.

There are two mining-related museums in Massa Marittima: the **Museum of Mining Art and History** in Piazza Mateotti (open Apr–Oct Tues–Sun 3.30–5pm, Nov–Mar by appointment only; entrance fee) and the **Mine Museum** in Via Corridoni (open Tues–Sun, Apr–Sept 10am–12.45pm, 3.30–5.45pm, Oct–Mar 10am–noon, 3–4.30pm; guided tours; entrance fee). The **Torre del Candeliere**, a clock tower dating to 1443 (open Tues–Sun, Apr–Oct 10am–1pm, 3–6pm, Nov–Mar 11am–1pm, 2.30–4.30pm; entrance fee) in Piazza Mateotti, offers great views across the city.

Gothic ruin

Heading east from Massa Marittima along the SS441 towards Siena takes you to what some have claimed as Italy's most impressive Gothic ruin. Located in a field, with the panorama of sky and fields to match its majesty, is the ruined **Abbazia di San Galgano** ❽. This roofless abbey, with grass for a nave and the sparsest of frescoes still clinging to its crumbling walls is definitely worth a visit. The best time to come is towards evening, when the coach tours have gone and the setting sun sends shafts of light through its windows. Concerts and operas are staged here in the summer (tourist office in the abbey).

On a nearby hill overlooking the abbey is the Romanesque church of Monte Siepi, built on the spot where St Galgano had a vision of Saint Michael and renounced his profession as a soldier to become a hermit, thrusting his sword into a rock. The event is illustrated by the frescoes of Ambrogio Lorenzetti that can be found in the adjacent, rectangular chapel. Siena is about 35 km (22 miles) from here on the SS73. ❑

The Abbey of San Galgano

Consecrated in 1288, the abbey of San Galgano was originally the main centre for the Cistercian Order that dominated this area in the 12th and 13th centuries, exerting influence across the whole of central Italy. Its abbot had the power of arbitration in the disputes between city-states, and its monks oversaw the building of Siena's Duomo as well as the accounts of Massa Marittima's free republic. But this period of power for the Cistercian Order was short-lived. In the mid-14th century, the abbey was ransacked by the English mercenary Sir John Hawkwood – an attack sanctioned by the pope, who was fearful of the Order's influence. Now in the hands of the papacy, the abbey's income was diverted to Rome, and slowly the building began to fall into disrepair.

Bouts of plague across the decades weakened the order further and by 1576 it is said that San Galgano was occupied by one solitary monk "who didn't even wear a robe". A lightning strike during a village Mass in 1778 saw the collapse of the campanile and marked the last service at San Galgano and the beginning of its final ruination.

RESTAURANTS

Massa Marittima

Il Brillo Parlante
Vicolo del Ciambellano 4
Tel: 0566-901274
The best way to approach a meal in this tiny restaurant – there are just four tables – is to ask what's available. The dishes are lovingly prepared and seasonal, and there's a good selection of fine wines. Booking essential. Closed Wed. €€€

Le Mura
Via Norma Parenti 7
Tel: 0566-940055
This large and busy restaurant has panoramic views towards Follonica and Elba, from both inside and out. The extensive menu incorporates typical Tuscan ingredients from the nearby wooded hills and fresh seafood from the coast beyond. Closed Tues. €€€

Osteria Da Tronca
Vicolo Porte 5
Tel: 0566-901991
A reasonably priced and popular family-run restaurant offering simple, well-prepared dishes cooked to traditional recipes by both *mamma* and her daughter. Booking recommended. Closed Wed. €€

Trattoria Dei Cavalieri
Via Norma Parenti 35
Te: 0566-902093
Well lit, friendly and with a pleasant atmosphere, this restaurant is both value for money and a joy to be in. Local dishes such as *tortelli maremmani* and *aquacotta* predominate. Booking essential. Closed Thur in low season. €€

Volterra

Da Badò
Borgo San Lazzaro 9
Tel: 0588-86477
Restaurant just outside the city, serving Volterran specialities. Featured prominently in guidebooks, so it is advisable to book. Closed Wed. €€

Don Beta
Via Matteotti 39
Tel: 0588-86730
www.donbeta.it
Ignore the yellow tablecloths, this is a great restaurant specialising in the traditional cuisine of the local huntsmen; try the *cinghiale* (wild boar) or *lepre* (hare). €

Il Pozzo Degli Etruschi
Via delle Prigioni 28-30
Tel: 0588-80608
www.ilpozzodeglietruschi.com
The simple medieval backdrop of this recently renovated eatery is echoed in the unpretentious and delicious Tuscan fare. In summer the shady inner courtyard is also open for dining. Closed Fri. €

Il Sacco Fiorentino
Piazza XX Settembre 18
Tel: 0588-88537
Pleasant and welcoming eatery in two parts: one side is a trattoria serving interesting Tuscan fare; the other is a wine bar with a shorter, cheaper, more traditional menu and snacks. Closed Wed and mid-Jan–end Feb. €–€€

Ombra della Sera
Via Gramsci 70
Tel: 0588-85274
Families and young Volterrans flock to this brightly lit, no-frills pizzeria, attracted by the buzzy atmosphere and excellent, reasonably priced pizza. The restaurant next door offers a quieter, more intimate atmosphere, and specialises in dishes based on truffles, mushrooms and local game. Closed Mon. €

Osteria Il Ponte
Via Massetana, San Lorenzo (5 km southwest of Volterra)
Tel: 0588-44160
Good, traditional home cooking in this welcoming *osteria* which also serves snacks. Closed Tues. €

Vecchia Osteria dei Poeti
Via Matteotti 55
Tel: 0588-86029
Central restaurant, popular with residents and tourists alike. Closed Thur. €€

PRICE CATEGORIES

Average cost of a three-course meal per person with a half-bottle of wine:
€ = under €25
€€ = €25–40
€€€ = €40–60
€€€€ = over €60

RIGHT: hearty bean dishes are a Tuscan staple.

SAN GIMIGNANO AND CHIANTI COUNTRY

An exploration of the ordered and harmonious landscape spanning the fertile hills between Florence and Siena, taking in the medieval skyscrapers of San Gimignano, the red-brick hill town of Certaldo, and the vineyards and villas along the Chianti trail

Perhaps the most spectacular sight anywhere in Tuscany is the town of **San Gimignano ❶**, famous for the sculptural quality of its skyline and richly rewarding – despite the huge number of visitors. It may be a cliché to call it a "Medieval Manhattan", but the famous towers thrusting up from the hill town do resemble miniature skyscrapers. This view is best appreciated from the approach roads to the town. Once you are there, it is the unspoilt townscape that bowls you over: almost nothing seems to have changed since the Middle Ages.

In its heyday the city had a total of 76 towers, only 14 of which remain. The towers were built in the 12th and 13th centuries by the *magnati*, or nobles, during the Guelf-Ghibelline conflicts. As well as defending the city, they served as status symbols: the higher the tower, the more rich and powerful its owner. The local 14th-century poet Folgore, who wrote during this period of relative wealth, described the "earthly pleasures" he encountered in the city, including "silk sheets, sugared nuts, sweets and sparkling wine". The arrival of the Black Death in 1348, however, put an end to silk sheets in San Gimignano until the 20th century. The diminished population fell under Florentine control, and this once important city became an economic backwater, bypassed by the Renaissance. While more civilised cities were exchanging towers for *palazzi*, San Gimignano destroyed nothing and built nothing. The city's misfortune has made it the best-preserved medieval city in Tuscany.

Exploring San Gimignano

The towers are concentrated around the **Piazza del Duomo** and **Piazza della Cisterna**, teeming with tourists all year round. They alone

Map on page 194

LEFT: view from a San Gimignano tower.
BELOW: a bountiful harvest.

make a visit here worthwhile, but the town possesses many other sights worth seeing. The Romanesque **Collegiata** (open Apr–Oct Mon–Fri 9.30am–7.30pm, Sat 9.30am–5pm, Sun 12.30–5pm, Nov–Mar Mon–Sat 9.30am–4.30pm, Sun opens at 12.30pm, no visits during mass; closed late Jan and late Nov; entrance fee) will detain you longest, as every inch of wall space is covered in frescoes. The north aisle has Bartolo di Fredi's dramatic scenes from the *Old Testament* (1367), while the opposite aisle has Lippo Memmi's *Life of Christ* (1333–41) and the nave the *Last Judgement* by Taddeo di Bartolo (1393–6). Contrast these Gothic-style narrative paintings with Ghirlandaio's lyrical Renaissance frescoes (1475) on the life of a local saint, in the chapel of Santa Fina.

Four museums

Next to the Collegiata, the **Museo d'Arte Sacra** (open Apr–Oct Mon–

Fri 9.30am–7pm, Sat 9.30am–5pm, Sun 12.30–5pm, Nov–Mar Mon–Sat 9.30am–4.30pm, Sun opens at 12.30pm; closed late Jan and late Nov; entrance fee) contains a variety of sacred art from the 13th to the 15th centuries.

Alongside is the **Museo Civico** (open daily Mar–Oct 9.30am–7.20pm, Nov–Feb 10am–5.50pm; entrance fee), housed in the Palazzo del Popolo, a forbidding fortress that served as the town hall. Completed in 1311, its tower, the **Torre Grossa**, is the tallest in the town (54 metres/175 ft) and the only one you can climb; the views of the Val d'Elsa from the top are spectacular. Among the museum's many good paintings is a set of early 14th-century frescoes by Memmo di Filippucci – rare in that they depict secular rather than religious scenes. Known as the *Wedding Frescoes*, they show a young bride and groom sharing a bath and climbing into their nuptial

TIP

To see San Gimignano at its best, it's worth considering an overnight stay in one of the characteristic hotels. Then you can savour the peaceful beauty of the town in the evening and early morning, after the coach trippers have gone.

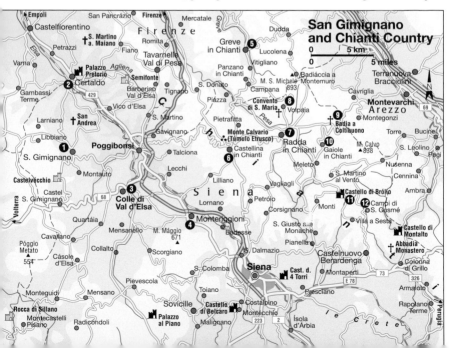

bed – an intimate glimpse into the private life of medieval Italy.

The former convent of Santa Chiara is now home to the **Museo Archeologico** (open daily 11am–5.45pm; entrance fee). Fascinating exhibits range from ceramic-and-glass vessels containing herbal remedies and healing lotions and potions, to Etruscan finds.

The nearby **Piazza della Cisterna** is a lovely triangular square with a 13th-century well and medieval *palazzi*. East of the square, on Via di Castello, is the **Museo della Tortura** (open daily 9.30am–7.30pm, winter Sat–Sun 10am–6pm; entrance fee), with a gruesome collection of medieval instruments of torture.

Every church in San Gimignano offers some reward, but perhaps the best is **Sant' Agostino** (open Apr–Oct daily 7am–noon, 3–7pm, Mar, Nov–Dec until 6pm, late Jan–Feb Tues–Sun 10am–noon, 3–6pm, Mon pm only) to the north of the town (near Porta San Matteo). Here, in Gozzoli's frescoes on the *Life of St Augustine* (1465), you will find the same love of colour, rich clothing

and exact portraiture as in Gozzoli's other frescoes such as *The Journey of the Magi* in the Palazzo Medici Riccardi in Florence *(see page 90)*.

A short walk along the city walls to the 14th-century fortress before leaving is worthwhile. This semi-derelict **Rocca** has views over tiered gardens and olive groves winding down to the "Vernaccia" vineyards.

The Val d'Elsa

A few kilometres north of San Gimignano, the medieval hill town of **Certaldo ❷** straddles the summit of a steep hill. To reach it, park in the lower town, Certaldo Basso, and take the *funicolare* up the steep slope to the upper town (closed to traffic). Certaldo Alto is a literary landmark as it was the home of Giovanni Boccaccio (1313–75), author of *The Decameron*, who died here in 1375. What is thought to have been his home was restored in 1823, bombed during World War II, and has now been rebuilt as the recently restored **Casa di Boccaccio** (open daily summer 9.30am–2pm, 2.30–7pm, winter 9.30am–4.30pm; entrance fee). The

Map on page 194

One of five circular towers in San Gimignano's city walls.

BELOW: San Gimignano newsagent.

Nectar of the Gods

The vine – along with olives and grain – became an integral part of Tuscany's agriculture very early in the region's history. The Etruscans were certainly enamoured with the fruits of the vine, as is evidenced by the wine cup found in an Etruscan tomb at Castellina in Chianti, and surviving Etruscan frescoes that depict scenes relating to Bacchus, the Roman god of wine. Monasteries played a large part in establishing a successful viticulture in the area – as they did through much of medieval Europe. Several old monastic sites – such as Badia a Coltibuono and Badia a Passignano – are still important wine estates today.

The wicker-covered Chianti flask, called a *fiascho*, is rarer these days in Italian restaurants than red-and-white check tablecloths. This emblem of the early days of Tuscan vine culture – now considered impractical, expensive to produce and a bit too "rustic" – has been superseded by an elegant square-shouldered bottle, reflecting the upgrading in quality of one of Italy's best-known wines.

If you order wine without referring to a wine list in a bar or restaurant in Tuscany, you will almost certainly be served the local *vino da tavola* (table wine) in a jug or carafe. It is always drinkable and often rather good. Now, however, Tuscany is much more conscious of its standing as a producer of higher-quality wines, and increasingly you will find a sophisticated list of superior Tuscan vintages.

Nevertheless, in wine terms, Tuscany is still synonymous with Chianti – to the chagrin of producers of the region's other fine wines. The heart of the Chianti district stretches in a large oval between Florence and Siena, with branches extending west towards Lucca and Pisa, south to Montalcino, southeast to Montepulciano, east to Arezzo and past Pontassieve, and north past Pistoia. The heartland is called Chianti Classico, covering the communes of Barberino Val d'Elsa, Castellina, Greve, Gaiole, San Casciano and Tavarnelle Val de Pesa.

The concern for the quality of wine has been evident in the Chianti Classico area since the 1700s, when grapes and wines began to be classified, and recommended methods of production were developed. The real mover in this area was Barone Bettino Ricasoli, who, in the mid-19th century, conducted experiments that led to a specific formula for making the wine. In 1924 a consortium, the Consorzio Chianti Classico, was founded to control production. To signify that a bottle was "Consorzio approved", a special sticker was placed around its neck carrying the symbol of the Consorzio, a black cockerel *(gallo nero).*

Once in the European Union, Italy had to develop a countrywide wine law. In line with EU regulations, "quality" wines were designated *Denominazione di Origine Controllata* (DOC), distinguishing them from their "lesser" brethren, called just *vino da tavola*. In 1984 Chianti joined the élite (including Brunello di Montalcino and Vino Nobile di Montepulciano) that were entitled to call their wines DOCG, the G standing for *e garantita*, "and guaranteed".

A few basics to keep in mind when shopping for wine in Tuscany: make sure it has the DOC designation; go for wines with family names or farm titles (avoid acronyms such as CA.VI.T) and look for the black cockerel label on the neck if you want a good Chianti. ❑

LEFT: the Sangiovese grape.

Map on page 194

differences between Certaldo Alto and Certaldo Basso are marked by the relative calm of the former, as traffic is limited. The red-brick town is crowned by the 15th-century **Palazzo Pretorio**, the front façade of which is studded with terracotta coats of arms. Exploration around the back of the town will reveal the early gateways, the portals of which are still intact and which lead down to steep, narrow approach lanes. The frescoed rooms of the **Palazzo del Vicario** (open summer daily 9.30am–2pm, 2.30–7pm, winter until 4.30pm; entrance fee) are worth visiting. The Palazzo also houses a delightful hotel and a Michelin-starred restaurant *(see page 201)*.

South of San Gimignano, **Colle di Val d'Elsa** ❸ is split between two sites. The lower "new" town is a busy, haphazard sprawl, whose centre of activity is the crystal factory – Colle is Italy's largest producer of crystal and fine glass, and there are plenty of shops selling it. The recent Museo del Cristallo (Via dei Fossi; May–Oct Tues–Sun 10am–noon 4–7pm, Nov–Apr Tues–Fri 3–7pm, Sat–Sun

10am–noon 3–7pm; entrance fee) tells its story. Follow the signs up to the ancient upper town. Here the main street is lined with 16th-century *palazzi* of unusual refinement, and, at one point, the stately procession of buildings is interrupted by a viaduct from which there are splendid views of the surrounding landscape.

More spectacular sights await in nearby **Monteriggioni** ❹, just off the N2 to Siena. The fortified town, encircled by walls and 14 towers, was built in 1213 to guard the northern borders of Sienese territory. Like Montepulciano, this little hill village is emblematic of the Tuscan landscape, and merits a short visit. It is seen at its best first thing in the morning, when you can enjoy a coffee on the main square before the coach parties arrive.

The Chiantigiana

The Chianti is a spiritual rather than a geographical location. Its shifting borders reflect the fluctuations in Florentine and Sienese power, but, although it lies in Siena province, its soul remains where it has always

In 1716 a decree issued by the Grand Duke of Tuscany defined the boundaries of the Chianti area and established the laws governing the production and sale of wine. Today this region is the world's oldest wine-producing league. The Chianti Classico area includes the communes of Barberino Val d'Elsa, Castellina, Greve, Gaiole, San Casciano and Tavernelle Val di Pesa.

BELOW: all the elements of a classic Tuscan landscape.

TIP

Cycling is an immensely popular way of touring Chianti country, and countless companies organise group or family holidays for people of all ages and abilities. You can also organise bike rental by the day or week through the Castellina in Chianti tourist office on Via Ferruccio (tel: 0577-741392; open daily 9am–1pm, 2.30–6.30pm).

BELOW: cyclists stop for souvenirs in Castellina.

been: on Florentine soil. It is a place whose turbulent history has shaped a scene of utter tranquillity, a harmony of tame hills and gentle people. In a place where nothing is essential viewing, everywhere is a glorious detour.

The SS222, known as the Chiantigiana, or Chianti Way, winds its picturesque way from Florence to Siena, through the heart of the region, offering archetypal scenes of cypress trees, olive groves and vineyards. First stop is the market town of **Greve** ❺ with an impressive arcaded square, Piazza Matteotti, topped with wrought-iron balconies dripping with geraniums. The shops under the arcades are crammed with the usual assortment of local foods, crafts and wines. The annual September Mostra Mercato del Chianti draws a large crowd.

An oft-missed jewel just five minutes' drive west of Greve is the ancient, tiny medieval walled town of **Montefioralle**, which was built as a feudal castle. Its narrow streets, stone houses and underpassages are beautifully preserved, and splendid views are to be had from the various *trattorie* in the town.

Next on the SS222 is **Castellina in Chianti** ❻. Castellina surveys symmetrical vineyards and wooded groves, a landscape dotted with low stone houses and Renaissance villas. New wine estates have been built from the remains of medieval castles. Villas have lazily domesticated the original castle or tower, but names like "La Rocca" or "La Torre" reveal the original function.

Castellina's name also reveals its medieval function as a Florentine outpost. In the late 13th century it was the first site of the Chianti League, a group of three Florentine feudal castles, each responsible for a third of the territory. The castle is now a fortified town hall hiding a small Etruscan museum and a warren of atmospheric backstreets with half-glimpsed views of the Chianti hills.

The other attraction is the **Enoteca La Bottega del Vino** (Via della Rocca 13; tel: 0577-741110; www.enobottega.it), the wine-tasting centre which gives advice on wine tours and *vendita diretta*, direct sales.

Chianti's capital

East of Castellina, **Radda in Chianti** ❼ retains its medieval street plan and imposing town hall. As in Castellina, the spontaneous rural architecture is more rewarding. Classical Medici villas with 16th-century windows and wells compete with romantic villas, constructed magpie-fashion from castles or Etruscan ruins. One 17th-century masterpiece is Villa Vistarenni, a white beacon of sophistication. The elegant loggias and the openness of the architecture symbolise the increasing wealth of the countryside and its proximity to urban Florence. In the tranquil Chianti, the country is richer and more civilised than the town.

From Radda a tortuous road climbs to **Volpaia** ❽, a pretty medieval village, with a ruined castle and Brunelleschi-style church. If Chianti villages and towns have little sense of identity and few artistic treasures, it is because they came into being with fully-fledged Florentine and Sienese identities, while military outposts like Radda had no time to develop artistically. Only the Chianti abbeys, endowed separately, had the independence to shape their own culture.

Abbey of the Good Harvest

Between Radda and Gaiole is the aptly named **Badia a Coltibuono** ❾ (Abbey of the Good Harvest; open May–Oct; closed am and Aug; tel: 0577-744832; www.coltibuono. com), set among pines, oaks, chestnuts and vines. Since the Dissolution of the Monasteries in 1810, this medieval abbey has belonged to one family. The lovely 15th-century cloisters, chapel and frescoed ceilings can be viewed as a guest of the Tuscan cookery school or bed and breakfast, while the 12th-century walls and bell-tower are open to all. Below the abbey are cellars filled with Chianti Classico, the abbey's traditional living. No less famous are the aromatic chestnut honey and olive oil. Much of the produce can be bought on the premises or savoured in the excellent abbey restaurant.

Chianti castles

Gaiole in Chianti ❿ is a newer riverside development in a wooded

Map on page 194

A winemaker promotes his produce at the Chianti wine festival held in Greve every September.

BELOW: café on Piazza Matteotti, Greve.

Map on page 194

The famous Chianti flask is no longer mass-produced for export. However, the nostalgic will be pleased to find rustic wicker fiaschi for sale throughout the region.

BELOW: San Gimignano through the early morning mist.

valley. It is a popular *villeggiatura*, a summer escape for hot Florentines in search of family-run hotels, home cooking and the familiar *gallo nero* (black cockerel) wine symbol. History lies in wait at Meleto and Vertine, unusual castles, and Barbischio, a medieval village, is a short walk away. Tempting footpaths marked *Sentieri del Chianti* lead all the way to Siena. With vineyards rising up gentle slopes, tranquil Gaiole and sleepy Greve are traditional Chianti.

The countryside from Gaiole south to Siena and east to Arezzo is higher, wilder and wetter. The wooded peaks are green and fresh with scents of thyme, rosemary and pine. Deep chestnut woods provide ideal cover for wild boar, recently reintroduced.

Of the many Florentine castles in the woods, **Castello di Brolio** ⓫ (open daily summer 9am–12.30pm, 3–6pm, winter reduced hours; entrance fee) is the most impressive – not least because of its views over the original Chianti vineyards stretching as far as Siena and Monte Amiata. On the medieval chessboard, every Florentine castle faced its

Sienese shadow. If the surviving castles are Florentine, it is because Siena lost the match and all its pieces. While Sienese Cereto and Cettamura are small heaps, Florentine Brolio and Meleto are resplendent. As a Florentine outpost, Castello di Brolio's past spans Guelf-Ghibelline conflicts, sacking by the Sienese in 1529 and German occupation and Allied bombing during World War II. The medieval walls are the castle's most striking feature, along with the 14th-century chapel, set in lush grounds. Brolio has long been controlled by the Ricasoli, Chianti landowners since the eighth century. Baron Bettino Ricasoli, Italian premier in 1861, founded the modern Chianti wine industry, a business continued by the present family (to visit the cellars and taste the wines, tel: 0577-730220; www.ricasoli.it).

The Chianti is a place for pottering and chance encounters, one of which is tiny **Campi di San Gusmé** ⓬, just south of Brolio. A short climb leads to a small tower, Romanesque church and views of tumbledown castles, villas and vineyards. ❑

RESTAURANTS

Castellina In Chianti

Albergaccio
Via Fiorentina 63
Tel: 0577-741042
www.albergacciocast.com
The dishes change, but the quality of the food – which is Tuscan with flair – remains the same. Booking advisable. Closed Sun, summers also Wed at lunch. €€

La Torre
Piazza del Comune
Tel: 0577-740236
Restaurant with terrace outside the fortress. Extensive menu of predictable Tuscan fare, but reasonable. Closed Fri. €€

Certaldo Alto

L'Antica Fonte
Via Valdracca 25
Tel: 0571-652225
www.tavernaanticafonte.it
Small, simple restaurant offering Tuscan specialities in a friendly and relaxed atmosphere. In summer there's additional seating in the garden opposite, with views across the Val d'Elsa. Booking essential. Closed Jan and Feb. €€

Osteria del Vicario
Via Rivellino 3
Tel: 0571-668228
www.osteriadelvicario.it
Pleasantly set in Romanesque cloisters, this Michelin-starred restaurant serves inventive variations on Tuscan and international dishes. Closed Sun dinner, Mon. €€€

Gaiole In Chianti

Badia a Coltibuono
Loc. Badia a Coltibuono
Tel/fax: 0577-749424
www.coltibuono.com
Set on a glorious rural wine estate, complete with 11th-century abbey. Specialities include home-made pasta with wild duck sauce and *antipasto della Badia*. Wine and oil from the estate is for sale. Popular with tourists on the Chianti trail. Closed Mon except May–Oct. €€€

Il Carlino d'Oro
Località San Regolo
Tel: 0577-747136
Family-run trattoria, far removed from the tourists that swarm around this part of the Chianti. Lunch only; closed Mon. €

Ristorante della Pieve (Castello di Spaltenna)
Località Spaltenna 13
Tel: 0577-749483
www.spaltenna.it
Magnificent restaurant in a hotel converted from a fortified monastery. Dishes use fresh local ingredients, and food is cooked in a wood-burning stove. Closed Nov–Mar. €€€€

Greve in Chianti

Bottega del Moro
Piazza Trieste 14r
Tel: 055-853753
www.labottegadelmoro.it
Restaurant serving good-quality traditional Tuscan fare. Try the *coniglio* (rabbit) or *trippa alla Fiorentina* (tripe) after a fresh pasta dish. Closed Mon. €€

Monterriggioni

Il Pozzo
Piazza Roma 20
Tel: 0577-304127
www.ilpozzo.net
Famous restaurant full of foreigners in summer, but deservedly popular, in a gem of a tiny walled town. Closed Sun evening, Mon, most of Jan and period in Aug. €€

Panzano in Chianti

Enoteca Baldi
Piazza Bucciarelli 25
Tel: 055-852843
Enoteca with impressive wine selection. Open for a light lunch or a late afternoon snack. €

Radda In Chianti

Le Vigne
Podere le Vigne Est
(1 km outside town)
Tel: 0577-738640
Beautifully located among vineyards, and serving great food, this is a real treat. Simple, reasonably priced rooms to rent above the restaurant. Closed mid-Nov–Feb. €€–€€€

Vignale
Via XX Settembre 23
Tel: 0577-738094
Restaurant housed in a converted farm building, serving refined and imaginative Tuscan cuisine. However, prices are high and tourists abound. Must book. €€€–€€€€

San Gimignano

Dorandò
Vicolo dell'Oro 2
Tel: 0577-941862
www.ristorantedorando.it
Stylish restaurant specialising in recipes with ancient origins. Closed Mon (except Easter–Nov) and 9 Dec–20 Feb. €€€€

Osteria delle Cantene
Via Mainardi 18
Tel: 0577-941966
New-wave trattoria where traditional and contemporary ideas successfully coexist. Try the local Vernaccia wine. Closed Wed and Jan. €€

Volpaia

La Bottega
Piazza della Torre 2
Tel: 0577-738001
A gorgeous spot for lunch on a maple-shaded terrace with views over the valley. The quality can vary, but the friendly service and prime location make up for any shortcomings. Closed Tues. €€

PRICE CATEGORIES

Average cost of a three-course meal per person with a half-bottle of wine:
€ = under €25
€€ = €25–40
€€€ = €40–60
€€€€ = more than €60

THE CHIANTI WINE TRAIL

A trip to Tuscany, home of the famous Chianti Classico and other fine Italian wines, is not complete without exploring some wine estates

What has become known as the Chianti area of Tuscany covers an enormous region, spanning seven different wine "zones". At its heart, in the hills between Florence and Siena, is Chianti Classico, while the remainder – the Colli Fiorentini, Colli Senesi, Colline Pisane, Colli Aretini, Rufina and Montalbano – spread out over central Tuscany.

The main centres in Chianti Classico are Greve, Panzano, Castellina, Gaiole, Fonterutoli and Radda – the official seat of the vintners' association known as the Consorzio del Marchio Storico. Scattered in and among these towns, many of them accessible off the picturesque route SS222, are innumerable vineyards and estates. Most of the estates welcome visitors. Treasure troves of art and history as well as wine, they are well worth exploring. *Toscana & Chianti News* (www.toscanaechiantinews.it), available at local hotels and restaurants, lists estates open for wine-tasting. Estate owners are usually proud to show off their wines and explain their particular methods of wine-making. They will discuss the astounding number of factors, from soil conditions to pruning and grafting, which come into play in order to produce the region's distinctive wines, as well as the science behind processes such as fermentation to ageing. Experimentation is constant, and the different schools of thought encountered along the way are fascinating. Any given winemaker could discuss for hours the pros and cons of various types of wood used in the barrels and casks for ageing and storage. But the best reason for visiting the vineyards is without question… the tasting. Sip, savour and enjoy.

ABOVE: Although chestnut was the traditional wood of the region, Chianti *normale* is now usually kept in oak barrels for several months. The smaller barrels are known as *barriques*; the larger are *botti*.

BELOW: The hills of Chianti are blanketed with vineyards; many of the wine estates are hundreds of years old.

ABOVE: Trebbiani and Malvasia grapes hang up to dry for Vin Santo, made in Chianti and other parts of Tuscany. The wine is fermented and aged for up to six years in small barrels, *orcaratelli*. This strong dessert wine is comparable to a good medium sherry.

LEFT: Hard-earned DOCG labels on bottles of Chianti Classico at Riecine estate near Gaiole. The wine here is made using both meticulous and classic methods.

THE ESTATES

Below are a selection of recommended wine estates in the Chianti region. The majority have shops where you can taste the wine before purchasing, but for a more memorable experience call the estate in advance to arrange a tasting *(degustazione)* combined with a tour of the vineyards and cellars. Good websites for up-to-date information on wine in the area are www.florencewine.it and www.chianticlassico.com.

Badia a Coltibuono
Gaiole in Chianti; tel: 0577-744832; www.coltibuono.com
This wine estate, run by the Stucchi Prinetti family, markets itself as a "wine resort" – visitors can eat, sleep and take courses within the former abbey. Tastings are available to pre-formed groups of 10 or more people.

Castello di Brolio
Gaiole in Chianti; tel: 0577-730220; www.ricasoli.it
Baron Ricasoli, whose descendants now run the Castello di Brolio, first designated the grape mixes to be used in Chianti wine. Today the famous estate can be visited by appointment.

Castello di Fonterutoli
Castellina in Chianti; tel: 0577-741385; www.mazzei.it
Owned by the family since the 15th century, Fonterutoli's wines have won several awards.

Castello di Gabbiano
Mecatale Val di Pesa; tel: 055-821 8059; www.gabbiano.com
The estate shop offers an opportunity to taste and purchase wine produced at Castello di Gabbiano. Tours can be organised on request.

Montevertine
Radda in Chianti; tel: 0577-738009; www.montevertine.it
The Manetti family only founded this small estate in 1967, but its quality wines are already famous. Call for details on tastings.

Vignamaggio
Greve; tel: 055-854661; www.vignamaggio.it
This *tenuta* is a wine estate and an *agriturismo*. Wine-tasting can be done at the shop, or combined with a pre-arranged guided visit.

SIENA

Siena's tumultuous history as arch-rival of Florence is written in the streets and squares, and resonates in the passionate souls of the Sienese. It is a magical Gothic city, full of pleasant surprises, but the glorious main square alone makes it worth a visit

From its striped marble Cathedral to its tunnelled alleys, brilliant Campo and black-and-white city emblem, Siena is a chiaroscuro city. In its surging towers it is truly Gothic. Where Florence is boldly horizontal, Siena is soaringly vertical; where Florence has large squares and masculine statues, Siena has hidden gardens and romantic wells. Florentine art is perspective and innovation, while Sienese art is sensitivity and conservatism. Siena is often considered the feminine foil to Florentine masculinity.

For such a feminine and beautiful city, Siena has a decidedly warlike reputation, nourished by sieges, city-state rivalry and *Palio* battles. The pale theatricality in Sienese painting is not representative of the city or its inhabitants: the average Sienese is no ethereal Botticelli nymph, but dark, stocky and swarthy.

A brief history

In keeping with Sienese mystique, the city's origins are shrouded in myths of wolves and martyred saints. According to legend, the city was founded by Senius, son of Remus, hence the she-wolf symbols in the city. St Ansano brought Christianity to Roman Siena and, although he was promptly tossed into a vat of hot tar and beheaded, he has left a legacy of mysticism traced through Sts Catherine and Bernardino to the present-day cult of the Madonna. The power of the Church came to an end when the populace rose up against the Ecclesiastical Council and established an independent republic in 1147. The 12th century was marked by rivalry in which the Florentine Guelfs usually triumphed over the Sienese Ghibellines.

In 1260 the battle of Montaperti routed the Florentines and won the Sienese ten years of cultural

Map on page 206

LEFT: Siena's Town Hall and Torre del Mangia, in the Campo.
BELOW: the glow of the rosy brick warms Siena's narrow passageways and arches.

The city is divided into three districts or terzi *(thirds) – The Terzo di San Martino, Terzo di Città and Terzo di Camollia. But this is purely an administrative division; Siena's true identity is inextricably linked to the* contrade, *the 17 medieval districts from which its social fabric is woven (see "Contrade Passions" box opposite).*

supremacy which saw the foundation of the University and the charitable "fraternities". The Council of the Twenty-Four – a form of power-sharing between nobles and the working class – was followed by the Council of Nine, an oligarchy of merchants which ruled until 1335. Modern historians judge the Nine self-seeking and profligate, but under their rule the finest works of art were either commissioned or completed, including the famous Campo, the Palazzo Pubblico and Duccio's *Maestà*.

The ancient republic survived until 1529, when the reconciliation

between the pope and the emperor ended the Guelf-Ghibelline feud. The occupying Spanish demolished the city towers, symbols of freedom and fratricide, and used the masonry to build the present fortress. The final blow to the republic was the long siege of Siena by Emperor Charles V and Cosimo I in 1554.

After the Sienese defeat, the city of Siena became absorbed into the Tuscan dukedom. As an untrusted member of the Tuscan Empire, impoverished Siena turned in on itself until the 20th century. Today, change is anathema to the

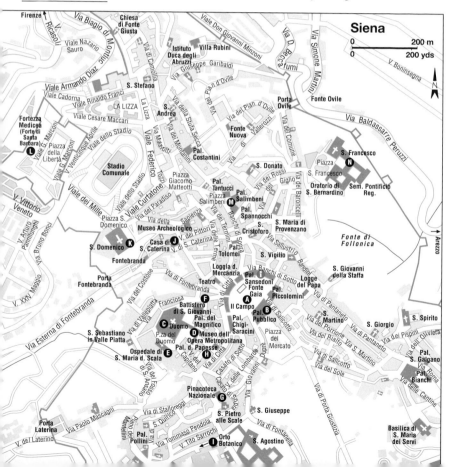

city: traditional landowning, financial speculation, trade and tourism are more appealing than new technology or industry. Siena has made a virtue of conservatism; stringent medieval building regulations protect the fabric of the city; tourism is decidedly low-key; old family firms such as the *Nannini* cake shop – Siena's most famous café – do a roaring trade with locals (and also produced Gianna Nannini, one of Italy's best-known female singers). It is a city with the psychology of a village and the grandeur of a nation.

Il Campo

All roads lead to **Il Campo Ⓐ**, the huge main central square, shaped like an amphitheatre – the Sienese say that it is shaped like the protecting cloak of the Virgin, who, with St Catherine of Siena, is the city's patron saint. From the comfort of a pavement café on the curved side of the Campo you can note the division of the paved surface into nine segments, commemorating the beneficent rule of the "Noveschi" – the Council of Nine which governed Siena from the mid-13th century to the early 14th, a period of stability and prosperity when most of the city's main public monuments were built.

The Campo is tipped with the Renaissance **Fonte Gaia** (Fountain of Joy). The marble carvings are copies of the original sculptures by Iacopo della Quercia, which are on display in Santa Maria della Scala *(see page 210)*. Beneath the fountain lies one of Siena's best-kept secrets – a labyrinth of medieval tunnels extending for 25 km (15½ miles), constructed to channel water from the surrounding hills into the city. The undergound aqueduct has two main tunnels: one leads to the Fonte Gaia and the other to the Fonte Branda, the best-preserved of Siena's many fountains, northwest of here. Parts of this subterranean system can be visited on a guided tour (ask at the tourist office).

At the square's base is the **Palazzo Pubblico Ⓑ**, the dignified Town Hall with its crenellated façade and waving banners, surmounted by the tall and slender tower. The Town Hall, which has

As an introduction to the city, a visit to the State Archives in the 15th-century Palazzo Piccolomini (Via Banchi di Sotto; open Mon–Sat, guided tours at 9.30am, 10.30am and 11.30am) provides a pictorial history of Siena through illuminated manuscripts and paintings.

BELOW LEFT:
Romulus, Remus and the she-wolf: Remus' son is said to have founded Siena.

Contrade Passions

Siena's cultural aloofness owes much to the *contrade*, the 17 city wards designated for now defunct administrative and military functions during the Middle Ages, which continue to act as individual entities within the city. To outsiders, the only real significance of the *contrade* appears to be in connection with the *Palio (see page 214)*, but their existence pervades every aspect of everyday life. Despite its public grandeur, much of Siena is resolutely working-class and attaches great weight to belonging to a community. Events such as baptisms and deaths are celebrated together, while the traditional Sienese will only marry within his or her *contrada*.

All over the city, the importance of the various *contrade* is evident. Little plaques set into the wall testify to which *contrada* you are in (dolphin, caterpillar, goose and so on). Each neighbourhood has its own fountain and font, as well as a motto, symbol and colours. The latter are combined in a flag, worn with pride and patriotism by the inhabitants and seen hanging and draped around buildings for important *contrada* events, most notably a *Palio* triumph.

The interior of the Duomo, a magnificent Gothic structure of banded black-and-white stone, with a superb floor of inlaid marble depicting themes not only from the Bible, but also from pagan myth and magic.

been the home of the commune since it was completed in 1310, is a Gothic masterpiece of rose-coloured brick and silver-grey travertine. Each ogival arch is crowned by the *balzana*, Siena's black-and-white emblem representing the mystery and purity of the Madonna's life.

The distinctive **Torre del Mangia** (open daily 10am–7pm, until 4pm Nov–mid-Mar; entrance fee) – named after the first bellringer, Mangiaguadagni, the "spendthrift" – is 87 metres high, and it's a 500-step climb to the top to enjoy glorious views of the pink piazza and Siena's rooftops. At the bottom of the tower, the **Cappella in Piazza** (Chapel in the Square) was erected in 1378 in thanksgiving for the end of the plague.

The city museum

Although bureaucrats still toil in parts of the Palazzo Pubblico, as they have for some seven centuries, much of the complex is now dedicated to the **Museo Civico** (open daily Mar–Oct 10am–7pm, until 5.30pm or 6.30pm Nov–mid-Mar;

entrance fee), which houses some of the city's greatest treasures. Siena's city council once met in the vast Sala del Mappamondo, although the huge globe that then graced the walls has disappeared. What remains are two frescoes attributed to the medieval master Simone Martini: the majestic mounted figure of Guidoriccio da Fogliano and the *Maestà*. Martini's *Maestà*, a poetic evocation of the Madonna seated on a filigree throne, has a rich, tapestry-like quality. The muted blues, reds and ivory add a gauzy softness. Martini echoes Giotto's conception of perspective, yet clothes his Madonna in diaphanous robes, concealing her spirituality in dazzling decoration.

Opposite is the iconic *Guidoriccio*, the haughty diamond-spangled *condottiero* (mercenary) reproduced on calendars and *panforte* boxes. But in recent years, despite Sienese denials, doubts have been cast on the authenticity of the fresco. Art historians maintain that a smaller painting uncovered below the huge panel is Martini's original,

and the Guidoriccio we see was executed long after the artist's death.

In the next room is a genuine civic masterpiece, Ambrogio Lorenzetti's *Effects of Good and Bad Government*, painted in 1338 as an idealised tribute to the Council of the Nine. The narrative realism and vivid facial expressions give the allegory emotional resonance. A wise old man symbolises the common good, while a patchwork of neat fields, tame boar and busy hoers suggests order and prosperity. Bad Government is a desolate place, razed to the ground by a diabolical tyrant, the Sienese she-wolf at his feet.

The Cathedral

Exiting the Campo, turn left and head up the hill via one of the winding streets to the Piazza del Duomo. The **Duomo ●** (open daily 10.30am–6pm; entrance fee) is Siena's most controversial monument, either a symphony in black-and-white marble or a tasteless iced cake, depending on your point of view. It began in 1220 as a round-arched Romanesque church, but soon acquired a Gothic façade festooned with pinnacles. Bands of black, white and green marble were inlaid with pink stone and topped by Giovanni Pisano's naturalistic statues.

The Cathedral interior is creativity run riot – oriental abstraction, Byzantine formality, Gothic flight and Romanesque austerity. A giddy chiaroscuro effect is created by the black-and-white walls reaching up to the starry blue vaults. The floor is even more inspiring: major Sienese craftsmen worked on the marble *pavimentazione* between 1372 and 1562. The finest are Matteo di Giovanni's pensive Sibyls and marble mosaics by Beccafumi. In order to preserve the floors, many of the most interesting scenes are covered by hardboard for most of the year and only revealed to the public for two months at the start of autumn (www.operaduomo.siena.it).

Nicola Pisano's octagonal marble pulpit is a Gothic masterpiece: built in 1226, it is a dramatic and fluid progression from his solemn **pulpit** in Pisa Cathedral. Off the north aisle is the decorative **Libreria Piccolomini**, built in 1495 to house the personal papers and books of Pope Pius II. The frescoes by Pinturicchio (1509) show scenes from the life of the influential Renaissance pope, a member of the noble Sienese Piccolomini family and founder of Pienza *(see page 219)*.

In the unfinished eastern section of the Cathedral is the **Museo dell' Opera Metropolitana ●** (open daily Mar–May and Sept–Oct 9.30am–7pm, June–Aug until 8pm, Nov–Feb 10am–5pm; entrance fee) and Pisano's original statues for the façade. In a dramatically lit room above is Duccio's *Maestà*, Siena's best-loved work, which was escorted from the artist's workshop to the Duomo in a torchlit procession; the largest known medieval panel painting graced the High Altar

Map on page 206

TIP

The Duomo's museum allows access to the parapets, which offer dazzling views of Siena – a more accessible alternative to the Torre del Mangia's panorama.

BELOW: The figure of Peace from the *Allegory of Good Government*, by Lorenzetti (1338).

BELOW: Siena's unmistakable Campo.

until 1506. The biggest panel depicts the Madonna enthroned among saints and angels, and, since the separation of the painting, facing scenes from the Passion. Although Byzantine Gothic in style, the *Maestà* is suffused with melancholy charm. The delicate gold and red colouring is matched by Duccio's grace of line, which influenced Sienese painting for the next two centuries. The Sienese believe that Giotto copied Duccio but sacrificed beauty to naturalism. The small panels do reveal some of Giotto's truthfulness and sense of perspective.

Opposite the Duomo on the piazza is the **Ospedale Santa Maria della Scala** ➊ (open daily mid-Mar–Oct 10am–6.30pm, Nov–Mar 10.30am–4.30pm; entrance fee). This former pilgrims' hospital, believed to have been founded in the 9th century, was in its day one of the most important hospitals in the world; it is now being turned into a major arts centre and exhibition space with restoration facilities. Used as a practising hospital until 1995, its main ward is adorned with

frescoes by Domenico di Bartolo. The city's **Museo Archeologico** (open mid-Mar–Oct Mon–Sat 10.30am–6.30pm, Nov–mid-Mar until 4.30pm; entrance fee), with its significant collection of Etruscan and Roman remains, is housed here; other rooms host temporary exhibitions.

A set of steps behind the Duomo leads down to Piazza San Giovanni, a small square dominated by the **Battistero di San Giovanni** ➏ (open Mar–May, Sept–Oct 9.30am–7pm, June–Aug until 8pm, Nov–Feb 10am–5pm; entrance fee), built beneath part of the Cathedral. Inside are frescoes and a beautiful baptismal font by Jacopo della Quercia.

Two art museums

There are two art museums in the vicinity of the Cathedral complex, at opposite ends of the scale of their content. The **Pinacoteca Nazionale** ➐ (Via San Pietro 29; open Tues–Sat 8.15am–7.15pm, Sun and Mon until 1.15pm and 1.30pm respectively; entrance fee) contains the finest collection of Sienese "Primitives" in the suitably Gothic Palazzo

Buonsignori. The early rooms are full of Madonnas, apple-cheeked, pale, remote or warmly human. Matteo di Giovanni's stylised Madonnas shift to Lorenzetti's affectionate *Annunciation* and Ugolino di Neri's radiant *Madonna*. Neroccio di Bartolomeo's *Madonna* is as truthful as a Masaccio.

As a variant, the grisly deaths of obscure saints compete with a huge medieval crucifix with a naturalistic spurt of blood. The famous landscapes and surreal Persian city attributed to Lorenzetti were probably painted by Sassetta a century later. But his *Madonna dei Carmelitani* is a sweeping cavalcade of Sienese life.

Those suffering from a surfeit of medieval sacred art can visit the **Palazzo delle Papesse** ⓗ (Via di Città 126; open Tues–Sun noon–7pm; entrance fee), a contemporary art gallery with changing exhibitions, which also offers a 360-degree view of Siena from its loggia.

For some outdoor space and greenery, turn left out of the gallery and head south to the **Orto Botanico** ⓘ (Via P.A. Mattioli 4; open Mon–Fri 8.30am–12.30pm, 2.30–5.30pm, Sat 8am–noon), a small botanical garden just inside the city walls. Opposite the Orto Tolomei is another little garden, with a view over the countryside and a sculpture which – although not obvious at first glance – outlines the shape of the city.

St Catherine trail

Slightly outside the historic centre, on Vicolo del Tiratoio, is the **Casa di Santa Caterina da Siena** ⓙ (Costa di Sant' Antonio; open daily 9am–12.30pm, 3–6pm), the home of Catherine Benincase (1347–80), canonised in the 15th century by Pope Pius II and proclaimed Italy's Patron Saint in 1939. The house, garden and her father's dye-works now form the "Sanctuary of St Catherine".

Inside the nearby **Basilica di San Domenico** ⓚ (open Apr–Oct 7am–6.30pm, Nov–Mar 9am–6pm) – a huge fortress-like church founded by the Dominicans – a reliquary containing the saint's head is kept in the Cappella Santa Caterina. The

St Catherine, the daughter of a Sienese dyer, devoted her early life to the needs of the poor and sick. She then turned to politics and dedicated herself to reconciling anti-papal and papal forces; she was instrumental in the return of Pope Gregory XI, exiled in Avignon, to Rome. All the places she visited, from the day of her birth, have been consecrated.

BELOW:
contrada procession in the Campo, by Vincenzo Rustici.

Map on page 206

Statue of Sallustio Bandini, founder of Siena's library, on Piazza Salimbeni.

chapel is decorated with frescoes depicting events in the saint's life, the majority completed by Sodoma in the early 16th century. The view from outside the Basilica across to the Duomo is spectacular.

The Fortress

From here it's a short walk to the Forte di Santa Barbara, also known as the **Fortezza Medicea** ⓛ, built by Cosimo I after his defeat of Siena in 1560. The red-brick fortress now houses an open-air theatre, provides glorious views of the countryside and contains the **Enoteca Italiana** (open Mon–Sat noon–1am; tel: 0577-288811). The latter, a wine exhibition and shop, offers visitors the chance to sample and buy from a wide range of Tuscan wines and have any questions answered about the winemaking process.

Via Banchi di Sopra, lined with fine medieval *palazzi*, is one of the three main arteries of the city centre (the other two being Via Banchi di Sotto and Via di Città). It links the Campo with the splendid **Piazza Salimbeni** ⓜ at its northern end.

The grand *palazzi* flanking the square are the head office of the Monte dei Paschi di Siena, one of the oldest banks in the world. Founded in 1472 and still an important employer, it is known as "the city father".

Basilica of St Francis

From the square, Via dei Rossi leads east to the **Basilica di San Francesco** ⓝ (open 7am–noon, 3.30–7pm). Now housing part of the University, the vast church exhibits fragments of frescoes by Pietro and Ambrogio Lorenzetti. Next door, the 15th-century **Oratorio di San Bernardino** (open mid-Mar–Oct 10.30am–1.30pm, 3–5.30pm; entrance fee), dedicated to Siena's great preacher, contains frescoes by Il Sodoma and Beccafumi.

At this extremity, as well as elsewhere, the city has well-preserved walls and gateways. Siena's compactness makes these easy to reach, offering the opportunity to wind through the narrow streets and stumble across hidden buildings and fountains on the way. ❑

BELOW: a more unusual view of Siena.

RESTAURANTS AND BARS

Restaurants

Al Mangia
Piazza del Campo 42
Tel: 0577-281121
www.almangia.it
In a wonderful position on the Campo, this restaurant serves good, classic Tuscan cuisine, popular with tourists and locals alike. Outside tables in summer. Closed Wed Nov–Feb. €€€–€€€€

Al Marsili
Via del Castoro 3
Tel: 0577-47154
www.ristorantealmarsili.it
Elegant restaurant in an ancient building with wine cellars cut deep into the limestone. Sophisticated cuisine, including gnocchi in duck sauce. Closed Mon in winter. €€–€€€

Antica Trattoria Botteganova
Via Chiantigiana 29
Tel: 0577-284230
This refined restaurant serves some of the finest cuisine in Siena. Specialities include local Tuscan delicacies, fish and delicious puddings. Closed Sun, period in Jan, early Aug. €€€–€€€€

Certosa di Maggiano
Strada di Certosa 82
Tel: 0577-288180
www.certosadimaggiano.com
This converted Carthusian monastery, now a hotel, serves gourmet food in a magical setting: a cloistered courtyard overlooking Siena. Closed Tues. €€€€

Da Guido
Vicolo del Pettinaio 7
Tel: 0577-280042
Veritable Sienese institution, set in medieval premises and popular with visiting VIPs. Traditional Sienese cuisine. Closed Wed and Jan. €€–€€€

Osteria del Castelvecchio
Via Castelvecchio 65
Tel: 0577-49586
Converted from ancient stables, this hostelry creates contemporary dishes with traditional flavours. Interesting wine list. Closed Tues. €€

Osteria Il Boccone del Prete
Via San Pietro17
Tel: 0577-280388
Family-run restaurant, serving Sienese dishes, in a pleasing setting. Closed Sun. €

Osteria Il Carroccio
Via Casato di Sotto 32
Tel: 0577-41165
Well-run quaint and tiny trattoria serving simple local dishes. Closed Tues dinner, Wed, Feb and 1 week in Nov. €

Osteria La Chiacchiera
Costa di S. Antonio 4
Tel: 0577-280631
Small, rustic *osteria* offering typical Sienese fare (try the thick *pici*). Closed Tues. €

Osteria La Taverna di San Giuseppe
Via G. Dupré 132
Tel: 0577-42286
www.tavernasangiuseppe.it
Delicious Tuscan fare in an atmospheric cavern with wooden furnishings. An antipasto is a must; delicious dishes using pecorino. Closed Sun. €–€€

Osteria Le Logge
Via del Porrione 33
Tel: 0577-48013
Restaurant set in a 19th-century grocer's shop, with an authentic dark-wood and marble interior, with such exotic offerings as duck and fennel and stuffed guinea fowl (*faraona*). Closed Sun and Jan. €€–€€€

Pizzeria di Nonno Mede
Via Camporegio 21
Tel: 0577-247966
Serves a good pizza and great desserts. Splendid view across to the Duomo, which is well lit in the evenings. Reservation recommended. €

Trattoria Papei
Piazza del Mercato 6
Tel: 0577-280894
Ideal place for sampling genuine Sienese home cooking in generous helpings. Closed Mon (except public holidays) and end July. €€

Tre Cristi
Vicolo di Provenzano 1–7
Tel: 0577-280608
www.trecristi.com
Elegant restaurant with a contemporary Mediterranean menu. Frescoed walls add to the atmosphere. Booking advised. Closed Sun in Aug. €€–€€€

Bars

Nannini (Banchi di Sopra) is an obligatory coffee stop on Siena's main shopping street. Opposite is **Caffè del Corso** – chic by day, boisterous by night. **Bar le Logge** (Via Rinaldini, at the end of Banchi di Sotto) is a non-touristy place to drink cappuccino. Once into Il Campo, numerous bars have food and drink to suit all tastes; the prices are elevated but the vantage point superb. To the left of the Palazzo Pubblico, **Gelateria Caribia** (Via Rinaldini) offers a multitude of ice cream flavours. **The Tea Room** (Via Porta Giustizia; closed Mon) is a cosy place for tea and cake, or a cocktail to accompany the live jazz. **Fonte delle Delizie** (Costa di San Antonio, near the Casa di Santa Caterina) makes delicious pastries. Further from the centre, **Il Masgalano** (Via del Camporegio, next to San Domenico) is a friendly place for coffees, light lunches or an *aperitivo*.

PRICE CATEGORIES

Average cost of a three-course meal per person with a half-bottle of wine:
€ = under €25
€€ = €25–40
€€€ = €40–60
€€€€ = over €60

THE PASSION OF THE *PALIO*

In little more than a minute, the Campo is filled with unbearable happiness and irrational despair as centuries-old loyalties are put to the test

It is strange how a race that lasts just 90 seconds can require 12 months' planning, a lifetime's patience and the involvement of an entire city. But Siena's famous *Palio* does just that, as it has done since the 13th century, when an August *Palio* made its debut. At that time, the contest took the form of a bareback race the length of the city. The bareback race run around the Siena's main square, the Piazza del Campo, was introduced in the 17th century. Today the *Palio* is held twice a year, in early July and mid-August. The *Palio*, which has been run in times of war, famine and plague, stops for nothing. In the 1300s, criminals were released from jail to celebrate the festival. When the Fascists were gaining ground in 1919, Siena postponed council elections until after the *Palio*. In 1943, British soldiers in a Tunisian prisoner-of-war camp feared a riot when they banned Sienese prisoners from staging a *Palio*; Sienese fervour triumphed.

Although, as the Sienese say, *"Il Palio corre tutto l'anno"* ("The Palio runs all year"), the final preparations boil down to three days, during which there is the drawing by lots of the horse for each competing ward *(contrada)*, the choice of the jockeys and then the six trial races – the last of which is held on the morning of the *Palio* itself. Although many do pack into the Campo for the actual race, other citizens cannot bear to watch it and cluster around the TV set in the *contrada* square or go to church to pray.

ABOVE: On the day of the *Palio*, the horses are taken to each *contrada* church for a blessing. The priest holds the horse's head and commands it, *"Vai e torni vincitore!"* ("Go and return victorious!").

LEFT: The words *"C'è terra in piazza"* ("There's earth in the Campo") are the signal to remove the colourful costumes from Siena's museums to feature in the great Historical Parade.

THE POWER OF THE *CONTRADE*

In Siena the *contrada* rules: ask a Sienese where he is from and he will say, *"Ma sono della Lupa"* ("But I'm from the Wolf *contrada*"). The first loyalty is to the city in the head, not to the city on the map.

Ten out of Siena's 17 *contrade* take part in each *Palio*: the seven who did not run in the previous race and three selected by lot. Each *contrada* appoints a captain and two lieutenants to run the campaign. In the *Palio*, the illegal becomes legal: bribery, kidnapping, plots and the doping of horses are all common.

Each of the *contrade* in the city has its own standard, many of which are displayed around the city during the *Palio* and play an important role in the ceremonial aspect of the event.

Flags, or standards, are a central theme of the *Palio* event. In fact, the *Palio* itself – the trophy of victory for which everyone is striving – is a standard: a silk flag emblazoned with the image of the Madonna and the coats of arms of the city, ironically referred to by the Sienese as the *cencio*, or rag. The *contrada* which wins the event retains possession of the *palio* standard until the next race.

ABOVE: The ruthless race lurches around the Campo three times. If a riderless horse wins, the animal is almost deified: it is given the place of honour in the victory banquet and has its hooves painted gold.

RIGHT: The Historical Parade, which is staged in the run-up to the main race, retraces Siena's centuries of struggle against Florence, from the glorious victory against its rival in 1260 to the ghastly defeat in 1560.

BELOW: A highlight of the *Palio* pageantry is the spectacular display of the flag-wavers, famous throughout Italy for their elaborate manoeuvres of twirling and hurling the huge standards dozens of feet in the air.

SOUTH OF SIENA

The route through the dramatic Crete region delivers you to the heart and soul of Tuscany. Pienza, Montalcino and Montepulciano are must-sees, but countless other lesser-known towns await discovery, while the hidden beauty of the Val d'Orcia river valley and the tortuous roads of Monte Amiata beckon the intrepid

The area just south of Siena is a primeval landscape of stark beauty. Appropriately called **Le Crete**, it is a moonscape of interlocking pale-clay hummocks and treeless gullies. In winter it is cold, bleak and even more crater-like. In summer the curvaceous terrain is softened by a deep green blanket. Sienese city dwellers love this barren landscape and are successfully discouraging local farmers from accepting European Union funds to flatten the land and grow wheat.

There is an extraordinary range of wildlife in the area: by day, wild deer roam by the Ombrone river; by night, porcupines and foxes are about in the woods. If intrepid walkers venture out in the late autumn evening they may meet a strange character with a couple of dogs, a torch and a harness. He is a truffle hunter, sniffing out truffles in the dampest ditches. More legal are the Sardinian peasants selling cheese. Unlike many Tuscans, Sardinians are prepared to live in remote, infertile places.

The best route through the Crete is the SS438 to Asciano, and the SP451 to Monte Oliveto Maggiore – empty roads through a barren landscape, dotted with striking hilltop farmhouses and lone cypresses. Known as the Accona desert in medieval times, it retains its spiritual remoteness.

Monte Oliveto Maggiore

After so much pale, undulating land, the red abbey of **Monte Oliveto Maggiore ❶** (open daily 9am–noon, 3.15–6pm, until 5pm in winter) is glimpsed through a wood of pines, oaks and olive trees. If the land appears to fall away from the abbey, it is not far from the truth: land erosion and frequent landslides provide a natural defence to the abbey's mystical centre. In 1313 Tolomei, a wealthy Sienese, abandoned the law for a life of prayer in the wilderness,

Map on page 218

LEFT: a timeless Tuscan landscape.
BELOW: church of San Biagio, Montepulciano.

TIP

The pretty walled village of Monticchiello offers fine views of Pienza, just 4km away. It is also renowned for the Teatro Povero – an annual play written and starring the villagers about life in rural Tuscany *(see page 39)*.

taking with him two fellow hermits. After a vision of white-robed monks, Tolomei established an Olivetan Order under Benedictine rule. The monks followed St Benedict's precept that "a real monk is one who lives by his own labour". Fortunately, a meagre diet, fervent prayer and lack of conversation stimulated the monks to artistic endeavour in the form of woodcarving, sculpture and manuscript design. As a noted artistic centre, the abbey invited Luca Signorelli and Il Sodoma to decorate the cloisters with scenes from St Benedict's life *(see box right)*.

The excitement of Sodoma aside, Monte Oliveto is a spiritual retreat. The austere refectory, the library cluttered with ancient manuscripts and books, the exquisite marquetry work of the choir stalls are as peaceful as the hidden walks deep into the woods. There is a restaurant, and former monastic cells are also available for overnight visitors (tel: 0577-707652; closed in winter).

Situated on a plain in the heart of the Crete, **Buonconvento** is worth a brief stop, if only to admire the imposing red 14th-century walls and massive medieval city gates of

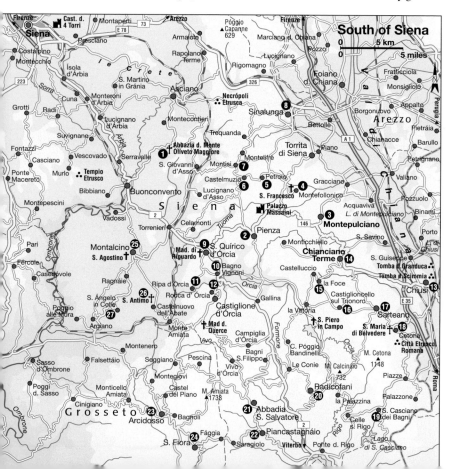

iron-bound wood. In 1366 Siena rebuilt the walls because, as a Sienese outpost, Buonconvento had been devastated. Today, the town is essentially a place for a leisurely introduction to truffles or game, or for a summer picnic in the peaceful gardens beside the town walls.

Utopian town

Pienza ❷ is an exquisite Renaissance doll's house. Although created by a humanist pope, Pius II, Pienza is almost too perfect to be human and too precious to be spiritual. Every fountain, piazza and painting is harmonious. Model citizens walk through streets as romantic as their names – Via dell'Amore, Via del Bacio, Via della Fortuna – streets of "love", "kiss" and "fortune".

Pienza's origins date back to 1458. When E.S. Piccolomini was elected pope, he could not resist playing God in his home village, Corsignano. He chose the noted Florentine architect, Bernardo Rossellino, to ennoble the hamlet in accordance with humanist principles. When the first masterpiece in modern town planning

emerged late and over budget, the Pope reduced his fraudulent architect to tears with his words, "You did well, Bernardo, in lying to us about the expense involved in the work… Your deceit has built these glorious structures; which are praised by all except the few consumed with envy."

Bernardo Rossellino was rewarded with a scarlet robe, 100 ducats and some new commissions. The decision to build a cathedral enabled the pope to rechristen Corsignano the village as Pienza the city – named, modestly, after himself. The result is what locals call a *città d'autore*, a city inspired by one vision. After Pienza, other cities in Tuscany or elsewhere are liable to look chaotic.

Much of the symmetry lies in the cathedral square, **Piazza Pio II**, and the slightly listing Duomo adds to the charm. Despite a Renaissance façade, the interior is late Gothic and decorated with mystical paintings from the Sienese school. In one central alcove is a chilling *Assumption* by Vecchietta, in which St Agatha holds a cup containing her breasts, torn off by the executioner.

Map on page 218

Pienza is famous for its homemade cheeses, especially pecorino and ricotta.

BELOW LEFT: one of the more spiritual. aspects of the St Benedict frescoes.

Il Sodoma's Frescoes

The main cloister of Monte Oliveto Maggiore *(see page 217)* is covered in frescoes on the *Life of St Benedict*, begun by Luca Signorelli in 1495 and completed by Sodoma from 1505. Of the two contemporaries, Signorelli had the more spiritual approach, but his loveliest work is a domestic scene portraying two monks being served by girls at an inn. In 1497, after only nine frescoes were completed, Signorelli left the rest for Il Sodoma to execute. Vasari adored Signorelli's spirituality as much as he loathed Il Sodoma's exuberance, hedonistic lifestyle and "licentious" fondness for "boys and beardless youths" which earned him his name. Il Sodoma's love of what Vasari called his Noah's Ark of "badgers, squirrels, apes, dwarf asses and Elba ponies" is often present, but his landscapes only come to life with the temptations of the flesh. His gaze rarely focuses on the main subject, but is deflected by the turn of an attractive leg, a mischievous smile, a perky badger or a soldier's buttocks. Needless to say, the inhibited monks preferred Signorelli's work to that of the man they labelled "Il Mataccio", imbecile or madman.

The Duomo's façade, the gracious arches, the well and the Palazzo Piccolomini, the pope's home, are just as Pius left them when he set off to fight the crusades, never to return. **Palazzo Piccolomini** (open Tues–Sun 10am–last entrance 6pm mid-Mar–mid-Oct, 4pm mid-Oct–mid-Mar; closed 7 Jan–mid-Feb and late Nov; guided tours only; entrance fee), now a museum, is lined with grand and homely treasures, including a library and arms collection. In the pope's bedroom, the intriguing book-holder, as cumbersome as a church lectern, is proof that the pope did not read in bed. The library opens onto a tranquil loggia with Etruscan urns, hanging gardens and a panorama stretching across the Orcia valley as far as Monte Amiata.

On the opposite side of the square, the **Museo Diocesano** (open Wed–Mon 10am–1pm, 3–6pm, Nov–mid-Mar Sat–Sun only; entrance fee) has a rich collection of medieval paintings, tapestries, and ornate gold- and silverware.

Just outside Pienza is the **Pieve di Corsignano**, a simple but coherent Romanesque church where Pope Pius II was baptised. You can ask for the key at the Pienza tourist office.

Cinquecento pearl

The winding road from Pienza up to **Montepulciano** ❸ – visible for miles around, with houses clustered on the sides of the hump of a hill on which it is built – is lined with *vendita diretta* signs, offering pecorino and wine. After Pienza, Montepulciano's asymmetrical design and spontaneous development give it the architectural tension that the earlier city lacks. If Pienza belongs to Rossellino, Montepulciano is Antonio da Sangallo's masterpiece.

Just outside and below the city walls, at the end of a long line of cypresses, lies Sangallo's church of **San Biagio**, the Renaissance building most at ease with its setting. The isolation focuses attention on the honey-coloured travertine, the Greek Cross design, the dome and the purity of the line. Sangallo's design skills rival Bramante's, not just in the church, the elegant well and the porticoed Canon's House, but else-

BELOW: Piazza Pio II, Pienza.

where in the city. The airy interior has a deeply classical feel, more akin to the Roman Pantheon than to a small Tuscan church.

Traffic is banned inside the city walls, but you can park outside San Biagio. It's a short but steepish walk from here into town. Alternatively, you can park in one of the many car parks at Montepulciano's eastern end and enter the town through the Porta al Prato, into Piazza Savonarola guarded by a statue of the Marzocco lion (symbol of Florentine power) on a column. From here the principal shopping street, Via di Gracciano nel Corso, leads up to the main square. Its lower end is lined with noble palaces. The Renaissance **Palazzo Bucelli**, at no. 73, is decorated with a mosaic of Etruscan urns and pots, a reminder of the city's ancient origins. The road continues upwards to **Piazza Grande**, the highest part of town and the highest spot culturally.

Florentine design has shaped the grand façades on Piazza Grande, but earlier Sienese Gothic touches are present in the interiors, double arches and doorways. Both styles reflect the city's buffeting between the two city-states and the eventual supremacy of Florence. On one side, the 15th-century **Palazzo Comunale** (Town Hall) has a Florentine Michelozzo façade adorning Sienese turrets. The **Tower** (open Mon–Sat 10am–6pm; entrance fee), modelled on that of Florence's Palazzo Vecchio, surveys the whole province: from Monte Amiata to Siena and even Lake Trasimeno. Once in the Palazzo, do not be deterred by the presence of a police station: the view, albeit restricted by iron railings, is legally yours.

Sangallo's **Palazzo Contucci** (open Mon–Sat 8.30am–1.30pm), on the other side of the square, still belongs to the aristocratic Contucci family, who produce Vino Nobile. In the **Cantine Contucci** (wine cellars; open Mon–Fri 8.30am–12.30pm, 2.30–6.30pm), Adamo, the wine master, will be delighted to expand on the entire noble history of the Contucci family and on his essential role on the Vino Nobile Wine-Tasting Committee. Vino Nobile, a smooth red wine with a hint of violets, was "ennobled" in

Pienza's reverence of Pope Pius is surpassed by Montepulciano's devotion to Poliziano. The renowned scholar, poet and resident tutor to Lorenzo de' Medici's children was named after the Latin term for the town – inhabitants of Montepulciano are called Poliziani. Poliziano eulogised the Montepulciano countryside in his Stanzas, which are thought to have inspired Botticelli's La Primavera.

BELOW:
Montepulciano's Etruscan origins are evident everywhere.

1549 when Pope Paul III's somme-lier proclaimed it "a most perfect wine, a wine for lords".

Between the two grand *palazzi*, at the top of wide steps, stands the **Duomo** (open daily 9am–noon, 4–6pm), which contains a master-piece of the Siena school: the huge *Assumption* triptych by Taddeo di Bartolo (1401) shines out above the high altar in the vast, gloomy nave.

A circular tour

Scattered among the rolling land-scape of Siena province are some beautiful villages, each with a sepa-rate identity and artistic treasures espied almost incidentally over the brow of a hill. A circular itinerary from Montepulciano unites a group of tiny villages once ruled by the Cac-ciaconti barons. **Montefollonico ❹**, 8 km (5 miles) northwest of Monte-pulciano, has a 13th-century frescoed church and one of the best restaurants in Italy, La Chiusa *(see page 231)*.

Petroio ❺, set on a rocky, wooded promontory, is a grand for-tified village on an old pilgrim route. In recent years it has been undergo-ing a revival thanks to its terracotta – examples of which adorn the city walls, Palazzo Pretorio and the medieval towers. Look out for the Canon's House, which contains a re-markable *Madonna and Child* by Taddio di Bartolo. Near the village is the intact **Abbadia a Sicille**, built by the Knights Templar as a refuge for knights on the way to the Holy Land. The adjoining Romanesque church is decorated with two Maltese crosses, but an Olivetan coat of arms marks the abolition of the Templars.

Set among farmland and woods, **Castelmuzio ❻** is a medieval village wrapped up in itself, its Museum of Sacred Art and its direct line to San Bernardo. Narrow shops in winding streets sell honey, salami and cheese made by an ageing pop-ulation of churchgoers.

Once a Cacciaconti fortress, aris-tocratic **Montisi ❼** commands a view over two valleys. Although the "low town" has a few young families and newer attitudes, the "high town" is a relic of medieval Italy. The vil-lage offers intriguing alleys, views, restaurants and two tiny Romanesque

TIP

Vino Nobile is excellent with two local peasant dishes: *bruschetta*, a toasted garlic bread drenched in olive oil, or *panzanella*, a bread salad with herbs.

BELOW: Montepulciano is bathed in a russet glow at sunset.

churches, one decorated with a Scuola di Duccio crucifix. A few apparently stark, uninviting farmhouses conceal wonderful frescoes and the occasional private chapel.

One can return to Montepulciano via **Sinalunga** ❽, a schizophrenic Tuscan town with a hideous "low town" but a pleasant "old town". The town's original name, Asinalunga, echoes its shape, "the long donkey". But in the lively market, pigs, not donkeys, are in evidence in the form of *porchetta*, the local speciality of roast pig flavoured with rosemary.

Val d'Orcia

The **Val d'Orcia** is a beautiful rural area at the southern border of Le Crete, but its villages have suffered from the desertion of the countryside in the 1950s and 1960s. **San Quirico d'Orcia** ❾ is a dignified valley town still waiting for its heyday. It survived an attack by Cesare Borgia's troops in 1502 and a World War II bombardment. The Romanesque **Collegiata**, made from sandstone and local travertine, has three remarkable portals. In the town,

there are a couple of churches worth seeing, and the frescoed rooms of the newly restored **Palazzo Chigi** are now open to the public (daily 8am–6.30pm; entrance fee).

Just south of San Quirico, off the SS2, **Bagno Vignoni** ❿ is a tiny but lively spa station, at its most evocative at dusk. The steam rises from the hot springs, and the yellowish light of the lanterns dimly illuminates the stone façades of the buildings lining the square, which is in fact a stone pool of sulphurous water, where both Lorenzo de' Medici and St Catherine once bathed. The hot springs were used by the Romans, and became public baths in medieval times. You are not allowed to bathe here now. However, the baths in Hotel Posta Marcucci are open to non-residents for a fee, and are also open at night on summer weekends.

From the pool, all senses are fulfilled at once: the imposing **Rocca d'Orcia** looms above; outside the pool of light, the sound of sheep and crickets reverberates; the softness of the hot, chalky water dissolves tiredness; and the smell of sulphur evapo-

Map on page 218

The Strada del Vino Nobile di Montepulciano is an association that promotes the local wines. As well as organising tours of the local vineyards and cellars they offer a range of cultural tours including visits to the Garden of Villa La Foce, the Montepulciano spa, and Siena's pottery workshops. Their office is on Piazza Grande (Mon–Sat 10am– 1pm, 3–6pm; tel: 0578-717484; www.stradavino nobile.it)

BELOW: chapel in a golden field outside Pienza.

Etruscan Art

Since there is no extant Etruscan literature, our knowledge of the living Etruscans is oddly dependent on a reading of their funerary art for clues. We know them as they would like to be known, these idealised aristocrats elevated by Greek myths. The women were depicted as pale while the men were uniformly reddish-brown, either suntanned or ritually painted. Friezes of serene married couples, tender lovers, absorbed wrestlers, erotic dancers or grieving warriors reflect the fullness of Etruscan life. Aristocratic Etruscan women had freedom and social status, as well as influence. They are frequently depicted attending banquets without their husbands, riding covered wagons to their landholdings and playing flutes or lyres at funerals. The men are rarely still: they charge through games, boar-hunts, processions, journeys, dances, banquets and diving competitions. The "ordinary" Etruscan is only glimpsed in passing: a prized blonde courtesan flits past dancing slaves; a serf mourns his dead master.

In keeping with primitive religions, natural forces were personified as gods of the sea, earth and rising sun. The Etruscans also re-invented Greek gods in their own image: Zeus, Hera and Athena were Tinia, Uni and Minerva. Oriental and Greek motifs coexisted: Egyptian sphinxes watched winged Etruscan demons pursue menacing Greek Furies.

But it is the tombs that remain as a cultural testimony to the power, wealth and beliefs of their owners. The tomb and mode of burial varied according to the local custom and period, but in general the rich were buried in decorated stone sarcophagi placed in chamber tombs, often decorated with lively frescoes, while the ashes of the poor were put in small urns in shallow graves. Tombs, in every shape and form, can be seen in the Etruscan necropolises: "temple" tombs at Saturnia; melon-shaped tombs at Cortona; oriental "trench" tombs at Vetulonia. At Sovana, "pigeon-hole" tombs are niches cut into the rock, while at Chiusi a mysterious labyrinth reputedly conceals the sarcophagus of Lars Porsenna, mythical king of the Etruscans.

In Etruscan funerary art, the man is often shown wearing his chains of office over his bare chest. He may hold an egg, container of the soul, or clutch the *patera*, a circular dish arguably symbolising the continuity of life. The bejewelled woman is surrounded by a mixture of feminine and sacred symbols: perfume boxes and earrings to beautify; a pomegranate or pine cone to symbolise either sexuality or death; a mirror to reflect her physical and spiritual perfection. In effect, these were portraits which were commissioned to show to the gods the noble patrons at their best.

Etruscan art is essentially regional; Arezzo had a reputation for *Arretino*, fine red pottery, and for its metalwork. The famous bronze Chimera remains a magical illusion: a goat's head springs from a lion's back and is seized by the lion's tail, suddenly transformed into a serpent's mouth. Chiusi boasts Canopic urns, cinerary urns with an idealised effigy of the deceased on the lid, while Cortona's bronze figurines represent Etruscan deities. Volterra's alabaster sarcophagi run the gamut of Etruscan demonology and Greek mythology, featuring sea monsters, Greek gods, beaked griffins and sirens. ❑

LEFT: the delicate eroticism of Etruscan dancers.

rates into the night air. After a swim, a short *passeggiata* around the old baths shows the well-restored square at its most romantic.

In the vicinity are three medieval fortresses – Ripa d'Orcia, Rocca d'Orcia and Castiglione d'Orcia. After the turning to Bagno Vignoni, **Ripa d'Orcia ⓫**, an enchanted castle (now a hotel; tel: 0577-897376; www.castelloripadorcia.com) set among cypress groves, comes into view. Although goats and pheasants are the commonplace fauna here, the locals nevertheless make claims that wolves roam the area.

Rocca d'Orcia ⓬, a fortified village once owned by the warring Salimbeni clan, has an impressive castle open to visitors. **Castiglione d'Orcia** offers more of the same: an atmospheric, well-preserved village, a ruined fortress and wonderful views. The abbey of Sant' Antimo *(see page 230)* can be reached from here. The mountain roads in the area are tortuous but beautiful.

The Etruscan towns

Although set among attractive low hills, **Chiusi ⓭** comes across as a rather unprepossessing town, devoid of Renaissance charm. The "low town" is a commercial centre and the shabby "high town" is endearing but overwhelmed by its glorious Etruscan past. Then, as now, the **Chiusini** were farmers, merchants and craftsmen, a spirit which predominates over artistry. Yet with a little Etruscan knowledge and much curiosity, the town is as fascinating as any in Tuscany. It boasts a complete underground city; an unrivalled collection of female cinerary urns; and the only tomb paintings in their original setting in Tuscany.

As one of the greatest city-states in the Etruscan League, Chiusi, or "Kamars", controlled the area from Lago di Trasimeno to Monte Amiata. After reaching its zenith as a trading centre in the 7th century BC, Etruscan Kamars became submerged by Roman Clusium and then by medieval Chiusi. The old city survives on three levels of civilisation: the Etruscan necropolis beneath the city hills; the Roman street-grid system below the Cathedral; and the medieval city above.

The **Museo Archeologico Nazionale** (open daily 9am–8pm; tel: 0578-20177; entrance fee) has one of the finest collections of its kind in Italy, which attests to the vitality of Kamars and shows a distinctly female bias in the outstanding female Canopic jars, cinerary urns and rounded *cippi* tombstones. The containers have Egyptian-style lids resembling human or animal heads. The Etruscans borrowed freely from the Greeks and Egyptians; the imitation Greek vases are less rational but more vigorous than the originals. A speciality of Chiusi is *bucchero*, glossy black earthenware, often in the form of vases with figures in relief. This pottery has a sophisticated metallic finish which cannot be reproduced by modern craftsmen.

Map on page 218

Chiusi's Cathedral, built from Etruscan and Roman fragments.

BELOW: the thermal pool in Bagno Vignoni.

Although much of the domestic pottery has a naturalness verging on the commonplace, the sarcophagi, the cinerary urns and the crouching sphinx reveal an underlying obsession with death and the appeasement of shadowy spirits.

A visit to the Etruscan tombs, 3 km (2 miles) outside town, can be arranged with the museum staff. The tombs contain sarcophagi, cinerary urns and, in the case of **Tomb of the Monkey**, rare wall-paintings of athletic games and domestic scenes.

In the Chiusi **Duomo**, three civilisations are visible at once: the "barbaric" Romanesque Cathedral is built from Etruscan and Roman fragments. The **Museo della Cattedrale** (open daily June–mid-Oct 10am–12.45pm, 4–6.30pm, mid-Oct–May Mon–Sat 10am–12.30pm, Sun 10am–12.30pm, 4–6pm; entrance fee) is of limited interest in itself, but your entrance ticket entitles you to a guided tour of a fascinating labyrinth beneath the Cathedral. The recently excavated tunnels are part of an Etruscan water system, cut into the rocks which provided natural filtration. The tour guide will lead you to a large Roman cistern dating from the 1st century BC, exiting at the bottom of the Cathedral bell-tower. Climb to the top for views of Monte Amiata, the Val d'Orcia and over to Lake Trasimeno in neighbouring Umbria.

Spa town

After underground Chiusi, **Chianciano Terme** is a breath of fresh air. Italians have flocked to this spa town since Roman times to enjoy the unique powers of *Acqua Santa*. The innovative Terme Sensoriali is one of a new breed of swish thermal spas that have appeared across Tuscany in recent years, replacing the old fashioned clinical establishments with world class spa resorts *(see pages 128 and 287)*.

This southern part of Siena province is positively bursting with Etruscan remains, and digging produces a continual flow of exciting finds. In Chianciano, well-marked walks lead to several recently discovered tombs and temples, and an excellent **Etruscan Museum** (open Tues–Sun 10am–1pm, 4–7pm, also

Mon in summer; tel: 0578-30471; entrance fee) contains many important and impressive finds, including an intact monumental tomb of a princess, lined with bronze and adorned with various gold and bronze artifacts. The large museum also features the remains from a spa complex dating from the 1st century BC, which was discovered in Chianciano and is thought to be the sacred magic spring that cured Emperor Augustus in 23 BC from a life-threatening stomach ailment.

An Anglo-Italian estate

Near the town are some of the loveliest walks and drives in Tuscany. Many walks start from **La Foce ⓯**, a 15th-century farmhouse which overlooks the fertile Val di Chiana and the desolate craters of the Val d'Orcia. The superb **gardens** here (open Wed Apr–Sept 3–7pm, Oct–Mar 3–5pm; entrance fee) were designed by the famous landscape gardener Cecil Pinsent. There are views across an Etruscan site to Monte Amiata and Monte Cetona. Its excellent strategic position meant that its owners, the Anglo-Italian Origos, used it as the partisans' refuge during World War II. Ongoing excavations on the property have uncovered some 200 Etruscan tombs. From here, a rough track leads to Petraporciana, the partisans' hidden headquarters, and to a primeval forest full of giant oaks, cyclamens, wild orchids or snowdrops: a perfect short spring or autumn walk.

Beside La Foce is **Castelluccio**, a castle – and summer concert venue – which commands the best-loved view in the province: a sinuous line of cypresses plotting an Etruscan route across the craters. When Prince Charles stayed at Villa La Foce, proud locals were not surprised to see him painting this view.

A short walk leads to **Pocce Lattaie** and prehistoric caves with dripping stalactites shaped like teats or nipples. These pagan caves were used in fertility rites and propitiatory offerings made to the gods. Be prepared to hire a guide (and a torch) from Chianciano.

Around Monte Cetona

From Chianciano, an idyllic rural drive leads via La Foce to Sarteano and Cetona, two small medieval and Etruscan towns. These views of desolate *crete*, fortified farmhouses and hazy Monte Amiata are captured by Paolo Busato in his celebrated photographs. It is worth sacrificing a hired car to the dirt roads, but the nervous can take the more direct route to Sarteano.

Castiglioncello sul Trionoro ⓰ is a tiny village with a *castello* and a church containing a Trecento Madonna. The village is set amid vast expanses of abandoned countryside in which Etruscan remains are uncovered by chance every few years.

Spilling over its double ring of city walls, **Sarteano ⓱** is a popular thermal centre which has retained its traditional identity. The town offers Etruscan remains, a grandiose 13th-

Map on page 218

TIP

Monte Cetona (1,148 metres/3,800 ft) is criss-crossed by woodland lanes and open tracks for walking, cycling and horse riding. A map of the network of mountain trails is available from the tourist offices of Cetona, San Casciano dei Bagni and Sarteano.

BELOW: the red earth of the Sienese landscape.

century Rocca and crumbling Renaissance *palazzi* built into the city walls. There is an interesting **Etruscan Museum** (open Tues–Sun 10.30am–12.30pm, 4–7pm; tel: 0578-269261 for information) but, contrary to rumours, the tomb of the Etruscan king Porsenna has never been discovered. In August each year, Sarteano holds a famous *Giostra* or tournament.

Cetona ⑱ clings to a richly wooded hill. The grand 18th-century houses on the plains are a relic of past prosperity, but Cetona is a refreshingly authentic Tuscan community. The broad traffic-free square is filled with locals going about their daily lives, free (as yet) of the wine, food and gift shops that are spreading like a rash over many of the better-known Tuscan towns. Although Cetona is noted for its textiles and copies of Etruscan vases, it now relies on *agriturismo* to keep its population from leaving. A short stay in a local farm with mountain walks, local cheeses and *bruschetti* drenched in olive oil is highly recommended.

A very scenic route, the Via della Montagna, goes from Cetona to the spa town of **San Casciano dei Bagni** ⑲ (take the high road north out of town and follow signs to Mondo "X"). En route, it's worth stopping at the beautifully restored **Convento di San Francesco**. It now houses a rehabilitation centre (Mondo "X"), but if you ring the bell, one of the occupants of the *comunità* will be happy to show you round.

The recently opened Fonteverde Thermal Resort on the edge of San Casciano dei Bagni offers a wide range of thermal therapies and beauty treatments, though the atmosphere is rather sterile, and the Medici villa has been converted into a swanky hotel (www.fonteverdespa.com).

Routes up to Monte Amiata

The varied approaches to Monte Amiata, southern Tuscany's highest peak, are at least as good as what awaits you on arrival. The fast Pienza to Abbadia San Salvatore route allows for a detour to the thermal baths at **Bagni San Filippo**, a bit ragged round the edges compared to the Fonteverde resort above, but more authentic for it.

The alternative route via Sarteano and **Radicofani** ⑳ was the one taken by both Dickens and Montaigne to a location second only to Volterra for natural drama. While the mountain villages have sports and leisure industries to thank for their revival, the villages on the edge of Amiata seem to be in permanent limbo, trapped rather than enhanced by a medieval identity. Dickens found Radicofani "as barren, as stony, and as wild as Cornwall, in England". Perched on a craggy basalt rock, it is the only place in Italy to possess a triple Medicean wall. The town overlooks *"Il Mare di Sassi"*, the "Sea of Stones", suitable only for very hardy sheep. Although an 18th-century earthquake destroyed much of the town, enough atmosphere remains.

BELOW: Monte Amiata.

The drive from Radicofani up to **Abbadia San Salvatore** ㉑ is via Le Conie, a tortuous road known as "Amiata's sentry". For those not interested in skiing, mountain walks and disused mercury mines, Abbadia is best-known for its much overrated **Abbazia** and its medieval "high town". The Romanesque **San Salvatore** (open summer Mon–Sat 7am–6pm, Sun 10.30am–6pm; closes 5pm in winter) is all that remains of a once magnificent abbey. Unfortunately it has been heavily restored, once in 16th-century baroque and again in 1925. A 12th-century *Crucifix* and the crypt with 36 columns remain relatively unspoilt. Geometric symbols, grapes, palm leaves, animals and Gordian knots decorate the pillars.

From Abbadia, a winding road with sharp bends and sheer drops leads to the top of **Monte Amiata**, 1,738 metres (5,700 ft) high. The wooded area around the extinct volcano has attractive walks. The Fosso della Cocca, a leafy tunnel, is the best place to spot unusual wildlife and vegetation.

Although **Castel del Piano** in neighbouring Grosseto province, set among pine forests and wild raspberries, is the oldest settlement in the area, **Piancastagnaio** ㉒ is a better base. Perched among chestnut groves, the town has a newly restored Rocca and Franciscan monastery.

Arcidosso ㉓ was the birthplace of a man called David Lazzaretti, "The Prophet of the Amiata". In the 19th century Lazzaretti created a revolutionary social and religious movement with its headquarters on **Monte Labro**, a lonely peak which forms part of a nature reserve where deer, chamois and wolves roam, and protected trees and wild flowers grow. The best time is autumn, when the crowds have left and the wild mushrooms appear.

Santa Fiora ㉔ is particularly delightful, and has fine works of art in the 12th-century Santa Fiora and Santa Lucilla churches, including some della Robbia ceramics.

Quintessential Sienese

In both temperament and identity, **Montalcino** ㉕ is certainly the most

Sienese shepherd.

BELOW: Montalcino.

Map on page 218

Brunello di Montalcino is one of Italy's best wines. Opportunities abound to taste and buy Brunello and the younger Rosso di Montalcino.

BELOW: Romanesque abbey of Sant'Antimo.

Sienese town in the province. In essence, its history is a microcosm of all Sienese history. From a distance Montalcino even looks like a Sienese Trecento painting: the landscape could be a background to a saint's life; in the foreground would be the fortress and scenes of rejoicing and celebration after a historic victory.

Montalcino has been known as "the last rock of communal freedom" since its time as the Sienese capital in exile between 1555 and 1559. After the fall of Siena, exiles gathered around Piero Strozzi and the Sienese flag. As a reward, Montalcinesi standard bearers have the place of honour in the procession preceding the *Palio* in Siena.

The magnificent 14th-century **Rocca** (open Apr–Oct daily 9am–8pm, Nov–Mar Tues–Sun 9am–6pm; free) is the key to Montalcino's pride. The approach is through olive groves and the slopes famous for Brunello wine. But the asymmetrical fortress, astride a spur of land, dominates the landscape. From its gardens there is a sense of boundless space and absolute freedom. In winter, the wind howls

over the massive walls and drives visitors to a different type of fortification in the **Enoteca** bar inside. This "National Wine Library" naturally serves Brunello, the first wine in Italy to be given the DOCG *denominazione* for excellence.

Architecturally, Montalcino offers a neoclassical Cathedral, a Gothic loggia, a Romanesque church and myriad intriguing alleys. The Duccio and della Robbia schools are well served by the Civic and Sacred museums. Most significant is the Palazzo Comunale, a mass of *Fiorentinità* finished off by a Sienese tower to prove that the Sienese always surpass the Florentines.

In spring, the area is very green, but yellow rape seed, poppies, sunflowers and grapes soon retaliate. Before leaving, try *pici*, home-made spaghetti, and sweet *sospiri* ("sighs") in a *fin de siècle* bar.

Sant'Antimo

Near by is **Sant'Antimo** ㉖, the remains of a Romanesque abbey founded by Charlemagne, set amidst cypresses in a peaceful valley. If the church is closed, try the sacristan in **Castelnuovo dell'Abate**, the village up the hill. Designed in the French and Lombard style, the abbey is built from local travertine, which resembles alabaster or onyx. The interior has a translucent quality and, as the light changes, turns luminously golden, white and brown.

Not far away, **Sant'Angelo in Colle** ㉗, a fortified hilltop village, once cast a dramatic shadow over Grosseto and other enemies. Until 1265 it was a Sienese outpost, but the tower is all that remains. Today it is a quiet medieval village.

Modern Siena province ends just there. As a frontier castle, Sant' Angelo looked down onto the plain which falls into Grosseto. After Siena province, Grosseto can look deceptively flat. ❑

RESTAURANTS

Montalcino

Osteria di Porta al Cassero
Via Ricasoli 32
Tel: 0577-847196
A local favourite. Try the polenta with wild boar sauce, a regional speciality. €€

Taverna Il Grappolo Blu
Via Scale di Moglio 1
Tel: 0577-847150
Intimate, well-run inn with a rustic atmosphere. Typical dishes include filling soups, rabbit dishes and pasta with *porcini*. Excellent wine list. Reserve. €€–€€€

Trattoria L'Angolo
Via Ricasoli, 9
Tel: 0577-848017
Among the over-priced restaurants of Montalcino, this well known trattoria remains a down-to-earth and fairly priced option. Good bean soup and home-made pasta. Closed Tues. €

Montefollonico

La Chiusa
Via Madonnina 88
Tel: 0577-669668
www.ristorantelachiusa.it
One of Tuscany's fanciest restaurants, set in an old oil mill on the outskirts of Montefollonico, with glorious views of the surrounding countryside. Seasonal dishes are lovingly prepared according to traditional recipes, using locally sourced ingredients and vegetables grown in the adjoin-

ing kitchen garden. 15 rooms to rent. Come here for a special occasion. Closed Tues. €€€€

Monte Oliveto

La Torre
Monte Oliveto Maggiore
Tel: 0577-707022
Tourists fill every table on the lovely shaded terrace of this restaurant by the Benedictine abbey, but the food is surprisingly good. Service is brusque but efficient. Picnic tables nearby. Closed Tues. €€

Montepulciano

Caffè Poliziano
Via di Voltaia nel Corso, 27
Tel: 0578-758615
www.caffepoliziano.it
Lovingly restored Art Nouveau café–restaurant in the historic heart of Montepulciano. It's a landmark, so often full, but worth trying to get a table, even if it's just for coffee. Glorious panoramic balcony. €–€€

La Grotta
Località San Biagio 16
Tel: 0578-757607
Once the home of architect Sangallo, and right next to his stunningly positioned church of San Biagio. Rustic Tuscan dishes, with French influence from the owner. *Alfresco* dining in summer. Closed Wed and Jan–Feb. €€€

Osteria Acquacheta

Via del Teatro 22
Tel: 0578-758443
www.acquacheta.eu
Authentic *osteria* serving uncomplicated, but flavoursome dishes such as *pici* (the local pasta) with wild boar ragù and tagliatelle with white truffles. Wine is sloshed into glass tumblers and your bill will be scribbled on the tablecloth. Excellent value, but book or be prepared to wait. €–€€

Monticchiello

La Porta
Via del Piano, 1
Tel/fax: 0578-755163
www.osterialaporta.it
Pleasant little *osteria* just outside the walled town of Monticchiello. Stop here for a snack and glass of wine, or a full meal, choosing from both traditional and more inventive dishes. Panoramic terrace. Closed Thur, most of Jan. €€

Pienza

La Buca delle Fate
Corso il Rossellino, 38/a
Tel: 0578-748272
Simple trattoria and bar in the lovely 16th-century Palazzo Gonzaga, on main thoroughfare through town. One of the best of Pienza's many eateries. Closed Mon. €

Proceno

La Fondue
Loc. Fosso Acquaviva

Tel/Fax: 0763-710163
After running restaurants in Atlantic City and Moscow, Neapolitan chef Francesco has chosen this scruffy hideaway by the border with Lazio as the unlikeliest of settings for a new venture. The food is simple but prepared with southern Italian flair. The decor needs work, but improvements are planned. Check out the photo gallery of celebrities he has fed. €€

Sinalunga

Le Coccole del-l'Amorosa
Località l'Amorosa 2 km (1 mile) south.
Tel: 0577-677211
www.amorosa.it
Superb restaurant in the hotel Locanda dell' Amorosa, romantically set in the stables of a medieval estate. The food is a mix of traditional and new, with a good choice. There is no better place to eat a *bistecca chianina* (farmed locally). Book well in advance. Closed Mon and Tues lunch.

PRICE CATEGORIES

Average cost of a three-course meal per person with a half-bottle of wine:
€ = under €25
€€ = €25–40
€€€ = €40–60
€€€€ = over €60

GROSSETO AND THE MAREMMA

Grosseto province has some of the most beautiful stretches of coast and wilderness areas in the region. The Maremma, "the marsh by the sea", is Tuscany's wild west, where cowboys and long-horned cattle roam. Inland, the marshy plains give way to densely wooded hills, where little towns seem to grow out of the tufa

Tuscany's southwestern corner, the Grosseto province, offers a wonderfully varied landscape, ranging from the flat plains around the provincial capital, Grosseto, to the thickly wooded peak of Monte Amiata, capped with snow throughout the winter months, to the smooth hills bordering the neighbouring province of Siena. The coastline has an unrivalled mix of Mediterranean flora and fauna, but the region is dominated by the marshy plain of the Maremma, stretching from the Piombino headland to Tuscany's border with Lazio. This coastal stretch of flat marshland backed by remote hills, famous for its horse-breeding, wild-boar hunting, Etruscan sites and austere inland villages, not to mention its rich cuisine, remains one of the least developed areas on the Tuscan tourist itinerary.

Abundant remains reveal that the Etruscans thrived in this area, cultivating the land and exploiting the mineral wealth of the nearby island of Elba. However, while the Romans continued to mine Elba for the iron they needed to make swords, they allowed the drainage and irrigation systems the Etruscans had put in place on the mainland to decay. By the Middle Ages, with territorial wars raging and the additional threat of Saracen invasion, the area had

become a near derelict malarial swamp where the average life expectancy was less than 20 years. Local populations migrated to the hills, where the air was sweeter and threat of invasion from the sea less imminent. It wasn't until the mid-19th century, with the draining of the swamps and land reclamation, that the revival of the Maremman lowlands began, spearheaded by the return of the *butteri* (Tuscany's tough cowboys) with their herds of long-horned cattle.

LEFT: the tufa town of Sorano.
BELOW: a solitary spot in the Maremma.

The pink-and-white candy-stripe façade of Grosseto's Cathedral overlooks Piazza Dante, the main hub of the town.

Grosseto

The provincial capital, **Grosseto ❶**, is a commercial and administrative centre, with little to recommend it from a touristic point of view. The town began life as a fortified citadel around 950, following the Saracen looting of the former capital, Roselle, less than 12 km (8 miles) away. For centuries, the low-lying citadel remained a backwater in the mosquito-infested plain, overshadowed by the larger, more powerful neighbouring strongholds of Massa Marittima and Pitigliano in the hills. Flattened by bombs in World War II, Grosseto's post-war regeneration resulted in an unappealing sprawl of factories and modern housing blocks. It is not the most inviting of towns; graffiti is rife and the old buildings of the historic centre unloved. However, if you are passing and have an interest in things Roman and Etruscan, the museum is worth a visit.

The *centro storico* is contained within an ancient hexagonal wall, one of town's few intact monuments, erected by the Medici in the 16th century. The bombastic **post office** building on Piazza Fratelli Rosselli was Mussolini's gift to Grosseto, but the hub of the city and its evening *passeggiata* is the Corso Carducci, a street lined with shops and cafés leading to **Piazza Dante**, the main square, dominated by the pink-and-white **Duomo**. Dedicated to San Lorenzo, the original Cathedral was built towards the end of the 13th century over an existing church constructed about 100 years earlier, but the pink-and-white building is the product of a heavy-handed restoration in the 19th century.

Most of the Cathedral's artworks have been transferred to the nearby **Museo Archeologico e d'Arte della Maremma** (Piazza Baccarini 3; open May–Oct Tues–Sun 10am–1pm, 5–8pm, Nov–Apr Tues–Sun

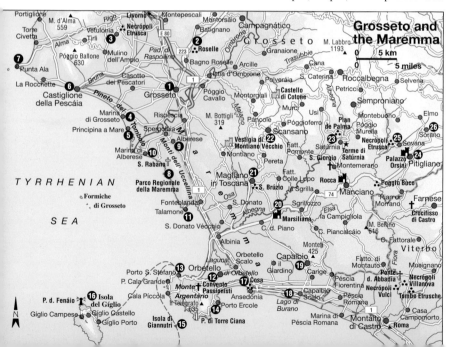

Map on page 234

10am–1pm, 4–7pm; entrance fee), one of the richest museums in the area. It has a fine collection of pre-Etruscan, Etruscan and Roman artefacts from the archaeological sites of Roselle, Vetulonia, Talamone, Pitigliano and Saturnia to the south. The top floor is given over to sacred art, mostly by Sienese artists. Among the most notable works are the lovely *Madonna delle Ciliege* (Madonna of the Cherries, *c*.1440–50), considered a Sassetta masterpiece, and a *Last Judgement* attributed to Guido da Siena (13th century), both from the Cathedral.

For Etruscan enthusiasts

The excavations at **Roselle ❷** (open daily 8.30am–sunset; entrance fee; follow signs to the ruins, not the town of Roselle), about 10 km (6 miles) northeast of Grosseto, reveal one of the most important Etruscan cities in northern Etruria. The paved streets, ruins of Etruscan taverns and workshops and the nearly intact circuit of Romano-Etruscan walls, as well as the outlines of the Roman forum and amphitheatre, are all very evocative. Most of the finds are on display in Grosseto's archaeological museum.

On the other side of the old Roman Via Aurelia (less romantically known as the N1), about 20 km (12 miles) north of Grosseto, the hilltop village of **Vetulonia ❸** lies above another ancient Etruscan city, Vetluna. The small excavated area (the *Scavi Città*) is more Roman than Etruscan. More interesting are the **tombs** (open summer 10.15am–6.45pm, winter 9.15am–4pm; archeological park same hours), 3km (2 miles) from the *Scavi Città*.

The coast

Grosseto is in the middle of a flat plain formed by the Ombrone river and is about 17 km (10 miles) from the sea. Many Grossetans have a second home along the coast, either in congested **Marina di Grosseto ❹** or in the more snobbish and quieter **Principina a Mare ❺**, hidden in a pine forest.

Some prefer the old fishing village of **Castiglione della Pescaia ❻**, where they can keep a sailing boat,

The Maremma's increasing reputation as a centre for wine-making and gastronomy has been endorsed by high profile French chef Alain Ducasse. He has transformed a former ducal residence near Castiglione della Pescaia into an elegant hotel with a superb restaurant (see page 276). Wine and olive oil are produced by the estate which is surrounded by ancient olive groves and vineyards.

BELOW: an early evening gathering on Grosseto's Piazza Dante.

TIP

The beaches within the Parco dell'Uccellina are among the most beautiful and unspoilt in Tuscany. To preserve this wilderness, the number of visitors is limited during the summer, and apart from the road to Marina di Alberese, cars are not permitted in the park. Transport from Alberese is arranged on buses. Visiting in the height of summer is ill-advised, as the weather becomes hot and humid, and there are tiny insects, *serafiche*, whose bite is painful.

BELOW: *butteri* rounding up horses.

ideally located at the foot of the mountains north of Grosseto. The harbour, crowded with fishermen's and tourists' boats, is believed to be the Etruscan Hasta, or Portus Traianus in Roman times. Overlooking the port is the Rocca Aragonese, with its walls and towers dating back to the 14th century. It's rather ordinary as beach resorts go, but has all the facilities you need.

The road connecting the resorts of Marina di Grosseto and Castiglione della Pescaia runs along the coast for a straight 10-km (6-mile) stretch separated from the sand and sea by a magnificent forest of umbrella pines known as the **Pineta del Tombolo**. You can leave your car by the roadside and take any of the footpaths through the umbrella pines to the lovely beach.

From here the road leads north to the Gulf of Follonica. The gulf's southern promontory is occupied by **Punta Ala ❼**, a semi-private resort with a flashy marina, upmarket hotels, golf clubs, horse riding and polo facilities. It's an attractive spot, but not really worth a detour, unless

you're into purpose-built resorts and want to hang out with moneyed Italians. Follonico, at the opposite extreme, is just plain ugly. If you are in the area and yearning for the seaside, **Cala Violino** is a quiet bay just before Follonico. Alternatively, there are some good beaches between Follonico and Piombino. Otherwise, at this point you're better off heading inland to **Massa Marittima** *(see page 189)* or back south to the beautiful Parco della Maremma.

"Park of the Little Bird"

The **Parco dell'Uccellina ❽**, also known as the **Parco Regionale della Maremma**, covers an area of around 60 sq. km (150 sq. miles), with about 20 km (12 miles) of coastline. The landscape is incredibly varied, ranging from salt marshes, sand dunes and open plains to rocky mountains, pine forests and Mediterranean maquis – dense scrubland characterised by rosemary, broom, sea lavender and holm oaks. Wild deer, boar and small mammals thrive in the undergrowth, while it is incredibly rich in birdlife – hence the name,

which means "Park of the Little Bird". Wading birds flock to the marshes around the mouth of the Ombrone river, and birds of prey circle the hills. The park is also an important pit-stop for birds migrating between Europe and Africa.

Down on the open fields and low-lying olive groves, herds of long-horned cattle and horses graze. They are reared by *butteri*, the tough Tuscan cowboys who settled in the region in the 19th century, after the swamps were drained and the land could be used for cattle grazing.

Evidence of human settlement here can be seen in the remains of a castle, the Benedictine monastery of **San Rabano**, and lookout towers used for the unfortunate soldiers posted here to watch for Saracen pirates and Spanish galleons.

The main entrance to the park is at **Alberese ❾**, where you have to leave your car. The visitor centre (open daily Mar–mid-June 8am–sunset, mid-June–mid-Sept 7.30am–sunset, mid-Sept–Mar 8.30 am–sunset; tel: 0564-407098; www.parcomaremma. it; entrance fee to park), where you

buy your entrance ticket, is full of information on the flora and fauna, and activities within the park. With your ticket you'll be given a map of the various way-marked trails you can follow, which range in levels of difficulty and duration, from gentle two-hour walks to day-long treks. Shuttle buses into the park leave from outside the visitor centre at regular intervals (times are posted outside the visitor centre), but be sure to check the time of the last bus back down.

Activities within the nature park include canoeing on the Ombrone river, sailing along the coast, riding across the mountains, birdwatching by the salt marshes and visiting the noble ruins of San Rabano and the many other towers strung out along the mountain tops, overlooking the sea, each with its story of marauding pirates and hidden treasures, going back to the times of the Saracens and Spanish galleons.

If time is limited or you'd rather not walk, you can take the one access road (you still need a ticket) from Alberese to **Marina di Alberese ❿**, a 6-km (4-mile) stretch of beach.

Map on page 234

Umbrella pines line many of the long, straight roads through the Maremman plains.

BELOW: fishing at Castiglione della Pescaia.

TIP

An annual rodeo is held in August, which brings American cowboys to Alberese. Other local festivals include the Sagra del Cinghiale (Boar Fair) in Montepescali, a summer opera festival in Batignano, the Sagra Pancolese (Local Gastronomic Fair) in Manciano, and the Sagra della Trippa (Tripe Fair) in Montemerano.

Just outside the southern boundaries of the park is the walled village of **Talamone** (18km/11 miles from Alberese), a small, low-key resort with some decent hotels and restaurants to choose from. You can gain access to the trails in the southern sector from nearby Caprarecce.

Argentario

It's a short drive from Talamone along the Aurelia-Etrusca (Grosseto–Rome highway) to **Monte Argentario**, a craggy peninsula that was once an island, thought to have been occupied by Roman moneylenders in the 4th century – *argentarius* in Latin is money-lender. From 1556 until 1815, Argentario existed as a separate state from the Grand Duchy of Tuscany, under Spanish rule. This kingdom encompassed the whole promontory and the existing ports of Orbetello, Talamone and Porto Azzurro, on the island of Elba. The Spanish legacy remains in architectural structures dotted throughout the area.

Monte Argentario gradually became attached to the land by two long sandbanks which built up over the centuries: Tòmbolo della Giannella and Tòmbolo di Feniglia. Both have fine beaches, but while Giannella is backed by a main road linking Porto Santo Stefano to the mainland, Feniglia is traffic-free and backed by protected pine forest. It's a 7-km (4-mile) walk or bike ride to the mainland.

Like two outstretched arms holding onto the mainland, the sandbanks embrace a lagoon, an important wintering spot for migrating birds. The lagoon is cut in half by a central causeway which links Argentario to the town of **Orbetello** , sited on a peninsula which projects into the lagoon from the mainland. The town's baroque architecture reflects its history as a 16th-century Spanish garrison town. The sea laps right up to the stout city walls, and visitors come from afar for the excellent fish restaurants found here and on Monte Argentario.

The rugged peninsula rises to a height of 635 metres (2,000 ft) and is cloaked in Mediterranean maquis, olive groves and vineyards. Apart

BELOW: Porto Santo Stefano.

from **Porto Santo Stefano** ⑬, most of the mountain has been spared from the property developers, but the exclusive villas outside the port towns remain the preserve of the rich. The coastline is extremely varied, but most of it is inaccessible, unless, of course, you are the owner of a yacht. The best way to enjoy Argentario is to stay in a hotel with a private beach. Otherwise, of the few beaches with public access, the nicest are Le Cannelle (roughly opposite Isola Rossa) and the beach to the left of the luxury hotel Il Pellicano, near Porto Ercole.

Porto Santo Stefano's busy harbour is crowded with small fishing boats and large yachts. It is an atmospheric town, with many shops, bars and fish restaurants. For a breathtaking and often hair-raising drive, the scenic coastal road from here (follow signs to La Panoramica) takes you along the clifftops, with spectacular views at every turn. The road is blocked by a rock fall beyond Cala Piccola and you have to turn back.

Porto Ercole ⑭ on the south side is Santo Stefano's smaller, supposedly more exclusive sister, but what was once a quiet fishing village is now overwhelmed by all the traffic that converges on it from sea and land. Its main attractions for landlubbers are the *centro storico* and the 16th-century Spanish fortress overlooking the harbour.

Island excursions

Santo Stefano has ferry connections with Giannutri and Giglio, two of the seven islands in the Archipelago Toscano *(see page 182)*. The archipelago was declared a nature reserve in 1996 – a move that, while obviously made to protect the environment, has created much controversy among both those involved with the tourist industry and local fishermen, whose rights have been restricted. Although swimming has not been affected, there are some areas where boats are not allowed to drop anchor.

Crescent-shaped **Giannutri** ⑮ is a tiny, flat, virtually uninhabited island 22 km (14 miles) away, where day trippers go to visit the ruins of a Roman villa – columns, mosaics, baths and a private pier.

Giglio ⑯, an hour's sail from Porto Santo Stefano, has more to offer. It is a playground for sailors and divers, and its proximity to Rome makes it a very popular weekend destination. Giglio is the second-largest island in Tuscany after Elba and has an impenetrable coastline with only one easily accessible port, Giglio Porto. A rocky road uphill leads to Giglio Castello, which dominates the landscape. Set among vineyards (which produce grapes for the very strong, distinctive local wine, Ansonica), it is a picturesque fortified settlement, with archways, alleyways and stairs carved from the rock. Giglio has a number of sandy beaches on its western side and is covered in typical Mediterranean vegetation: aromatic herbs and plants, and orange and lemon groves.

Map on page 234

It's always worth packing a pair of binoculars. Apart from being useful for close inspection of frescoes, in this area they will be handy for some rewarding birdwatching. The Orbetello lagoon and Parco dell'Uccellina are among the few places along the Italian coast which provide refuge for a wide variety of native and migratory birds.

BELOW: an old coastal watchtower on Giglio island.

The Maremma is famous for its brigands. One notorious bandito, Domenico Tiburzi, a local Robin Hood, was executed in 1896. There was disagreement over whether he could be buried in consecrated ground, and eventually a typical Italian compromise was reached: he was buried at the edge of a cemetery with his head in sacred ground, and the rest of his body outside.

BELOW: bathing in the Cascate del Gorello.

Cosa to Capalbio

Back on the mainland coast, across the Aurelia from the town of **Ansedonia** are the important Roman remains of **Cosa** ⑰ (daily 9am–7pm) built on top of what was originally an Etruscan settlement. Excavations have revealed a main street, a forum, a walled acropolis and *capitolium* with magnificent views out to sea; the site is somewhat overgrown and has a melancholy air.

Below the promontory is the silted-up Roman port and the Tagliata Etrusca, the Etruscan Cut – a canal in fact built by the Romans to drain the **Lago di Burano** ⑱. This protected lake is another favourite stopping place for thousands of migratory birds *(see page 284)*.

Inland lies **Capalbio** ⑲, one of the first towns on the hills bordering Lazio (Rome's province). Capalbio is a popular getaway among wealthy Italians, who have bought up every corner of the village and turned it into a fashionable summer refuge from the capital. It is famous for its food, and several excellent restaurants specialise in local dishes of wild boar and other game. The woodland around Capalbio is managed as a game reserve, and a game festival is held here every September.

Near by is the magical **Giardino dei Tarocchi**, or Tarot Garden (open daily 2.30–7.30pm in summer, 1st Sat of month 9am–1pm in winter; entrance fee), created by French sculptor Niki de Saint Phalle, who died in 2002, and inspired by the arcane symbolism of tarot. The park displays 22 fantastic, brightly coloured sculptures covered in mirror and mosaic, glinting in the sun among the flowers and fountains.

Fortified towns

Across the densely wooded hills north of Capalbio is the flat plain of the river Albegna, now completely drained, which leads to the castle of **Marsiliana** ⑳, once an Etruscan town and now the only property left belonging to the Corsini family, who originally owned the entire area. Most of these swamps were expropriated by the state, drained and then distributed to small landowners.

Spa therapy

Tuscany has an ancient spa tradition. Etruscans worshipped water and were believers in water rituals and herbal cures, but it was the Romans who perfected water cures, pioneering the virtues of moving between the hot and cold of the caldarium, tepidarium and frigidarium. The steaming thermal waters that gush from the ground are channeled into spa pools. These waters stimulate, re-mineralise, relax and revive the body, with sodium and magnesium nourishing bones, while the therapeutic mud is collected at the source of the spring, and used in natural face and body treatments. The top Tuscan spas are pampering as well as curative. *(For a list of Tuscany's best spas, see page 287).*

Map
on page
234

North of here lies **Magliano in Toscana** ㉑, a fortified medieval village perched above olive groves. Both civil and religious architecture show a strong Romanesque influence, with Gothic and Renaissance additions. A perfect example of the blend of styles is San Giovanni Battista, a Romanesque church with Gothic side windows and a Renaissance façade.

A few kilometres further inland, **Scansano** ㉒, a breezy hill village with a separate fortified section (*oppido*), was once the summer capital of the province, when all the administrative powers were moved from malarial Grosseto during the hot season. It is now famous for the fine DOC wine, Morellino di Scansano, and there are several *cantine* for wine-tasting.

Spa town

Travelling eastwards across hills and moors inhabited by *butteri* (cowboys) and Maremman cattle, you come to Montemerano, another typically Tuscan walled town, with 15th-century fortifications. From here you can take the road to the ancient Roman town of **Saturnia** ㉓. On the approach to the town, around a sharp curve, you will glimpse – and smell – the **Cascate del Gorello**, a steaming waterfall where you can bathe in hot sulphur springs. Alternatively, you can soak car-weary limbs in the thermal swimming pools of the nearby Terme di Saturnia, a modern spa and luxury hotel. Further on, Saturnia itself is a quiet little village, drowsy under the immense weight of its past. It was the Etruscan Aurinia, and then came under Roman control in 280 BC. The village is centred around a large oak-ringed piazza with one or two notable *trattorie*.

Tufa towns

Sorano, Sovana and Pitigliano are three southern Tuscan jewels situated above dramatic cliffs of soft, porous tufa covered in a thick jungle of fern, ivy and evergreen trees. The roads here, hewn out of the hills, are an experience in themselves. The winding stretch between Sovana and Pitigliano, which rises spectacularly above it, is particularly memorable.

The Equinos Association (www.cavallo maremmano.it) organises horse-trekking and butteri *shows in the Maremma. The Via Equestre Grossetana is a 1,000-km (620-mile) network of bridlepaths, with 43 equestrian tourism centres (www.via equestregrossetana.it)*

BELOW: Pitigliano.

Map on page 234

Ciborium from the 8th or 9th century inside Sovana's exquisite Romanesque church of Santa Maria.

BELOW: farm outbuilding and view of the surrounding countryside, near Sovana.

In the mid-18th century **Pitigliano** ㉔ was one of the the most important settlements in southern Tuscany. This majestic town is built on a hill of volcanic tufa and straddles a vast aqueduct with wine and olive-oil cellars carved out of the hillside below. It is laid out around two parallel streets that run along its length, crossed by 60 narrower streets which intersect with tiny alleys. Pitigliano used to be called "little Jerusalem", because it was a refuge for Jews fleeing from religious persecution in the Papal states. Even today the Jewish quarter of the city, which has the oldest Italian synagogue, remains distinct. It is one of the few places in Italy where you can find kosher wine or turkey "ham" *(billo)*, a Jewish speciality.

The town is centred around a magnificent citadel built by the Orsini in the 16th century. **Palazzo Orsini** houses an **Etruscan Museum** (open 2 weeks before Easter–2 Nov, 26 Dec–2 Jan Tues–Sun 10am–1pm, 3–7.30pm, or by appointment; tel: 0564-614067; entrance fee), containing finds from the nearby Etruscan site of Poggio Buco.

Before leaving, dip into one of the bars and enjoy a glass of Bianco di Pitigliano from the tufa wine cellars.

Sovana ㉕, a few kilometres away, is a tiny one-street village with two outstanding proto-Romanesque churches. The surrounding area is scattered with Etruscan tombs, hidden in the surrounding woods. These are best seen with a guide.

Situated above a deep ravine with a roaring stream and waterfall is medieval **Sorano** ㉖, which is also built on a tufa outcrop. Unfortunately, some of the buildings have begun to collapse into the steep valleys around the city, but the great majority of Sorano can be seen without danger.

Visible from every corner of Grosseto province on a clear day, particularly in snowy winter, is **Monte Amiata** *(see page 228)*, the highest peak in Tuscany south of Florence. It is a dormant volcano, with hot geysers on its slopes and underground waters that supply the spa at Saturnia. Monte Amiata is a refreshing escape during the hot summer months and a popular local ski resort in winter. ❑

RESTAURANTS

Capalbio

Il Fontanile dei Caprai
7 km (4.5 miles) from Capalbio on the Marsiliana road
Tel: 0564-896526
This country restaurant and its jovial owner are full of rustic charm. Tasty Maremman dishes made from locally sourced ingredients. Open weekends for lunch and dinner and from mid-June–mid-Sept, 26 Dec–8 Jan in the evenings too. €€

Castiglione della Pescaia

La Griglia
Via delle Rocchette
Tel: 0564-941402
Modest trattoria with good food. Their specialty is the mixed grilled fish platter. €€
La Terrazza
Corso Della Libertà 49
Tel: 0564-934617
Reliable restaurant and pizzeria. Open in spring and summer only. €

Grosseto

Gli Attortellati
Strada Provinciale Trappola 39   Tel: 0564-400059
Fixed menu that changes daily according to what is in season. Delicious food, but best to avoid the acidic house wine. €€
Il Canto del Gallo
Via Mazzini 29
Tel: 0564-414589
Tiny trattoria in the old town walls. Organic pro-

duce features strongly. Closed Sun and two weeks in Feb. €€

Montemerano

Da Caino
Via Canonica 3
Tel: 0564-602817
www.dacaino.it
One of the best restaurants in Tuscany. Exquisite and creative food, specialising in wild mushrooms and truffles. Must book. Closed Wed, Thur lunch, late Jan–late Feb and 2 weeks in July. €€€€

Orbetello

Osteria dell Lupacante
Corso Italia 103
Tel: 0564-867618
One of Orbetello's many good fish restaurants. Serves creative dishes *alla siciliana*. Closed Wed Sept–June. €€€
Osteria Il Nocchino
Via Lenzi 64
Tel: 0564-860329
Squeeze yourself into this tiny fish restaurant and tuck into such salty fresh dishes as salt cod and chick peas or sea food risotto. Evenings only. Closed Tues and weekend lunchtimes in winter. €€

Pitigliano

Trattoria del Grillo
Via Cavour, 18
Tel: 0564-615202
Authentic trattoria, by the aqueduct, mixing Tuscan classics with local flour-

ishes so you might follow good old *bruschetta* or *pici*, with escalopes in Pitigliano wine. Honestly priced and packed with locals. Closed Tues. €

Porto Santo Stefano

Il Moletto
Via del Molo
Tel: 0564-813636
www.moletto.it
The last in a long line of fish restaurants along the marina's main drag. Share a seafood platter while watching the port activity. Closed Wed. €€

Saturnia

Due Cippi-da Michele
Piazza Vittorio Veneto 26/A
Tel: 0564-601074
Maremman dishes in a patrician *palazzo*. Closed Tues. €€–€€€

Sovana

Taverna Etrusca
Piazza del Pretorio 16
Tel: 0564-616183
Local specialities served in a medieval dining room. Closed Wed. €€
Scilla
Via del Duomo
Tel: 0564-616531
The bright and elegant hotel/restaurant has a more contemporary feel than the Taverna Etrusca and offers a vegetarian menu. Closed Tues. €€

AREZZO AND EASTERN TUSCANY

Known for its gold, art and antiques, Arezzo city is one of the wealthiest in Tuscany, and the province is equally well-off in terms of prosperous farms and villages. The source of the Arno is here, too, in an area of great natural beauty known as the Casentino

The landscape of the province of Arezzo is rugged, with steep, thickly wooded valleys that shield its towns and villages from view. To the north, the Casentino is a remote area of chestnut woods, vineyards and monasteries; to the south are the prosperous farms of the fertile Val di Chiana. To the west, across the Pratomagno ridge, lies the Arno valley, which becomes more and more industrialised as you near Florence. At the heart of the province, its capital, Arezzo, was one of the most important towns in the Etruscan federation, thanks to its strategic position on a hill at the meeting point of three valleys. Today, it is one of Tuscany's wealthiest cities, known for its gold art and antiques, and boasts a large number of jewellers, antique shops and furniture restorers.

Arezzo city

Arezzo ❶ is rich in buildings, monuments and works of art of all eras. The old hilly part of the city is the most picturesque, with its massive main square, the **Piazza Grande** ❹, so far from being level that its numerous slopes and steps present a severe test even to the sober. On the first Sunday of every month, this square is the venue for an **antiques market**, the largest and oldest of its kind in Italy. Stalls cover the square, run around the base of the Duomo and spill into the cobbled **Corso Italia** ❸, the city's main shopping street.

Rising from the southern side of the square, sitting on the Corso, is the **Santa Maria della Pieve** ❻ (open daily 8am–1pm, 3–7pm) with its "tower of a hundred holes", so named because of the filigree pattern of arches piercing the belfry. This is one of the most beautiful Romanesque churches in all Tuscany.

Maps
City: 246
Area: 248

LEFT: view of Poppi.
BELOW: detail from the *Legend of the True Cross* fresco cycle by Piero della Francesca.

A spiritual fresco

Two blocks west you will find the church of **San Francesco** 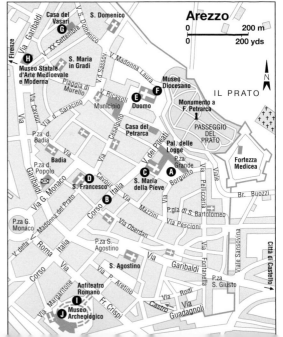 (open Mon–Fri 9am–6.30pm, Sat until 5.30pm, Sun 1–5.30pm) where you can see Piero della Francesca's restored *Legend of the True Cross* (1452–66) (guided tour Mon–Sat 10am; advance booking necessary; tel: 0575-352727; entrance fee). This masterful fresco cycle weaves together a complex story in which the wood of the Tree of Knowledge (from which Adam and Eve ate the apple) becomes the wood of the cross on which Christ died, and which was later discovered by the Empress Helena, mother of the Emperor Constantine the Great, who converted to Christianity and made it the state religion of the Roman Empire in AD 313.

The Cathedral

Medieval monuments cluster together in the northern part of the city, where you will find the **Duomo** (open daily 6.30am–noon, 3–6.30pm), sheltered by the encircling walls of the Grand-Duke Cosimo's 16th-century Fortezza, now a public park with fine views of the town and the Casentino beyond. The Duomo's construction, mainly from the late 13th to the early 16th centuries, has been described as one of the most perfect expressions of Gothic architecture in Italy. The Gothic façade, however, is fake and dates from 1914.

The real highlight of the Cathedral are the 16th-century stained-glass windows by Guillaume de Marcillat, a French artist who made Arezzo his home. Other great works here are the 14th-century tomb of Guido Tarlati, which flanks the *St Mary Magdalene* fresco by Piero della Francesca. This work can be contemplated in comparative peace, unlike the frescoes in San Francesco. The **Museo Diocesano** (open Thur–Sat 10am–noon; entrance fee), behind the

BELOW: browsing the antique stalls.

Cathedral, contains medieval crucifixes and Vasari frescoes.

Vasari trail

Further west is the **Casa del Vasari** ⓖ (open Mon, Wed–Sat 9am–7pm, Sun 9am–1pm; entrance fee), the attractive house that Giorgio Vasari – painter, architect and author of *The Lives of the Artists* (1550) – built for himself and decorated with frescoes of the artists he most admired.

Close by is the **Museo Statale d'Arte Medioevale e Moderna** ⓗ (open Tues–Sun 8.30am–7.30pm; entrance fee), housed in the 15th-century Palazzo Bruni. Spread across three floors, its varied collection includes an excellent display of majolica pottery, frescoes and examples of the Arezzo goldsmiths' work, alongside paintings by Vasari and modern works by local artists.

Roman Arezzo

Last but not least, in the flat southern part of the city you will find the **Anfiteatro Romano** ⓘ (open daily 8.30am–7.30pm, request to be accompanied by museum custodian;

Maps
City: 246
Area: 248

entrance fee). The Roman Arretium was originally an Etruscan city, but in 294 BC it became a Roman settlement, a convenient resting post on the Via Cassia between Rome and Florence. The site was later plundered to build the city walls and churches, and the perimeter wall is all that remains.

A section of the amphitheatre walls was incorporated into an Olivetan monastery (near the station), now occupied by the excellent **Museo Archeologico** ⓙ (open daily 8.30am–7.30pm, more restricted hours in winter; entrance fee), which features some of the finest examples anywhere of the Aretine ware for which Arezzo has long been famous. This high-quality Roman pottery once competed with the more famous Samian ware as the crockery of choice on aristocratic Roman dinner tables.

Piero della Francesca trail

East of Arezzo, the Upper Tiber valley is tightly enclosed at its northern end by the Alpe di Catenaia and the Alpe della Luna. Two important

Piazza Grande is the scene of the Giostra del Saracino, a historic jousting tournament held twice a year, in June and September.

BELOW: the Corso.

Piero della Francesca's 1463 masterpiece, the Resurrection, *was hailed by Aldous Huxley as "the best picture in the world".*

towns for Piero della Francesca enthusiasts are here. **Sansepolcro** 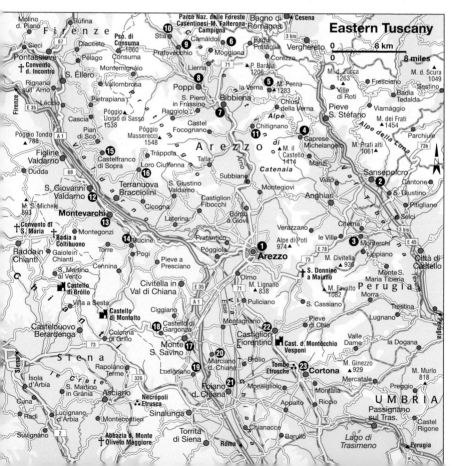 is famous for two things: as the town where Buitoni pasta is produced and as the birthplace of the great Renaissance artist. The old town huddled behind crumbling ramparts is an important artistic centre. The quiet, narrow streets are linked by four ancient gates, the best-preserved of which is the Porta Fiorentina.

In the town centre, at the junction of Piazza Torre di Berta and Via Matteotti, is the **Duomo** (open daily 8am–12.30pm, 3–6.30pm). Dedicated to St John the Evangelist, it

began life in the 11th century as a monastic abbey. A wide range of excellent artworks cover the walls of the interior, including a tabernacle by the della Robbia school. Perugino's *Ascension of Jesus* is also here.

But the reason most people make the pilgrimage here is to see Piero della Francesca's greatest work, the *Resurrection*. The fresco was nearly destroyed by the Allies during World War II as they bombarded Sansepolcro, believing the Germans were still occupying the town. It was thankfully saved from destruction by the villagers, who surrounded it with sandbags. Today, this intense, brooding work is displayed in the **Museo Civico** (open daily June–Sept 9am–1pm, 2.30–7.30pm, Oct–May 9.30am–1pm, 2.30–6pm; entrance fee), in Via degli Aggiunti, alongside the **Madonna della Misericordia**, another della Francesca masterpiece.

Other key buildings to look out for are the 16th-century Palazzo delle Laudi (the Town Hall) and the Palazzo Gherardi, begun in 1300, both in Via Matteotti, and the Palazzo Pretorio opposite Piazza Garibaldi.

From Sansepolcro, the della Francesca trail leads south to **Monterchi ❸**, where a former schoolhouse displays his striking *Madonna del Parto* in the **Museo Madonna del Parto** (open Tues–Sun 9am–1pm, 2–7pm, until 5pm in winter; entrance fee). The Madonna, heavily pregnant and aching, has unbuttoned the front of her dress, while above, two angels hold up the entrance to the tent in which she stands.

Michelangelo's birthplace

Northwest of Sansepolcro, on a steep slope above the Tiber, is the hamlet of **Caprese Michelangelo ❹**, birthplace of Michelangelo. Protected by an almost complete set of walls, this cluster of rustic buildings – which includes the Buonarroti house, the old town hall where Michelangelo's father was the Florentine governor, and the tiny chapel in which Michelangelo was baptised – are interesting more for their connections than for their contents. The views over Alpine countryside explain why Michelangelo attributed his good brains to the mountain air he breathed as a child.

The Casentino

The Casentino is the name given to the little-known region of the Upper Arno valley that runs from the eastern side of the Consuma Pass down to the source of the river just north

of Arezzo. It is an area of great natural beauty, enclosed by high mountains, cloaked in fir, chestnut and beech woods, and concealing ancient monasteries and farming villages. You have no choice but to explore it at a leisurely pace. The narrow, winding, rural roads are slow going, and with views at every turn, the temptation to stop and admire them is hard to resist.

At its remoter edges this region cannot have changed much since the 13th century, when St Francis took to a lonely, desolate crag on the wooded slopes of **Monte Penna** at **La Verna ❺**, using a niche between two huge boulders as a hermitage. The mountain was given to the Franciscan Order as a free gift by a local devotee, Count Orlando da Chiusi di Casentino, who had been inspired by one of St Francis's sermons. On this spot in 1224 St Francis is supposed to have received the stigmata while he was praying. Today, in the middle of the ancient forest, a Franciscan sanctuary still occupies the rock. Assembled around a tiny piazza is a collection of monastic buildings, including one

Portrait of a turbaned Michelangelo, by Giuliano Bugiardini, 1522.

BELOW: detail from the *Resurrection*, by Piero della Francesca.

The Parco Nazionale delle Foreste Casentinesi is one of Italy's newest national parks and is heavily promoted in the region. It lies along the Apennine ridge that forms the border between Tuscany and Emilia Romagna. There are waymarked trails through the park, and a number of *agriturismo* establishments if you want to spend a few days exploring the woods and mountains *(for more information, see page 64)*.

BELOW: in Tuscany, shop decoration is an art form.

large church containing yet more fine terracotta sculptures by the gifted della Robbia family.

Sixteen kilometres (10 miles) northeast of La Verna, high in the spectacular woodland, cut by mountain streams and waterfalls, is another more ancient monastery, **Camáldoli** ❻ (open daily 9am–1pm, 2.30–7pm; until 7.30pm in summer; tel: 0575-556012). It was founded in 1012 by San Romualdo (St Rumbold), a former member of the Benedictine Order, who founded a strict community of hermits. The monastery is still inhabited, and the monks run a welcoming café here. The old cloister **pharmacy** (open 9am–12.30pm, 2.30–6pm), with its mortars and crucibles, is a pleasing relic of past times and now sells soaps and liqueurs made by the monks.

Another 300 metres (1,000 ft) up the mountain (a beautiful hour-long walk), above the monastery is the **Eremo**, a hermitage consisting of nothing more than a small baroque church and ten cells, each surrounded by a high wall and a tiny kitchen garden. Here the hermits still live in

solitude and silent contemplation. The church and St Rumbold's cell are open to visitors (daily 8.30–11.30am, 2.30–6.30pm; tel: 0575-556021), but access to the monks' quarters is closed.

After immersing yourself in the silence and isolation of Camáldoli, a visit to noisy **Bibbiena** ❼ will bring you sharply back to the modern world. At its heart is a typical Tuscan hill town, but its inner charms are hidden by the modern sprawl around it. Bibbiena is the Casentino's main commercial centre, best-known for its own particular brand of salami and as a centre for industry related to tobacco production. Buildings of note in the historic centre include the church of **San Lorenzo** (open daily 8am–6pm), which has some richly decorated della Robbia panels, and the church of **Sant'Ippolito Martire** (open daily 8am–7pm) which has a fine triptych by Bicci di Lorenzo. Near by is the Renaissance **Palazzo Dovizi**, home of Cardinal Dovizi, who, as Cardinal Bibbiena, became the secretary of Pope Leo X. Bibbiena's central piazza offers distant views to Camáldoli and Poppi – the latter is the gateway to an interesting area of castles and fortified towns.

Casentino castles

This region was continually fought over by the Guelf Florentines and the Ghibelline Aretines. A decisive battle in 1289 which firmly established the dominance of the former over the latter is marked by a column on a site called **Campaldino**, just between Castel San Niccolò and Poppi.

Poppi ❽ surveys the surrounding countryside from its hilltop perch, dominated by the brooding **Castello dei Conti Guidi** (open daily 10am–5pm Nov–mid-Mar, until 6pm mid-Mar–Oct, until 7pm July–Aug), the most important medieval monument in the Casentino. Built in the 13th century for the powerful Guidi

counts who ruled most of the area, the castle's design was based on that of the Palazzo Vecchio in Florence, and it is thought likely that Arnolfo di Cambio was the architect. The courtyard and stairway are impressive, and the Florentine frescoes may be viewed on request. The ancient streets of this quiet town are lined with arcades linked by steep steps and decorated with finely carved capitals and stone seats. There's a Romanesque church and a few shops selling locally made copper pots.

Off in the distance, on a hill above the village of **Pratovecchio ➒**, birthplace of Paolo Uccello, is the 11th-century **Castello di Romena** (open in summer or by appointment; tel: 0575-520516), another Guidi castle. The noble family gave refuge to Dante here after his expulsion from Florence at the beginning of the 14th century. Of the 14 towers that Dante would have seen at the castle, only three remain.

Standing on a lonely slope, a stone's throw from the castle, **Pieve di Romena** (visits by appointment with the custodian; tel: 0575-583725)

is one of the most important Romanesque churches in Tuscany. Beneath its apse, which dates from 1152, excavations have revealed the remains of an Etruscan building as well as two earlier churches. The finely carved capitals atop the gigantic granite columns in the nave make reference to the four Evangelists and to St Peter.

Back down in Pratovecchio, you'll find the headquarters of the Casentino national park (Via G. Brocchi 7; tel: 0575-50301; www.parcoforeste casentinesi.it; *see tip opposite*).

To the north and guarding the source of the Arno (Monte Falterona) is the medieval town of **Stia ➓**, with a pretty porticoed piazza. Here stand the ruins of the **Castello di Porciano** (open mid-May–mid-Oct Sun 10am–noon, 4–7pm, or by appointment; tel: 0575-582635), another Guidi stronghold which stood guard over the Arno valley.

The Castello di Romena is visible from up here. Whereas these monuments are all easily accessible, the fortified remains at Castel Castagnaia, with the nearby ruined Roman

Fiat's classic Cinquecento "Bambino" is still a much-loved runaround, perfect for the narrow streets of small towns like Poppi.

BELOW: view across Poppi from the Palazzo Pretorio.

TIP

East of the Arno and skirting the western edge of the high Pratomagno ridge is the panoramic road known as the Strada dei Sette Ponti, or Road of the Seven Bridges. The winding route passes through several medieval towns, including Castelfranco di Sopra, Loro Ciuffena to the south and the abbey at Vallombrosa *(see page 120)* to the north.

BELOW RIGHT: the white Chianina cattle are highly prized for their beef.

temple, both to the west of Stia, are harder to reach. The road peters out, and they can only be reached on foot through rough, stony countryside.

Remains of yet another Guidi castle can be seen in the tiny village of **Montemignaio**. There's not much left to see, but the village church has Ghirlandaio's *Virgin and Child with the Four Church Elders*.

On the slope of the forested Pratomagno ridge, south of Bibbiena, is the restored castle at **Chitignano ⓫**. The medieval remains were rebuilt in the 18th century. There are other ruined castles at Talla and Subbiano.

The Valdarno

There are two possible routes through the Arno valley between Florence and Arezzo. The SS69 runs parallel to the river and provides the quickest access to the Valdarno's sights, though traffic here can be heavy. More scenic is the road that skirts the Pratomagno ridge on the eastern side of the Arno. It's full of twists and turns, but the views are rewarding.

In the Middle Ages, the Valdarno was bitterly fought over by the Ghi-

bellines and the Guelfs. At the close of the 13th century pressure was exerted on the Florentines by the war-like Aretine bishops, who controlled powerful strongholds in the Arno valley. In an effort to resist them, the Florentines built three fortresses, which were really fortified towns, at San Giovanni Valdarno, Terranuova and Castelfranco di Sopra.

Halfway between Florence and Arezzo, **San Giovanni Valdarno ⓬** was fortified as a bulwark against the Aretines, but little evidence remains of its former military function. Today it is a lively industrial centre with a prominent display of architectural and artistic wealth. The central piazza and arcaded Palazzo Comunale were designed by Arnolfo di Cambio. The nearby church of **Santa Maria della Grazia** (open daily; free) contains a *Virgin and Child with the Four Saints* by Masaccio, who was born here in 1401. Just outside the town, the Renaissance monastery of Montecarlo houses an *Annunciation* by Fra Angelico.

In prehistoric times the Arno basin was one big lake, and farmers today

Val di Chiana and Its Cattle

The Val di Chiana is the most extensive valley in the Apennine range. In prehistoric times, the area between Monte San Savino and Cortona was submerged in water. It was drained by the Etruscans, but by the late Middle Ages the whole valley had become a swamp, and for refuge from malaria, as well as from marauding, hostile armies, the people took to the hills, barricading themselves behind high defensive walls on precipitous outcrops of rock.

Today Val di Chiana is a prosperous, malaria-free zone of rich farmland which is mainly used to rear one of Italy's two prized breeds of cattle for meat – Chianina, which is native to Tuscany. (The other is Razza Piemontese from Piedmont.) The Chianina cow grows quickly to a large size, so that it is butchered when the steer is a grown calf. The meat is firm and tasty, with a distinctive flavour. For any beef- loving Italian, *bistecca alla Fiorentina* – a huge, tender Val di Chiana T-bone steak, grilled over an open fire seasoned with nothing more than crushed peppercorns, salt, and a hint of garlic and olive oil, served very rare – is the ultimate steak.

Maps
City: 246
Area: 248

frequently dig up fossil remains and bones of long extinct animals. At **Montevarchi** ⑬, south of San Giovanni Valdarno, is the **Accademia Valdarnese** (closed for restoration until 2010), an important museum of prehistory, which houses an impressive collection of fossilised remains from the Pliocene period discovered in this stretch of the Arno valley. Apart from the museum and the church, there is not much to detain the traveller here, though in the hills to the south of the town, above **Bucine** ⑭, there is a beautiful hexagonal font in the church of tiny **Galatrona**, covered with reliefs of the *Life of St John the Baptist*.

Unlike San Giovanni Valdarno, **Castelfranco di Sopra** ⑮, across the Arno (also fortified for the Florentines by Arnolfo di Cambio), retains its military character; the Porta Fiorentina gate is as forbidding as it ever was, and many of the 14th-century streets and buildings have survived.

About 10 km (6 miles) south of Castelfranco on the scenic Strada dei Sette Ponti (Road of the Seven Bridges) is **Loro Ciuffenna** ⑯, a medieval village positioned on a chasm cut by the Ciuffenna river. A couple of kilometres away is the rural Romanesque church of **Gropina**, dating from the early 13th century, noted for the carvings of animals, figures and geometrical patterns on the pulpit and columns. From here the picturesque route to **Talla**, where you'll find another ruined castle, crosses into the Casentino.

Val di Chiana

The broad flat valley south of Arezzo is known as the Val di Chiana, a fertile plain surrounded by hills and picturesque towns, where cattle are bred to supply the restaurants of Florence with the raw ingredient of *bistecca alla Fiorentina* (steak Florentine). **Monte San Savino** ⑰, on the edge of the Val di Chiana, has been a citadel since Etruscan times, although the fortifications that survive date from the Middle Ages. In 1325 the inhabitants were unable to fend off a ruthless Aretine mob who razed the town as punishment for their Guelf sympa-

Colourful contemporary ceramics can be found in and around Cortona.

BELOW: Castiglion Fiorentino.

Church and square in Lucignano, famous for its unique concentric street plan.

thies. It was subsequently rebuilt. Its once large Jewish community was wiped out – many were burned at the stake – for resisting the French army in 1799. Progress has hardly touched Monte San Savino; it retains medieval and Renaissance houses, of which the **Palazzo Comunale**, with a façade by Antonio da Sangallo the Elder and a fine **museum** (open Nov–Mar Wed–Fri 9am–1pm, Sat–Sun also afternoons 4–7pm, Apr–Oct Wed–Fri 9am–1pm, 4–7pm, Sat–Sun until 7.30pm, Tues am only), is the most important.

Other important landmarks here include the **Loggia del Mercato** by Sansovino and the churches of Santa Chiara and Sant' Agostino.

The wild hills northwest of the town shelter a feudal retreat, the **Castello di Gargonza** ⓲. This 13th-century *borgo* or walled village, on the western slope of Monte Palaz-zuolo, dominates the Chiana valley and is the centre of a vast wooded estate producing oil and wine. The walled settlement has been converted into a hotel and restaurant complex (www.gargonza.it). The converted cottages, tiny cobbled streets, a chapel, a baronial tower, attractive gardens and a magnificent view down to the Chiana all make Gargonza a very pleasant retreat.

South of Monte San Savino is **Lucignano** ⓳. Originally an Etruscan stronghold, the concentric arrangement of streets around a fortress make it unique among Tuscan hill towns. With a few exceptions Lucignano's buildings (13th–18th-century) are perfectly preserved, as is the Gothic church of San Francesco. The 14th-century **Palazzo Comunale** (open Tues–Sun 10am–12.30pm, 3.30–7pm, until 5.30pm in winter; entrance fee) contains frescoes from the Sienese and Aretine schools, as well as some examples of finely worked gold ornaments for which the province of Arezzo has long been famous, including the beautiful 14th-century *Tree of Lucignano,* richly embellished with jewels.

Fortified villages

Marciano della Chiana ⓴, 6 km (4 miles) northeast, another tiny village of great character, was also fortified

Maps
City: 246
Area: 248

in the Middle Ages. Much of the castle remains intact, as do the walls and a gateway with a clock tower built into it. Three km (2 miles) to the southeast is the octagonal chapel of **Santa Vittoria**, designed by Ammannati to mark the spot where the Florentines defeated the Sienese in 1554.

Foiano della Chiana ㉑ clings prettily to the side of the hill. Much of it dates from the 15th–16th centuries, though traces of medieval defences can be seen around the edge of the town. At Cisternella, about 3 km (2 miles) to the northeast of the centre, are the remains of what is believed to have been a Roman bathhouse.

From here, looming large in the distance, is the fortified village of **Castiglion Fiorentino** ㉒, bounded by thick walls and dominated by the **Cassero Fortress** (open Tues–Sun 10am–12.30pm, 4–6pm, weekends until 7pm; entrance fee). This well-preserved medieval settlement has an unusually high number of churches. The oldest of these, the Pieve Vecchia (the oldest church), has a Signorelli fresco of the *Deposition of Christ* (1451), and the 13th-century church of San Fran-cesco contains a sculpted version.

Other sacred works and gold and silverware from the surrounding churches can be seen in the **Pinacoteca Comunale** (open Tues–Sun 10am–12.30pm, 4–6pm, until 7pm Sat–Sun; entrance fee). On the old market square are Vasari's famous **loggias**. The stone arches frame a fine vista of the rooftops and surrounding countryside.

Just outside the village is the fine octagonal temple of **Santa Maria della Consolazione**.

Cortona

Close to the Umbrian border, 30 km (18 miles) south of Arezzo, **Cortona** ㉓ is one of the oldest and and most enchanting hill towns in Tuscany. It was founded by the Etruscans, who were among the first to appreciate its lofty heights. The Romans colonised it, the Aretines sacked it in 1258, and in 1409 it was sold to the Florentines, which linked it from then onwards to the fortunes of the Grand Duchy of Tuscany. By the 15th century, Cortona had become a major centre of power.

Cortona is perched majestically on a ridge of Monte Sant'Egidio, 650 metres (2130 ft) above the Val di Chiana. The road from the valley floor to the city winds its way through terraced olive groves and vineyards, past villas, farms, monasteries and churches surrounded with ilexes and cypresses. But Cortona's main attraction lies in the steepness of its crooked streets, linked by stone staircases, which work their way painfully to the Medici fortress at the top.

The town is entered from the relatively flat Piazza Garibaldi and Via Nazionale, which lead to Piazza Signorelli, with its 13th-century **Palazzo Comunale** (Town Hall) and the **Museo dell'Accademia Etrusca** (open daily 10am–7pm in summer, Tues–Sun until 5pm in winter;

Frances Mayes's books Bella Tuscany *and* Under the Tuscan Sun *(now a lavishly shot film) have elevated Cortona, site of her home, to celebrity status.*

BELOW: the lofty heights of Cortona.

Maps
City: 246
Area: 248

One of a number of celebrated artists from Cortona, Luca Signorelli (1450–1523) produced frescoes for Orvieto Cathedral, and was summoned to the Vatican to complete frescoes in the Sistine Chapel. In a tiny courtyard below the Medici Fortress, the church of San Nicolò houses his wonderful standard of the Deposition.

BELOW: the domed church of Santa Maria della Grazia, below Cortona.

entrance fee). This rewarding museum has two star exhibits: the lovely fresco of *Polymnia*, generally considered to be a fine Roman painting of the Muse of Song until recent research proved it to be an 18th-century forgery; and a genuine Etruscan chandelier dating from 300 BC.

West of the piazza is the 16th-century Cathedral and its companion, the **Museo Diocesano** (open daily 10am–7pm in summer, Tues–Sun until 5pm in winter; entrance fee), which contains some rare masterpieces by Fra' Angelico, Lorenzetti and Luca Signorelli.

Returning to the town centre, it is worth seeking out Via Janelli with its row of brick buildings with overhanging upper storeys – some of Tuscany's oldest surviving medieval houses. Other picturesque streets to look out for include the Via Ghibellina and Via Guelfa.

It's a steep climb up to the **Basilica di Santa Margherita**, which contains the remains of Santa Margherita, the town's patron saint. She was a farmer's daughter who joined the Third Order of St Francis

and founded a convent and hospital. The citizens of Cortona still make pilgrimages up the winding stone-flagged streets to her tomb to offer her prayers during hard times.

The **Medici Fortress** above is overgrown and rarely open, but the views from up here are splendid, and it's a fine spot for a picnic.

Lake Trasimeno

One side of Cortona's public gardens opens to a belvedere with sweeping views. As you look south you will notice a glistening body of water. This is **Lago di Trasimeno**, Italy's fourth-largest lake, which lies in neighbouring Umbria. Its shallow waters are surprisingly clean and, in summer, full of swimmers, boaters and windsurfers. There was a day, though, in 217 BC when the lake waters ran red with the blood of the Roman legions, more than 16,000 of whom were slaughtered by Hannibal's troops. Today the scene is considerably more peaceful, especially on the southern shore, which is generally less crowded. A number of fine fish restaurants line the lake. ❑

RESTAURANTS

Arezzo

Antica Osteria L'Agania
Via Mazzini 10
Tel: 0575-295381
Very pleasant and hugely popular family-run trattoria serving good, homely Tuscan fare. Excellent value. Closed Mon, except June–Aug. €–€€

Buca di San Francesco
Via San Francesco 1
Tel/fax: 0575-23271
www.bucadisanfrancesco.it
A famous cellar restaurant adjoining San Francesco church, with Trecento frescoes and a Roman-Etruscan pavement below. The lovely, medieval atmosphere is matched by straightforward, rustic, tasty cuisine. Closed Mon evening and Tues. €€

Il Cantuccio
Via Madonna del Prato 76
Tel/fax: 0575-26830
Vaulted basement restaurant run by the Volpi family who produce their own wine and olive oil. Try the *bistecca*, perhaps with deep-fried *porcini* mushrooms. Closed Wed. €€

Il Torrino
Strada dei Due Mari 1
Tel: 0575-360649
www.iltorrino.com
Eight km (5 miles) along the San Sepolcro road, this restaurant is worth seeking out for the good food and wonderful view. Truffles in season. Closed Mon. €€

La Lancia d'Oro
Piazza Grande 18/19
Tel: 0575-21033
Excellent Arezzo cuisine features here in this pleasing, central restaurant. In summer you can dine al fresco. Closed Sun evening, all day Mon and 5–25 Nov. €€–€€€

La Torre di Gnicche
Piaggia San Martino 8
Tel: 0575-352035
www.latorredignicche.it
Just off the northern corner of the main square, this tiny little wine bar is an excellent choice for a cheap and simple meal – a hearty *ribollita*, or a platter of cheese – with a glass of wine from a long list of excellent selections. Popular with the antique dealing fraternity. Closed Wed. €

Cortona

Il Falconiere
Loc. San Martino 370 (4km/2½ miles north of Cortona)
Tel: 0575-612679
www.ilfalconiere.it
In a lovely setting in the hills, this elegant hotel makes you feel as though time stands still. Good, imaginative cuisine includes both fish and meat dishes and service is excellent. Lovely panoramic terrace. Reserve in advance. €€€€

La Grotta
Piazzetta Baldelli 3
Tel: 0575-630271
A well-established family-run trattoria with local food and a warm welcome. Alfresco dining in summer. Popular with tourists. Closed Tues. €€

Osteria del Teatro
Via Maffei 2
Tel: 0575-630556
www.osteria-del-teatro.it
Simple, but delicious food, a fine location in a 15th-century *palazzo* and friendly service make this one of Cortona's nicest eateries. Closed Wed. €€–€€€

Lucignano

Osteria da Totò
Piazza del tribunale 6
Tel: 0575-836763
www.trattoriatoto.it
Run by well-known chef Lorenzo Totò, the cuisine takes its inspiration from traditional Italian cooking. Closed Tues. €–€€

Mercatale di Cortona

Mimmi
Via Pietro della Cortona 2931
Tel: 0575-619029
A wonderful dining experience: arrive early to sit down to never-ending dishes of home made Tuscan cuisine, cooked in a wood fired oven. Vegetables from the kitchen garden and good local wines. Closed 1 week in Nov. €

PRICE CATEGORIES

Average cost of a three-course meal per person with a half-bottle of wine:

€ = under €25
€€ = €25–40
€€€ = €40–60
€€€€ = over €60

TRANSPORT

GETTING THERE AND GETTING AROUND

GETTING THERE

By Air

From the UK, low-cost airlines like Ryanair and Easyjet operate from many of Italy's smaller provincial airports, thus making travel between the UK and Italy easy as well as opening up Italian routes to greater competition. In addition to the national airline, Alitalia, many major scheduled airlines run direct flights to Italy, as well as charter flights which tend to offer lower fares and often fly to more convenient provincial airports than scheduled ones.

From the US, the main carriers are Alitalia, Delta, United and US Airways, which fly to Rome, Milan and Venice. European airlines such as British Airways and Air France also fly to Italy, with a stopover.

The country has two airports designed for intercontinental flights: **Roma Leonardo da Vinci** (known as Fiumicino) and **Milano Malpensa**.

Pisa's Galileo Galilei Airport is the usual airport for international visitors to Florence. Getting from Pisa to Florence is easy and cheap *(see page 259).*

Florence's Peretola-Florence (also known as Amerigo Vespucci) is set 4 km (2 miles) northwest of the city centre. Some international flights land here, but these tend to be more expensive than flights to Pisa. Meridiana operates regular flights between Florence and the UK (www.meridiana.it).

Bologna Airport is a further alternative; it is conveniently located for Florence and Tuscany (there's a direct train to Florence and Arezzo).

By Rail

Rail travel is a slow and not particularly cheap option unless you are travelling as part of the Inter-Rail scheme (providing a month's unlimited rail travel in Europe for anyone under the age of 26 at a very reasonable price). When travelling from Great Britain via Paris (the usual route when travelling to Florence or Rome, for example), it is necessary to change in Paris (from Gare du Nord to Gare de Lyon).

ES (Eurostar), EC (EuroCity), IC (Inter City) and TEE (Trans Europe Express) trains are top-of-the-range trains running between the main Italian and European cities. A special supplement is charged and seat reservation is obligatory.

You can check your routes on the official Italian railway website: www.trenitalia.it, and get more info at www.trenitaliaplus.com.

In the UK, for information and train bookings, contact the Rail Europe call centre tel: 08705-848848; or visit the ticket office at 178 Piccadilly, London W1 open Mon–Fri 10am–6pm, Sat until 5pm; or log on to www.rail europe.co.uk.

Visitors from the US and Canada can also buy tickets and passes in advance through rail Europe. Visit www.raileurope.com or tel: 08708-302008. Another useful website is www.traintraveling.com.

By Road

When calculating the cost of travelling to Italy by car, allow for the price of motorway tolls as well as accommodation en route and petrol. The quickest cross-Channel car ferries are from Dover to Calais. The Channel Tunnel transports cars on the train between Folkestone and Calais (Eurotunnel, tel: 08705-353535; www.euro tunnel.com). The usual route from France to Italy is via Paris and the Mont Blanc Tunnel (between Chamonix and Courmayeur) or from Switzerland through the Gran San Bernardo Tunnel (between Bourg St Pierre and Aosta). Some of the alpine passes are seasonal, so check the viability of your route with the tourist board or a motoring organisation before setting off.

To take your car into Italy, you will need your current driving licence, your vehicle registration document and insurance certificate. You are also required to carry a warning triangle in case of breakdown. Headlights should be illuminated at all times. Some petrol stations require payment in cash, not credit card. Keep cash handy for *autostrada* tolls too.

The AA and RAC in the UK give up-to-date advice on Channel crossings, with or without a car, and also driving on the continent.

In the US, the AAA provides information on travel in Italy.

By Coach

Travelling to Italy from the UK by coach is not much cheaper than going by air. National Express Eurolines runs coaches from London Victoria, via Paris and Mont Blanc, to Aosta, Turin, Genoa, Milan, Venice, Bologna, Florence and Rome. To book from London, contact: National Express, Victoria Coach Station, Buckingham Palace Road, London SW1, tel: 08705-514 3219; www.nationalexpress.co.uk.

GETTING AROUND

On Arrival

Pisa Airport The international airport, Galileo Gallilei (tel: 050-849111) has its own railway station. Trains take five minutes into Pisa Centrale and one hour for the 80 km (50 miles) to Florence (www.trenitalia.com). Bus LAM "rosso" ("the red line") also links the airport with Pisa Centrale rail station. There is a frequent coach service between the airport (departing from outside the Arrivals hall) and Florence's Santa Maria Novella train station (www.terravision.it). Car hire is available from the airport, and so are taxis. A toll-free *superstrada* links Pisa airport with Florence. **Peretola (Amerigo Vespucci) International Airport** (tel: 055-30615) in northwest Florence is connected by bus (Vola

in Bus) to the SITA bus company depot not far from Santa Maria Novella station; the journey time is about 20 minutes.

By Air

Alitalia offers a huge range of internal flights from both Florence and Pisa airports. These are supplemented by Meridiana's domestic services, which are usually a bit cheaper.

By Rail

For information 24 hours daily call 89 20 21 or visit www.trenitalia.it. The state-subsidised railway network is a relatively cheap and convenient form of transport for travelling between major cities in Tuscany. The principal Rome–Milan line is convenient for Bologna, Florence and Arezzo, while the Rome–Genoa line serves Pisa, Livorno and Grosseto. The Florence–Siena route is much faster by coach than by train.

Note that Pisa and Florence both have several train stations: **Pisa Centrale** station serves Pisa city while **Pisa Aeroporto** serves the airport. In Florence, **Santa Maria Novella** is the main station for the city, although the second station, **Rifredi**, is served by several *Eurostar* trains.

Categories of Trains

Eurocity: these trains link major Italian cities with other European cities – in Germany and Switzerland, for instance. A supplement is payable on top of the ordinary rail fare.

Eurostar Italia and Alta Velocità: these swish, high-speed trains have first- and second-class carriages (supplements payable).

Intercity: this fast service links major Italian cities. Intercity Plus is the latest fleet of plush new fast trains. A supplement is payable; reservations required.

Interregionali: these inter-regional trains link cities within different regions (e.g. Tuscany and Umbria) and stop reasonably frequently.

Regionali: these regional trains link towns within the same region and stop at every station.

Tickets

Booking

Reservations are mandatory for superior trains (such as Eurostar and Eurocity) and tickets should be purchased in advance. Other tickets with compulsory supplements should be purchased at least three hours in advance. You must date-stamp *(convalidare)* your rail ticket before beginning the journey at one of the small machines at the head of the platforms. Failure to do so may result in a fine. If you wish to upgrade to first class or a *couchette*, you can pay the conductor the difference.

Expect long lines for tickets at major stations, but, for a small fee, they can also be purchased from many travel agents. There are automatic ticket machines at major stations, although these are often out of order. Payment can be made either by cash or by credit card.

Wagons Lits/Carrozze Letto (sleeping cars) are found on long-distance trains within Italy, as well as on trains to France, Austria, Germany, and Switzerland. Reservations are essential.

Special Offers

There are a wide variety of train tickets and special offers available, which vary constantly and with the season. Some of the more established are:

The Trenitalia Pass: available for foreign visitors, it allows between 3 and 10 days unlimited travel on the Italian State Railway network, within a two-month period.

Group fares: groups of between 6 and 24 people can benefit from a 20 percent discount.

Youth fares: students aged between 12 and 26 can buy a yearly *Carta Verde* – "green card". This season ticket entitles them to a 10 percent discount on national trains and a 20 percent discount on international trips.

TRANSPORT

ACCOMMODATION

ACTIVITIES

A – Z

LANGUAGE

Children's fares: children under four travel free; children aged between 4–12 are eligible for a 50 percent discount on all trains but must pay the full supplement for Intercity and Eurocity trains.
Pensioners' fares: the over-60s can buy a *Carta d'Argento*. Valid for a year, this "silver card" entitles them to a 15 percent discount on all train tickets.

Railway Stations

The main railway stations are open 24 hours a day and are integrated with road and sea transport. They provide numerous services, including telecommunications, left luggage, food and drink, tourist information and porters (luggage trolleys are hard to find).
Florence: The train information office at Santa Maria Novella station is next to the waiting room. The train reservation office is just inside the building (open daily 6am–10pm). There is a left luggage counter, where pieces of luggage are left at your own risk. The station also has an air terminal where you can check in for Pisa airport. There are bars and a pharmacy in the main hall, and shops on the lower level.
Siena: The railway station has an information office, counter for left luggage (and bicycles) and restaurant. Immediately outside the station is a bus ticket office and a tourist office. However, Siena's railway station is outside the town centre. More useful, and with faster services and a greater range of local destinations, is the coach service, with coaches leaving from Piazza San Domenico to Florence and various other Tuscan towns.

By Coach

Coaches are very comfortable and often quicker than trains. Especially convenient is the Rapida bus to Siena, running several times a day. Provincial bus companies include (websites in Italian only):
CPT, via A. Bellatalla 1, Ospedaletto Pisa; tel: 0508-84111 or free information line: 800-012773; www.cpt.pisa.it (for travel in Pisa Province).
CAP, Piazza Duomo 18, Prato; tel: 0574-6081; www.capautolinee.it (for travel in Tuscany and other parts of Italy).
Lazzi, Piazza Stazione 3r, Florence; tel: 055-215155; www.lazzi.it (for travel in Tuscany).
Rama, Via Topazio 12, Grosseto; tel: 0564-475111; www.griforama.it (for travel around Grosseto and Tuscany).
Sita, Via S. Caterina da Siena 15, Florence; tel: 800-001311; www.sitabus.it (for travel in Tuscany and Italy in general).
SENA, Sottopassaggio (Underpass) la Lizza, Siena; tel: 0577-283203; www.sena.it (for travel to and from Tuscany, great for Siena–Rome).

Tuscan Island Ferries

Numerous ferries ply the waters between the mainland and the islands of the Tuscan archipelago (Elba, Giglio, Capraia, Gorgona and Pianosa). Services from Piombino to Elba are regular throughout the day – every half hour in the summer – but during the peak months, especially August, you should book in advance. At other times you can turn up and buy your ticket direct from the harbour office. The journey time for the car ferry is just under an hour. Hydro-foil services for foot passengers only are less frequent but take around 35 minutes.

The biggest operator is **Toremar**, which connects Piombino to Portoferraio, Porto Azzuro, Rio Marina and Cavo. For information and bookings from Italy tel: 892123, from abroad, tel: (+39) 081-017 1998, Portoferraio office, tel: 0565-918080. For online bookings go to www.toremar.it or www.visitelba.com.

Moby Lines, the other main operator, runs a regular service between Piombino and Portoferraio. For information and bookings: tel: 199 303040, Portoferraio office, tel: 0565-9361. Online bookings: www.mobylines.it.

Toremar also operates services from Livorno to Capraia and Gorgona, from Piombino to Pianosa, and from Santo Stefano on the Argentario peninsula to the island of Giglio.

City Transport

Local Buses/Trams

Buses within each province are cheap and plentiful. Tickets can be bought at designated offices, tobacconist's, bars and newspaper stands. They are purchased in booklets or singly, and have to be stamped by a machine on the bus at the start of a journey. Failure to do so risks a fine. All provincial bus services are routed past the railway station in every town.

In **Florence**, a range of tickets for the city's buses and new tram system is available from the ATAF office (Piazza Stazione; tel: 800-424 800): 60-minute, multiple (four singles), 3-hour, 24-hour, 3-day, 5-day, 7-day and monthly.

Rather confusingly for English-speakers, **Siena's** city/regional bus service is called TRA-IN.

Pisa province bus times are displayed on a board in Pisa's APT office on Piazza Garibaldi. Just outside Pisa Centrale Station, on the left, is a ticket window where bus tickets are sold.

Sightseeing Buses

Numerous sightseeing tours are offered in all the main cities. Florence: **City Sightseeing Italy** (Piazza Stazione 1; tel: 055-264 5363; www.city-sightseeing.it) offer a tour to Fiesole and a tour to Piazzale Michelangelo, both with multilingual commentary. Tickets are valid for 24 hours, allowing you to hop on and off at numerous points around the city. Details of other tours are available locally.

Taxis

Taxis are plentiful in all towns and tourist resorts. They wait in special ranks at railway stations and main parts of the city but can always be called by telephone. If you call a taxi by phone, the cost of the journey begins then. (In Florence, tel: 4390, 4242 or 4798 for Radio Taxi.) Meters display the fares: the fixed starting charge varies and extra charges are payable for night service, service on Sunday and public holidays, luggage and journeys outside the town area.

In Florence, there are taxi ranks in Via Pellicceria, Piazza di San Marco and Piazza Santa Trinità and outside Stazione di Santa Maria Novella.

Cycling and Mopeds

Mopeds and bicycles are the most efficient way to get around the narrow streets of Florence, Siena and Lucca. They can be hired in the main cities. Try to find one with good brakes and a stand. You may be asked to leave an identity card or passport as security. Below is a list of some outlets:

Florence: The brand new **Bike Sharing** initiative allows cyclists to borrow bikes from 50 distribution points 300 meters away from one another. First half hour is free. Or you can rent a bike from Florence by Bike, Via San Zanobi 120r; tel: 055-488992; www.florencebybike.it. Alinari, Via San Zanobi 38r; tel: 055-280500; www.alinarirental.com.

Siena: Perozzi, Via del Romitorio 5 (near the Lizza park), tel: 0577-223157; www.perozzi.it. Amici della Bicicletta di Siena, c/o Public Assistance, Viale Mazzini 95, tel: 0577-45159; www.adbsiena.it.

Lucca: Barbetti, Via Anfiteatro 23, tel: 0583-954444; Cicli Bizzarri, Piazza S. Maria, 32; tel: 0583-496031.

Driving

To ease traffic congestion, many city centres are closed to most vehicles. Since cities like Florence, Montepulciano and Pistoia have introduced partial or complete city-centre driving bans (at least for non-residents), it makes sense to leave the car in the car parks on the edge of the historic centre.

State highways in Tuscany include the No. 1 "Aurelia", which runs north–south, to the west of Pisa. National motorways *(auto-strade)*: the A11, the "Firenze–mare", and the A12, the "Sestri Levante–Livorno". Both of these are toll roads. The two *superstrade* (Florence–Siena and the Florence–Pisa–Livorno) are toll-free.

Car Hire

The major rental companies (Hertz, Avis, Europcar, etc.) have representation in most cities and resorts. The smaller local firms offer cheaper rates but cars can only be booked on the spot. Booking in advance, often as part of a fly-drive package, is usually cheaper than hiring on arrival.

Rates normally allow unlimited mileage and include breakdown service. Basic insurance is included but additional cover is available at fixed rates. Most firms require a deposit and often take and hold a credit card payment until the return of the car. You will usually be asked to return the car with a full tank of petrol; do so, as if the rental company has to fill the tank, they charge a premium for the petrol.

Licences and Insurance

Licences: Drivers must have a driving licence issued by a nation with a reciprocal agreement with Italy. The pink EU licence does not need an Italian translation. All other licences do need a translation, obtainable (free) from motoring organisations and Italian tourist offices. It is a legal requirement in Italy that documents pertaining to the driver and the car are kept on one's person.

Insurance: if you are bringing your own vehicle, check that your insurance covers you in Italy. A Green Card, obtainable from your insurance company, is not obligatory within the EU and does not give any extra cover, but it is an internationally recognised document, which may be helpful if you have an accident.

Rules of the Road

Italy drives on the right. Road signs are international, with a few local differences:

Road signs: ALT is a stop line on the road for road junctions; STOP is for a pedestrian crossing.

Precedence: at crossroads, motorists must give precedence to vehicles on their right, except on recently built roundabouts, when those already on the roundabout have priority. If a motorist approaching a crossroads finds a precedence sign (a triangle with the point downwards) or a Stop sign, he/she must give precedence to all vehicles coming from both the right and left.

Parking: Outside cities and towns, parking on the right-hand side of the road is allowed, except on motorways, at crossroads, on curves and near hilly ground not having full visibility. Illegally parked vehicles will be towed away, and incur a hefty fine. To find a car park in an Italian town online, look on www.parcheggi.it; for Florence go to www.firenzeparcheggi.it. There is a "parcheggio scambiatore" in Viale Europa (south Florence) – drivers can park their cars here and get a bus, hire a bike or take part in the car-sharing scheme to get into the centre. Special "tourist" rates (24 hours and nightly tickets) are available at the "Parterre" (Piazza della Libertà), "Oltrarno" (Porta Romana), and "Beccaria" garages.

Breakdowns and accidents: In case of a breakdown, dial 116. On motorways, telephones are 2 km (1 mile) apart, with special buttons to call for the police and medical assistance. Both have to be contacted if an accident involves an injury.

Motorways

Access signs to the motorways, unlike those of other European countries, are in green, not blue. Motorways tolls can be high. There is rarely a hard shoulder on Italian motorways, and often there are only two lanes. Accidents are frequent, so take extra care.

ACCOMMODATION

WHERE TO STAY

Choosing a Hotel

The quality and choice of accommodation in Tuscany is extremely varied. Visitors can choose between a city *palazzo*, grand country villa, or historic family-run hotel, a rented apartment or villa, a bucolic farm-stay holiday *(agriturismo)* or even, in the most popular cities, a private home stay. (This is not known as bed and breakfast since breakfast is not usually provided.)

Hotel rooms generally need to be booked well in advance in Florence and Siena. During local summer festivals, particularly the Sienese *Palio* and Arezzo's *Giostra*, rooms are very scarce. Attractive accommodation in the centre of Volterra and San Gimignano is popular, so early booking is advisable.

There is a huge variation in what you get for your money. A moderately priced hotel in Florence may be an adequate 3-star *pensione*, whereas the same money could buy you a luxurious 4-star room in a grand country house off the tourist track.

Generally speaking, "high season" in Tuscany is May to September. However, in towns, this does not necessarily include August. In Florence, for instance, many of the more expensive hotels reduce their prices during this month. It can sometimes pay to bargain.

Many hotels with restaurants insist on a half- or full-board arrangement, especially in the high season. This ploy is particularly prevalent on the islands (e.g. Elba), in seaside resorts (e.g. Forte dei Marmi), in spa resorts (e.g. Montecatini Terme and Chianciano Terme), and where accommodation is in short supply.

Hotel Listing

The hotel recommendations listed on pages 265–277 are grouped to correspond to the Places chapters. The towns and hotels within each section are listed alphabetically.

In the case of Florence and Siena, where so many hotels are available, the listing is subdivided into price categories. Other cities' hotels have price indicators at the end of their descriptions.

These refer to the cost of a standard double room for one night during high season, usually including breakfast; the ranges are as follows:

€ = below €100
€€ = €100–200
€€€ = €200–300
€€€€ = over €300

Private Home Stays

This is a fairly new development in Tuscany but it is a good way of meeting the locals while paying modest prices. In Florence and Siena, the homes are carefully graded from simple to luxurious.

In Florence, contact AGAP (Associazione Gestori Alloggi Privati) at Via de' Neri 9, 50122 Florence, tel: 055-505 1012. In Siena, request the Affittacamere (private lodgings) booklet of addresses from the tourist office (APT, Piazza Campo 56, Siena, tel: 0577-280551). The list includes private accommodation in the whole of Siena Province, including San Gimignano, Montalcino and the Sienese Chianti.

Agriturismo

Farm stays *(agriturismo)* are an excellent way of experiencing the Tuscan countryside while staying on a farm or a wine estate. Standards vary widely from simple, rustic accommodation at low prices to relatively luxurious surroundings, complete with swimming pool. Before booking, check the website if they have one or insist on a description or a photo, since many may be modern and fail to match up with the visitor's romantic image of Tuscany. Some farms, however, are genuine 16th-century wine and oil estates. There is usually the opportunity to buy local produce on site and meals are sometimes provided. For obvious reasons, you will normally need a car to make the most of a farm stay.

Reservations: during peak season, it is best to book in advance. Official accommodation tends to be booked for a minimum of one week, but individual arrangements for weekends and overnight stays are often possible, especially during mid- and low season.

Every local tourist authority produces farm-stay booklets. Or you can browse the following websites: www.agriturismo.com, www.agriturismo.net and www.agriturist.it (Italian only).

Rural Stays

These overlap with farm stays but can include country houses or even entire restored medieval villages (such as Sovicille, near Siena). In general, there is a working farm attached to the accommodation or at least the opportunity to sample or buy wine, oil and local products grown on the estate. As with farm stays, the accommodation offered can vary from simple rooms to self-contained apartments. The owners often use the profits from letting to reinvest in the restoration of the family estate or village. With rural stays, the emphasis is on country living in traditional buildings rather than in luxurious villa accommodation.

Many of the owners may speak basic English, French or German, but at least a smattering of Italian is appreciated. Always request detailed descriptions and directions.

Local tourist offices are a good source for recommendations *(see pages 292–3)*. Extensive listings, supported by images, can also be found on www.agriturismo.com and www.agriturismo.net. The following

are some typical examples of rural stays, but are just a handful among countless options:

La Ripolina, Località Pieve di Piana, 53022 Buonconvento, Siena Province; tel: 0577-282280; www.laripolina.it. Most of the holiday apartments are in converted farmhouses; one is in a fortified abbey with its 10th-century wall. Fresh farm produce available.

Agriturismo Podere San Lorenzo, Via Allori 80, 56048 Volterra, Pisa; tel: 0588-39080; www.agriturismo-volterra.it. Podere San Lorenzo is a working olive farm that has nine guest apartments in the farmhouse. Organic produce from its garden is used in the preparation of delicious meals served in an old Franciscan chapel. Cooking classes are available and there is a chemical-free swimming pool.

San Savino, Val di Chio, Località Santa Lucia 89/a, 52043 Castiglion Fiorentino, Arezzo Province; tel: 0575-651000; www.agriturismo-sansavino.it. This restored 11th-century monastery overlooks a lake, olive groves and woods and offers several apartments (plus pool and stables).

Villa Igea, Torre Alta, 55060 Ponte del Giglio, Lucca province; tel: 0583-353122; www.villa-igea.biz. This charming traditional Tuscan villa and cottage is set among woodland and olive groves overlooking a valley. Home produced extra virgin olive oils and tastings.

La Parrina, km 146 Via Aurelia, Località Parrina, 58010 Albinia, Grosseto province; tel: 0564-862636; www.parrina.it. This long-established agricultural estate is set among vineyards, olive groves and orchards. The rooms and dining rooms are decorated with an unfussy elegance that makes you feel right at home. To prove you're on a working farm you may be woken early by the sound of tractors. Rooms and apartments; swimming pool, chapel, farm shop, restaurant and wine tasting, and bicycles.

Villa and Apartment Rentals

One of the most popular ways of visiting Tuscany is to stay in a rented villa or apartment. They do not come cheap, but you have the benefit of independence, and the freedom to cook for yourself using delicious fresh Tuscan produce. Prices vary enormously, depending on the season and the luxuriousness of the accommodation. The following agencies deal with rentals:

At Home in Italy, tel: (212) 421-9165; www.athomeabroadinc.com. This US-based company sources quality hotels and apartments in Italy and around the world.

The Best in Italy, tel: (0039) 055-223064; www.thebestinitaly.com. A Florence-based lettings agency offering luxurious villas and *palazzi* with pools, tennis courts, stables, domestic staff and other such luxuries.

Caffelletto, tel: (0039) 02-331 1814/331 1820; www.caffelletto.it. This Milan-based company offers a selection of villas, castles, stylish country manors and city apartments, some on a bed and breakfast basis, others self-catering. They also produce an annual guide to Bed and Breakfasts in Italy (*Italian Bed and Breakfasts, a Caffelletto guide,* by Michele Ballarati, Margherita Piccolomini and Anne Marshall, pub. Rizzoli). The 2006 edition is also available in English.

Cottages to Castles, tel: (0044) 01622-775236; www.cottagestocastles.com. UK-based with agents in many countries.

Cross-Pollinate, www.cross-pollinate.com; e-mail: info@cross-pollinate.com. Website run by an enterprising American couple in Rome offering a network of private guesthouses, B&Bs and apartments for Florence, Rome and Venice.

Cuendet, tel: (0039) 0577-576330; www.cuendet.com. Monterrigioni-based company with a good selection of Tuscan villas and apartments.

Hello Italy, tel: (0044) 01483-419964; www.helloitaly.co.uk. A small company with a good selection of villas and houses, particularly recommended for the Lunigiana region.

Invitation to Tuscany, tel: (0044) 020-8742 8552; www.invitationtotuscany.com. UK-based but with agents in many countries.

Windows on Italy, tel: (0039) 055-268510; www.windowsonitaly.com. Agency run by the Ferragamo fashion house, with the focus on more exclusive properties.

Castles and Monasteries

Accommodation is available in a variety of castles and palaces. Standards will vary from very simple to luxurious. A list of places can be obtained from the ENIT (Italian State Tourist Offices abroad, *see page 292*) or enquire at the local tourist office.

Many convents, monasteries and other religious institutions offer simple accommodation for tourists and pilgrims. Monte Oliveto Maggiore is just one example *(see page 217)*. Each provincial tourist office should be able to supply you with a full list.

Youth Hostels

A list of youth hostels is available from ENIT (Italian National Tourist Offices, *see page 292*) and places can be booked through them or through local Tuscan tourist offices. Alternatively, contact the Associazione Italiana Alberghi per la Gioventù, Via Cavour 44, 00184 Rome, tel: 06-487 1152, www.ostellionline.org. The main city youth hostels in Tuscany are:

Arezzo

Villa Severi, Via F. Redi 13; tel: 0575-299047.

Cortona

San Marco, Via Maffei 57; tel: 0575-601765; www.cortonahostel.com

Florence

Archi Rossi, Via Faenza 94r; tel: 055-290804 www.hostelarchirossi.com

Villa Camerata, Viale Augusto Righi 2–4; tel: 055-601451

Santa Monaca Hostel, Via Santa Monaca 6; tel: 055-268338; www.ostello.it

Sette Santi, Viale dei Mille 11; tel: 055-504 8452; www.7santi.com

Youth Hostel Firenze 2000, Viale R. Sanzio 16; tel: 055-233 5558

Lucca

Ostello San Frediano, Via della Cavallerizza; tel: 0583-469957; www.ostellolucca.it. Near Piazza Anfiteatro in the centre of town.

Pisa

Centro Turistico Madonna dell'Acqua, Via Pietrasanta 15; tel: 050-890622. Madonna dell'Acqua is a few kilometres out of town, so take bus no. 3 from the station.

Siena

Ostello della Gioventù "Guidoriccio", Via Fiorentina 89; tel: 0577-52212. Guidoriccio is appealing, but it lies 2 km (1 mile) outside the city: catch bus no. 10 or 15 from Piazza Matteotti and ask to be let off at Lo Stellino.

Camping

For a free list of campsites contact the Federazione Italiana Campeggiatore, Via Vittorio Emanuele II, 50041 Calenzano, Firenze; tel: 055-882391; www.federcampeggio.it.

Florence

Michelangelo, Viale Michelangelo 80, tel: 055-681 1977. Open Apr–Oct, crowded in high season. No. 13 bus from station. Good facilities; 320 pitches.

Camping Panoramico, Via Peramonda 1, Fiesole; tel: 055-599069; www.florencecamping.com. Terraced site in Fiesole, outside Florence. Open all year.

Ostello Via Camerata, Viale Augusto Righi 2–4; tel: 055-601451. Next door to the hostel is a campsite, Villa Camerata, which is also open all year round. No. 17B bus from station.

Pisa

Campeggio Torre Pendente, Viale delle Cascine 86; tel: 050-561704; www.campingtorrependente.it. Open Apr–mid-Oct. No. 5 bus from the station.

Camping Internazionale, Via Litoranea 7, Marina di Pisa; tel: 050-35211. Facilities include a private beach, bar and pizzeria.

Siena

Campeggio "Siena Colleverde", Strada di Scacciapensieri 47; tel: 0577-332545; www.campingcolleverde.com. Open end Mar–end Oct. Two km (1 mile) from the city; no. 8 bus.

There are also companies which organise camping holidays in Tuscany. In the UK these include:

Eurocamp Travel, Hartford Manor, Greenbank Lane, Northwich, Cheshire CW8 1HW, tel: 0870-901 9410; www.eurocamp.co.uk.

Keycamp, Hartford Manor, Greenbank Lane, Northwich, Cheshire CW8 1HW, tel: 0870-700 0740; www.keycamp.co.uk.

Caravan and Camper Hire

In Tuscany, caravans and camper vans are available for hire from **Caravanmec**, Via Cupola 281, Peretola, Florence, tel: 055-315101; www.caravanmec.it, although there are other companies too.

FLORENCE

Deluxe (€€€€)

Continentale
Vicolo dell'Oro 6r
Tel: 055-27262
www.lungarnohotels.com
Chic hotel in the Ferragamo mini-chain. The shades of pink and pistachio in the lobby set the tone for the fabulous retro-style interiors. Ideal location near the Ponte Vecchio with rooms overlooking the Arno. The Sky Lounge offers spectacular views across the Florentine skyline.

Gallery Hotel Art
Vicolo dell'Oro 5
Tel: 055-27264000
www.lungarnohotels.com
Another classy boutique hotel in the Ferragamo stable. Sleek decor and central location. The lobby and trendy Fusion Bar host regular photography and contemporary art exhibitions.

Grand Hotel
Piazza Ognissanti 1
Tel: 055-27161
www.westin.com
Smaller than its sister hotel (the Excelsior, across the square) but almost as grand, housed in an elegant 19th-century palace overlooking the Arno. Recently refurbished.

Grand Hotel Villa Medici
Via Il Prato 42
Tel: 055-277171
www.villamedicihotel.com
Convenient hotel near the train station with a pool, gym, gardens and large airy rooms.

Helvetia & Bristol
Via dei Pescioni 2
Tel: 055-26651
www.royaldemeure.com
One of the best of the luxury small hotels in the city, with many illustrious names numbered among its guests. Supremely comfortable rooms and suites; excellent restaurant. Delightful winter garden.

Kraft
Via Solferino 2
Tel: 055-284273
www.krafthotel.it
Ideally placed for music lovers, a stone's throw from the opera house, and performers often stay here. Rooftop pool and excellent restaurant.

Regency
Piazza d'Azeglio 3
Tel: 055-245247
www.regency-hotel.com
Five-star luxury in an elegantly converted Florentine palazzo situated in a quiet, leafy square, a short walk from the main sights. Rooms are welcoming and comfortable. Cool, shady garden. Good restaurant.

Savoy
Piazza della Repubblica 7
Tel: 055-27351
www.hotelsavoy.it
Beautiful and elegant 5-star hotel in the heart of the city, close to the Duomo and main museums, galleries and fashion houses. Comfortable spacious rooms with contemporary and stylish Italian decor.

Torre di Bellosguardo
Via Roti Michelozzi 2
Tel: 055-229 8145
www.torrebellosguardo.com
Bellosguardo ("beautiful view"), the hill on which this Renaissance villa was built, is only 15 minutes' walk up from Porta Romana, but a world away. This quiet and roomy hotel has frescoed reception rooms and charmingly decorated bedrooms with antiques and quirky details. Secluded swimming pool and delightful grounds with lily pond.

Villa la Vedetta
Viale Michelangiolo 78
Tel: 055-681631
www.villalavedettahotel.com
Deluxe hotel in a panoramic position near Piazzale Michelangelo. Rooms are elegant and well-equipped; Michelin-starred restaurant.

Westin Excelsior
Piazza Ognissanti 3
Tel: 055-27151
www.westin.com
The grandest hotel in Florence – a lavishly furnished 19th-century building on the banks of the Arno. You can look forward to sumptuous bedrooms, many with grand marble bathrooms, and there is a panoramic rooftop restaurant.

Expensive (€€€)

Astoria
Via del Giglio 9
Tel: 055-239 8095
www.boscolohotels.com

Completely refurbished hotel near the station, with grand dimensions and elaborate decor.

Beacci Tornabuoni
Via de' Tornabuoni 3
Tel: 055-212645
www.hoteltornabuoni.it
Deluxe guest house, comfortable and very welcoming, although some rooms are on the small side. Flower-filled rooftop terrace for breakfast and drinks. Half-board terms compulsory. Particularly popular with Americans.

Botticelli
Via Taddea 8
Tel: 055-290905
www.hotelbotticelli.it
Close to the central San Lorenzo market, this three-star hotel is both comfortable and appealing, with all the mod cons you could want but also well

PRICE CATEGORIES

These refer to the cost of a standard double room during high season, usually including breakfast.

€ = under €100
€€ = €100–200
€€€ = €200–300
€€€€ = more than €300

preserved 16th-century features, including vaulted ceilings and frescoes. Friendly staff.

Grand Hotel Baglioni
Piazza dell' Unità Italiana 6
Tel: 055-23580
www.hotelbaglioni.it
Classic hotel retaining its air of discreet elegance while providing extremely comfortable rooms. Fine gardens and rooftop restaurant. Popular with the business community.

Hermitage
Vic. Marzio 1, Piazza del Pesce
Tel: 055-287216
www.hermitagehotel.com
Delightful hotel behind the Ponte Vecchio. Personal attention from staff. Lovely roof garden views.

J&J
Via di Mezzo 20
Tel: 055-26312
The setting of this small hotel – in a modest street near Santa Croce – belies the luxury within. Housed in a former convent near Sant'Ambrogio, all 19 rooms and suites are highly individual, romantic and chic. Lovely old cloister for summer breakfasts and evening drinks.

Loggiato dei Serviti
Piazza della SS Annunziata 3
Tel: 055-289592
www.loggiatodeiservitihotel.it
Atmospheric hotel facing the Innocenti hospital across a traffic-free piazza. Sangallo's 16th-century *palazzo* houses 38 rooms and suites and an annexe, all tastefully furnished. One of the city's best-loved and most refined hotels. No garden.

Marignolle Relais & Charme
Via di San Quiricino 16

Tel: 055-228 6910
www.marignolle.com
A few minutes to the south of Florence, this charming hotel with pool is comfortable and handy for exploring the surrounding area.

Monna Lisa
Borgo Pinti 27
Tel: 055-247 9751
www.monnalisa.it
This Renaissance *palazzo*, furnished with antiques, drawings and sculpture, is a popular choice. There is a delightful garden and private parking.

Morandi alla Crocetta
Via Laura 50
Tel: 055-234 4747
www.hotelmorandi.it
Tiny *pensione* tucked away in a backstreet near the university, housed in a former convent. Antiques, parquet flooring and colourful rugs; 10 bedrooms, two with private terraces. Book well in advance.

Porta Faenza
Via Faenza 77
Tel: 055-214287
www.hotelportafaenza.it
Comfortable, family-run hotel, with all mod cons, near the central market. Private garage (rare in this part of town).

Moderate (€€)

Alessandra
Borgo SS Apostoli 17
Tel: 055-283438
www.hotelalessandra.com
An old-fashioned, simple *pensione* conveniently situated near the Ponte Vecchio. Many of the 25 spacious rooms are furnished with antiques.

Annalena
Via Romana 34
Tel: 055-222402

www.hotelannalena.it
A discreet *pensione* in a 15th-century *palazzo*, originally built as a refuge for widows of the Florentine nobility. Opposite the rear entrance to the Boboli Gardens. Some rooms have balconies looking onto the horticultural centre.

Aprile
Via della Scala 6
Tel: 055-216237
www.hotelaprile.it
Much more appealing than most hotels near the station, this is an ex-Medici palace complete with frescoes, a pleasant breakfast room and garden. Rooms range from simple to reasonably grand.

Casci
Via Cavour 13
Tel: 055-211686
www.hotelcasci.com
Frescoed *quattrocento palazzo*, family-run and enjoying a welcoming atmosphere. Five minutes' walk north of the Duomo.

Classic Hotel
Viale Machiavelli 25
Tel: 055-229351
www.classichotel.it
Elegant, pinkwashed villa with lovely rooms, a conservatory and pretty gardens, situated on a tree-lined avenue just above the Porta Romana. Excellent value.

Davanzati
Via Porta Rossa 5
Tel: 055-286666
www.hoteldavanzati.it
Centrally located, this tastefully refurbished hotel has 21 quiet rooms all with a laptop and internet connection. Clean rooms and helpful service. A great deal.

Fiorino
Via Osteria del Guanto 6
Tel: 055-210579
www.hotelfiorino.it
Located in the centre of the city, this unpretentious hotel has a pleasant family atmosphere.

Giada
Canto de'Nelli 2
Tel: 055-215317
www.hotelgiada.it
Friendly *pensione* near San Lorenzo market. Some rooms overlook the Medici Chapels.

Liana
Via Alfieri 18
Tel: 055-245303
www.hotelliana.it
Lovely hotel some way north of centre in the former British Embassy, but not far from Santa Croce. Rooms vary from simple to elegant with frescoed ceilings and original floors. Good breakfast and pretty garden. Private car park.

Mario's
Via Faenza 89
Tel: 055-216801
www.hotelmarios.com
One of the most attractive of the many *pensioni* in Via Faenza, behind the central market. Decorated in rustic Tuscan style, with comfortable bedrooms (quieter at the rear). Friendly.

Orto de'Medici
Via San Gallo 30
Tel: 055-483427
www.ortodeimedici.it

PRICE CATEGORIES

These refer to the cost of a standard double room during high season, usually including breakfast.
€ = under €100
€€ = €100–200
€€€ = €200–300
€€€€ = more than €300

Attractive little neo-classical *palazzo* near Piazza San Marco, with grand public rooms. Simpler bedrooms, most with private baths; lovely breakfast room leading onto a terrace.

Palazzo Benci
Piazza Madonna degli Aldobrandini 3
Tel: 055-213848
www.palazzobenci.com
Patrician *palazzo*, traditionally the seat of the Benci family, recently restored but retaining original features.

Pensione Bretagna
Lungarno Corsini 6
Tel: 055-289618
www.bretagna.it
Suitably, this is a favourite with British business travellers. Drops a price bracket in low season.

Residenze Johlea and Antica Johlea
Via San Gallo 80/76
Tel: 055-463 3292
www.johanna.it
These two residences are set in a nice area

around San Marco. They retain an authentic Tuscan feel, but are equipped with more modern conveniences than their cheaper sister residence (Johanna 1) near San Lorenzo *(see below)*.

Silla
Via de'Renai 5
Tel: 055-234 2888
www.hotelsilla.it
An elegant arched courtyard leads to this first-floor hotel in a quiet, relatively leafy area south of and overlooking the Arno.

Torre Guelfa
Borgo SS Apostoli 8
Tel: 055-239 6338
www.hoteltorreguelfa.com
Elegant, recently refurbished hotel with a grand "salon", pastel-shaded bedrooms, a sunny breakfast room and the tallest privately owned tower in the city.

Villa Azalee
Viale Fratelli Rosselli 44
Tel: 055-214242
www.villa-azalee.it

Pleasant, 19th-century villa near the station, with the feel of a private house, set in a garden full of azaleas and camelias. Private garage; bicycles for hire.

Villa Belvedere
Via Benedetto Castelli 3
Tel: 055-222501
www.villabelvederefirenze.it
Exceptionally friendly and modern hotel; south of the city. Sunny rooms, a pretty garden and lovely views across Florence. Amenities include pool and tennis court.

Inexpensive (€)

Relais Cavalcanti
Via Pellicceria 2
Tel: 055-210962
www.relaiscavalcanti.com
Simple guesthouse near the Palazzo Davanzati. Very few hotel amenities – basically just a bed, but the rooms are clean, nicely decorated and cheap.

Staff are helpful, although not always present. In high season it enters the next price bracket.

Relais del Duomo B&B
Piazza dell'Olio 2
Tel: 055-210147
www.relaisdelduomo.com
Four roomed B&B just a stone's throw from the Duomo. Rooms are clean and all have private bath and TV. Can be noisy at times but it's a good deal for Florence, especially during low season when prices drop.

Residenza Johanna 1
Via Bonifacio Lupi 14
Tel: 055-481896
www.johanna.it
The cheapest of a group of four great-value-for-money residences across the city. Rooms are clean and comfortable even though there are few mod cons and breakfasts are do-it-yourself. In an unmarked building in a quiet street near Piazza Libertà.

AROUND FLORENCE

Artimino

Paggeria Medicea
Viale Papa Giovanni XXIII 1
Tel: 055-875141
www.artimino.com
Grand hotel in the former stables of a restored Medici villa, nestling between olive groves and vineyards near Carmignano, 24 km (15 miles) west of Florence. Very good restaurant and a farm shop selling local produce and wine. There are also a number of apartments available for weekly rental.
€€€

Candeli

Villa La Massa
Via La Massa 24
Tel: 055-62611
www.villalamassa.com
Some 7 km (4 miles) north of Florence, this cluster of beautifully converted 17th-century villas radiates elegance. Riverside restaurant; swimming and tennis. Free shuttle service for guests from the hotel to the Ponte Vecchio.
€€€€

Fiesole

Pensione Bencistà
Via Benedetto da Maiano 4

Tel: 055-59163
www.bencista.com
Delightful 14th-century villa, decorated with antiques and rustic furnishings. Reliable restaurant; half-board is compulsory. Flower-decked terrace with panoramic views over Florence. €€

Villa Fiesole
Via Beato Angelico 35
Tel: 055-597252
www.villafiesole.it
Comfortable but chic hotel with frescoes, panoramic views and pool. Full wheelchair access. €€

Villa San Michele
Via Doccia 4
Tel: 055-567 8200
www.villasanmichele.com
One of the finest and most expensive hotels in Tuscany. Supposedly designed by Michelangelo, this former

TRANSPORT

ACCOMMODATION

ACTIVITIES

A – Z

LANGUAGE

Franciscan monastery enjoys harmonious lines and heavenly views of the city, particularly from the loggia and restaurant. Spacious grounds; pool; piano bar. The plush suites have jacuzzis. **€€€€**

Galluzzo

La Fattoressa
Via Volterrana 58
Tel: 055-204 8418
www.lafattoressa.it
Old farmhouse converted into simple but comfortable bed and breakfast accommodation with double and triple rooms. Dinner prepared on request. Very friendly family-run place. Just southwest of Florence and conveniently situated for the *autostrada*. **€€**

Relais Certosa
Via Colle Romole 2
Tel: 055-204 7171
www.florencehotelcertosa.it
Former hunting lodge (once attached to the 14th-century Carthusian monastery) near Florence, now a welcoming residence, with spacious grounds and views of the medieval charterhouse. Tennis courts and swimming pool. **€€€**

Impruneta

Villa Cesi
Via delle Terre Bianche
Tel: 055-231101
www.villacesi.it
A stone's throw from Impruneta's main square, the 28 rooms of this modern hotel profit from a restaurant and swimming pool. There are prettier towns to spend a night in but this is a decent place to stay if you're in the area and needing a bed. **€€**

Molino del Piano

Hotel Il Trebbiolo
Via del Trebbiolo 8
Località Olmo
Tel: 055-830 0583
www.iltrebbiolo.it
Delightful 3-star hotel 14 km (9 miles) from Florence. The villa is set amid olive groves, with cosy little rooms and an annexe with cooking facilities. The hotel restaurant offers solid Tuscan cuisine. **€€**

Poggio a Caiano

Hotel Hermitage
Via Ginepraia 112
Tel: 055-877 7085

www.hotelhermitageprato.it
Nice, if business-like hotel set on a hill, close to the Medici Villa; handy for exploring the surrounding area. Members receive discount at the Le Pavoniere golf course near Prato. Restaurant; swimming pool in summer. Good value. **€–€€**

Prato

Villa Rucellai
Via di Canneto 16
Tel: 0574-460392
www.villarucellai.it
This mellow, medieval villa northeast of the town is an oasis in Prato's industrial landscape. An informal but elegant bed and breakfast establishment with a family house atmosphere. Swimming pool, chapel and garden. Very good value for money. **€**

Sesto Fiorentino

Villa Villoresi
Via Campi 2, Colonnata di Sesto Fiorentino
Tel: 055-443212
www.villavilloresi.it
Gracious villa, a world away from the ugly industrial suburb of Sesto which surrounds

it. Complete with chandeliers and frescoes, plus the longest loggia in Tuscany. Restaurant and pool. **€€**

Trespiano

Villa Le Rondini
Via Bolognese Vecchia 224
Tel: 055-400081
www.villalerondini.it
Secluded villa in a wonderful setting, overlooking the Arno valley just 4 km (2 miles) from Florence. Lovely views over the city from the swimming pool, set in an olive grove. Restaurant. Bus link to the city. **€€€**

Vicchio

Villa Campestri
Via di Campestri 19
Tel: 055-849 0107
www.villacampestri.it
Imposing Renaissance villa in a wonderful, rural setting in the Mugello, 35 km (25 miles) north of Florence. Impressive public rooms, excellent food and a relaxed atmosphere. Bedrooms in the main villa are quite grand; those in the annexe less so. Pool, horse riding. **€€–€€€**

PISTOIA PROVINCE

Abetone

Bellavista
Via Brennero 383
Tel: 0573-60028
www.bellavista-abetone.it
Typical wood and stone mountain building with panoramic views, close to the centre of Abetone and ski lifts. Comfortable and spacious rooms. Seasonal opening. **€€**

Regina
Via Uccelliera 5
Tel: 0573-60257
Pleasant 19th-century villa within an attractive setting. 3-star. **€–€€**

Monsummano Terme

Grotta Giusti Spa Hotel
Via Grotta Giusti 1411
Tel: 0572-90771
www.grottagiustispa.com

Historic spa hotel centred on a handsome villa set in sprawling parkland with its own thermal spring and natural caves. The resort's steamy grottoes were dubbed "the eighth wonder of the world" by the operatic Giuseppe Verdi. Excellent spa facilities and Ayurvedic massage. Next to the

Montecatini golf course. **€€€€**

La Speranza
Via Grotta Giusti 162
Tel: 0572-51313
Basic *pensione* with well-maintained garden. Good option if you're passing through and all you want is a bed for the night. €

Montecatini Alto
Casa Albertina e Mario
Via Fratelli Guermani, 12
Tel: 0572-900238
www.casaalbertina.it
Charming 13th-century villa in the medieval walled village. The individually designed rooms are cosy, and some have balconies. Excellent breakfast served in the little garden surrounded by orange and lemon trees with great views over Montecatini Terme. €€

Montecatini Terme
Florio
Via Montebello 41
Tel: 0572-78343
Montecatini Terme is overrun with hotels. This one with its own garden is a good moderately priced option. €
Grand Hotel Plaza e Locanda Maggiore
Piazza del Popolo 7
Tel: 0572-75831
www.hotelplaza.it
Flashy 4-star hotel with good facilities including a pool. Special deals for families. €€
Torretta
Viale Bustichini 63
Tel: 0572-70305
www.hoteltorretta.it
A modern, family-run hotel with a pool; special diets catered for. €

Pescia
Azienda Agricola Marzalla
Via Collecchio 1
Tel: 0572-490751
Unpretentious, family-run *agriturismo* in the hills. With a pool, and a pleasant *trattoria* nearby. Weekly basis only in high season. €

Pistoia
Il Convento
Via San Quirico 33
Tel: 0573-452651/2
www.ilconventohotel.com
Tranquil hotel, formerly a Franciscan monastery. The dining room was once the monks' refectory and the bedrooms their cells; some have a terrace. Breakfast is served in the cloister in fine weather. Includes a lovely garden

surrounded by woodland, a swimming pool, a good restaurant and a chapel. Five km (3 miles) from town. €€
Hotel Patria
Via Crispi 8
Tel: 0573-25187
www.patriahotel.com
Welcoming small hotel in the city's historic centre. Parking permits available. €
Villa Vannini
Villa di Pitecchio
Tel: 0573-42031
www.villavannini.it
Delightful villa some 6 km (4 miles) north of Pistoia, with the atmosphere of a private house. Elegant and comfortable bedrooms; fine food; wonderful walks in the woods. Good value. €–€€

LUCCA AND THE VERSILIA

Lucca
Alla Corte degli Angeli
Via Degli Angeli 23
Tel: 0583-469204
www.allacortedegliangeli.com
A sister hotel to the San Martino *(see below)*, this delightful tiny hotel is also within the city walls, close to the Piazza dell'Anfiteatro. Each of the six rooms has a flower theme and provides splendid views over the city roofs. €€
Antico Casale Toscano
Località Piaggia 10
Tel: 340-360 0646
www.anticocasaletoscano.com
This charming typical Tuscan farmhouse is set in the hills above Lucca among olive groves in a working farm. Rooms are available on a nightly basis from Nov–Mar and on a

weekly basis Apr–Oct. Teresa organises special free cookery evenings including tastings of her own extra virgin olive oil during the summer. €
Diana
Via del Molinetto 11
Tel: 0583-492202
www.albergodiana.com
Centrally located hotel off Piazza San Martino; a pleasant budget option. €
San Martino
Via della Dogana 9
Tel: 0583-469181
www.albergosanmartino.it
Warm, welcoming little hotel in a quiet location, within the city walls, a stone's throw from the Duomo. Nearby private carparking organised by the hotel. Excellent value. €–€€

Hotel Carignano
Via per Sant'Alessio,
3680 Carignano
(5 km/3 miles outside Lucca)
Tel: 0583-329618
www.hotelcarignano.it
This family-run hotel is set in a quiet, hilly location outside Lucca, within easy reach of the sea and mountains. Rooms are large and bright. €–€€
Hotel Ilaria e Residenza dell'Alba
Via del Fosso 26
Tel: 0583-47615
www.hotelilaria.com
Ideally located in the historic centre and set in splendid grounds, this very stylish hotel is dedicated to comfort and good service. The annexe, Residenza dell'Alba, is located in the former medieval

church of the Annunziata. Large bedrooms offer every modern amenity coupled with a historic interior. €€–€€€

TRANSPORT
ACCOMMODATION
ACTIVITIES
A – Z
LANGUAGE

La Luna
Via Fillungo Corte
Compagni 12
Tel: 0583-493634
www.hotellaluna.com
Family-run hotel in the historic centre just steps away from the Piazza dell'Anfiteatro. **€€**

La Romea (B&B)
Vicolo delle Ventaglie 2
(corner of Via S. Andrea)
Tel: 0583-464175
www.laromea.com
Small, very pleasing establishment on the first floor of a medieval *palazzo* in the historic centre. The two young hosts Giulio and Gaia are most helpful. Five rooms all with private bathrooms and air-conditioning. Generous breakfast. **€€**

Piccolo Hotel Puccini
Via di Poggio 9
Tel: 0583-55421
www.hotelpuccini.com
A small and very popular three-star hotel just around the corner from Puccini's birthplace, crammed with mementos of the maestro. Excellent value. **€**

Stipino
Via Romana 95
Tel: 0583-495077
www.hotelstipino.com
Simply decorated, 2-star hotel graced with a personal touch. **€**

Villa Rinascimento
Loc. Santa Maria del Giudice,
Via del Cimitero 532b
Tel: 0583-378292
www.villarinascimento.it
Rustic villa with a lovely garden and

swimming pool, on a hillside 9 km (5 miles) west of Lucca. **€€**

Torre del Lago

Butterfly
Belvedere Puccini 24/26
Tel: 0584-341024
There aren't many places to stay in Torre del Lago itself, but this restaurant on the central piazza has rooms overlooking the Lake and is very close to the theatre. **€**

Viareggio

London
Viale Manin 16
Tel: 0584-49841
Very pleasant family-run hotel in a former Liberty-style *palazzo*. Good sized public rooms and 33 very

comfortable bedrooms. **€€**

Locanda le Monache
Piazza XXIX Maggio 36
Camaiore (10 km/6 miles from Viareggio)
Tel: 0584-989258
www.lemonache.com
A traditional Tuscan restaurant with 15 rooms housed in a former monastery. The rooms are of a good size, albeit simply furnished. **€**

Plaza e de Russie
Piazza d'Azeglio 1
Tel: 0584-44449
www.plazaederussie.com
Liberty-style hotel, one of the most luxurious in this seaside resort. Beautiful rooms and lovely view from the elegant roof restaurant. **€€–€€€**

GARFAGNANA AND LUNIGIANA

Bagni di Lucca

Azienda Agriturismo La Torre
La Torre, Fornoli
Tel: 0583-805297
www.latorreagriturismo.com
Set among olive and chestnut groves, this delightful farmhouse can accommodate up to 15 people in six apartments. Simply furnished in traditional Tuscan style with lovely views over the rolling countryside. Good home cooking and swimming pool. **€–€€**

Barga

Alpino
Via G. Pascoli 1
Tel: 0583-723336
This 3-star hotel in the lower, busier half of town has been offering a warm welcome for over 100 years. The

seven rooms and two suites have all been recently refurbished. Restaurant. **€€**

Castelnuovo di Garfagnana

La Lanterna
(1km/half a mile east at Monache-Piano Pieve)
Tel: 0583-639364
www.hotellalanterna.com
Set in a peaceful, green location, with 22 plain but comfortable rooms and a large restaurant. A good base for exploring the Garfagnana. **€**

Fivizzano

L'Albergo Ristorante Pieve San Paolo
Località Pieve San Paolo
Tel: 0585-949800
A small, family-run *albergo* in the heart of magnificent mountain

scenery. Very welcoming. **€–€€**

Hotel Terme
Via Noce Verde (Equi Terme)
Tel: 0585-97830
A 3-star hotel set in the beautiful Parco Naturale delle Alpi Apuane. The scenery makes up for the somewhat dated decor. There are 60 bedrooms and two swimming pools with spa treatments. **€–€€**

Il Giardinetto
Via Roma 151
Tel: 0585-92060
Rather eccentric hotel/restaurant, full of character and characters. Traditional Tuscan food. **€**

Licciana Nardi

Del Pino
Via Bastia 37, Lunigiana
Tel: 0187-475041

Quiet, comfortable modern *pensione* in a mountain village, surrounded by pine trees. **€**

Pontremoli

Hotel Napoleon
Piazza Italia, 2bis
Tel: 0187-830544
www.hotelnapoleon.net
Set in the heart of Pontremoli, this family-run hotel has lovely views of the Apennines. Elegant restaurant. **€**

PISA AND ENVIRONS

Cascina Sant'Anna

Hotel Villa Guelfi
Via Tosco Romagnola 1301
Località Santa Anna Cascina
Tel: 050-778032
www.pisaonline.it/hotelvillaguelfi
Villa built in typical
19th-century Pisan
style. Just 8 km (5
miles) outside Pisa
and convenient for the
Pisa–Florence motor-
way. €€

Massa Pisana

Villa La Principessa
Via Nuova per Pisa, 1616
Tel: 0583-370037
Exclusive 4-star man-
sion open Apr–Oct. Old-
fashioned elegance;
modern comforts.
Swimming pool, lovely
garden. €€€

Palaia

Borgo di Colleoli
Palaia
Tel: 0587-622 524
www.ilpalazzocolleoli.com
Combination of hotel
and self-catering accom-
modation. Rooms are
spacious and the "ham-
let" enjoys a gorgeous
setting in well mani-
cured grounds sur-
rounded by rolling hills.
Pisa is a short drive
away; the coast about
an hour and a half.
Good for families. Two
swimming pools.
€€–€€€

Pisa

Albergo Helvetia
Via Don Gaetano Boschi 31
Tel: 050-553084
This small budget hotel
is situated in a particu-
larly quiet area and yet
it's right on the Piazza
dei Miracoli's doorstep.
Only half of the 29

rooms, have private
bathrooms. Pleasant
courtyard garden. Plain
but cheap. €

Ariston
Via Cardinale Maffi 42
Tel: 050-561834
www.hotelariston.pisa.it
The best thing about
this hotel is its position,
literally in the shadow of
the Leaning Tower. The
rooms are of an accept-
able standard, but the
service can be
unfriendly. €€

Grand Hotel Duomo
Via Santa Maria 94
Tel: 050-561894
www.grandhotelduomo.it
Comfortable, business-
like hotel, close to the
Piazza dei Miracoli.
Restaurant; private
garage. €€€

Hotel Locanda La Lanterna
Via S .Maria 113
Tel: 050-830305
www.locandalalanterna.com
Pleasant, no-frills bed
and breakfast hotel,
close to the Leaning
Tower. Very good value
for money. €

Hotel Novecento
Via Roma 37
Tel: 050-500323
www.hotelnovecento.pisa.it
Elegant hotel in the his-
toric heart of Pisa, a
ten-minute walk from
the Leaning Tower.
Rooms are stylish and
the little garden is a
peaceful retreat.

Hotel Relais dell'Orologio
Via della Faggiola 12/14
Tel: 050-830361
www.hotelrelaisorologio.com
Conveniently located
between the Campo dei
Miracoli and Piazza dei
Cavalieri, this gracious
14th-century manor

house has been trans-
formed into a stylish
and elegant boutique
hotel with just 21 indi-
vidually decorated
rooms. Romantic court-
yard garden. A luxurious
treat. €€€€

Royal Victoria
Lungarno Pacinotti 12
Tel: 050-940111
www.royalvictoriahotel.it
The most characterful
hotel in the city opened
in 1842 and played
host to Dickens and
other Grand Tourists. It
has been in the same
family for generations.
The current custodians
have retained its
authentic old-fashioned
atmosphere and charm.
Rooms overlooking the
Arno are in great
demand, though they
can be noisy. Garage.
Bikes for hire. €€

Touring
Via Puccini 24
Tel: 050-46374
www.benotel.com/italy/pisa/touring
Well run, if dowdy hotel
across the Arno from
the main sights, but
near the station. €€

Villa Kinzica
Piazza Arcivescovado 2
Tel: 050-560419
www.hotelvillakinzica.it
Remarkably positioned
hotel, two minutes' walk
from the Leaning Tower.
Many original features
remain, though some
rooms need attention
and service can be
brusque. Own restaur-
ant/pizzeria. €–€€

San Giuliano Terme

Villa Corliano
Strada Statale Abetone 50
Tel: 050-818193
www.corliano.it

Faded villa of grand
dimensions, half way
between Pisa and Lucca.
Informal, with plenty of
atmosphere. A find.
Restaurant attached. €€

Tirrenia

Atlantico Continental Hotel
Largo Belvedere 26
Tel: 050-37031
Four-star luxury hotel
with pool, private beach
and tennis court. Good
amenities but lacks a
bit of atmosphere. €€€

Bristol
Via delle Felci 38
Tel: 050-37161
www.bristol.it
Three-star, unpreten-
tious and comfortable
hotel with pool and ten-
nis court. €€

Grand Hotel Golf
Via dell'Edera 29
Tel: 050-957018
www.grandhotelgolf.it
Rather impersonal 4-
star hotel but it has its
own golf course and is
right by the sea. €€

PRICE CATEGORIES

The price categories
refer to the cost of a
double room during
high season, usually
including breakfast.
€ = under €100
€€ = €100–200
€€€ = €200–300
€€€€ = more than €300

TRANSPORT

ACCOMMODATION

ACTIVITIES

A – Z

LANGUAGE

LIVORNO AND THE MAREMMA PISANA

Casale Marittimo
Il Poggio
Località Il Poggio
Tel: 0586-652308
www.ilpoggio.org
Agriturismo on the road from Bibbona offering small apartments. Ideal base for exploring the area, especially for families with children. **€**

Livorno
Gran Duca
Piazza Micheli 16

Tel: 0586-891024
www.granduca.it
Attractive hotel (for Livorno) on the seafront with views over the old harbour. A good place to stay if you are catching an early ferry. Fitness centre with pool, spa and sauna. **€€**

Montenero
La Vedetta
Via della Lecceta 5
Tel: 0586-579957

www.hotellavedetta.it
Modern hotel in Livorno hills. Rooms are basic but views are expansive. Near the sanctuary of Madonna di Montenero. **€**

Sassetta
Campo di Carlo
Via Campagna Nord 62
Tel: 0565-794257
www.campodicarlo.it
Child-friendly guesthouse in the heart of the

country, not far from Sassetta and within easy reach of the sea. Six lovely rooms. **€**

ELBA

Capo Sant' Andrea
Hotel Ilio
Via Sant'Andrea 5
Tel: 0565-908018
www.ilio.it
This welcoming 19-room hotel is a hidden gem among the many small establishments stacked up on the hillside around Capo Sant' Andrea. As with many of the Elban hotels, half-board is obligatory, but the restaurant is excellent and pre-dinner cocktails on the terrace add an extra touch. Mountain bikes for rent.**€–€€**

Marciana
Bel Tramonto
Località Patresis
Tel: 0565-908027
www.valverdehotel.it
Modern hotel with lovely swimming pool and grounds. Most rooms have balconies overlooking the sea. **€**

Portoferraio
La Hermitage
Località Biodola
Tel: 0565-936911
www.hotelhermitage.it
Large and lively resort hotel, founded in the 1950s. **€€€**
Hotel Mare
Località Magazzini

Tel: 0565-933069
www.elba-on-line.com
This peaceful hotel, located just across the bay from Portoferraio, is part of a tiny village with its own marina. Excellent restaurant and friendly hotel staff. Rooms are simple and clean. **€**
Hotel Scoglio Bianco
Località Viticcio
Tel: 0565-939036
www.scogliobianco.it
Low-key whitewashed hotel in one of Elba's quieter corners. Great sunset views from the terraces. Half-board obligatory, but still good value. **€**

Villa Ottone
Località Ottone
Tel: 0565-933042
www.villaottone.com
Refined hotel in a gleaming white 19th-century villa just east of Portoferraio. Beautifully tended grounds and a poolside restaurant. **€€**

VOLTERRA AND ENVIRONS

Massa Marittima
Albergo il Sole
Corso della Libertà 43
Tel: 0566-901959
Simple hotel in an old *palazzo* in the medieval heart of the town. **€**
Villa Il Tesoro
Località Volpaia
Tel: 0566-92971

www.villailtesoro.com
Romantic hamlet 7km (4 miles) outside Massa Marittima, surrounded by vineyards and olive groves, offering glorious views. Accommodation in spacious suites, some with terraces. **€€€**

Volterra
Nazionale
Via dei Marchesi 11
Tel: 0588-86284
www.albergonazionalevolterra.it
Ancient palazzo, a hotel since 1890, just round the corner from the Piazza dei Priori. Rooms are non-descript but

comfortable. Balconies have fabulous views. €

San Lino
Via San Lino 26
Tel: 0588-85250
www.hotelsanlino.com
Monastic building whose original austerity has been softened by a successful conversion into a 4-star hotel. Swimming pool and garage. €

Villa Nencini
Borgo Santo Stefano 55
Tel: 0588-86386
www.villanencini.it
Pleasant stone villa just outside the town walls, with a garden and pool, as well as a restaurant and an *enoteca*. €€

Villa Palagione
Località Palagione
Tel: 0588-39014
www.villa-palagione.com

Aristocratic villa, 7 km (4 miles) from Volterra, converted into a hotel and cultural centre specialising in group activities (cooking, wine tasting, painting, horse riding, walking, language courses, etc), but individuals are welcome. Beautiful frescoed rooms. Bicycles for hire. €€

Villa Riotti
S.P. Monte Volterrano
Tel: 0588-88053
www.hotelvillariotti.it
This 15th-century villa sits on a hillside, 2 km (1 mile) from the centre of Volterra. The 15 rooms are simply furnished; garden and swimming pool with views over the Cecina valley. €

SAN GIMIGNANO AND CHIANTI COUNTRY

Castellina in Chianti

Belvedere di San Leonino
Località San Leonino
Tel: 0577-740887
www.hotelsanleonino.com
Imposing 15th-century country house surrounded by olive trees and vineyards. Swimming pool. €€

Colle Etrusco Salivolpi
Via Fiorentina 89
Tel: 0577-740484
www.hotelsalivolpi.com
Well-restored farmhouse with an appealing garden and uncontrived rustic decor – original beams, whitewashed walls, terracotta tiles and decorative ironwork. €

Collelungo
Località Castellina in Chianti
Tel: 0577-740489
www.collelungo.com
Lovingly restored stone farmhouse divided into comfortable apartments (named after the Siena *contrade*) for 2–4 people. Barbecue and pool. Minimum stay: three nights. €€

Le Piazze
Località Le Piazze
Tel: 0577-743190
www.locandalepiazze.it
Converted 17th-century farmhouse with ter-

races and gardens. Rustic furnishings and luxurious bathrooms. Meals on request. €€

Tenuta di Ricavo
Località Ricavo 4
Tel: 0577-740221
www.ricavo.com
A highly rated hotel occupying a series of rustic houses in a medieval hamlet, 5 km (3 miles) from Castellina. Pool; good quality restaurant. Open Apr–Oct. €€

Villa Casalecchi
Località Casalecchi
Tel: 0577-740240
www.villacasalecchi.it
Three-star hotel, set in a 19th-century villa, surrounded by oak trees. Pool, tennis courts, restaurant. Open Mar–Oct. €€

Certaldo Alto

Osteria del Vicario
Via Rivellino 3
Tel: 0571-668228
www.osteriadelvicario.it
Well-known restaurant with five simple rooms in a pretty hilltop town. €

Colle di Val d'Elsa

Villa Belvedere
Via Senese
Tel: 0577-920966
www.villabelvedere.com

Delightful 18th-century villa surrounded by a large park. Excellent restaurant. €€

Hotel Arnolfo
Via F. Campana 8
Tel: 0577-922020
www.hotelarnolfo.it
Occupies a 15th-century *palazzo* in a commanding position at the top of town, though rooms are basic. €

Gaiole in Chianti

Castello di Spaltenna
Via Spaltenna 13
Tel: 0577-749483
www.spaltenna.it
Formidable fortified monastery, now a luxurious hotel with an excellent restaurant, indoor and outdoor pools, gym, Turkish bath, sauna and tennis court. Supremely comfortable, individualistic rooms. €€€

L'Ultimo Mulino
Loc. La Ripresa di Vistarenni
Tel: 0577-738520
www.ultimomulino.it
Atmospheric hotel in a converted mill. An ideal setting for exploring Chianti; pool. €€

Greve In Chianti

Albergo del Chianti
Piazza Matteotti 86
Tel: 055-853763

www.albergodelchianti.it
Small, pleasant hotel with pool, garden and a friendly atmosphere. €€

Monteriggioni

Hotel Monteriggioni
Via 1 Maggio 4
Tel: 0577-305009
www.hotelmonteriggioni.net
A couple of village houses have been converted into an elegant hotel with a garden and pool, in a pretty walled town 10 km (6 miles) north of Siena. €€€

PRICE CATEGORIES

The price categories refer to the cost of a double room during high season, usually including breakfast.
€ = under €100
€€ = €100–200
€€€ = €200–300
€€€€ = more than €300

Panzano in Chianti

I Fagiolari
Case Sparse
Tel: 055-852351
Mobile: 335-612 4988
www.fagiolari.it
This small restored Tuscan farmhouse is surrounded by olive trees and forest. The friendly owner, Giulietta, gives cooking classes and can prepare meals for guests. All four rooms have private bath and cosy decor. There's also a separate cottage for rent. Swimming pool. **€€**

Villa Le Barone
Via San Leolino 19
Tel: 055-852621
www.villalebarone.com
Aristocratic villa in the Chianti hills filled with family antiques, giving the feel of a private house. Some rooms have their own terrace. Facilities include swimming pool, tennis court and a good restaurant. Half-board rates. **€€–€€€**

Villa San Giovese
Piazza Bucciarelli 5
Tel: 055-852461
www.villasangiovese.it
Well restored villa in the Florentine Chianti, with rooms in a converted traditional farmhouse. Noted restaurant and wines. **€€**

Radda in Chianti

Relais Fattoria Vignale
Via Pianigiani 9
Tel: 0577-738012
www.vignale.it
Discreetly elegant old manor house with a relaxed atmosphere. Excellent wine produced on site; bar and restaurant in the old wine cellars; pool. **€€€**

San Casciano Val di Pesa

Il Borghetto
Via Collina 23, Montefiridolfi
Tel: 055-824 4442
www.borghetto.org
Very welcoming *agriturismo* with homely rooms and apartments, part of a working wine and olive oil estate. Swimming pool; cookery classes. **€€**

San Gimignano

L'Antico Pozzo
Via San Matteo 87
Tel: 0577-942014
www.anticopozzo.com
Charming old townhouse in the heart of the medieval town, carefully restored and simply but tastefully furnished. **€€**

Hotel La Cisterna
Piazza della Cisterna 23
Tel: 0577-940328
www.hotelcisterna.it
Medieval *palazzo* with a fine restaurant. The best rooms have views of the main piazza or across the valley. One of the most atmospheric and popular hotels in town. **€€**

Hotel Pescille
Località Pescille
Tel: 0577-940186
www.hotelpescille.it
Converted manor house 3 km (2 miles) southwest of San Gimignano. Some rooms have a balcony with views of the medieval towers. Swimming pool; tennis. **€€**

Villa San Paolo
Strada per Certaldo
Tel: 0577-955100
19th-century hillside villa, 5 km (3 miles) from San Gimignano, with attractive rooms, terraced grounds and a fitness centre. **€€€**

SIENA

Deluxe (€€€€)

Certosa di Maggiano
Strada di Certosa 82
Tel: 0577-288180
www.certosadimaggiano.com
Just outside Siena, this 14th-century Carthusian monastery – the oldest in Tuscany – has been converted into a 5-star hotel adorned with antiques. Set in olive groves with an outdoor pool, tennis courts, a prestigious restaurant and original features.

Grand Hotel Continental
Banchi di Sopra 85
Tel: 0577-56011
www.royaldemeure.com
Majestic hotel, recently restored with fine frescoed interiors, set in the heart of Siena. Covered courtyard, restaurant and wine bar.

Expensive (€€€)

Garden
Via Custoza 2
Tel: 0577-567111
www.gardenhotel.it
Just north of Siena, this 16th-century patrician villa houses a prestigious hotel with a formal, Italian garden and a pool. Four-star rooms available too. Good for families. Drops a price bracket in low season.

Villa Scacciapensieri
Via Scacciapensieri 10
Tel: 0577-41441
www.villascacciapensieri.it
Supremely elegant villa hotel in lovely grounds 3 km (1½ miles) north of the city. Sophisticated interior, bedrooms with rural views, and a panoramic city view from the restaurant terrace.

Moderate (€€)

Albergo Chiusarelli
Via Curtatone 15
Tel: 0577-280562
www.chiusarelli.it
Slightly decaying, genteel villa in a garden with a car park. Near the bus station.

Antica Torre
Via Fiera Vecchia 7
Tel: 0577-222255
www.anticatorresiena.it
A tiny, atmospheric hotel, essentially a conversion of a 17th-century tower, with a small garden and

private car park. Only 12 rooms, so book early.

Duomo
Via Stalloreggi 38
Tel: 0577-289088
www.hotelduomo.it
Situated right in the heart of the historic centre, this 18th-century *palazzo* has a cloistered, intimate atmosphere. Some rooms have views of the cathedral and Sienese hills.

Santa Caterina
Via Enea Silvio Piccolomini 7
Tel: 0577-221105
www.hscsiena.it
Friendly 3-star hotel set in a garden just outside the city walls, near Porta Romana, about a 15-minute walk to the centre. Breakfast is served on a lovely verandah with views across the Sienese hills. Roadside rooms

can be noisy.
Palazzo Ravizza
Pian dei Mantellini 34
Tel: 0577-280462
www.palazzoravizza.it
Historic townhouse with frescoed ceilings, a good restaurant and lovely gardens with views over the Tuscan hills. Well chosen antiques in the bedrooms. Welcoming public rooms.

Inexpensive (€)

Albergo Centrale
C. Angiolieri 26
Tel: 0577-280379
Clean and spacious 2-star hotel, a stone's throw from the Campo.
Piccolo Hotel Etruria
Via delle Donzelle 3
Tel: 0577-288088
www.hoteletruria.com
Friendly, family-oriented hotel with simple but

clean rooms divided between two townhouses. Good value.
Tre Donzelle
Via delle Donzelle 5
Tel: 0577-280358
www.tredonzelle.carbonmade.com
Facilities are limited and rooms are basic, but clean and comfortable. For a hotel so near the Campo it's excellent value.

SOUTH OF SIENA

Bagno Vignoni

Adler Thermae Spa
Via Ara Urcea 43
Tel: 0577-889 001
www.adler-thermae.com
Child-friendly resort, noted for its spa facilities and good Tuscan cuisine. €€
La Locanda del Loggiato
Piazza del Moretto 30
Tel: 0577-888925
www.loggiato.it
This romantic 6-roomed B&B in the Val D'Orcia is a perfect place for couples to stay if wine-tasting in the nearby villages. Has its own wine bar. No children. €€

Cetona

Locanda di Anita
Piazza Balestrieri, 5
Tel: 0578-237075
www.lalocandadianita.it
Charming little inn and bar set back from the main square. Guests are also given a special pass for access to the luxury Fonteverde spa in San Casciano dei Bagni (see page 287). €€

Castiglione d'Orcia

Bagni San Filippo
Tel: 0577 872982

www.termesanfilippo.it
As a delightful embodiment of a time-warp spa that works, this affordable spot provides friendly service, low-key bedrooms, hearty Tuscan cuisine – and the restorative water and mud treatments, of course. €€

Montalcino

Il Giglio
Via Saloni 5
Tel: 0577-846577
www.gigliohotel.com
Small family-run hotel suspended above the city walls. Its 12 rooms all offer fabulous views over the lush Val d'Orcia. €€
Il Marzocco
Piazza Savonarola 18
Tel: 0578-757262
www.albergoilmarzocco.it
Medieval palazzo with fine, if old-fashioned rooms, some of which have balconies with fine valley views. €

Montepulciano

Il Borghetto
Via Borgo Buio 7
Tel: 0578-757535
www.ilborghetto.it
Three 16th-century palazzi in the heart of

town, converted into a hotel. Rooms are small, but comfortable. Be sure to request one with views over the valley. Cosy sitting room with a big fireplace and resident cat. The owner is also a tour guide. €€
Palazzo Contucci
Pizza Grande 13
Tel: 0578-757006
www.residenzecontucci.it
This palatial 16th-century building designed by Sangallo still belongs to the aristocratic Contucci family. The Contessa rents out an apartment above the wine cellars. €€

Pienza

Antica Locanda
Corso Il Rossellino 72
Tel: 0578-493110
www.anticalocanda.toscana.nu
Small, but comfortable bed and breakfast, with some rooms overlooking the valley. €
Piccolo Hotel
Via Circonvallazione 7
Tel: 0578-749402
www.piccolohotellavalle.it
Popular, comfortable 3-star hotel. Some rooms have panoramic balconies with fine views over the Val

d'Orcia. €–€€
Il Chiostro di Pienza
Corso Il Rosellino 26
Tel: 0578-748400
www.relaisilchiostrodipienza.com
Beautifully converted medieval convent, with a quiet cloister, in the heart of Pienza. Also runs a good restaurant. Very welcoming. €€–€€€

Ripa d'Orcia

Castello di Ripa d'Orcia
Località Castiglione d'Orcia
Tel: 0577-897376

PRICE CATEGORIES

The price categories refer to the cost of a double room during high season, usually including breakfast.
€ = under €100
€€ = €100–200
€€€ = €200–300
€€€€ = more than €300

www.castelloripadorcia.com
Peaceful medieval hamlet, dominated by a tower, parts of which have been converted into hotel rooms and apartments. *Trattoria* with panoramic terrace views. Closed Dec–Feb. **€€**

Hotel Palazzuolo
Via Santa Caterina 43
Tel: 0577-897080
www.hotelpalazzuolo.it
Surrounded by lush countryside, with terrace and swimming pool; Tuscan cuisine a speciality. Free use of mountain bikes. **€**

Sinalunga
Locanda dell'Amorosa
Località l'Amorosa
Tel: 0577-677211
www.amorosa.it
Renaissance hamlet, complete with chapel, converted into a first-class hotel. Romantic setting; superb

restaurant; high prices. **€€€–€€€€**

Soviclle
Borgo Pretale
Tel: 0577-345401
www.borgopretale.it
Beautifully restored hamlet. Homely apartments and restaurant. **€€€**

GROSSETO AND THE MAREMMA

Albinia
La Parrina
Km 146 Via Aurelia
Tel: 0564-862626
www.parrina.it
Genuine *agriturismo* set among vineyards, olive groves and orchards on the Maremman plains. It has retained the traditional décor of a country estate. Excellent buffet breakfast on garden terrace. Swimming pool, chapel, farm shop and bicycles. **€€–€€€**

Castiglione della Pescaia
Albergo Tirreno
Via Ansedonia 69
Tel: 0564-933796
www.hoteltirrenocastiglione.it
Clean hotel with 12 rooms. Tariff includes room and board – meals are at the tasty restaurant on the premises. **€**
L'Andana
Tenuta La Badiola
Tel: 0564-944800
www.andana.it
The former estate of Tuscan grand duke Leopold II has been transformed into a supremely refined hotel with an excellent restaurant, by one of France's most celebrated chefs, Alain Ducasse, who has also set up his own winery here. The height of luxury. **€€€€**

Isola del Giglio
Pardini's Hermitage
Cala degli Alberi, Giglio Porto
Tel: 0564-809034
www.hermit.it
Pleasant, secluded island retreat with 12 small rooms and well tended gardens. Accessible by boat from Giglio Porto. Relaxed atmosphere, friendly welcome and good facilities. Half-board only. **€€**

Montemerano
Villa Acquaviva
Strada Scansanese 10 Nord (2 km/1 mile from Montemerano)
Tel: 0564-602890
www.relaisvillaacquaviva.com
Family-run villa near Saturnia with a lovely garden and comfortable rooms. Mountain bikes available for hire. Swimming pool. **€€**

Porto Ercole
Don Pedro
Via Panoramica 7
Tel: 0564-833914
www.hoteldonpedro.it
Long-established family-run hotel with views over the port below. The decor is rather old-fashioned, but it is well positioned. Half-board preferred. Open Easter–Sept. **€€**
Hotel Il Pellicano
Località o Sbarcatello
Tel: 0564-858111

www.pellicanohotel.com
Chic hotel enjoying a superb, isolated clifftop position. Bedrooms are housed in various buildings; terraces lead down to the private beach. Tennis courts and swimming pool. Weekly barbecues in summer. An expensive treat. **€€€€**

Porto Santo Stefano
Torre Di Cala Piccola
8km (5 miles) from Porto Santo Stefano on the Strada Panoramica, Argentario
Tel: 0564-825111
www.torredicalapiccola.com
Charming cliff-top hotel, built around a 17th-century Spanish lookout tower. Rooms and apartments with private beach and superb sea views. Open Mar–Oct. **€€€€**

Saturnia
Hotel Villa Clodia
Via Italia 43
Tel: 0564-601212
www.hotelvillaclodia.com
Centrally located three-star hotel with lovely view and swimming pool, within walking distance of the spa. Good value. **€**
Terme di Saturnia
Via della Follonata
Tel: 0564-600111
www.termedisaturnia.it

Luxury hotel and spa resort (*see page 287*). The thermal pool and treatment centre is open to non-residents. **€€€–€€€€**

Sovana
La Scilla
Via del Duomo 5
Tel: 0564-616531
www.scilla-sovana.it
Eight bright and elegant rooms in a pretty tufa-stone hotel.
Albergo Ristorante Taverna Etrusca
Piazza del Pretorio
Tel: 0564-616183
Excellent small restaurant with comfortable rooms. **€**

Talamone
Hotel Capo d'Uomo
Via Cala di Forno 7
Tel: 0564-887077
Cliff-top hotel with balconies overlooking the sea and access to a private rocky beach. Within easy reach of the Parco dell'Uccellina. **€€**

AREZZO AND EASTERN TUSCANY

Arezzo

Continentale
Piazza G. Monaco 7
Tel: 0575-20251
www.hotelcontinentale.com
A centrally located
3-star hotel, with good
facilities, comfortable
rooms and a lovely
roof terrace. Popular
among business travellers. **€€**

Hotel Patio
Via Cavour 23
Tel: 0575-401962
www.hotelpatio.it
Innovative hotel in an
old *palazzo* in the historic heart of Arezzo,
not far from San
Francesco. The colourful decor of each of the
seven rooms was
inspired by the writings
of widely travelled
novelist Bruce Chatwin.
€€

Val di Colle
Località Bagnoro, Scopeto
Tel: 0575-365157
www.valdicolle.it
A meticulously restored
14th-century house,
sitting on a hilltop 4 km
(2½ miles) from the
centre of Arezzo. There
are eight elegant
bedrooms decorated
with a rustic theme.
Antique furniture sits
harmoniously alongside
the modern art. Golfers
can use the driving
range and 9-hole putting
green on the premises.
€€€

Bibbiena

Albergo Borgo Antico
Via Cappucci 2
Tel: 0575-536445
www.brami.com
Welcoming hotel-restaurant in the centre of
Bibbiena, with comfortable, if non-descript

bedrooms. Good base
for exploring the
Casentino area. **€**

Castiglion Fiorentino

Villa Schiatti
Località Montecchio 131
Tel: 0575-651440
www.villaschiatti.it
Situated in the
panoramic hills between
Arezzo and Siena,
equipped with pool,
restaurant and terrace
offering splendid views
over the Tuscan countryside. **€–€€**

Cortona

Il Falconiere
Località San Martino.
Tel: 0575-612679
www.ilfalconiere.it
Luxurious country
retreat set in olive
groves 3 km (2 miles)
above Cortona. Firstclass restaurant. **€€€**

Rugapiana Vacanze
Via Nazionale 63
Tel: 0575-630364
www.tuscanytravel.net/rugapiana
Rooms and apartments
for short or longer
stays, in central
Cortona. Guests can
use the facilities at an
agriturismo just outside
town. **€€**

San Michele
Via Guelfa 15
Tel: 0575-604348
www.hotelsanmichele.net
Centrally situated, comfortable hotel housed in
an impressively
restored Renaissance
palace. **€€**

Foiano della Chiana

La Lodola
Via Piana 19
Tel: 0575-649660
www.lalodola.com

Bed and breakfast in an
18th-century farmhouse. The rooms are
lovingly decorated by
the antique dealer
owners – some of the
furniture is for sale. **€€**

Gargonza

Castello di Gargonza
Monte San Savino
Tel: 0575-847021
www.gargonza.it
Attractive fortified
village near Arezzo, with
a frescoed chapel and
castle walls, converted
into a hotel with separate apartments. The
13th-century buildings
overlook the Val di
Chiana. The restaurant,
with large terrace,
specialises in game.
€€

Loro Ciuffenna

Villa Cassia di Baccano
Via Setteponti Levante 132
Tel: 055-977 2310
www.villacassiadibaccano.it
Stylishly converted villa
17 km (11 miles) from
Arezzo, offering comfortable airy apartments on a weekly
basis, and suites on a
daily basis. Numerous
services and a swimming pool. Lovely views.
€€–€€€

Monterchi

B&B Il Colle
Località. Il Colle 4b
Tel: 0575-709856
www.bedandbreakfastilcolle.com
Former farmhouse
which has been well
converted into a homely
bed and breakfast.
Living room, terrace
and kitchen available.
Open fire makes it
cosy in colder weather.
€€

Sansepolcro

Relais Oroscopo
Via Togliatti 68
Tel: 0575-734875
www.relaisoroscopo.com
Located on the outskirts of Sansepolcro,
3-star hotel with individually decorated
rooms and a renowned
restaurant. **€–€€**

Regello

Villa Rigacci
Via Manzoni 75
Tel: 055-865 6718
www.villarigacci.it
Country house hotel in
a pleasant setting, off
the scenic "Road of
the Seven Bridges"
and handy for the
Rome–Florence
motorway. Sophisticated Mediterranean
food, extensive
grounds and a
swimming pool. Good
base for designer outlet shopping – there
are malls in nearby
Leccio and Montevarchi. **€€**

TRANSPORT

ACCOMMODATION

ACTIVITIES

A – Z

LANGUAGE

ACTIVITIES

THE ARTS, NIGHTLIFE, FESTIVALS, SPORTS AND SHOPPING

THE ARTS

Archaeological Sites

There are various places of archaeological interest in Tuscany. These include **Etruscan** (8th–2nd century BC) sites at Volterra, Fiesole, Arezzo, Chiusi, Vetulonia and on the island of Elba. There is an archaeological museum in Florence and other museums in Volterra, Chiusi, Cortona, Asciano, Grosseto and Massa Marittima.

Notable **Roman** (8th century BC–5th century AD) remains can be seen at Fiesole, Cosa, Roselle, Volterra and Arezzo.

Art and Architecture

Art

Renaissance art is, of course, what Tuscany is most famous for. The most outstanding Renaissance collections are in Florence, in the **Uffizi Gallery**, the **Pitti Palace Gallery** and the **San Marco Museum**.

Works of art from the late Renaissance and Mannerist periods, the baroque, the neoclassical and romantic, and also the 20th century are exhibited at most galleries and museums in the main cities of the region.

The exciting new **La Strozzina** gallery in the restored cellars of the Palazzo Strozzi has finally put Florence on the contemporary art map. The **Palazzo Strozzi** itself is a major exhibition site focussing on high profile art exhibitions.

Architecture

Tuscany is a treasure trove of architectural history *(see the feature on pages 54–59)*.
● Churches and civil buildings from the **Romanesque** period can be found at Pisa, Florence, Lucca, Siena, Pistoia and Arezzo.
● The most important **Gothic** buildings are in Florence, Siena, Pisa, Pistoia and Arezzo.
● Tuscany also abounds in religious and secular **Renaissance** buildings, Florence being the most important centre.

Sightseeing

Details of important museums and art galleries are in the *Places* section of this book. Be sure to take advantage of multientrance tickets where possible.

Florence

There are stands in shops and cafes where free leaflets detailing events and exhibitions can be picked up. Examples are *Informacittà* and *Vivi Firenze*.

The Friends of Florentine Museums Association (Via degli Alfani 39, tel: 055-293007) has 12,000 members. They arrange museum visits 9–11pm in the summer, with orchestral recitals.

For those who plan to visit a lot of museums in Florence, consider a membership to Amici degli Uffizi. Prices vary for individuals, families and students – members get free and privileged entrances (no queues) to Polo Museale Fiorentino museums and theatre discounts. See www.amicidegliuffizi.it for more information.

It is advisable to reserve Uffizi and Accademia tickets in advance, especially in high-season *(see tip on page 87)*.

Entry prices for museums and galleries vary greatly, with the Uffizi the most expensive. State museums are closed on Monday while most other museums close on Tuesday or Wednesday. Most museums also close on 1 May.

Every year, in the spring, Florence has a "culture week" *(La Settimana di Beni Culturali)*, when all the state museums are free. Enquire at the tourist office for more information.

Walking tours are an excellent way to gain more insight into the city. Context Florence (tel: 06-482 0911; www.contextflorence.com) organises private and small group walks and special site visits with local scholars.

Pisa

The main sites may be easily visited on foot or by local bus. Buy a joint ticket to see all the sights on the Campo dei Miracoli. A horse and carriage ride is a pleasant introduction to the city; prices are negotiable.

Siena

The tourist office can provide a list of authorised guides. With one week's notice, you can visit any of the *Contrada* (district) museums that celebrate the *Palio* and the ancient city traditions: the numbers are available on www.paliodisiena.biz.

Listings

The Florentine is the city's free bi-weekly English language newspaper. Issues can be found around town or downloaded from their website (www.theflorentine.net). Articles cover current events in Florence and event listings. The monthly publication, *Firenze Spettacolo* also has a complete listing of city events; although in Italian the listings themselves are usually straightforward. *Events* is another popular listings magazine, or you can check the entertainment pages of *La Nazione*, the regional newspaper, or the Tuesday edition of the national paper, *La Repubblica*. If you read Italian well, then get *Toscana Qui*, and *Firenze ieri, oggi, domani*.

Music, Ballet and Opera

Florence

The *Maggio Musicale* music festival (www.maggiofiorentino.it), held from mid-May to the end of June, is a big event with top names in concert, ballet and opera performing in various venues throughout the city. Tickets are available from the Teatro Comunale, Corso Italia 16, tel: 055-211158, and this is where most of the events are staged, although concerts are held throughout the summer in

cloisters, piazzas and the Boboli Gardens.

During the *Estate Fiesolana* – Fiesole's summer festival – concerts, opera, ballet and theatre are held in the town's Roman amphitheatre. Classical concerts are also held in many of the city churches.

The principal venue for chamber music concerts in Florence is the **Teatro della Pergola**, Via della Pergola (tel: 055-226 4335; www.pergola.firenze.it), a superb example of a 17th-century theatre (inaugurated in 1656). These concerts are generally held at weekends, and are well publicised.

The **Fiesole Music School** in San Domenico also holds a concert series (tel: 055-597 8527; www.scuolamusica.fiesole.fi.it) and the Orchestra Regionale Toscana's lively concert series runs December–May.

Florence's **Teatro Verdi**, Via Ghibellina 99 (tel: 055-212320; www.teatroverdifirenze.it) is the venue for a wider range of entertainment, from light opera and ballet to jazz and rock concerts.

The Orchestra da Camera Fiorentina stages bi-monthly classical concerts in the Bargello and the church of Orsanmichele. Their schedule is available at www.orcafi.it.

The Florence Dance Festival, held in late June/early July, features well-known national and international names along with up-and-coming dancers and choreographers (tel: 055-289276; www.florencedance.org for information).

Lucca

Puccini e la sua Lucca is a permanent festival dedicated to Giacomo Puccini, with concerts in the Basilica di San Giovanni. Tickets available at the church on performance days from 6pm; www.puccinielasualucca.com.

Pisa

Pisa's opera season runs at the Teatro Verdi from October to February. Tel: 050-941111 or visit www.teatrodipisa.pi.it.

Pistoia

Held every July, the Pistoia Blues Festival hosts big-name blues, jazz and rock artists for three days of concerts.

Siena

Public performances of rare, unpublished and new music are held in August each year during the Sienese Music Week.

Arezzo

Every July, the Arezzo Wave Love Festival brings a variety of Italian and world famous musicians to Tuscany to perform free concerts in a five-day music fest.

Theatre

In addition to the main theatres, **Teatro della Pergola** *(see left)* and **Teatro Verdi** (Via Ghibellina 99, tel: 055-212320; www.teatroverdifirenze.it), there are numerous smaller companies performing regularly in Florence, but most productions are Italian. The **Teatro Metastasio** in Prato is another place to see high-quality drama productions (tel: 0574-6084; www.metastasio.net). Look out for the listings in *Firenze Spettacolo*.

Ticket Sales

Useful ticket agencies in Florence are **Agenzia Box Office**, Via Alamanni 39, tel: 055-210804 (open Mon 3.30–7.30pm; Tues–Sat 10am–7.30pm); **Rinascente**, 4th Floor, Piazza della Repubblica, tel: 055-292508 (open Tues–Sat 1.30–7.30pm). In Prato, tickets can be purchased from **Dischi Niccoli**, Via Cairoli 19, tel: 0574-27890. It is best to go in person to buy tickets for all events from opera to rock music.

Cinema

Almost all films are dubbed into Italian, but there are a few cinemas that occasionally show original versions, screenings by organisations such as the British Institute and the odd film festival or special season which will use sub-titles rather than dubbing. The main cinema for foreigners is the **Odeon** (Piazza Strozzi, tel: 055-214068), which shows recent films in English on Mondays, Tuesdays and Thursdays and is packed with foreign students and expatriates. During the summer a number of films are shown in the open air – see the tourist office for details.

NIGHTLIFE

Tuscany's cities offer a wide variety of music and entertainment, especially in the summer when there are any number of festivals around the region (see page 280). In Florence, bars and clubs are set up in the warm weather in several piazzas, often with live music. There are a number of late-night bars and clubs dotted around town, but most of the bigger clubs are on the outskirts. Nightclubs come and go, so it's best to ask around for recommendations.

The following places are all in Florence. Elsewhere, the local tourist offices (see page 292) are your best bet for finding out about local clubs and bars, concerts, festivals and other events. Note that most clubs close on Monday; very few get going before 10pm.

Bars and Live Music

Astor
Piazza del Duomo 20r, tel: 055-284305. Cocktail bar with dance floor, frequented by Americans.
Be Bop
Via dei Servi 76r. Cocktail bar with live music: country, blues and jazz.
Il Caffè
Piazza Pitti 9, tel: 055-239 6241. Chic and refined: a cosy spot to chat to friends, day or evening.
Caffè Cibreo
Via del Verrocchio 5r, tel: 055-234 5853. Atmospheric annexe to the famous restaurant, ideal for anything from a morning coffee to a late-night digestivo. Closed Sun and Mon.

Caruso Jazz Café
Via Lambertesca 14/16r, tel: 055-281940. Relaxed café with art exhibitions and live music Wed–Fri. Closed Sun.
Dolce Vita
Piazza del Carmine, tel: 055-280018; www.dolcevitaflorence.com. Fashionable and crowded bar in the bohemian Oltrarno quarter.
Fusion Bar
Vicolo dell'Oro 3, tel: 055-2726 6987. Swanky bar in the Gallery Hotel Art perfect for aperitifs and sushi.
Golden View
Via dei Bardi 58r, tel: 055-214502. Restaurant with a view of Ponte Vecchio that turns into a bar after the dinner crowd finishes. Live jazz music.
Hemingway
Piazza Piattellina 9r, tel: 055-284781. Elegant café with comfy chairs and books to browse.
Jazz Club
Via Nuova dei Caccini 3, tel: 055-247 9700. Relaxed basement bar with live music daily. Small fee to become a member.
Moyo
Via dei Benci 23r, tel: 055-247 9738. Swanky cocktail bar in the Santa Croce area with outside seating and delicious cocktails.
Piccolo Caffe
Borgo Santa Croce 23r, tel: 055-200 1057. Primarily a gay bar, but also a friendly café which provides welcome relief from unwanted attention for women.
Il Rifrullo
Via San Niccolò 55r, tel: 055-234 2621. The long bar groans with munchies during cocktail hour and there is an open fire in the back room. Great cocktails.
Roses
Via del Parione 26r, tel: 055-287090. Florence's first sushi bar; sophisticated, good for cocktails and long drinks.
Slowly
Via Porta Rossa 63, tel: 055-264 5354. Trendy cocktail bar with a great aperitif buffet.
I Visacci
Borgo Albizi 80r, tel: 055-200 1956. Pleasant art café with

friendly staff, relaxed music and a good selection of wines and cocktails.

Nightclubs

Central Park
Via Fosso Macinante 1, Parco delle Cascine, tel: 055-353505. Possibly the trendiest club in Florence. Open Thurs–Sat.
Dolce Zucchero
Via Pandolfini 36/38r, tel: 055-247 7894. One of the few clubs in the city centre, it operates a drinks card whereby you pay on exit.
Doris
Via de' Pandolfini 26r, tel: 055-246 6775. Centrally located, multi-level club with music ranging from soft and romantic to high-energy and aggressive.
Maracanà
Via Faenza 4, tel: 055-210298; www.maracana.it. A lively Latino club. Closed Mon.
Meccanò
Viale degli Olmi 1, tel: 055-331371. One of Florence's oldest and most famous discos. Vast dance floor, bar and lounge areas.
Tabasco
Piazza Santa Cecilia 3, tel: 055-213000. Men only; this was the first gay bar in Italy.
Tenax
Via Pratese 46r, tel: 055-308160. Popular club and live music venue.
YAB
Via Sassetti 5r, tel: 055-215160; www.yab.it. Fashionable disco-pub.

FESTIVALS

Arezzo

Last Sunday in June and first Sunday in September: Giostra del Saracino – Mounted knights attack a wooden effigy of a Turk.

Cortona

July/August: Cortona Summer Festival – arts festival.
15 August: Sagra della Bistecca – Feast of the Beefsteak.

September (first half of the month): antiques exhibition.

Florence

Easter Day: *Scoppio del Carro*, the Explosion of the "Carriage" (actually fireworks on a float). Colourful musical processions.
Ascension Day: *Festa del Grillo*, Festival of the Crickets in the Cascine park. Sale of crickets and sweets.
End of April: Flower Show, Parterre, near Piazza Libertà – a riot of colour.
May and June: *Maggio Musicale Fiorentino* – performances of opera, ballet and classical music.
Saturday in late June: *Notte Bianca in Oltrarno* – all-night festivities, music and food in and around Piazza Santo Spirito.
June–September: *Estate Fiesolana* in Fiesole (just outside Florence) – music, dance, opera, cinema and theatre.
24 June: *San Giovanni* – Florence's patron saint's day, with a holiday in the city and an evening firework display near Piazzale Michelangelo.
June–July: *Calcio in costume* (*Calcio Fiorentino*) – football in medieval costume in Piazza Santa Croce.
7 September: night festival of the *Rificolona* (lanterns) – procession of carts, lanterns and singers.
First three weeks of December: *German Christmas Market* – Piazza Santa Croce becomes a festive German market with decorations, mulled wine, sausage and beer, and German sweets.

Livorno

Late July/August: *Effetto Venezia* – lively 10-day festival in the city's Venetian quarter. The little canals provide the setting for street theatre, music and food.

Lucca

July: Summer festival with big name bands in Piazza Anfiteatro.
September – first weekend. Festival of Flowers.
September: *Luminaria di Santa Croce* – a religious procession.

Lucignano

Last two Sundays in May: *Maggiolata Lucignanese* – festival that includes a procession of carts decorated with allegorical scenes in flowers.

Massa Marittima

Sunday following May 20 and the **second Sunday in August**: *Balestro del Girifalco* – crossbow competition.

Montalcino

Last Sunday in October: *Sagra del Tordo* – Thrush Festival. Pageant, costume ball, banquet and archery at the fortress.

Monticchiello

Last 15 days of July: *Il Teatro Povero* – "The Poor Theatre" presents a performance written by locals about locals.

Pescia

September (even numbered years): Biennial Flower Show.

Pienza

August/September: "Meeting with a Master of Art" in the council chamber of the Town Hall.
First Sunday of September: *Fiera del Cacio* – a fair devoted to Pienza's famous cheese.

Pisa

May and **June**: concerts at various annual festivals and fairs, especially during the *Gioco del Ponte* on the last Sunday of June.
16–17 June: *Luminaria di San Ranieri* – thousands of candles light up buildings along the Arno. Boat race in the evening of the second day.
Last Sunday in June: *Gioco del Ponte*.
Mid-September to end October: The annual *Anima Mundi International Festival of Sacred Music* takes place in Pisa Cathedral. Tel: 050-387 2229/2210; www.opapisa.it.

Pistoia

25 July: *Giostra dell'Orso* – a mock battle between a wooden bear and 12 knights in costume on Piazza del Duomo.

San Gimignano

July–September: Summer Fair, *Estate Sangimignanese* – varied programme of events, including ballet, concerts and cinema.

Siena

28-30 April: Feast of St Catherine.
2 July and **16 August**: *Palio* traditional horse race. For tickets and hotel bookings, write to the tourist office six months in advance.
Mid-July–August: *Incontri in Terra di Siena* – chamber music festival featuring quality concerts held in stunning settings south of Siena.
August: Sienese Music Week – performances of opera, symphonies and chamber music.
13 December: *Festa di Santa Lucia* – ceramics festival.

Torre del Lago

July and **August**: Puccini Opera Festival, near the composer's villa on Lake Massaciuccoli.

Viareggio

February: *Carnevale* – one of the best carnivals in Italy.

Volterra

First Sunday in September: *Torneo di Tiro con la Balestra* – crossbow tournament.

OUTDOOR ACTIVITIES

Sources of Information

For information about **green tourism** and **outdoor activities**, first contact the nearest office of ENIT, the Italian national tourist board *(see page 292)*.

For trekking or cycling routes (with map and suggested hostels and mountain refuges), request the *Turismo Natura Toscana* booklet from Regione Toscana, Via di Novoli 26, 50127 Firenze, tel: 055-438 3822. (It also gives tips for other activities, from horse-riding to climbing and caving.)

In English, the most comprehensive guide to green tourism is *Wild Italy* (by Tim Jepson, Sheldrake Press, 2005). Recommended local guides (in various languages) are: *Italia a Cavallo (Italy on Horseback)* published by Edizioni Demomedia and available from bookstores (or tel: 055-282162). The same publishers also produce *Toscana Verde (Green Tuscany), The Chianti and Il Mangia Firenze (Eating in Florence Province)*.

Hiking

Hiking (usually called "trekking" in Italian) is a popular activity in Tuscany. Serious hikers can follow the Italian Alpine Club (CAI or Club Alpino Italiano: www.cai.it) paths, which criss-cross the region. There is a branch of the CAI in Florence (Via della Mezzetta 2m, tel: 055-612 0467; www.caifirenze.it), or you can contact the local tourist office for information.

Two long-distance paths, **Apuane Trekking** (a four-day trek) and the **Grande Escursione Apenninica** (GEA, taking 25 days end to end), have well-marked trails and can be joined at various points. Shorter waymarked trails (such as those in the Maremma or Chianti regions) tend to be less well signposted, so take good local maps (such as those produced by CAI).

All walkers should bear in mind that there is no public right of way across private property. Be particularly vigilant during the hunting season, especially on Sundays. If travelling without a car, forward planning is required. City to city transport is generally fine (often quicker by bus than train) but rural transport is poor: either of the "two buses a day" variety or simply non-existent.

Areas to Explore

The following are guidelines to some of the more accessible areas of natural beauty.
Abetone and the Tuscan-Emilian border
Abetone makes a good base for exploring this forested mountain region, also known as the Alto Appennino. The town has a profusion of Swiss chalet-style hotels. The picturesque medieval centres of Fiumalbo and Cutigliano make good alternative bases but have fewer facilities and lack Abetone's more dramatic alpine views.
Transport: by public transport, it is quicker to reach Abetone by bus from Modena (in Emilia-Romagna) than by other routes.
Apuan Alps (Alpi Apuane)
Maps and information on mountain refuges are available from Massa, Carrara and most coastal tourist offices. Numerous one-day hikes are available through the Alps, with typical starting points being the villages of Stazzema and Levigliano on the western flanks of the mountains. Almost as appealing is a car journey along the winding mountain roads towards the interior.

Arezzo/Pratovecchio

The Parco Nazionale delle Foreste Casentinesi (www.parks.it) straddles Tuscany and Emilia Romagna. The park headquarters is at Pratovecchio, Via G. Brocchi 7, tel: 0575-50301. Alternatively, contact the Arezzo tourist office for more information.

Lunigiana and Garfagnana

Serious hikers should request the *Trekking in Lunigiana* map, with long-distance trails beginning in Aulla, Fosdinovo, Frignoli and Sassalbo. To appreciate the rural atmosphere, avoid staying in such fashionable coastal resorts as Forte dei Marmi. Instead, choose the Garfagnana hinterland, where Castelnuovo di Garfagnana is picturesque, and Barga, the main town, makes a pleasant base. Both are convenient for Parco dell' Orecchiella, the national park, 15 km (9 miles) north of Castelnuovo di Garfagnana. San Pellegrino in Alpe, 16 km (9½ miles) north-east of Castelnuovo, is appealing in summer and winter.
Transport: coastal transport is good, with transport into the Garfagnana hinterland less so. If you are planning to explore Garfagnana and Lunigiana by train or bicycle, a small branch line connects Lucca with Aulla and allows bicycles on the train.
The Maremma
If you want to be by the sea, stay in Santo Stefano, Talamone or Orbetello. Otherwise, opt for a ranch or farm near the park.
Transport: visitors using public transport should go to Orbetello (by bus or train) or to Monte Argentario (by bus from Grosseto). To visit the nature reserve is trickier: by train to Alberese station (only a couple of trains a day, from Grosseto), then a taxi.

The Mugello

Up-to-date information is available at www.mugellotoscana.it. Alternatively, request the *Green Heart of Tuscany* booklet from tourist offices in the region.

Avoid staying in Borgo San Lorenzo, the main town, which is not very attractive, or in the semi-industrialised valleys. Instead, choose the countryside or such villages as Vicchio.
Transport: for those who wish to explore the Mugello by train or bicycle, the Faenza–Florence train service stops at stations along the Apennine ridge (Vicchio, Marradi, Ronta), ideal places to begin trekking.

Green Sites

These include nature reserves, caves, botanical gardens and museums of rural life. The classification of Italian conservation areas is chaotic and confusing. In theory, the Arcipelago Toscano (Tuscan Archipelago, including Elba and the other islands) is a National Park but in reality much remains unprotected. Illegal hunting continues in the larger parks. The best-run sanctuaries tend to be the smallest, often those administered by the Worldwide Fund for Nature (WWF) or by LIPU, the Italian bird protection society (for which there is a great need).

TRANSPORT · ACCOMMODATION · ACTIVITIES · A – Z · LANGUAGE

Abetone

On the Tuscan-Emilian border Abetone is the main ski and summer resort in the northern Apennines *(see page 284)*. It is also the centre for information on GEA long-distance trails and shorter botanical rambles. For details, contact the Abetone tourist office.

The Apuan Alps and Lunigiana

The **Frignoli Botanical Gardens** near Sassalbo (tel: 0187-422598) have an arboretum and display the full range of plants grown in the Apuan Alps. In **Aulla**, in Lunigiana, there is an interesting natural history museum and ecological centre set in historic Brunella castle (open daily summer 9am–noon, 4–7pm; winter 9am–noon, 3–6pm; entrance fee; tel: 0187-400252), as well as neighbouring botanical gardens. From Aulla, visitors can organise tours of glacial moraines, karst gorges and caves.

Garfagnana

Here, **Parco dell'Orecchiella**, 15 km (9 miles) north of Castelnuovo di Garfagnana, is the chief regional park in the Lucca stretch of the Apennines. The main entry point is Corfino. There are also **botanical gardens** at Villa Collemandina, Pania di Corfino (tel: 0584-644911). The local visitors' centre (tel: 0583-619002) includes a civilised mountain refuge and suggested nature trails. For general information, contact the Comunità Montana Garfagnana (tel: 0583-644911) or the tourist office in Barga, the region's main town.

The **Orrido dei Bottri reserve** is a narrow gorge with sheer cliff faces that can be crossed by serious hikers.

Livorno Province

In Livorno, the **Oasi di Bolgheri** is the best bird and wildlife sanctuary, a mixture of scrub, lakes and marshy grasslands. This WWF reserve is home to native and migratory birds and small mammals such as wild boar. The reserve lies 10 km (6 miles)

south of Cecina and is reached by train to Bolgheri. Contact Marina di Cecina or Livorno provincial tourist offices for details.

Lucca Province

Bottaccio Wood, outside Castelvecchio di Compito, is a marshland nature reserve good for birds and best visited in spring (tel: 0583-65008).

The Maremma

In the Maremma region, the **Centro Visite Parco Naturale della Maremma**, or Parco dell'Uccellina (tel: 0564-407098) is closed to traffic. Entry points are Marina di Alberese (the coast) or Alberese (the landward side, with the park ticket office and small museum). The Marina entrance gives access to the park via the excellent beach. The Alberese entrance provides access to the park on foot or by means of the park shuttle bus. In addition to short trails, there are longer trails of 5 or 4 km (3 or 2½ miles, lasting about three hours). The waymarked paths are not wholly reliable. It is advisable to take drinking water and a picnic. In Alberese, canoes can be hired to explore the canals, and horse-riding is also available.

Lago di Burano (tel: 0564-898829), further south, offers one of the best bird-watching opportunities in Tuscany. This is the southern-most of two lagoons beside the peninsula of Monte Argentario. This WWF lagoon is home to falcons, cormorants, the black-winged stilt, purple and grey herons, with peregrines, ospreys and marsh harriers using the lagoons as feeding grounds. (By road, the reserve is at the Capalbio Scalo exit on the SS1; by rail, travel to the small Capalbio station.) For details of opening times, contact the Maremma national park (as above) or Grosseto provincial tourist office.

The Mugello

In the Mugello, the hamlet of Grezzano has **Casa d'Erci**, which is a farmhouse converted into a

museum of rural life and peasant culture. Check opening times on 055-92519.

Pisa Province

Here, the lakeside habitat at **Lago di Massaciuccoli** is home to migratory and wintering wildfowl as well as native species, including flamingos, geese, ducks, cranes and terns. The region's lone surviving lagoon has suffered from intensive shooting but survives nonetheless. For details of opening times and tours, contact Pisa provincial tourist office.

For more information, see also Nature Parks, pages 64–5.

Horseriding

There are over 40 centres belonging to the National Association of Equestrian Tourism (FITE-TREC-ANTE; Piazza A. Mancini 4, 00196 Rome, tel: 06-326 50230; www.fitetrec-ante.it) or to the Federazione Italiana Sport Equestri (Viale Tiziano 74, Rome, tel: 06-323 3826; www.fise.it).

Here are some suggestions for riding near Tuscany's main cities: **Maneggio Belvedere**, Località. Filetta 58010 Sorano (Grosseto), tel: 0564-615465; www.maneggio belvedere.it.

Club Ippico Senese, Località Pian del Lago, Siena, tel: 0577-318677; www.clubippicosenese.it.

For horse-riding centres elsewhere in Tuscany, call the **Centro Ippico Toscano**, Via Vespucci 5r, Florence, tel: 055-315621.

Fishing

For **freshwater fishing** foreigners need a temporary membership of FIPS (Federazione Italiana della Pesca Sportiva) and a government licence issued by the Provincial Administration. **Sport fishing** can be practised both from the shore and from a boat. In some ports, a special permit is required from the Harbourmaster's Office. Every provincial town has an office to give advice and notice of restrictions on fishing times and places.

Golf

There are some decent courses in Tuscany; the best include: **Golf Club Ugolino**, Via Chiantigiana, Grassina, tel: 055-230 1009; www.golfugolino.it **Montecatini Golf and Country Club** (18 holes), Via dei Brogi 32, Località Pievaccia, Monsummano Terme, tel: 0572-62218; www.montecatinigolf.com **Cosmopolitan Golf and Country Club**, Viale Pisorno 60, Tirrenia-Pisa, tel: 050-33633; www.cosmopolitangolf.it **Golf Club Punta Ala**, tel: 0564-922121; www.puntaala.net/golf

Skiing

Tuscany has a major ski resort at Abetone in the Apennines, north of Pistoia, extending over four valleys with 30 km (19 miles) of trails. For information on ski passes, pistes, etc., call Azienda Autonoma Soggiorno e Turismo in Abetone, tel: 0573-630145.

Watersports

At all Tuscan sea resorts it is possible to water-ski and row with hired boats. Yacht chartering facilities are also available in the resorts of Marina di Pisa and Tirrenia, and Porto Azzurro, Elba.

Diving

Diving is very popular in Tuscany, the best areas being around the Argentario on the southern coast, and the islands Giglio, Giannutri, Elba and Capraia. There is red coral, a huge variety of Mediterranean underwater flora and even a couple of wrecks off Giannutri. Many of the seaside ports in the area have diving clubs which take boats out regularly.
Elba Diving Centre, Marciana Marina, tel: 0565-904256; www.elbadiving.it.
Giglio Diving Club, Via della Torre Campese, tel: 0564-804065; www.geocities.com/gigliodiving.

Swimming Pools

Many Tuscan hotels, villas and *agriturismo* places have swimming pools and there are public pools in most towns, although these often have limited opening hours. Public swimming pools in Florence:
Piscina Le Pavoniere, Viale della Catena 2, tel: 055-362233. Open during the summer. There is also a bar and pizzeria here.
Piscina Nannini, Lungarno Aldo Moro 6, tel: 055-677521. Olympic-size pool which is open air during the summer months.
Siena has its own **Piscina Comunale**, Piazza G. Amendola, tel: 0577-47496.

Spectator Sports

Football is the national sport. Almost every city and village has a team and the most important national championship is the "Serie A" (Premiership), the winner of which is eligible to play in the Champions' League, against other top European teams. If you want to see a game, check the newspaper listings, but it is difficult to get tickets for a big match.
Horse racing is also popular and there is a racecourse in Florence's Cascine park: **Ippodromo le Cascine**, tel: 055-226076.
For tickets for any sporting event, consult the local tourist office or, alternatively, buy the pink *Gazzetta dello Sport* newspaper, which gives the lowdown on what's on when and how to book.

SHOPPING

What to Buy

The quality of goods in Italy, especially Tuscany, is very high and prices generally reasonable. Suggested buys are:
Fashions: dresses, suits, hats, gloves, linen, silk ties and shirts, scarves, knitwear, designer labels *(see outlet shopping below)* and jewellery.

Leather goods: prices are not rock bottom but the quality is often excellent and the designs appealing. Shoes and handbags are particularly good buys, but there are also boxes and belts, luggage, briefcases and wallets.
Cloth: silk, linen, wool and cotton.
Handicrafts: lace and tablecloths; pottery, ceramics and porcelain; gold and silver ware; alabaster and marble objects; woodwork; straw and raffia goods; glass and crystal work; art books and reproductions; marbled paper; rustic household goods; prints; antiques; reproduction furniture.
Alcohol: regional wines – along with the well-known Chianti, Montalcino and Montepulciano, wines from the coastal Maremma such as Sassicaia and Ornellaia, and other regions are gaining an international reputation; Italian spirits, liqueurs and aperitifs, such as Grappa or Liquore Strega.
Food: cold-pressed olive oil, herbs, locally made pasta, farmhouse cheeses, bottled vegetables, truffles, dried mushrooms, cured ham, salami, etc.

Shopping Hours

Food stores and general shops open 8.30am–1pm and 3.30 or 4–7.30pm. They stay open a little later in the summer. Many of the bigger supermarkets stay open through lunch and close at around 8pm. Department stores and other shops in bigger cities stay open all day (9.30am–7.30/8pm), and there is now limited Sunday trading in some places. Many clothing shops are closed on Monday mornings.

Where to Shop

Chain stores such as Oviesse and Standa can be found in most towns in Tuscany, and the upmarket Rinascente is in Florence.
Open-air markets are held usually once or twice a week in almost all tourist resorts and towns.
Supermarkets are found in most of the resorts and in all big

towns, but are less common in smaller towns and villages. **Tobacconist's shops** (called *tabaccai*) sell postage stamps and *schede* (telephone cards), alongside cigarettes and tobacco.

Outlet Shopping

The Arno Valley is the cradle of many clothes factories for some of Italy's top designer labels. They tend to be located between Pontassieve and Incisa Val d'Arno and have retail outlets where there are bargains of up to 60 percent discount. Get there early for the best buys and be prepared to queue. Avoid weekends. The best retail outlets, within easy reach of Florence and Arezzo, include:

The Mall, Via Europe 8, Leccio Regello, tel: 055-865 7775. Gucci, Giorgio Armani, Sergio Rossi, Yves Saint Laurent, Bottega Veneta, Loro Piana, Agnona, Tod's, Hogan, La Perla, Salvatore Ferragamo, Ungaro, Ermenegildo Zegna, Valentino, Alexander McQueen, Balenciaga, Burberry, Fendi, Stella McCartney, Yohji Yamamoto.
Fendi, Via Pian dell'Isola 66, Rignano sull'Arno, tel: 055-834981. Especially good for accessories.
Barberino, Via Meucci snc, Barberino del Mugello, tel: 055-842161. New outlet of over 100 stores including some designer fashion and other chain stores: Bottega Verde, Bruno Magli, Coccinelle, D&G, Furla, Fornarina, Guess, Missoni, Pinko, Prada, Puma.
Dolce e Gabbana, Via Santa Maddalena 49, Santa Maria Maddalena tel: 055-833 1300. Everything from accessories and clothes to household designer goods.
Prada, Località Levanella, Montevarchi tel: 055-91901. A good selection, but they operate a strict queuing system.

For more information on outlet shopping go to www.outlet-firenze.com. Dedicated fashionistas might consider investing in a copy of *Lo Scopri Occasioni*

(published in English as *Designer Bargains in Italy*), which has over 1000 outlet addresses. Visit www.scoprioccasioni.it.

Shopping in Florence

Despite tourism, consumerism and high labour costs, Florence still has a reputation as a city with high standards of craftsmanship in many spheres, from silver jewellery to marbled paper. If you wish to visit craftsmen at work, consult the tourist office and ask for their booklets on crafts; these will list the main craftspeople still practising in the city. For example, the **Santa Croce leather school**, on Piazza Santa Croce, is a popular place for visitors to watch skilled Florentine leather-workers.

Many artisan workshops can be found in the Oltrarno neighbourhood, near Pitti Palace and Piazza Santo Spirito.

Antiques

There are two main areas for antiques shops: Via Maggio and the surrounding streets in the Oltrarno and Borgo Ognissanti, west of the centre. There is a wide choice of goods, but you are unlikely to find a bargain.

Books

Edison, Piazza della Repubblica 27, tel: 055-213110; www.libreria edison.it. Large bookshop with an extensive range of language and guidebooks. Open until midnight.
Feltrinelli Internazionale, Via Cavour 12/20r, tel: 055-219524. The most comprehensive and respected bookshop in Florence, with a range of foreign language books and guides.
Seeber-Melbookstore, Via Cerretani 16r, tel: 055-287339; www. melbookstore.it. A range of books and music as well as a café.
The Paperback Exchange, Via delle Oche 4r, tel: 055-293460; www.papex.it. Just south of the Duomo, this is no ordinary bookshop: it stocks just about every book ever written on Florence. They also have a vast stock of

quality second-hand English and American paperbacks.

Boutiques

Florence is full of top designer boutiques. The most elegant street is the Via de' Tornabuoni where Gucci, Valentino and other big names in fashion have their outlets. Other exclusive streets are the Via Calzaiuoli and Via Roma (both have a stunning range of leather goods), Via della Vigna Nuova and Via del Parione.

The top designer shops are:
Giorgio Armani, Via Tornabuoni 48r, tel: 055-219041. For a more affordable Armani, visit Emporio Armani, Piazza Strozzi 14–16r, tel: 055-284315.
Dolce e Gabbana, Via della Vigna Nuova 27r, tel: 055-281003. Sexy, stylish, often outrageous clothes.
Enrico Coveri, Lungarno Guicciardini 19, tel: 055-264476. Flamboyant, colourful clothes.
Ferragamo, Via de' Tornabuoni 2, tel: 055-271121. The famous Florentine shoemakers have now branched out into accessories and clothes. Upstairs, the **Ferragamo Museum** (open Wed–Mon 10am–6pm) hosts various exhibits showing Ferragamo's influence on shoe style.
Gucci, Via de' Tornabuoni 73r, tel: 055-264011. The range has expanded, but belts and handbags remain their trademark.
Prada, Via de' Tornabuoni 51–55r and 67r, tel: 055-283439. Gorgeous accessories and shoes.
Emilio Pucci, Via de' Tornabuoni 20–22r, tel: 055-295 8082. Famous for its retro prints, beautiful scarves and dresses.
Raspini, Via Roma 25r, tel: 055-213077. Upscale boutique carrying top brands.
Valentino, Via dei Tosinghi 52r, tel: 055-293142.
Versace, Via de' Tornabuoni 13r, tel: 055-296167. Haute couture by Donatella.
Also worth checking out are:
Echo, Via dell'Oriuolo 37r, tel: 055-238 1149. An interesting selection of women's clothing arranged by colour.

TRANSPORT

ACCOMMODATION

ACTIVITIES

A – Z

LANGUAGE

Cavalli, Via de' Tornabuoni 83r, tel: 055-239 6226. The Florentine designer's store with a stylish café, Giàcosa.

Ethic, Borgo Albizi 37, tel: 055-234 4413. One of few fashionable boutiques to offer clothing at reasonable prices.

Christian Dior, Via de' Tornabuoni 57r, tel: 055-266911.

Hogan, Via de' Tornabuoni 97r, tel: 055-274 1013.

Trussardi, Via de' Tornabuoni 34/36, tel: 055-265 4648.

Ceramics

Sbigoli Terracotte, Via Sant' Egidio 4r, tel: 055-247 9713. Good choice of hand-painted ceramics in traditional and contemporary designs.

Fabrics

Antico Setificio, Via L. Bartolini 4, tel: 055-213861. Fabrics made traditionally, above all silk, still woven on 18th-century looms.

Casa dei Tessuti, Via de' Pecori, 20–24, tel: 055-215961. Fine silks, linens and woollens in an historic Florentine store.

Gloves

Madova, Via Guicciardini 1r, tel: 055-239 6526. Every kind of glove you could imagine and all of them beautifully made.

Jewellery

There is still a flourishing jewellery trade in Florence (particularly on the Ponte Vecchio and in Oltrarno, on the south side of the river), though most gold jewellery is now made in Arezzo.
The following traditional goldsmiths and silversmiths remain:

Brandimarte, Via Bartolini 18r, tel: 055-239381. Handcrafted silver goods and jewellery in a large store. Good prices.

Donato Zaccaro, Sdrucciolo de' Pitti 12r, tel: 055-212243.

Gatto Bianco, Borgo SS Apostoli 12r, tel: 055-282989. Contemporary designs in gold and silver.

Marzio Casprini, Via Rosso Fiorentino 2a, tel: 055-710008. Silversmith.

Exclusive Jewellery

If you can afford to push the boat out, these establishments are well worth adding to your itinerary:

Buccellati, Via de' Tornabuoni 71r, tel: 055-239 6579.

Bulgari, Via de' Tornabuoni 56r, tel: 055-286635.

Torrini, Piazza del Duomo 10r, tel: 055-230 2401.

Leather

Quality ranges from the beautifully tooled creations of local artisans to shoddy goods aimed at undiscerning tourists. For top-of-the-range quality (and prices), you should start with the designer boutiques in the Via de' Tornabuoni or shops in streets around the Piazza della Repubblica. Try the following outlets:

Il Bisonte, Via del Parione 31r, tel: 055-211976. Leather goods at high prices.

Furla, Via della Vigna Nuova 47r, tel: 055-281416. Bags and accessories in contemporary designs.

Raspini, Via Roma 25–29, tel: 055-213077. Superb leather bags and coats.

For more down-to-earth prices, head for the **San Lorenzo market** northwest of the Duomo, where numerous street stalls sell shoes, bags, belts and wallets; you can also try the Santa Croce area.

Marbled Paper

Marbled paper is very closely associated with Florence and many of the designs echo ancient themes or Medici crests. With their beautiful colours, vibrant patterns and particular smells, the shops are a joy to visit.

Giulio Giannini e Figlio, Piazza Pitti 37r, tel: 055-280814. Florence's longest-established marbled paper shop.

Il Papiro, Via Cavour 55r, tel: 055-215262; Piazza del Duomo 27r, tel: 055-281628.

Il Torchio, Via de' Bardi 17, tel: 055-234 2862. Cheaper than some other shops, you also see the artisans at work.

Markets

Many neighbourhoods have a weekly market. Try the following:
Straw Market (Mercato del Porcellino): hand-embroidered work, Florentine straw, leather goods, wooden objects and scarves.

Flea Market (Mercato delle Pulci, Piazza dei Ciompi): basically junk, but great fun.

Sant'Ambrogio (Piazza Ghiberti): fruit and veg, food and clothes.

San Lorenzo Market (Mercato di San Lorenzo, Piazza San Lorenzo): the covered market sells vegetables, fruit, meat and cheeses etc., while the surrounding streets are filled with stalls selling clothes, shoes, leather and jewellery.

Cascine Market (Mercato delle Cascine, Tuesday mornings only): produce, household goods and clothing.

Artisan Market (Piazza Santo Spirito, 2nd Sun of the month, Sept–June): craft market with some organic food.

Pharmacy

Officina Profumo Farmaceutica di Santa Maria Novella, Via della Scala 16, tel: 055-216276. Housed in a frescoed chapel, this fascinating shop was founded by monks in the 16th century. It sells herbal remedies, beautifully packaged perfumes, shampoos, lotions and room scents.

Shoes

Florence is still a good place to buy shoes at reasonable prices.
Cresti, Via Roma 9r, tel: 055-214150. Beautiful shoes at much lower prices than at Ferragamo.

Ferragamo, Via de' Tornabuoni 16r, tel: 055-292123. Italy's most prestigious shoemaker, providing hand-tooled shoes and beautifully crafted ready-to-wear collections.

Francesco, Via di Santo Spirito 62r, tel: 055-212428. Hand-made shoes in classic designs tooled by a traditional craftsman.

The roads leading from the Duomo to Santa Maria Novella station have a good range of slightly cheaper shoe shops.

Shopping in Siena

Clothes and Shoes

The main shopping streets in Siena are Banchi di Sopra and Via di Città. They are lined with chain and individual stores selling a range of clothes and footwear.

Crafts

Wrought-iron and copper, ceramics, crystal and stained glass provide a wide choice. **Giogi Leonardo & Co**, at Antica Siena, Piazza del Campo 28, tel: 0577-46496, sells beautiful blue and yellow porcelain, while **Il Papiro** (Via di Città) sells handmade paper and gifts. **Acquarelli Originali** (Via Monna Agnese 14–16), a tiny store near the Duomo, sells hand-painted watercolours.

Food and Wine

Siena is known for its **confectionery**, particularly *panforte*, which is made from a sweet dough, flavoured with vanilla and full of candied citrus fruits. The most famous maker of such specialities is **Nannini**, at Piazza Matteotti 21 and Piazza del Monte 95/99, and **Bar Pasticceria Nannini** at Via Banchi di Sopra 24 (www.pasticcerienannini.it).

Siena Province produces a variety of good **wines** including Chianti, Brunello di Montalcino and Nobile di Montepulciano. The Permanent Italian Wine Exhibition in Fortezza Medicea (tel: 0577-288497; www.enoteca-italiana.it), displays and sells regional wines.

OTHER ACTIVITIES

Children

Tuscany has much to offer children of all ages, from medieval castles to ice creams galore and plenty of child-friendly restaurants. There are several good parks, nature reserves and numerous opportunities for horse-riding, cycling and swimming. Much of the coast of Tuscany, particularly the well equipped resorts near Viareggio and the beaches on islands such as Elba, is also great for children.

Tuscan festivals can be fun, especially the Lenten carnivals, the horse races, the jousting, boat pageants, and all the tiny food festivals *(see pages 280–1)*. To find out what's on, above all in summer, check the listings in *La Repubblica* or *La Nazione* as well as enquiring at the tourist offices. If you read Italian, buy *Firenze Spettacolo*, which has a good children's section: *Città & Ragazzi*.

Some of the suitable places in Tuscany for children are:
The Boboli Gardens *(Giardini di Boboli)* are fun for children to clamber around. There is an amphitheatre, strange statues and grottoes, and a handy café.
The Museo dei Ragazzi in Palazzo Vecchio offers special children-friendly tours of the Palace led by actors in costume, as well as activities and workshops.
The Cascine, Florence's other main park with a tiny zoo.
Giardino dei Tarrocchi, near Capalbio, is a bizarre garden full of colourful fantasy figures.
Ludoteca Centrale, Via Fibbiai 2, Florence, tel: 055-247 8386, is a fun children's centre with games, music and audiovisual equipment for the under-sixes.
Pinocchio Park *(Parco di Pinocchio)* at Collodi, near Pisa, is an obvious, if old-fashioned choice for children, tel: 0572-429342. Open 8.30am–sunset.
Pistoia Zoo, Via Pieve a Celle, Pistoia, tel: 0573-911219; www.zoodipistoia.it. Compact zoo, but one of the region's best.
Zoo Fauna Europa, just south of Poppi, tel: 0575-529079. A conservation centre for such breeds as the lynx and the Apennine wolf. Open 8am–sunset.
Canadian Island, Via Gioberti 15, Florence, tel: 055-677567. You can leave your children here if you (or they) are fed up with dragging around the sights. They can play with Italian children in an English-speaking environment.

Spas

Tuscany has a large number of spas, offering a range of health and beauty treatments from mud baths to hydro-massage or just the opportunity to relax in hot springs. The Italian Tourist Office (ENIT) has a complete list of facilities available; www.turismo.toscana.it (look at the *Terme e Golf* section). The Consorzio Terme di Toscana, presso Terme di Montecatini (Via Manzoni 5, tel: 0572-910357; www.termeditoscana.com) also provides information. Here is a list of Tuscany's top spas:
Bagni di Pisa, San Giuliano Terme; tel. 050-88501; www.bagnidipisa.com. Atmospheric spa resort, with distant views of the Leaning Tower – a romantic retreat.
Grotta Giusti Spa Resort, Monsummano Terme; tel. 0572-90771; www.grottagiustispa.com Historic spa resort spread around an elegant villa that is proud of its restorative spa caverns, innovative treatments and award-winning head barman.
Fonteverde Natural Spa Resort, San Casciano dei Bagni; tel. 0578 57241; www.fonteverdespa.com. Equally strong in Mediterranean and Oriental treatments, this spa is one of the best in the country.
Petriolo Spa & Resort , Pari - Civitella Paganico; tel. 0564 9091; www.atahotels.it/petriolo Timeless resort within easy reach of Siena, offering everything from an Ayurvedic massage to sweating in a dry-ice cave.
Terme di Saturnia Spa & Golf Resort, Saturnia; tel. 0564 600111; www.termedisaturnia.it Fed by historic springs, this pampering spa boasts a recreation of Ancient Roman baths, elegant suites and an 18-hole golf course.
Terme Sensoriali, Parco Acqua Santa, Chianciano Terme; tel: 0578 68480; www.termesensoriali.it Innovative spa matching imaginative aesthetics with an eclectic approach, from classic treatments based on the healing powers of the thermal springs to therapies inspired by Ayurveda.

A–Z

AN ALPHABETICAL SUMMARY OF PRACTICAL INFORMATION

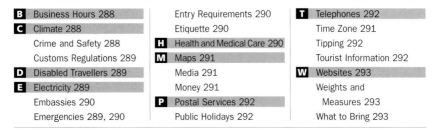

B usiness Hours

Shops in the main cities open Monday to Friday 8.30am–1pm and 3.30–7.30pm. The majority open on Saturday, and several are open on Sunday too, especially in high season. Some shops in coastal resorts and tourist centres now stay open all day throughout the summer and have Saturday and Sunday opening. Stores in most cities will close for at least two weeks around the *Ferragosto* holiday on 15 August. This is especially true of smaller cities not on the coastline.

Food shops are closed on Wednesday afternoons in winter and Saturday afternoons in summer. Clothes shops are closed on Monday mornings. Offices are usually open 8am–1pm and 2–4pm, although many have more extensive opening hours.

On Italian national holidays, all shops and offices are closed.

C limate

The Tuscan climate is pleasantly mild in the spring and autumn, cool and wet in the winter, and very hot near the sea and on low-lying land in the summer, with a pleasant warmth in the hills. There is very little wind except for on the Tyrrhenian coastline around Marina di Pisa and Tirre-nia, but surprise storms can be very heavy at any time of the year, and flooding in a number of places has caused severe dam-age in the past. The rainfall in Tuscany is generally higher than in most other parts of Italy. The temperature is slightly lower than in other areas, making it more agreeable in summer though somewhat colder in winter.

The weather in Florence can be extreme. The city is situated in a bowl, surrounded by hills, with the Arno cutting through it, and this accounts for the high degree of humidity that is often a feature of midsummer. The worst of the humidity is likely to occur between mid-July and mid-August with temperatures climbing well into the 30s Celsius (90s Fahren-heit).

Crime and Safety

Although violent crime is rare, in recent years, much crime in the north has tended to be gang- or drug-related. With increasing numbers of immigrants in Italy,

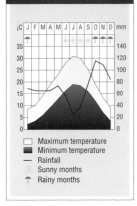

CLIMATE CHART

☐ Maximum temperature
■ Minimum temperature
— Rainfall
☀ Sunny months
☂ Rainy months

the harassment of so-called "foreigners" (essentially immigrants from former Yugoslavia, Eastern Europe, Albania or Africa) is unfortunately on the increase in a country traditionally unused to dealing with immigrants.

The main problem for tourists is petty crime, from pickpocketing and bag-snatching to the theft of objects left unattended in cars; it is wise to have insurance coverage against this and to take basic, sensible precautions against theft. If driving, lock your car and never leave luggage, cameras or other valuables inside. This applies particularly in major cities

If you are the victim of a crime (or suffer a loss) and wish to claim against your insurance, it is essential to make a report at the nearest police station as soon as possible and get documentation to support your claim. When you need a policeman, dial **113** (or **112** for the *Carabinieri*, the national police force).

Customs Regulations

Examination of luggage, passports, currency and hand baggage may take place on both entering and leaving Italy at airports, ports and borders. For-malities may also be also carried out on trains. Registered luggage may be sent to towns with Customs Offices: examination takes place at the destination.

It is no longer possible to buy duty-free or tax-free goods on journeys within the EU; VAT and duty are included in the purchase price. Shops at ports and airports will sell goods duty- and tax-paid to those travelling within the EU; in practice, many shops have chosen not to pass on price increases since the sale of duty-free goods within the EU was abolished.

There are no longer any limits on how much you can buy on journeys within the EU, provided it's for your own personal use. But there are suggested limits, and if you exceed them Customs may seize your goods if you can't prove they are for your own use. The guidance levels are:
● 3,200 cigarettes or 400 cigarillos or 200 cigars or 1 kg of smoking tobacco;
● 10 litres of spirits; 20 litres of fortified wine; 90 litres of wine; 110 litres of beer.

Duty-frees are still available to those travelling outside the EU.

Professional photographers must carry an ATA Carnet (issued in the UK through the London Chamber of Commerce, 33 Queen Street, London EC4R 1AP, tel: 020-7248 4444) for temporary importation of equipment.

D isabled Travellers

Despite difficult cobbled streets and poor wheelchair access to many tourist attractions and hotels, many people with disabilities visit Florence and Tuscany every year.

However, unaccompanied visitors will usually experience some difficulty, so it is best to travel with a companion.

Conditions and disability awareness are improving slowly in Tuscany (as well as in Italy in general), although the situation is certainly not ideal, and access is not always easy. More museums now have lifts, ramps and adapted toilets, newer trains and buses are accessible (although wheelchair users may need help when boarding), and recent laws require restaurants, bars and hotels to provide the relevant facilities. These laws, however, do not always cover access to those facilities. In 2004, Siena became the first Italian city to have an itinerary for the deaf. The brochure, *Siena in Lingua dei Segni*, is available from the tourist information centre, as is information about the facilities offered by sights and museums.

The Accessible Guide to Florence, by Cornelia Danielson (Xlibris Corporation publishers, 2004) provides very detailed information on museums, restaurants, hotels and more for disabled travellers to Florence.

For drivers with disabilities, there are plenty of reserved parking places in towns, and these are free.

In the UK, you can obtain further information from RADAR, 12 City Forum, 250 City Road, London EC1V 8AF; tel: 020-7250 3222; www.radar.co.uk. In the US, contact SATH, 5th Avenue, Suite 610, NY 10016; tel: 212-447 7284; www.sath.org.

E lectricity

Italy uses 220v and two pin plugs. Adaptors for British three-pin appliances can be pur-

EMERGENCY NUMBERS

Fire Brigade: 115.
Medical Aid/Ambulance: 118.
Police Immediate Action: 112.
General Emergency: Fire, Police or Ambulance (replies are in foreign languages in the main cities): 113.
Automobile Club d'Italia (ACI):
• 24-hour breakdown: 803-116.
• 24-hour information line: 1518.

chased from airports or department stores in the city. You will need a transformer to use 100–120 volt appliances.

Embassies

Australian Embassy: Via Antonio Bosio 5, 00161 Roma; tel: 06-852721.
UK Embassy: Via XX Settembre 80a, 00187 Roma; tel: 06-4220 0001.
UK Consulate: Lungarno Corsini 2, 50123 Firenze; tel: 055-284133.
US Embassy: Via Vittorio Veneto 119a, 00187 Roma; tel: 06-46741.
US Consulate: Lungarno A. Vespucci 38, 50123 Firenze; tel: 055-266951.

Emergencies

Useful Florence Contacts

Heart Emergency Mobile Coronary Unit: 055-214444.
Ambulances (Misericordia) Piazza Duomo 19–20: tel: 188 or 055-212222.
Tourist Medical Service 24-hour home visits, with English- or French-speaking doctors: Via Lorenzo il Magnifico 59, tel 055-475411.
Lost Property Via F. Veracini 5, tel: 055-334802.
Automobile Club d'Italia (ACI) tel: 055-24861.
Car pound – if your car is towed away – tel: 055-422 4142.
Police Headquarters (Questura) – the place to visit in the event of thefts, lost passports, etc., Via Zara 2, tel: 055-49771.
Tourist Police (Polizia Assistenza Turistica) are at Via Pietrapiana 50r, tel: 055-203911, and have interpreters on hand to assist.
Associazione Volontari Ospedalieri, Florence, tel: 055-234 4567. This group of volunteers will translate (free) for foreign patients.

Useful Siena Contacts

Siena Hospital Nuovo Policlinico di Siena, Località le Scotte, Viale Bracci, tel: 0577-585111.
Police Station (Questura), Via del Castoro 6, tel: 0577-201111 – open 24 hours a day.
Pronto Soccorso (Misericordia), Via del Porrione 49, Siena, tel: 0577-21011, or dial 118 in an emergency.
Lost Property Via Casato di Sotto 23, tel: 0577-292426.
Associazione Volontari Ospedalieri, Siena, tel: 0577-247869.

Entry Requirements

Visas and Passports

Subjects from European Union countries require either a passport or a Visitor's Identification Card to enter Italy. A visa is not required. Holders of passports from most other countries do not require visas for stays of less than three months, except for nationals of Eastern European countries, who need to obtain visas from the Italian Embassy in their own country.

Police Registration

A person may stay in Italy for three months as a tourist, but police registration is required within three days of entering Italy. If staying at a hotel, the management will attend to the formality. Although this regulation seems to be rarely observed, it is advisable that you carry a set of passport photos in case you need them for registration.

You are legally obliged to carry a form of identification (passport, driving licence, etc.) with you at all times. This rule is often flouted but bear in mind that it would be unwise to call the police or attempt to report a problem (e.g. theft) unless you are carrying appropriate identification.

Etiquette

Tuscans are generally friendly and will appreciate efforts to speak the language. Any attempt to rush or pressure them, however, will be regarded as the height of bad taste, and whatever you want will take longer. Almost everything is done on the basis of personal favours or contacts so any personal recommendations you can muster will always come in useful.

H ealth

UK visitors are entitled to medical treatment in Italy provided they have a European Health Insurance Card (tel: 0845-606 2030, visit www.dh.gov.uk, or obtain an application form from the post office). There are similar arrangements for citizens of other European Union countries. As few Italians have faith in their own state health service, it may be advisable to take out insurance for private treatment in case of accident.

Vsitors from outside the EU are strongly advised to take out adequate holiday and medical insurance to provide full cover during their stay abroad.

In high summer, the weather can be very hot; sunscreen, shady hats and mosquito repellent are recommended.

Medical Services

Pharmacies: The staff in chemist's shops (farmacie) are usually very knowledgeable about common illnesses and sell far more medicines without prescription than in some other countries (even so, most drugs still require a prescription). Pharmacies are identified by a cross, often red or green and usually in neon.

Normal pharmacy opening hours are Mon–Fri 9am–1pm and 4pm–7pm. Every farmacia posts a list of the local chemists who are on emergency duty on to their pharmacy window. The following are chemist's shops which are open 24 hours in Florence:

Farmacia Comunale 13, in Florence station, tel: 055-216761.

Farmacia Molteni, Via Calzaiuoli 7r, tel: 055-215472.

Farmacia all'Insegna del Moro, Piazza San Giovanni 20r, tel: 055-211343.

In addition, you can call 800-420707 to find out which chemists are on the night rota.

First Aid Service (*Pronto Soccorso*) with a doctor is found at airports, railway stations and in all hospitals. See box on page 289 for numbers to call in an emergency.

M aps

Touring Club Italiano does a good fold-out map of the Tuscany region showing major and minor roads. The Siena and Florence tourist offices supply reasonable city maps. *Insight Guide Fleximaps* are also available for Florence and Tuscany.

Media

Each large Italian town has its own newspaper. *La Stampa*, *Il Corriere della Sera*, and *La Repubblica* also have a national following. *La Nazione* is the paper favoured by most Tuscans for regional matters.

Television is deregulated in Italy. In addition to the state network, RAI (which offers three channels), there are about 1,000

channels, of which the main ones are Canale 5, Rete 4, Italia 1, Telemontecarlo and Video Music.

There are several useful publications for visitors to Tuscany, including *The Florentine*, a bi-weekly English language paper focusing on current events and city life, and *Firenze Spettacolo*, a monthly listings magazine in Italian (with some listings also in English), focusing on nightlife, clubs, bars and the live arts in Florence.

Money Matters

In common with the other Eurozone countries of the EU, Italy's monetary unit is the Euro (€), which is divided into 100 cents. The currency is available in 500, 200, 100, 50, 20, 10 and 5 euro notes, and 2-euro, 1-euro, 50-cent, 20-cent, 10-cent, 5-cent, 2-cent and 1-cent coins.

Italy is a society that prefers cash to credit cards, except for large purchases, or, for instance, hotel bills. In the case of petrol stations, more modest restaurants and smaller shops, it is usual to pay in cash. Check beforehand if there is any doubt. Most shopkeepers and restaurateurs will not change money, so it is best to change a limited amount when you arrive, especially if it is the weekend, when banks are closed. Try to avoid changing money in hotels, where the commission tends to be higher than in banks.

Travellers' Cheques

Although travellers' cheques are gradually being replaced by credit cards, euro, dollar or sterling travellers' cheques are easy to cash, subject to a commission, but remember that you will be required to present your passport. In some cases they can be used in exchange for goods and services in shops and hotels.

Cash Machines and Credit Cards

Given the long queues for money-changing in Italy, it is simplest to

get cash from cashpoint machines, which are now widely available. Most Maestro cards work in Italian machines, with your normal PIN number, as do credit cards, though you may sometimes have to look for particular "Bancomats" (cashpoint machines) that take your card.

In cities, many restaurants, hotels, shops and stores will take major credit cards, but in rural areas especially, you may be able to pay only in cash.

Banks

Banks offer the best exchange rates (small exchange booths often charge up to 3 percent commission) and are normally open Mon–Fri 8.30am–1.30pm. Some banks also open in the afternoon 2.30pm–4.30pm. Outside these hours and at weekends you can use automatic exchange machines to change cash. There is a high concentration of banks in Florence, including foreign banks, to the west of Piazza della Repubblica, around Via Tornabuoni.

Florence
Banca Commerciale Italiana, Via Tornabuoni 16.
Banca d'Italia, Via dell'Oriuolo 37/39.
Banca Toscana, Corso 6.
Credito Italiano, Via Vecchietti 11.
Cassa di Risparmio di Firenze, Via Bufalini 6.

Siena
Banca Nazionale del Lavoro, Via Vittorio Veneto 43.
Banca di Roma, Via dei Termini 37.
Cassa di Risparmio di Firenze, Piazza Tolomei 11.
Monte dei Paschi di Siena, Via Banchi di Sopra 84.

Exchange Offices

Florence

Change Underground, Piazza Stazione 14, Int. 37 (under the station).

Post Office, Via Pellicceria 3 (1st floor), near Piazza della Repubblica. Open Mon–Sat 8.15am–7pm.

Siena

Viaggi Seti (Piazza del Campo 56) – changes notes and travellers' cheques.

Coop "Siena Hotels Promotion" (Piazza San Domenico) – changes notes and travellers' cheques.

Forexchange (Via di Città 80-82) – changes notes and traveller's cheques and processes Western Union transfers.

P ostal Services

Main post offices in major towns are open all day; otherwise the hours are 8am–1.30pm (12.30pm Saturday). Stamps are sold at post offices and tobacconist's shops *(tabacchi)*.

There is also a courier service for sending important documents world-wide in 24/48 hours. This service is only available at major post offices. In Florence these are at Via Pellicceria 3 (main post office) and Via Alamanni 20r (by the station).

Poste Restante

Correspondence addressed c/o Post Office with FERMO POSTA added to the name of the locality will be held for collection (for 30 days). Letters are held at the local Central Post Office and will be handed over the Fermo Posta counter on proof of identity – usually a passport – and a fee.

T elecommunication

Telephones

Most public telephones accept phonecards *(carte telefoniche or schede telefoniche)* and these are available from tobacconists or post offices in various denomi-

nations; few telephones now accept coins. From some bars, and from post offices, you can call *scatti* (ring first, pay later according to the number of units or *scatti* used).

Italy has an extremely high ownership of mobile phones and in the major cities, such as Florence, it is possible to hire one.

For long-distance calls, the cheapest time to telephone is between 10pm and 8am Monday to Saturday, and all day Sunday.

For directory enquiries dial 12. For international enquiries, call 176 and to make a reverse charges (collect) call, dial 170.

When dialling Italy from abroad, dial the country code (0039) and the area code **including** the initial zero. In Italy, when calling numbers either inside or outside your area, dialling must always be preceded by the area code including the zero. The area code for Florence is 055 and for Pisa the area code is 050.

● **1 January** – *Capodanno* (New Year's Day).
● **6 January** – La Befana (Epiphany)
● **Easter** – *Pasqua*.
● **Easter Monday** – *Pasquetta*.
● **25 April** – *Anniversario della Liberazione* (Liberation Day).
● **1 May** – *Festa del Lavoro* (Labour Day).
● **24 June** – *San Giovanni* (St John the Baptist) – in Florence only.
● **15 August** – *Ferragosto* (Assumption of the Virgin Mary).
● **1 November** – *Ognissanti* (All Saints' Day).
● **8 December** – *Immacolata Concezione* (Immaculate Conception).
● **25 December** – *Natale* (Christmas Day).
● **26 December** – Santo Stefano (Boxing Day).

E-mail, Internet and Fax

Most large hotels offer internet, e-mail and fax facilities. There are numerous internet cafés around Florence, including the chain Internet Train which allows you to connect using their computers or your own laptop. Most main post offices and stations have fax facilities.

INTALCABLE provides international telegram services; telegrams may be dictated over the phone.

Tipping

Most Italian restaurants levy a *coperto* of around €2 per person – a cover charge for linen, bread and service – and so tipping isn't as common as in other countries. However, in pricier places a tip of around 10 percent is an appropriate indication of appreciation of good service. Only in the finest hotels, and for lengthy stays, is it customary to tip bellboys, maids and head waiters. You may wish to note that according to Italian law, you should keep the bill with you until you are at least 100 metres (300 ft) from the restaurant.

Tourist Board

The Italian State Tourist Board, known as ENIT (Ente Nazionale per il Turismo), provides tourist information. ENIT's headquarters are in Via Marghera 2/6 Rome (tel: 06-49711; www.enit.it).
In the UK, ENIT, 1 Princes Street, London W1R 2AY; tel: 020-7408 1254; fax: 020-7493 6695.
In the US, ENIT, Suite 1565, 630 Fifth Avenue, New York, NY 10111; tel: 212-245 4822; fax: 212-586 9249. There are also offices in Chicago, Los Angeles and Canada.
Website: www.italiantourism.com

Tourist Offices

Tourist information is available at the Azienda di Promozione Turistica (APT), the main tourist office in each provincial capital. In addition, there is a tourist office (*Uffi-cio di Turismo*) in most towns. In small places, the *Comune* holds tourist information and some commercial banks and travel agencies publish tourist guides. The Touring Club Italiano (TCI), with offices in almost every town, provides free information about the area.

Arezzo Province

Arezzo: Piazza Risorgimento 116, Arezzo, tel: 0575-23952; Piazza della Repubblica 28, tel: 0575-377678.
Cortona: Via Nazionale 42, tel: 0575-630352.
www.apt.arezzo.it

Florence Province

Florence: Via Manzoni 16, 50121 Firenze, tel: 055-23320; Via Cavour 1r, tel: 055-290832; Borgo Santa Croce 29r, tel: 055-234 0444; and Piazza della Stazione 4, tel: 055-212245.
www.firenzeturismo.it
Fiesole: Via Portigiani 3/5, tel: 055-598720.

Grosseto Province

Grosseto: Viale Monterosa 206, tel: 0564-462611.
www.lamaremmafabene.it

Livorno Province

Livorno: Piazza Cavour 6, 57100, tel: 0586-204611. There is also the Harbour Information Office, Porto Mediceo, tel: 0586-895320.
www.costadeglietruschi.it
Elba: Calata Italia 26, Portofer-raio, tel: 0565-914671.
www.aptelba.it

Lucca Province

Lucca: Piazza Guidiccioni 2, tel: 0583-91991; Piazza Santa Maria 35, tel: 0583-919931; Vecchia Porta San Donato, Piazzale Verdi, tel: 0583-442944.
www.turismo.provincia.lucca.it
Bagni di Lucca: Via E. Wipple, tel: 0583-804557.
Viareggio: Viale Carducci 10, tel: 0584-962233.

Massa-Carrara Province

Marina di Massa: Lungomare Vespucci 24, tel: 0585-240046.
Marina di Carrara: Via Garibaldi 41d, tel: 0585-632519.
www.aptmassacarrara.it

Pisa Province

Pisa: Via Matteucci, tel: 050-929777; Piazza Arcivescovado 8, tel: 050-560464;
www.pisa.turismo.toscana.it
Volterra: Piazza dei Priori 20, tel: 0588-87257.

Pistoia Province

Pistoia: Piazza del Duomo 1, tel: 0573-21622.
www.pistoia.turismo.toscana.it
San Marcello Pistoiese:
Via Marconi 70, tel: 0573-630145.

Prato Province

Prato: Piazza Santa Maria delle Carceri 15, tel: 0574-24112.
www.prato.turismo.toscana.it

Siena Province

Siena: Piazza del Campo 56, 53100, tel: 0577-280551.
www.terresiena.it

W ebsites

Useful websites are given throughout the book. The following is just a selection of the many additional sites on Italy, Florence and Tuscany that are available on the web:

Tuscany Tourist Information:
www.turismo.toscana.it
Database on all Italian museums: www.museionline.com
Florence: www.firenzemusei.it, www.polomuseale.firenze.it.
Best routes in Italy:
www.autostrade.it, www.rac.co.uk, www.theaa.com.
Plan your journey from one Italian destination to another.
Piazze d'Italia:
www.mediasoft.it/piazze
Visit different squares in Italy, including virtual tours. Information plus hotels and restaurants: www.firenzeturismo.it.

Agriturismo in Tuscany:
www.agriturismo.regione.toscana.it
Official site giving information on rural farm stays in this popular area.
General Information: www.itwg.com
Events: www.firenzespettacolo.it, www.theflorentine.net

Weights and Measures

The metric system is used for weights and measures.
Multiply by the following:

Centimetres to inches	0.4
Metres to feet	3.3
Metres to yards	1.1
Kilometres to miles	0.6
Kilograms to pounds	2.2

Italians refer to 100 grams (about a quarter of a pound) as *un etto*; 200 grams are therefore *due etti*.

Liquid measurements are in litres. One litre is 1.75 imperial pints.

Temperatures are given in Celsius (Centigrade).

What to Bring

Towns like Florence, Lucca and Siena are sophisticated, so take something smart for shopping or dining out, although jackets and ties are rarely required for men. It can rain unexpectedly wherever you are, so a raincoat is an essential piece of clothing; it should be large enough to cover anything worn, and light enough to be folded and carried.

Decent dress is required when visiting religious buildings: men and women are expected to have their arms covered, and shorts are frowned upon. Women often carry a headscarf as a simple head covering. Sun hats are also recommended as protection.

Shoes need to be sturdy but comfortable and suitable for walking – especially on cobbled streets and for climbing steps.

Binoculars are a good idea for nature studies and viewing architectural details and frescoes.

TRANSPORT

ACCOMMODATION

ACTIVITIES

A – Z

LANGUAGE

LANGUAGE

UNDERSTANDING ITALIAN

Language Tips

In Tuscany, the Italian language is supplemented by regional dialects. In large cities and tourist centres you will find many people who speak English, French or German. It is well worth buying a good phrase book or dictionary, but the following will help you get started. Since this glossary is aimed at non-linguists, we have opted for the simplest options rather than the most elegant Italian.

Pronunciation and Grammar Tips

Italian speakers claim that pronunciation is straightforward: you pronounce it as it is written. This is approximately true but there are a couple of important rules for English speakers to bear in mind: *c* before *e* or *i* is pronounced "ch", e.g. *ciao, mi dispiace, coincidenza. Ch* before *i* or *e* is pronounced as "k", e.g. *la chiesa*. Likewise, *sci* or *sce* are pronounced as in "sheep" or "shed". *Gn* in Italian is rather like the sound in "onion", while *gl* is softened to resemble the sound in "bullion".

Nouns are either masculine (*il*, plural *i*) or feminine (*la*, plural *le*). Plurals of nouns are most often formed by changing an *o* to an *i*

and an *a* to an *e*, e.g. *il panino, i panini; la chiesa, le chiese.*

Words are stressed on the penultimate syllable unless an accent indicates otherwise, generally speaking.

Like many languages, Italian has formal and informal words for "You". In the singular, *Tu* is informal while *Lei* is more polite. For visitors, it is simplest and most respectful to use the formal form unless invited to do otherwise. There is, of course, rather more to the language than that, but you can get a surprisingly long way towards making friends with a few phrases.

Basic Communication

Yes *Sì*
No *No*
Thank you *Grazie*
You're welcome *Prego*
Alright/Okay/That's fine *Va bene*
Please *Per favore* or *per cortesia*
Excuse me (to get attention) *Scusi* (singular), *Scusate* (plural)
Excuse me (to get through a crowd) *Permesso*
Excuse me (to attract attention, e.g. of a waiter) *Senta!*
Excuse me (sorry) *Mi scusi*
Could you help me? (formal) *Potrebbe aiutarmi?*
Certainly *Ma, certo*

Can I help you? (formal) *Posso aiutarLa?*
I need ... *Ho bisogno di ...*
I'm sorry *Mi dispiace*
I don't know *Non lo so*
I don't understand *Non capisco*
Could you speak more slowly, please? *Può parlare piu lentamente, per favore?*
Could you repeat that please? *Può ripetere, per piacere?*
What? *Quale/come?*
When/why/where? *Quando/perchè/dove?*
Where is the lavatory? *Dov'è il bagno?*

Greetings

Hello (Good day) *Buon giorno*
Good afternoon/evening *Buona sera*
Good night *Buona notte*
Goodbye *Arrivederci*
Hello/Hi/Goodbye (familiar) *Ciao*
Mr/Mrs/Miss *Signor/Signora/Signorina*
Pleased to meet you (formal) *Piacere di conoscerLa*
Do you speak English? *Parla inglese?*
I am English/American *Sono inglese/americano*
Canadian/Australian *canadese/australiano*
How are you (formal/informal)? *Come sta/come stai?*
Fine thanks *Bene, grazie*

Telephone Calls

the area code *il prefisso*
May I use your telephone, please? *Posso usare il telefono?*
Hello (on the telephone) *Pronto*
My name's *Mi chiamo/Sono*
Could I speak to...? *Posso parlare con...?*
Can you speak up please? *Può parlare più forte, per favore?*

In the Hotel

Do you have any vacant rooms? *Avete camere libere?*
I have a reservation *Ho fatto una prenotazione*
I'd like... *Vorrei...*
   a room with twin beds *una camera a due letti*
   a single/double room (with a double bed) *una camera singola/doppia (con letto matrimoniale)*
   a room with a bath/shower *una camera con bagno/doccia*
for one night *per una notte*
for two nights *per due notti*
How much is it? *Quanto costa?*
Is breakfast included? *E compresa la prima colazione?*
half/full board *mezza pensione/pensione completa*
Do you have a room with a balcony/view of the sea? *C'è una camera con balcone/con una vista del mare?*
Is it a quiet room? *E una stanza tranquilla?*
Can I see the room? *Posso vedere la camera?*
Can I have the bill, please? *Posso avere il conto, per favore?*
Can you call me a taxi, please? *Può chiamarmi un tassì/taxi, per favore?*

Eating Out

Bar snacks and drinks

I'd like... *Vorrei...*
coffee *un caffè* (*espresso*: small, strong and black)
un caffellatte (like *café au lait* in France)

un caffè lungo (weak, served in a tall glass)
un corretto (laced with alcohol, probably brandy or grappa)
tea *un tè*
herbal tea *una tisana*
hot chocolate *una cioccolata calda*
orange/lemon juice (bottled) *un succo d'arancia/di limone*
fizzy/still mineral water *acqua minerale gassata/naturale*
with/without ice *con/senza ghiaccio*
red/white wine *vino rosso/bianco*
beer *una birra*
milk *latte*
a (half) litre *un (mezzo) litro*
ice cream *un gelato*
sandwich *un tramezzino*
roll *un panino*
Cheers *Salute*

In a Restaurant

I'd like to book a table *Vorrei riservare una tavola*
Have you got a table for...? *Avete una tavola per ...?*
I have a reservation *Ho fatto una prenotazione*
lunch/supper *il pranzo/la cena*
I'm a vegetarian *Sono vegetariano/a*
Is there a vegetarian dish? *C'è un piatto vegetariano?*
May we have the menu? *Ci dia la carta?*
wine list *la lista dei vini*
home-made *fatto in casa*
What would you like? *Che cosa prende?*
What would you recommend? *Che cosa ci raccomanda?*
home-made *fatto in casa*
What would you like as a main course/dessert? *Che cosa prende di secondo/di dolce?*
What would you like to drink? *Che cosa desidera da bere?*
a carafe of red/white wine *una caraffa di vino rosso/bianco*
the dish of the day *il piatto del giorno*
cover charge *il coperto/pane e coperto*
The bill, please *Il conto per favore*
Is service included? *Il servizio è incluso?*

Menu Decoder

Antipasti (hors d'oeuvres)

antipasto misto **mixed hors d'oeuvres** (including cold cuts, possibly cheeses and roast vegetables)
buffet freddo **cold buffet**
caponata **mixed aubergine, olives and tomatoes**
insalata caprese **tomato and mozzarella salad**
insalata di mare **seafood salad**
insalata mista/verde **mixed/green salad**
melanzane alla parmigiana **fried or baked aubergine** (with parmesan cheese and tomato)
mortadella/salame **salami**
peperonata **grilled peppers** (drenched in olive oil)

Primi (first courses)

Typical first courses include soup, risotto, gnocchi or numerous varieties of pasta in a wide range of sauces.
il brodetto **fish soup**
i crespolini **savoury pancakes**
gli gnocchi **dumplings**
la minestra **soup**
il minestrone **thick vegetable soup**
pasta e fagioli **pasta and bean soup**

EMERGENCIES

Help! *Aiuto!*
Stop! *Fermate!*
I've had an accident *Ho avuto un incidente*
Watch out! *Attenzione!*
Call a doctor *Per favore, chiama un medico*
Call an ambulance *Chiama un'ambulanza*
Call the police *Chiama la Polizia/i Carabinieri*
Call the fire brigade *Chiama i pompieri*
Where is the telephone? *Dov'è il telefono?*
Where is the nearest hospital? *Dov'è l'ospedale più vicino?*
I would like to report a theft *Voglio denunciare un furto*

il prosciutto (cotto/crudo) **ham** (cooked/cured)
i tartufi **truffles**
la zuppa **soup**

Secondi (main courses)

Typical main courses are fish-, seafood- or meat-based, with accompaniments *(contorni)* that vary greatly from region to region.

La carne (meat)

allo spiedo **on the spit**
arrosto **roast meat**
al ferro **grilled without oil**
al forno **baked**
al girarrosto **spit-roasted**
alla griglia **grilled**
stufato **braised, stewed**
ben cotto **well-done** (steak, etc.)
al puntino **medium** (steak, etc.)
al sangue **rare** (steak, etc.)
l'agnello **lamb**
il bresaolo **dried salted beef**
la bistecca **steak**
il maiale **pork**
il manzo **beef**
l'ossobuco **shin of veal**
il pollo **chicken**
la salsiccia **sausage**
saltimbocca (alla romana) **veal escalopes with ham**
le scaloppine **escalopes**
lo stufato **stew**
il sugo **sauce**

Frutti di mare (seafood)

Beware the word *"surgelati"*, meaning frozen rather than fresh.
affumicato **smoked**
alle brace **charcoal grilled/ barbecued**
alla griglia **grilled**
fritto **fried**
ripieno **stuffed**
al vapore **steamed**
le acciughe **anchovies**
l'aragosta **lobster**
il branzino **sea bass**
i calamari **squid**
i calamaretti **baby squid**
i crostacei **shellfish**
le cozze **mussels**
il fritto misto **mixed fried fish**
i gamberi **prawns**
i gamberetti **shrimps**
il granchio **crab**
il merluzzo **cod**
le ostriche **oysters**

il pesce **fish**
il pesce spada **swordfish**
il polipo **octopus**
il risotto di mare **seafood risotto**
le sarde **sardines**
la sogliola **sole**
le seppie **cuttlefish**
la triglia **red mullet**
la trota **trout**
il tonno **tuna**
le vongole **clams**

I legumi/la verdura (vegetables)

a scelta **of your choice**
i contorni **accompaniments**
ripieno **stuffed**
gli asparagi **asparagus**
la bietola **similar to spinach**
il carciofo **artichoke**
le carote **carrots**
i carciofini **artichoke hearts**
il cavolo **cabbage**
la cicoria **chicory**
la cipolla **onion**
i funghi **mushrooms**
i fagioli **beans**
i fagiolini **French (green) beans**
le fave **broad beans**
il finocchio **fennel**
l'insalata mista **mixed salad**
l'insalata verde **green salad**
la melanzana **aubergine**
le patate **potatoes**
le patatine fritte **French fries**
i peperoni **peppers**
i piselli **peas**
i pomodori **tomatoes**
le primizie **spring vegetables**
il radicchio **red lettuce**
la rughetta **rocket**
i ravanelli **radishes**
gli spinaci **spinach**
la verdura **green vegetables**
la zucca **pumpkin/squash**
gli zucchini **courgettes**

I dolci (desserts)

al carrello **(desserts) from the trolley**
un semifreddo **semi-frozen dessert (many types)**
la bavarese **mousse**
la cassata **Sicilian ice cream with candied peel**
un gelato **ice cream**
una granita **water ice**
una macedonia di frutta **fruit salad**

il tartufo (nero) **(chocolate) ice cream dessert**
il tiramisù **cold, creamy rum and coffee dessert**
la torta **cake/tart**
lo zabaglione **dessert made with eggs and Marsala wine**
lo zuccotto **ice cream liqueur**
la zuppa inglese **trifle**

La frutta (fruit)

le albicocche **apricots**
le arance **oranges**
le banane **bananas**
il cocomero **watermelon**
le ciliege **cherries**
i fichi **figs**
le fragole **strawberries**
i frutti di bosco **fruits of the forest**
i lamponi **raspberries**
la mela **apple**
il melone **melon**
la pesca **peach**
la pera **pear**
il pompelmo **grapefruit**
le uve **grapes**

Basic foods

l'aceto **vinegar**
l'aglio **garlic**
il burro **butter**
il formaggio **cheese**
la frittata **omelette**
la grana **parmesan cheese**
i grissini **bread sticks**
l'olio **oil**
la marmellata **jam**
il pane **bread**
il pane integrale **wholemeal bread**
il parmigiano **parmesan cheese**
il pepe **pepper**
il riso **rice**
il sale **salt**
le uova **eggs**
lo zucchero **sugar**

Sightseeing

Si può visitare? **Can one visit?**
Suonare il campanello **ring the bell**
aperto/a **open**
chiuso/a **closed**
chiuso per la festa **closed for the festival**
chiuso per ferie **closed for the holidays**
chiuso per restauro **closed for restoration**

Is it possible to see the church? *E possibile visitare la chiesa?*
Where can I find the custodian/sacristan/key? *Dove posso trovare il custode/il sacristano/la chiave?*

At the Shops

What time do you open/close? *A che ora apre/chiude?*
Closed for the holidays (typical sign) *Chiuso per ferie*
Pull/push (sign on doors) *Tirare/spingere*
Entrance/exit *Entrata/uscita*
Can I help you? (formal) *Posso aiutarLa?*
What would you like? *Che cosa desidera?*
I'm just looking *Sto soltanto guardando*
How much does it cost? *Quant'è, per favore?*
Do you take credit cards? *Accettate carte di credito?*
I'd like... *Vorrei...*
this one/that one *questo/quello*
I'd like that one, please *Vorrei quello lì, per cortesia*
Have you got ...? *Avete ...?*
We haven't got (any) ... *Non (ne) abbiamo...*
Can I try it on? *Posso provare?*
the size (for clothes) *la taglia*
What size do you take? *Qual'è Sua taglia?*
the size (for shoes) *il numero*
expensive/cheap *caro/economico*
It's too small/big *E troppo piccolo/grande*
I (don't) **like it** *(Non) mi piace*
I'll take it/I'll leave it *Lo prendo/Lo lascio*
This is faulty. Can I have a replacement/refund? *C'è un difetto. Me lo potrebbe cambiare/rimborsare?*
Anything else? *Altro?*
Give me some of those *Mi dia alcuni di quelli lì*
a (half) kilo *un (mezzo) chilo*
100 grams *un etto*
200 grams *due etti*
more/less *più/meno*
with/without *con/senza*
a little *un pocchino*
That's enough *Basta così*

Types of shops

bank *la banca*
bureau de change *il cambio*
chemist's *la farmacia*
food shop *l'alimentari*
leather shop *la pelletteria*
market *il mercato*
news-stand *l'edicola*
post office *l'ufficio postale*
supermarket *il supermercato*
tobacconist *il tabaccaio*
travel agency *l'agenzia di viaggi*

Travelling

Transport

airport *l'aeroporto*
arrivals/departures *arrivi/partenze*
boat *la barca*
bus *l'autobus/il pullman*
bus station *l'autostazione*
car *la macchina*
ferry *il traghetto*
first/second class *prima/seconda classe*
flight *il volo*
left luggage office *il deposito bagagli*
motorway *l'autostrada*
no smoking *vietato fumare*
platform *il binario*
railway station *la stazione (ferroviaria)*
stop *la fermata*

At the station

Can you help me please? *Mi può aiutare, per favore?*
Where can I buy tickets? *Dove posso fare i biglietti?*
at the ticket office/at the counter *alla biglietteria/allo sportello*
What time does the train leave? *A che ora parte il treno?*
What time does the train arrive? *A che ora arriva il treno?*
Can I book a seat? *Posso prenotare un posto?*
Is this seat free/taken? *E libero/occupato questo posto?*
I'm afraid this is my seat *E il mio posto, mi dispiace*
You'll have to pay a supplement *Deve pagare un supplemento*
Do I have to change? *Devo cambiare?*

Where does it stop? *Dove si ferma?*
You need to change in Firenze *Bisogna cambiare a Florence*
Which platform does the train leave from? *Da quale binario parte il treno?*
The train leaves from platform one *Il treno parte dal binario uno*
When is the next train/bus/ferry for Pisa? *Quando parte il prossimo treno/pullman/traghetto per Pisa?*
How long does the crossing take? *Quanto dura la traversata?*
What time does the bus leave for Siena? *Quando parte l'autobus per Siena?*
Next stop please *La prossima fermata per favore*
Is this the right stop? *E la fermata giusta?*
The train is late *Il treno è in ritardo*
Can you tell me where to get off? *Mi può dire dove devo scendere?*

Directions

right/left *a destra/a sinistra*
first left/second right *la prima a sinistra/la seconda a destra*
Turn to the right/left *Gira a destra/sinistra*
Go straight on *Va sempre diritto*
Go straight on until the lights *Va sempre diritto fino al semaforo*
opposite/next to *di fronte/accanto a*
up/down *su/gìu*
traffic lights *il semaforo*
Where is ...? *Dov'è ...?*
Where are ...? *Dove sono ...?*
How do I get there? *Come si può andare?* (or: *Come faccio per arrivare a ...?*)

On the Road

petrol *la benzina*
petrol station/garage *la stazione servizio*
oil *l'olio*
Fill it up please *Faccia il pieno, per favore*
lead free/unleaded/diesel *senza piombo/benzina verde/diesel*
My car won't start *La mia macchina non s'accende*
My car has broken down *La macchina è guasta*

FURTHER READING

Art and History

The Architecture of the Italian Renaissance, by Peter Murray. Thames and Hudson.
Autobiography, by Benvenuto Cellini. Penguin Classics.
Catherine de Medici: a Biography by Leonie Frieda. Phoenix
A Concise Encyclopedia of the Italian Renaissance, edited by J.R. Hale. Thames and Hudson.
Etruscan Places, by D.H. Lawrence. Olive Press.
The Florentine Renaissance and *The Flowering of the Renaissance* by Vincent Cronin. Fontana.
The High Renaissance and *The Late Renaissance and Mannerism*, by Linda Murray. Thames and Hudson.
The Italian Painters of the Renaissance, by Bernard Berenson. Phaidon Press.
Lives of the Artists, vols. 1 & 2, by Giorgio Vasari. Penguin Classics.
Machiavelli, by Anglo Sydney. Paladin.
The Merchant of Prato, by Iris Origo. Penguin.
Painter's Florence, by Barbara Whelpton Johnson.
The Rise and Fall of the House of Medici, by Christopher Hibbert. Penguin.
Siena: A City and its History, by Judith Hook. Hamish Hamilton.
Silvio Berlusconi: Television, Power and Patrimony, by Paul Ginsborg. Verso Books.

Travel Companions

A Room with a View, by E.M. Forster. Penguin.
D.H. Lawrence and Italy, by D.H. Lawrence. Penguin.
The Italians, by Luigi Barzini. Hamish Hamilton.
Italian Hours, by Henry James. Century Hutchinson.
Love and War in the Apennines, by Eric Newby. Picador.
The Love of Italy, by Jonathan Keates. Octopus.
Pictures from Italy, by Charles Dickens. Granville Publishing.
The Stones of Florence, by Mary McCarthy. Penguin.
Under the Tuscan Sun and the sequel *Bella Tuscany*, by Frances Mayes. Bantam

SEND US YOUR THOUGHTS

We do our best to ensure the information in our books is as accurate and up-to-date as possible. The books are updated on a regular basis using local contacts, who painstakingly add, amend and correct as required. However, some details (such as telephone numbers and opening times) are liable to change, and we are ultimately reliant on our readers to put us in the picture.

We welcome your feedback, especially your experience of using the book "on the road". Maybe we recommended a hotel that you liked (or another that you didn't), or you came across a great bar or new attraction we missed.

We will acknowledge all contributions, and we'll offer an Insight Guide to the best letters received.

Please write to us at:
Insight Guides
PO Box 7910
London SE1 1WE
Or email us at:
insight@apaguide.co.uk

The Villas of Tuscany, by Harold Acton. Thames and Hudson.

Other Insight Guides

Europe is comprehensively covered by over 400 books published by Apa Publications. They come in a variety of series, each tailored to suit different needs.

Insight Guides, the main series of guides that Apa publishes, provide the reader with a cultural background, plus comprehensive travel coverage linked to photography and maps. The series includes titles on Italy, Southern Italy and Northern Italy, Sicily, Tuscany, the Italian Lakes and Sardinia. Italian destinations in Insight's detailed and colourful **City Guides** series include Rome, Florence and Venice. The itinerary-based **Insight Step by Step Guides**, written by local hosts, come complete with a pull-out map. Titles include The Italian Lakes, Florence and Rome. **Insight Smart Guides** give you the facts about a destination in a very digestible form and feature numerous Italian titles.

ART & PHOTO CREDITS

4Corners Images 236
AFP/Getty Images 40
akg-images 245, 249T
akg-images/Erich Lessing 51, 52
akg-images/Rabatti-Domingie 18, 47
akg-images/S. Domingie 3, 8B
The Art Archive 50
The Art Archive/Baroncelli Chapel Santa Croce, Florence/Daglio Orti 44
The Art Archive/Duomo Florence/Dagli Orti 53
The Art Archive/Galleria degli Uffizi Florence/Dagli Orti 42, 45, 46
The Art Archive/Museo Storico Topografico Firenze Com'era Florence/Dagli Orti 24
The Art Archive/Palazzo Pubblico Siena/Dagli Orti 5T, 21R, 209
Rosemary Bailey 152T
Gaetano Barone 23
Claudio Beduschi/Cuboimages 128
Mark Bolton Photography/Alamy 137
The Bridgeman Art Library 4C, 5B, 6B, 9CR, 22, 26, 43, 56, 118, 249
Celentano/laif/Camerapress 39
Stefano Cellai/SIME-4Corners Images 244
CuboImages/Alamy 239
CuboImages/Robert Harding Picture Library 130, 166, 167, 175
Cornelia Doerr/Photolibrary 12/13
Ettore Ferrari/epa/Corbis 33
Jerry Dennis/Apa 82, 85, 89, 96T, 116
ENEL 187
Guglielmo Galvin 7T, 64, 178T, 179T, 181T
Guglielmo Galvin & George Taylor/Apa back cover CL, CR & B, 6T, 17, 61, 120T, 124T, 129T, 130T, 140T, 146T, 150T, 151, 152, 154, 169, 207, 208T, 210, 212
Bertrand Gardel/hemis.fr 38
Getty Images 29, 30
Patrizia Giancotti 148, 168, 233, 241T
Frances Gransden/Apa 20, 54, 88T, 114T

Albano Guatti 7BL, 16, 37, 63, 123, 135, 138, 139, 174, 204, 225T
Herbert Hartmann 19
John Heseltine 184, 189
Peter Horree/Alamy 129
Alain Le Garsmeur 224, 226
Mary Liz Austin/Getty Images 228
Lombardi Siena 21L
Enrico Martino 85T, 191
Metropolitan Opera Archives 139T
Anna Mockford & Nick Bonetti 176, 179, 180
Anna Mockford & Nick Bonetti/Apa 1, 2/3, 4T, 7CL, 8TL, 8TR, 9CL, 14, 36, 41, 55, 57, 58, 59, 62, 67, 70L, 70R, 71, 72/73, 74/75, 76, 83, 84, 86, 86T, 87, 88, 90, 91, 91T, 92, 92T, 94, 95, 95T, 96, 112, 113, 115, 115T, 117, 118T, 119, 120, 122, 125, 125T, 126, 127T, 132, 133, 134T, 136, 137T, 140, 142, 143, 145, 146, 147, 149, 150, 157, 158, 159, 161, 162, 170, 171, 171T, 172, 173, 174T, 185, 186, 188, 192, 193, 195, 195T, 196, 197L, 197R, 198, 199, 199T, 200, 200T, 205, 208, 212T, 216, 217, 219, 219T, 221, 222, 223, 225, 229, 229T, 230, 230T, 232, 234, 235, 237, 237T, 238, 240, 241, 242, 242T, 243, 246, 247, 247T, 250, 251, 251T, 253, 253T, 254, 254T, 255, 256, 257
Monte dei Paschi di Siena 211
Cathy Muscat 170T, 177, 181, 183, 190
Museum Guarnacci 7R
National Portrait Gallery 28
Michael Newton 227
Photolibrary.com 66, 127
Sergio Pitamitz/Corbis 220
Pisa Tourist Office 9T, 155, 164
Andrea Pistolesi 99
Pitti Gallery, Florence 69
Guido Alberto Rossi /Getty Images 10/11
Santa Maria Novella, Florence 48
Lizzie Shepherd/Alamy 60
Sipa Press/Rex Features 32
Hubert Stadler/Corbis 163
Team/Alinari/Rex Features 31
Topham Picturepoint 35
Bill Wassman 65

Pages 100/101: akg-images/Rabatti Domingie 100BL, 101BL, The Art Archive 100BR, 101TL, 101TR, The Bridgeman Art Library 100/101. Pages 102/103: akg-images 102TL, akg-images/Rabatti Domingie 102BL, 103TR, The Bridgeman Art Library 103CR, Corbis 102CR. Pages 104/105: The Art Archive 104/105, Jerry Dennis/Apa 104BL, 105BL, 105CR, Anna Mockford & Nick Bonetti/Apa 104CR. Pages 106/107: akg-images/Rabatti Domingie 106BL, 106CR, 107CL, 107BR, The Art Archive 107TR. Pages 108/109: akg-images/Rabatti Domingie 108CL, The Bridgeman Art Library 109CL, Corbis 108TR, 109TL, 109CR. Pages 110/111: The Art Archive 110CL, 111TR, The Bridgeman Art Library 110/111, Corbis 111BR, Jerry Dennis/Apa 110BR, Topham Picturepoint 111BL. Pages 202/203: G Galvin & G Taylor/Apa 202TL, Anna Mockford & Nick Bonetti/Apa 202CR, Mick Rock/Cephas Picture Library 202BR, 202/203, 203TR, 203CL, 203BC. Pages 214/215: Michael Freeman 215TR, 215BL, 215BR, Foto/Maria Appiani 214CR, 214BC, Simeone Huber/Getty Images 214/215.

TOURING MAP: akg-images/S. Domingie-M. Rabbatti bronze Chimera, Jon Arnold Cover, All others Anna Mockford & Nick Bonetti/Apa

Cartographic Editor: Zoë Goodwin
Map Production: Phoenix Mapping, James Macdonald and Mike Adams
© 2006 Apa Publications GmbH & Co. Verlag KG, Singapore Branch

Production: Linton Donaldson and Mary Pickles.

GENERAL INDEX

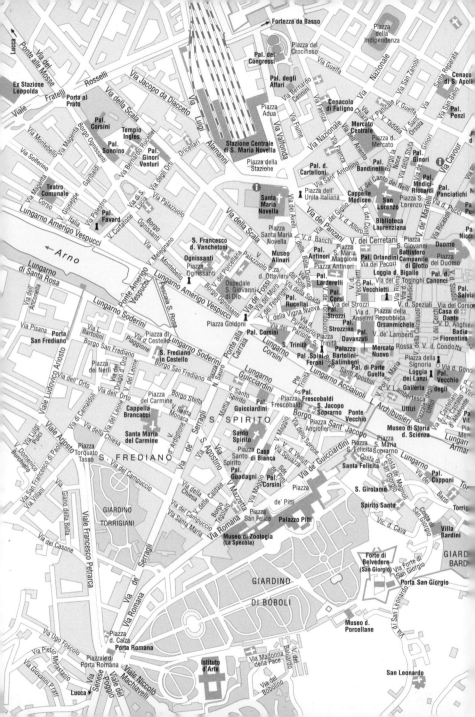